Folk Classification

Folk Classification:

A Topically Arranged Bibliography of
Contemporary and Background References
Through 1971

Harold C. Conklin

Department of Anthropology
Yale University
1972

Available from

Department of Anthropology
Yale University, New Haven, Conn. 06520

Price $4.00

C O N T E N T S

  * other than 1. or 2.

** other than 7. or 8.

Introduction

This bibliography of some 5000 entries includes references to (1) analyses of specific systems of folk classification, (2) discussions and comparisons of such analyses, and (3) theoretical and practical background literature on classification in general and in various subject fields. These references are arranged alphabetically under ten topical headings selected to minimize multiple listings. Only works published through 1971 are included. Although an effort was made to list at least some representative sources from as broad a spectrum of folk classificatory fields as possible, there are undoubtedly many gaps and omissions. The nature of these limitations as well as the history, purpose, scope, and organization of this compilation are discussed briefly below.

Since 1955, I have prepared several sets of references for courses and seminars in folk science or ethnoscience. In each case, I have emphasized ethnographic materials on the folk classification of biological and other environmental phenomena. With a view to revising my 1967 version of these bibliographies (containing about 1400 entries) in some more generally available form, I solicited comments, criticisms, corrections, substitutions, additions, and other suggestions. Many students and colleagues responded generously and helpfully (see acknowledgments below). However, despite periods of intense effort on the part of various friends and assistants, field work and other duties have considerably delayed the final compilation of this revision.

In order to reduce the necessary duplication of references under different headings I experimented with various topical arrangements of the materials processed by 1968. Though certainly not totally satisfactory, the most efficient breakdown appeared to be the one followed here: a general section, plus nine specific sections which may be considered as comprising three tripartite subdivisions:

0. Principles of classification

1. Kinship and related topics ⎫
2. Archeological classification ⎬ culturally domi-
                                     nated content
3. Anthropological classification
       (other than 1. or 2.) ⎭

4. Ethnobotany ⎫
5. Ethnozoology ⎬ biologically domi-
                     nated content
6. Ethnomedicine ⎭

7. Orientation ⎫
8. Color ⎬ physically domi-
              nated content
9. Sensation (other than 7. or 8.) ⎭

Partly due to the bibliography's considerable increase in size, attempts at further subdivision, cross-referencing, and overall annotation regretfully had to be abandoned. However, checking for accuracy, consistency, representative coverage, and appropriate cross-listing was continued.

The main purpose in compiling these sets of references has been to provide students of folk classification with an introduction to the contemporary and historical literature on the multiplicity of problems, modes of analysis, and types of classificatory relations encountered in various domains. I have given special emphasis to references which contain evidence or some discussion of either inherent aspects of particular folk classifications, or classificatory principles directly or indirectly applicable to the analysis of folk systems.

The problems of meaning and of content faced by the field ethnographer are rarely unique. Thus my intent in including nonanthropological works on classification has been largely heuristic. This holds not only for linguistics and biosystematics, but also in fields apparently less directly related to cultural categorizations. For example, the way a crystallographer or microbiologist treats multidimensionality or reticulate connectivity-- both theoretically and in such practical matters as notational systems and methods of data display--may provide invaluable suggestions for the handling of similar relational problems encountered in the semantic structure of particular folk classifications.

Whenever references inescapably fall under two or more of the ten bibliographic headings, they are so listed. Otherwise, there is no cross-referencing between sections and a minimum of cross-referencing within any single section. No topic is covered completely and undoubtedly many useful sources have been missed. In general, standard references such as lexicons and encyclopedias are not listed. Ethnographic dictionaries, textbooks, readers, reviews, reprints of articles, and available dissertations are indicated by only a small sampling of the extant literature. With these limitations in mind, however, the general range for each of the ten sections can be outlined briefly. To facilitate use of the bibliography, the numerical tagging of these ten lists, from 0. through 9., is followed in the secondary enumeration at the top of each section page, (e.g., [7:41] indicates 'page 41 of section 7.').

0. Principles of Classification. This section contains references to theoretical and methodological discussions of systems of folk classification, and to general and analytical works containing evidence or discussions of similar problems in linguistics, psychology, philosophy, logic, mathematics, and biosystematics; and in related fields. Not included are works concerned with subject matter falling entirely under one of the sections 1. to 9.

1. Kinship and Related Topics. Included in this section are references to works on folk systems of kin categorization and similar ethnosociological classifications. (Some overlap with section 3.)

2. Archeological Classification. This section lists references to works which exemplify or provide discussions of artifactual and contextual problems of classification in archeology. (Some overlap with section 3.)

3. Anthropological Classification (other than 1. or 2.) This residual section includes references to works in social and cultural anthropology which treat problems of classification in areas not emphasized in other sections of this bibliography. Social, economic, technological, and comparative topics are represented. On the social use of language and naming there is some overlap with 0. and 1.; on the technological side there is also some overlap with 2.

4. Ethnobotany (including systematic botany). Because of similar content, works on both biological and cultural classification of plants are combined in this section. Much of the "ethnobotanical" literature also sampled here provides evidence of, but little direct attention to, folk classification. (Some overlap with 0., 5., and 6.)

5. Ethnozoology (including systematic zoology). Similarly, works on both biological and cultural classification of animals are found in this section. Again,

the range of publications sampled includes "ethnozoo-logical" reports where there is little direct analysis of folk classification. (Some overlap with O. and 4.)

6. Ethnomedicine (including medical classification). In this section, both medical and ethnographic references to works on systems of disease categorization, treatment (use of medicinal plants, etc.), anatomical classification, and related topics are included. (Some overlap with 4.)

7. Orientation. Listed in this section are works on folk systems of time reckoning, spatial location, measuration, navigation, meteorology, astronomy, ethnogeography, general environmental and ecological relations, and deixis. Some standard classificational references in geological, geographical, and similar fields are included. (Some overlap with O.)

8. Color. This section includes accounts of color categorization, color naming, and related topics, in terms of particular systems of folk classification, comparative studies, and technical research in psychophysics, colorimetry, etc.

9. Sensation (other than 7. or 8.) This final section contains references to works on the categorization of sound, smell, taste, touch, visual form, and related topics. The relatively small size of this section reflects the extent of the available literature, especially that specifically concerned with folk

categorization of these noncolorimetric aspects of sensory experience.

Partial subject guide. A rough indication of the range of topics represented (including those mentioned above), and of the section(s) in which at least some exemplars are most likely to be found is provided in the following synoptic index of a sampling of (a) topics or fields, (b) entities classified, and (c) loci of classifications.

(a) Topics or fields:
    anatomy   6.
    archeology   2.
    art   3.
    astronomy   7.
    bacteriology   4.
    biology   0. 4. 5.
    biosystematics   0. 4. 5.
    botany   0. 4.
    calendric systems   7.
    cartography   7.
    chemistry   9.
    classification in general   0.
    clinical classification   6.
    clustering   0.
    colorimetry   8.
    computation   0. 7.
    counting systems   7.
    cross-cultural classification   3.
    crystallography   0.
    cuisine   9.
    cultural anthropology   1. 2. 3.
    cybernetics   0.
    deixis   7.

design   0.
distance   7.
ecology   7.
economics   3.
economic botany   4.
environment   7.
ethnobotany   4.
ethnogeography   7.
ethnology   3.
ethnomedicine   6.
ethnomineralogy   7.
ethnoscience   0. 3.
ethnosociology   1. 3.
ethnozoology   5.
faceted classification   0.
folklore   3.
folk science   0. 4. 5.
geography   7.
geology   7.
gesture   7. 9.
graph theory   0.
hydronomy   7.
identification   0. 4. 5.
indexing   0.
information retrieval   0.
keys   0. 4. 5.
kinesics   0. 3. 9.
kinship   0. 1. 3.
law   3.
lexicography   0.
linguistics   0. 7.
logic   0.
mathematics   0.
measurement   7.
medicine   6.
meteorology   7.

vision   8. 9.

zoology   0. <u>5</u>.

(b) Entities classified:

animals   5.

artifacts   2. 3.

body parts   6.

colors   8.

crops   4.

directions   7.

diseases   6.

ethnic units   3.

foods   9.

land forms   7.

names   0. 7.

personal names   1. 3.

place names   7.

plants   4.

pronominals   0. 7.

social categories   3.

soils   7.

symbols   3.

(c) Loci of classifications:

catalogs   3.

dictionaries   0.

ethnographic dictionaries   3.

field guides   4. 5. 7.

thesauri   0.

libraries   <u>0</u>. 3.

Acknowledgments.   Support for the compilation of this bibliography has come from a number of sources: the National Science Foundation, the Concilium on International and Area Studies and the Department of Anthropology at Yale University, and the Institute for Advanced

16

Study in Princeton.

Since 1967, many individuals have offered helpful advice. Myrdene Anderson, Marc Bornstein, Allen R. Maxwell, William C. Sturtevant, Michiko Takaki, and Tzvetan Todorov have provided especially detailed criticism, suggestions, and assistance in various ways. Specific comments, corrections, or suggested additions have also been received from C. Adams, R. N. Adams, P. O. Afable, J. Barrau, L. Bartoshuk, K. Basso, B. Berlin, M. Black, M. Bromley, I. R. Buchler, R. N. H. Bulmer, J.-P. Caprille, K.-C. Chang, B. N. Colby, M. D. Coe, G. Condominas, H. Cutler, R. M. W. Dixon, R. C. Dunnell, A. Feinstein, R. D. Fogelson, M. L. Forman, C. O. Frake, R. C. Freedman, D. H. French, P. Friedrich, C. Geertz, E. A. Hammel, E. Hamp, C. B. Heiser, Jr., R. N. Henderson, J. K. Hollyman, R. Jakobson, F. G. Lounsbury, P. Maranda, G. A. Miller, R. Needham, P. Newman, T. O'Leary, L. I. Paradis, D. R. Pilbeam, R. Price, P. C. Reynolds, I. Rouse, H. W. Scheffler, A. M. Schenker, T. A. Sebeok, L. R. Stark, W. Straatmans, A. Strickon, E. Stump, K. Thomson, K. Waage, J. B. Watson, O. Werner, R. W. Wescott, T. W. Whitaker, G. Williams, H. Woodbury, F. J. F. Wordick, and M. Zigmond. Others who have helped in the preparation of this revision include Elizabeth O. Kyburg, Marian F. Griffiths, Rebecca M. Bettis, Cecile C. Doty, Leticia V. Mobley, Shari T. Grove, and Jean M. Conklin.

0. Principles of Classification

[Including references to pertinent works in
semantics, linguistics, psychology, philosophy, logic, mathematics and biosystematics;
and items which deal directly with general
problems in the analysis of systems of folk
classification.]

Ableson, R. P. and M. J. Rosenberg
    1958   Symbolic psycho-logic: a model of attitudi-
            nal cognition. Behavioral Science 3.1:1-13.
            Ann Arbor.

Abercrombie, M. L. J.
    1960   The anatomy of judgment. 156 pp. New York:
            Basic Books.

Abraham, Samuel
    1969   On linguistics, logic, and semiotics.
            Linguistics 49:5-10. The Hague.

Abraham, Samuel and Ferenc Kiefer
    1966   A theory of structural semantics. (Janua
            Linguarum, Series Minor 49.) 98 pp. The
            Hague: Mouton.

Adams, Robert P.
    1970   Contour mapping and differential systematics
            of geographical variation. Systematic
            Zoology 19.4:385-390. Lawrence, Kans.

Adanson, Michel
    1763   Familles des plantes. 2 vols. Paris:
            Vincent.

Agassiz, Louis
    1859   Essay on classification. 381 pp. London:
            Longman, Brown, Green, Longmans, and Roberts.
            (1962 reprint, 268 pp. Cambridge: Belknap
            Press of Harvard University Press.)

Akhmanova, Ol'ga S.
    1957   Ocherki po obshchej i russkoj leksikologii.
            (Essays on general and Russian lexicology.)
            295 pp. Moscow: State Pedagogical Publish-
            ing House of the Ministry of Education of
            the RSFSR.

Alexander, Christopher
    1964   Notes on the synthesis of form. 215 pp.
            Cambridge: Harvard University Press.

Alexandre, Pierre
1961   Note sur quelques problèmes d'ethnolinguistique. L'Homme 1.1:102-106. Paris.

Allen, W. Sidney
1953   Relationship in comparative linguistics.
Transactions of the Philological Society,
pp. 52-108. Oxford.

1965   Classification and language. Classification
Society Bulletin 1.1:13-21. Leicester, Engl.

Alston, Ralph Eugene and B. L. Turner
1963   Biochemical systematics. 404 pp. Englewood
Cliffs, N. J.: Prentice-Hall.

Alston, William P.
1964   Philosophy of language. 113 pp. Englewood
Cliffs, N. J.: Prentice-Hall.

Amadon, Dean
1966a   Another suggestion for stabilizing nomenclature. Systematic Zoology 15.1:54-58.
Lawrence, Kans.

1966b   The superspecies concept. Systematic
Zoology 15.3:245-249. Lawrence, Kans.

1968   Further remarks on the superspecies concept.
Systematic Zoology 17.3:345-346. Lawrence,
Kans.

Ampère, André Marie
1834   Essai sur la philosophie des sciences; ou,
exposition analytique d'une classification
naturelle de toutes les connaissances
humaines. lxx, 272 pp. Paris: Bachelier.

Anderson, Edgar
1940   The concept of genus: II. A survey of
modern opinion. Bulletin of the Torrey
Botanical Club 67.5:363-369. New York.

1954   Efficient and inefficient methods of measuring species differences. Pp. 93-106 in
Statistics and mathematics in biology,
edited by O. Kempthorne et al. Ames:
Iowa State College Press.

Anderson, Richard C. and David P. Ausubel, editors
1965   Readings in the psychology of cognition.
xii, 690 pp. New York: Holt, Rinehart,
and Winston.

Andrew, R. J.
1962   Evolution of intelligence and vocal mimick-
        ing. Science 137.3530:585-589. Washington.

Andrews, C. Lesley
1970   Science teaching and ethnoscience: a
        review. Search 1.5:802-805. Sydney.

Anglin, Jeremy M.
1970   The growth of word meaning. Foreword by
        Howard W. Johnson. (MIT Research Monograph
        No. 63.) xiii, 108 pp. Cambridge, Mass.
        and London: MIT Press.

Anonymous
1969   Classification and information control.
        Papers from the Classification Research
        Group, 1960-1968. (Library Association
        Research Pamphlet No. 1.) 130 pp. London.

Antal, László
1961   Sign, meaning, context. Lingua 10.2:211-
        219. Amsterdam.

1963   Questions of meaning. (Janua Linguarum,
        Series Minor No. 27.) 95 pp. The Hague:
        Mouton.

1964   Content, meaning and understanding. 63 pp.
        The Hague: Mouton.

Anthony, Edward M., Jr.
1954   An exploratory inquiry into lexical clusters.
        American Speech 29.3:175-180. New York.
        (Reprinted 1958, pp. 128-133 in Readings in
        applied English linguistics, edited by
        H. B. Allen. New York: Century Crofts.)

Apostel, Léo, Benoit Mandelbrot, and Albert Morf
1957   Logique, langage et théorie de l'information.
        With an introduction by Jean Piaget. (Bib-
        liothèque Scientifique Internationale:
        Études d'épistémologie genétique, No. 3.)
        vi, 207 pp. Paris: Presses Universitaires
        de France.

Apresjan, Ju. D.
1962   O ponjatijakh i metodakh strukturnoj
        leksikologii. (On the concepts and methods
        of structural lexicology.) Pp. 141-162 in
        Problemy strukturnoj lingvistiki. Moscow:
        USSR Academy of Sciences.

[0:4]

Apresjan, Ju. D. (cont.)
    1966   Analyse distributionnelle des significations
            et champs sémantiques structurés. Langages
            1:44-74. Paris.

    1969   Syntaxe et sémantique. Langages 15:57-66.
            Paris.

Aranguren, José Luis
    1967   Human communication. Translated from the
            Spanish by Frances Partridge. 255 pp.
            Toronto: McGraw-Hill.

Ardener, Edwin
    1971   Introductory essay: social anthropology and
            language. Pp. ix-ci in Social anthropology
            and language, edited by E. Ardener. London:
            Tavistock.

Ardener, Edwin, editor
    1971   Social anthropology and language. (Associa-
            tion of Social Anthropologists Monographs,
            10.) ci, 318 pp. London: Tavistock.

Ariel, S.
    1967   Semantic tests. Man (n.s.) 2.4:535-550.
            London.

Arlotto, Anthony T.
    1968   On defining "monosyllabism." Journal of the
            American Oriental Society 88.3:521-522. New
            Haven.

Arrow, Kenneth J.
    1951   Mathematical models in the social sciences.
            Pp. 129-154 in The policy sciences, edited
            by D. Lerner and H. O. Lasswell. Stanford:
            Stanford University Press.

Asch, Solomon E.
    1955   On the use of metaphor in the description
            of persons. Pp. 22-38 in On expressive
            language, edited by H. Werner. Worcester:
            Clark University.

    1958   The metaphor: a psychological inquiry.
            Pp. 86-94 in Person perception and inter-
            personal behavior, edited by R. Tagiuri
            and L. Petrullo. Stanford: Stanford
            University Press.

Ashby, W. Ross
    1958   Requisite variety and its implications for

the control of complex systems. Cybernetica
1.2:83-99. Namur, Belgium.

Atherton, Pauline, editor
1965   Classification research: proceedings.
(International Federation for Documentation
Publications, No. 370.) x, 563 pp. Copenhagen: Munksgaard.

Auber, Jacques and Maurice Soulé
1957   La Langue malgache en trente familles de
mots. Essai de regroupement systématique
de thèmes de la langue malgache. 235 pp.
Tananarive: Imprimerie Officielle.

Austerlitz, Robert
1959   Semantic components of pronoun systems:
Gilyak. Word 15.1:102-109. New York.

Austin, John Langshaw
1962   How to do things with words. (William
James Lectures, Harvard University, 1955.)
166 pp. Cambridge: Harvard University
Press.

Ayer, Alfred Jules
1946   Language, truth, and logic. 2d revised
(1936) edition. 160 pp. London: V. Gollane.

1947   Thinking and meaning. 28 pp. London:
H. K. Lewis. (Reprinted 1963, London:
University College.)

Bach, Emmon
1965   Structural linguistics and the philosophy
of science. Diogènes 51:111-128. Montreal.

Baldinger, Kurt
1966   Sémantique et structure conceptuelle. (Le
Concept "Se Souvenir.") Cahiers de Lexi-
cologie 8.1:3-46. Paris.

Banerjee, Nikunja Vihari
1963   Language, meaning and persons. 173 pp.
London: Allen and Unwin.

Barbosa, Alice Príncipe
1969   Teoria e prática dos sistemas de classifi-
cação bibliográfica. (Obras didáticas No.
1.) 441 pp. Rio de Janeiro: Instituto
Brasileiro de Bibliografia e Documentação.

Bar-Hillel, Yehoshua
1954   Logical syntax and semantics. Language
        30.2:230-237. Baltimore.

Barker, Roger G.
1968   Ecological psychology: concepts and methods
        for studying the environment of human
        behavior. vi, 242 pp. Stanford: Stanford
        University Press.

Barker, Roger G., editor
1963   The stream of behavior: explorations of its
        structure and content. 352 pp. New York:
        Appleton-Century-Crofts.

Barker, Roger G. and Louise Shedd Barker
1961   Behavior units for the comparative study of
        cultures. Pp. 457-476 in Studying personal-
        ity cross-culturally, edited by B. Kaplan.
        New York: Row, Peterson.

Barker, Roger G. and Herbert F. Wright
1954   Midwest and its children: the psychological
        ecology of an American town. viii, 532 pp.
        Evanston, Ill.: Row, Peterson.

Baron, Naomi
1971   Semantic relations between verbs and cognate
        objects. Stanford Occasional Papers in
        Linguistics 1:140-152. Stanford.

Barthes, Roland
1971   Elements of semiology. Translated by
        Annette Lavers and Colin Smith. 111 pp.
        New York: Hill and Wang.

Bartlett, Harley Harris
1940   The concept of genus: I. History of generic
        concept in botany. Bulletin of the Torrey
        Botanical Club 67.5:349-362. New York.

Bartlett, Harley Harris et al.
1940   The concept of genus: I-V. Bulletin of the
        Torrey Botanical Club 67.5:349-389. New
        York.

Barton, Allen H.
1955   The concept of property-space in social
        research. Pp. 40-53 in The language of
        social research, edited by P. F. Lazersfeld
        and M. Rosenberg. Glencoe, Ill.: Free Press.

Basilius, Harold
  1952   Neo-Humboldtian ethnolinguistics. Word
          8.2:95-105. New York.

Basso, Keith H.
  1967   Semantic aspects of linguistic accultura-
          tion. American Anthropologist 69.5:471-477.
          Menasha.

  1968   The western Apache classificatory verb sys-
          tem: a formal analysis. Southwestern Jour-
          nal of Anthropology 24.3:252-266. Albuquer-
          que.

  1970   Review of Cognitive anthropology, edited by
          Stephen A. Tyler. American Anthropologist
          72.3:611-613. Menasha.

Basson, Anthony Henry and Daniel John O'Connor
  1960   Introduction to symbolic logic. viii, 175
          pp. Glencoe, Ill.: Free Press.

Bastian, Jarvis
  1959   Review of Words and things, by Roger Brown.
          Word 15.2:353-356. New York.

Bather, Francis Arthur
  1927   Biological classification; past and future.
          Quarterly Journal of the Geological Society
          of London 83:lxii-civ. London.

Battig, William F. and William E. Montague
  1969   Category norms for verbal items in 56 cate-
          gories: a replication and extension of the
          Connecticut category norms. Journal of Ex-
          perimental Psychology Monograph 80.3(Part
          2):1-46. Lancaster, Pa.

Baum, John D.
  1964   Elements of point set typology. 150 pp.
          Englewood Cliffs, N. J.: Prentice-Hall.

Bazell, Charles Ernest
  1949   On the problem of the morpheme. Archivum
          Linguisticum 1:1-15. Glasgow. (Reprinted
          in Bobbs-Merrill Reprint Series in Language
          and Linguistics No. 4. Indianapolis.)

  1953   Le Sémantique structurale. Dialogues No. 3:
          120-132. Istanbul.

  1954a   The choice of criteria in structural lin-
          guistics. Word 10.2-3:126-135. New York.

Bazell, Charles Ernest (cont.)
1954b   The sememe. Litera I:17-31. Istanbul.

Bazell, C. E., J. C. Catford, M. A. K. Halliday, and
         R. H. Robins, editors
1966   In memory of J. R. Firth. xi, 500 pp.
         London: Longmans.

Beckenbach, Edwin F.
1964   Network flow problems. Pp. 348-365 in
         Applied combinatorial mathematics, edited
         by E. F. Beckenbach. New York: John Wiley.

Beckenbach, Edwin F., editor
1964   Applied combinatorial mathematics. viii,
         608 pp. New York: John Wiley.

Beckner, Morton
1959   The biological way of thought. viii, 200 pp.
         New York: Columbia University Press.

Beekman, John
1968a   Eliciting vocabulary, meaning, and colloca-
         tions. Notes on Translation No. 29:1-11.
         Tlalpan, México, D. F.

1968b   Implicit information and translation. Notes
         on Translation No. 30:3-14. Tlalpan,
         México, D. F.

1968c   Classifying translation problems. Notes on
         Translation No. 30:15-18. Tlalpan, México,
         D. F.

1969   Metaphor and simile. Notes on Translation
         No. 31:1-22. Hidalgo, Mexico.

Bellert, Irena and Waclaw Zawadowski
1970   Preliminary attempt at outlining a system of
         linguistic signs in terms of the theory of
         categories. Pp. 232-243 in Sign·language·
         culture, (Janua Linguarum, Series Maior 1),
         edited by A. J. Greimas et al. The Hague
         and Paris: Mouton.

Belloc, Hillaire
1931   On translation. 44 pp. Oxford: Clarendon.
         (Reprinted 1959, The Bible Translator 10:
         83-100. London.)

Bendix, Edward Herman
1966   Componential analysis of general vocabulary:

the semantic structure of a set of verbs in English, Hindi, and Japanese. (International Journal of American Linguistics 32.2 [Part 2]; Publication 41, Indiana University Research Center in Anthropology, Folklore, and Linguistics.) x, 190 pp. Bloomington.

Bendor-Samuel, John T.
1961   The verbal piece in Jebero. (Supplement to Word, Monograph No. 4.) 120 pp. New York.

Bennett, David C.
1968   English prepositions: a stratificational approach. Journal of Linguistics 4.1:153-172. London.

1969   A stratificational view of polysemy. 18 pp. New Haven: Linguistic Automation Project, Yale University.

Benveniste, Émile
1966a   Formes nouvelles de la composition nominale. II. Composition et synopsie. Bulletin de la Société de Linguistique de Paris 61:90-95. Paris.

1966b   Convergences typologiques. L'Homme 6.2: 5-12. Paris.

Berg, R. F.
1966   On the origin of verbal thinking: factors that might have contributed to the acquisition of language by man. Linguistics 28: 5-49. The Hague.

Berge, Claude
1964   The theory of graphs and its applications. 247 pp. London: Methuen; New York: John Wiley. (First published in France 1958; first published in Great Britain 1962.)

Berlin, Brent
1967   Categories of eating in Tzeltal and Navaho. International Journal of American Linguistics 33.1:1-6. Baltimore.

1968   Tzeltal numeral classifiers; a study in ethnographic semantics. (Janua Linguarum, Series Practica 70.) 243 pp. The Hague: Mouton.

1970   A universalist-evolutionary approach in

semantics. Bulletins of the American Anthropological Association 3.3(Part 2): 3-18. Washington.

Berlin, Brent, Dennis E. Breedlove, and Peter H. Raven
1966   Folk taxonomies and biological classification. Science 154.3746:273-275. Washington.

1968   Covert categories and folk taxonomies. American Anthropologist 70.2:290-299. Menasha.

Berlin, Brent and A. Kimball Romney
1964   Descriptive semantics of Tzeltal numeral classifiers. Pp. 79-98 in Transcultural studies in cognition, (American Anthropologist 66.3[Part 2], Special Publication), edited by A. K. Romney and R. G. D'Andrade. Menasha.

Bernstein, Basil
1962a   Linguistic codes, hesitation phenomena and intelligence. Language and Speech 5(Part 1):31-46. Teddington, England.

1962b   Social class, linguistic codes and grammatical elements. Language and Speech 5(Part 4):221-240. Teddington, England.

1964   Elaborated and restricted codes: their social origins and some consequences. American Anthropologist 66.6(Part 2):55-69. Menasha.

Berry, Brian Joe Lobley
1958   A note concerning methods of classification. Annals of the Association of American Geographers 48.3:300-303. Albany.

Berry, Brian Joe Lobley and Duane F. Marble
1968   Spatial analysis. xi, 512 pp. Englewood Cliffs, N. J.: Prentice-Hall.

Bertalanffy, L. von
1955   An essay on the relativity of categories. Philosophy of Science 22.2:243-263. Baltimore.

Bès, Gabriel G.
1967   Parenté génétique et parenté typologique. La Linguistique 3.2:139-150. Paris.

Bickerton, Derek
 1969   Prolegomena to a linguistic theory of meta-
         phor. Foundations of Language 5.1:34-52.
         Dordrecht.

Bierstedt, Robert
 1959   Nominal and real definitions in sociological
         theory. Pp. 121-144 in Symposium on socio-
         logical theory, edited by L. Gross. Evans-
         ton and White Plains: Row, Peterson.

Bierwisch, Manfred
 1967   Some semantic universals of German adjecti-
         vals. Foundations of Language 3.1:1-36.
         Dordrecht.

 1969   On certain problems of semantic representa-
         tions. Foundations of Language 5.2:153-184.
         Dordrecht.

 1970   Semantics. Pp. 166-184 in New horizons in
         linguistics, edited by J. Lyons. Harmonds-
         worth, England: Penguin Books.

Birch, L. C. and P. R. Ehrlich
 1967   Evolutionary history and taxonomy. System-
         atic Zoology 16.3:282-285. Lawrence, Kans.

Black, Mary B.
 1963   On formal ethnographic procedure. American
         Anthropologist 65.6:1347-1351. Menasha.

Black, Mary and Duane Metzger
 1965   Ethnographic description and the study of
         law. Pp. 141-165 in The ethnography of law,
         (American Anthropologist 67.6[Part 2],
         Special Publication), edited by L. Nader.
         Menasha.

Black, Max
 1949   Language and philosophy: studies in method.
         xiii, 264 pp. Ithaca: Cornell University
         Press.

 1959   Linguistic relativity: the views of Benjamin
         Lee Whorf. Philosophical Review 68:228-238.
         Ithaca.

 1962   Models and metaphors: studies in language
         and philosophy. 267 pp. Ithaca: Cornell
         University Press.

Black, Max (cont.)
1969   The labyrinth of language. 220 pp. New
        York and Toronto: New American Library.

Black, Max, editor
1962   The importance of language. 169 pp. Engle-
        wood Cliffs, N. J.: Prentice-Hall.

Blackwelder, Richard E.
1955   Review of The language of taxonomy, by John
        R. Gregg. Systematic Zoology 4.1:41-42.
        Baltimore.

1967   A critique of numerical taxonomy. Systemat-
        ic Zoology 16.1:64-72. Lawrence, Kans.

1969   Reply to Randal and Scott. Systematic Zool-
        ogy 18.4:468-472. Lawrence, Kans.

Blackwood, Beatrice
1970   The classification of artefacts in the Pitt
        Rivers Museum, Oxford. (Occasional Papers
        on Technology 11.) 94 pp. Oxford: Oxford
        University Press.

Blagden, John Frederick
1968   Thesaurus compilation methods. Aslib Pro-
        ceedings 20.8:345-349. London.

Blaut, James M.
1970   Geographic models of imperialism. Antipode:
        A Radical Journal of Geography 2.1:65-85.
        Worcester, Mass.

Bliss, Henry
1929   The organization of knowledge and the system
        of the sciences. Introduction by John Dewey.
        xx, 433 pp. New York: Henry Holt.

Bloch, Bernard and George L. Trager
1942   Outline of linguistic analysis. (Special
        Publications of the Linguistic Society of
        America.) 82 pp. Baltimore: Waverly Press.

Bloomfield, Leonard
1914   An introduction to the study of language.
        335 pp. New York: Henry Holt.

1933   Language. 564 pp. New York: Henry Holt.
        (First edition 1914, q.v.)

1936   Language and ideas? Language 12.2:89-95.
        Baltimore.

1942   Philosophical aspects of language. Pp. 173-
        177 in Studies in the history of culture;
        the disciplines of the humanities. Menasha:
        American Council of Learned Societies.

1943   Meaning. Monatshefte für deutschen Unter-
        richt 35:101-106. Madison, Wisc.

1944   Secondary and tertiary responses to language.
        Language 20.2:45-55. Baltimore.

Boas, Franz
1911   Introduction. Pp. 1-83 in Part 1 of Handbook
        of American Indian languages, (Bulletin of
        the Bureau of American Ethnology, No. 40),
        edited by F. Boas. Washington.

Bock, Philip K.
1964   Social structure and language structure.
        Southwestern Journal of Anthropology 20.4:
        393-403. Albuquerque.

Bock, Walter J.
1969   Nonvalidity of the "phylogenetic fallacy."
        Systematic Zoology 18.1:111-115. Lawrence,
        Kans.

Bodde, Dirk
1939   Types of Chinese categorical thinking.
        Journal of the American Oriental Society
        59.2:200-219. New Haven.

Boguslawski, A.
1970   On semantic primitives and meaningfulness.
        Pp. 143-152 in Sign·language·culture, (Janua
        Linguarum, Series Maior 1), edited by A. J.
        Greimas et al. The Hague and Paris: Mouton.

Bohannan, Paul
1956   On the use of native language categories in
        ethnology. American Anthropologist 58.3:
        557. Menasha.

Bohr, Niels
1939   Natural philosophy and human cultures.
        Nature 143.3616:268-272. London.

Bolinger, Dwight L.
1963   The uniqueness of the word. Lingua 12.2:
        113-136. Amsterdam.

1965   The atomization of meaning. Language 14.4:
        555-573. Baltimore.

[0:14]

Boole, George
    1847   The mathematical analysis of logic. 82 pp.
            Cambridge. (Reprinted and elaborated in
            1854; reprinted in 1948, New York: Philo-
            sophical Library.)

    1854   An investigation of the laws of thought.
            v, 424 pp. London: Macmillan.

Boons, Jean-Paul
    1967   Synomymie, antonymie et facteurs stylistiques.
            Communications 10:167-188. Paris.

Borko, Harold, editor
    1962   Computer applications in the behavioral
            sciences. 633 pp. Englewood Cliffs, N. J.:
            Prentice-Hall.

Bortoft, Henri
    1968   Language, will and the fact. Systematics
            6.3:201-224. London.

Boulding, Kenneth Ethwart
    1956   The image. 176 pp. Ann Arbor: University
            of Michigan Press.

Bousfield, A. K. and W. A. Bousfield
    1966   Measurement of clustering and of sequential
            constancies in repeated free recall. Psycho-
            logical Reports 19:935-942. Missoula, Mont.

Bousfield, W. A. and B. H. Cohen
    1955   The occurrence of clustering in the recall
            of randomly arranged words of different
            frequencies of usage. Journal of General
            Psychology 52:83-95. Provincetown.

Bousfield, W. A., B. H. Cohen, and G. A. Whitmarsh
    1958   Associative clustering in the recall of words
            of different taxonomic frequencies of occur-
            rence. Psychological Reports 4:39-44.
            Missoula, Mont.

Bradshaw, John
    1967   Some New Testament key words in Samoan.
            The Bible Translator 18:75-82. London.

Braine, Martin D. S.
    1960   Problems and issues in the study of concep-
            tual development. 35 pp. Washington:
            Department of Clinical and Social Psychology,
            Walter Reed Army Institute of Research.

Braithwaite, Richard Bevan
1960   Scientific explanation: a study of the
(1953) function of theory, probability and law in
        science. x, 374 pp. New York: Harper.

Bréal, Michel Jules Alfred
1897   Essai de sémantique (science des significa-
        tions). 349 pp. Paris: Hachette. (Eng-
        lish translation 1900, Semantics: studies
        in the science of meaning. London and New
        York: Holt.)

Bright, Jane O. and William Bright
1965   Semantic structures in northwestern Califor-
        nia and the Sapir-Whorf hypothesis. Pp. 249-
        258 in Formal semantic analysis, (American
        Anthropologist 67.5[Part 2], Special Publica-
        tion), edited by E. A. Hammel. Menasha.

Bright, William
1968a   Language IV: Language and culture. Inter-
        national Encyclopedia of the Social Sciences
        9:18-22. New York: Macmillan and Free Press.

1968b   Toward a cultural grammar. Pp. 20-29 in
        Indian linguistics, Vol. 29 (Katre Felicita-
        tion Volume, Part 1), edited by A. M. Ghatage
        et al. Poona: Deccan College, Linguistic
        Society of India.

Bright, William, editor
1966   Sociolinguistics: proceedings of the UCLA
        Sociolinguistics Conference, 1964. (Janua
        Linguarum, Series Maior 20.) 324 pp. The
        Hague: Mouton.

Broadfield, A.
1946   The philosophy of classification. vii, 102
        pp. London: Grafton.

Bronowski, Jacob and Ursula Bellugi
1970   Language, name, and concept. Science 168.
        3932:669-673. Washington.

Bross, Irwin D. J.
1964   Prisoners of jargon. American Journal of
        Public Health 54.6:918-927. New York.

Brough, John
1953   Some Indian theories of meaning. Transac-
        tions of the Philological Society, pp. 161-
        176. Oxford.

Brower, Reuben A., editor
    1959   On translation. xii, 298 pp. Cambridge:
            Harvard University Press.

Brown, Roger W.
    1956   Language and categories. Pp. 247-312 (Appen-
            dix) in A study of thinking, by J. S. Bruner
            et al. New York: John Wiley.

    1958a   Words and things. xviii, 398 pp. Glencoe,
            Ill.: Free Press. (Reprinted 1968, New York:
            Free Press; London: Collier-Macmillan.)

    1958b   How shall a thing be called? Psychological
            Review 65.1:14-21. Lancaster, Pa.

    1965   The semantic system; language, thought, and
            society. Pp. 306-349 (Chapter 7) in Social
            psychology, by R. W. Brown. New York: Free
            Press; London: Collier-Macmillan.

Brown, Roger W. and Marguerite Ford
    1961   Address in American English. Journal of
            Abnormal and Social Psychology 62.2:375-385.
            Baltimore.

Brown, Roger W. and Albert Gilman
    1960   The pronouns of power and solidarity. Pp.
            253-276 in Aspects of style in language,
            edited by T. A. Sebeok. Cambridge: MIT
            Press; New York: John Wiley.

Brown, Roger W. and Eric H. Lenneberg
    1954   A study in language and cognition. Journal
            of Abnormal and Social Psychology 49.3:454-
            462. Baltimore.

Bruner, Jerome S.
    1957   Going beyond the information given. Pp. 41-
            70 in Contemporary approaches to cognition,
            by J. S. Bruner et al. Cambridge: Harvard
            University Press.

Bruner, Jerome S. et al.
    1957   Contemporary approaches to cognition: a
            symposium held at the University of Colorado.
            210 pp. Cambridge: Harvard University Press.

Bruner, Jerome S., Jacqueline J. Goodnow, and George A.
            Austin
    1956   A study of thinking. With an appendix on
            language by Roger W. Brown. 330 pp. New
            York: John Wiley.

Bruner, Jerome S., Rose R. Olver, and Patricia M.
      Greenfield
  1966   Studies in cognitive growth. xviii, 343 pp.
            New York: John Wiley.

Buchanan, Robert Earle
  1969   Critique of "Nomenifers: are they christened
            or classified?" Systematic Zoology 18.3:343-
            344. Lawrence, Kans.

Buchanan, Robert Earle et al., editors
  1958   International code of nomenclature of bacte-
            ria and viruses. Revised edition. 180 pp.
            Ames: Iowa State University Press.

Buchler, Ira R. and R. Freeze
  1966   The distinctive features of pronominal sys-
            tems. Anthropological Linguistics 8.8:78-
            105. Bloomington, Ind.

Buchler, Ira R. and Henry A. Selby
  1970   Animal, vegetable, or mineral? Pp. 213-234 in
            Échanges et communications; mélanges offerts à
            Claude Lévi-Strauss à l'occasion do son 60ème
            anniversaire, edited by J. Pouillon and P.
            Maranda. The Hague and Paris: Mouton.

Buck, Roger C. and David L. Hull
  1966   The logical structure of the Linnean hier-
            archy. Systematic Zoology 15.2:97-111.
            Lawrence, Kans.

  1969   Reply to Gregg. Systematic Zoology 18.3:
            354-347. Lawrence, Kans.

Bühler, Karl
  1934   Sprachtheorie. Die Darstellungsfunktion der
            Sprache. xvi, 434 pp. Jena: Fischer.

Bull, William E.
  1948   Natural frequency and word counts; the falla-
            cy of frequencies. Classical Journal 44.8:
            469-484. St. Louis, Mo.

Bullock, A. A.
  1968   What is a new taxon? Taxon 17.5:504-506.
            Utrecht.

Bulmer, Ralph N. H.
  1970   Which came first, the chicken or the egg-head?
            Pp. 1069-1091 in Échanges et communications;
            mélanges offerts à Claude Lévi-Strauss à

l'occasion de son 60ème anniversaire, edited by J. Pouillon and P. Maranda. The Hague and Paris: Mouton.

Bulmer, Ralph N. H. (cont.)
1971   Science, ethnoscience and education. Papua and New Guinea Journal of Education 7.1:22-23. Sydney.

Burke, Kenneth
1962   What are the signs of what?: a theory of 'entitlement.' Anthropological Linguistics 4.6:1-23. Bloomington, Ind.

Burks, Arthur W.
1949   Icon, index and symbol. Philosophy and Phenomenological Research 9:673-689. Buffalo.

Burling, Robbins
1962   A structural restatement of Njamal kinship terminology. Man 62:122-124 (Art. 201). London.

1963   Garo kinship terms and the analysis of meaning. Ethnology 2.1:70-85. Pittsburgh.

1964a   Cognition and componential analysis: God's truth or hocus-pocus? American Anthropologist 66.1:20-28. Menasha.

1964b   Burling's rejoinder. American Anthropologist 66.1:120-122. Menasha.

1965   How to choose a Burmese numeral classifier. Pp. 243-264 in Context and meaning in cultural anthropology, edited by M. E. Shapiro. New York: Free Press; London: Collier-Macmillan.

1969   Linguistics and ethnographic description. American Anthropologist 71.5:817-827. Menasha.

1970   Man's many voices: language in its cultural context. xi, 222 pp. New York: Holt, Rinehart and Winston.

Burma, Benjamin H.
1949a   The species concept: a semantic review. Evolution 3.4:369-370. Lancaster, Pa.

1949b   Postscriptum [see Burma 1949a, Mayr 1949].
         Evolution 3.4:372-373. Lancaster, Pa.

1954   Reality, existence, and classification: a
         discussion of the species problem. Madroño
         12:193-209. Berkeley.

Burns, John M.
1968   A simple model illustrating problems of
         phylogeny and classification. Systematic
         Zoology 17.2:170-173. Lawrence, Kans.

Bursill-Hall, G. L.
1960   Levels analysis: J. R. Firth's theories of
         linguistic analysis I. Journal of the Cana-
         dian Linguistic Association 6.2:124-135.
         Toronto.

Busacker, Robert G. and Thomas L. Saaty
1965   Finite graphs and networks: an introduction
         with applications. xiv, 283 pp. New York:
         McGraw-Hill.

Buyssens, Eric
1967   La Communication et l'articulation linguis-
         tique. 175 pp. Brussels: Presses Universi-
         taires de Bruxelles.

1970   The common name and the proper name. Pp. 21-
         23 in Studies in general and Oriental linguis-
         tics: presented to Shirô Hattori on the
         occasion of his sixtieth birthday, edited by
         R. Jakobson and S. Kawamoto. Tokyo: TEC
         Company.

Cain, Arthur James
1956   The genus in evolutionary taxonomy. System-
         atic Zoology 5.3:97-109. Baltimore.

1958   Logic and memory in Linnaeus's system of
         taxonomy. Proceedings of the Linnean Society
         of London 169.1-2:144-163. London.

1959a   Deductive and inductive methods in post-
         Linnaean taxonomy. Proceedings of the
         Linnean Society of London 170.2:185-217.
         London.

1959b   The post-Linnaean development of taxonomy.
         Proceedings of the Linnean Society of London
         170.3:234-244. London.

Cain, Arthur James (cont.)
    1959c   Taxonomic concepts. Ibis 101.3-4:302-318.
             London.

Cain, A. J. and G. A. Harrison
    1958   An analysis of the taxonomist's judgment of
             affinity. Proceedings of the Zoological
             Society of London 131:85-98. London.

Calame-Griaule, Geneviève
    1965   Ethnologie et langage; la parole chez les
             Dogon. 590 pp. Paris: Gallimard.

Caless, T. W.
    1969   Subject analysis matrices for document
             classification. Classification Society
             Bulletin 2.1:29-37. Leicester, England.

Calvet, Louis-Jean
    1970   Arbitraire du signe et langues en contact:
             les systèmes de numération en bambara, dioula
             et malinké. La Linguistique 6.2:119-123.
             Paris.

Camin, Joseph H. and Robert R. Sokal
    1965   A method for deducing branch sequences in
             phylogeny. Evolution 19.3:311-326.
             Lawrence, Kans.

Camp, W. H.
    1951   Biosystematy. Brittonia 7.3:113-127.
             New York.

Campbell, Brenton
    1967   Linguistic meaning. Linguistics 33:5-23.
             The Hague.

Cancian, Frank
    1963   Informant error and native prestige ranking
             in Zinacantan. American Anthropologist
             65.3:1068-1075. Menasha.

Capell, A.
    1960   Language and world view in the northern
             Kimberley, Western Australia. Southwestern
             Journal of Anthropology 16.1:1-21.
             Albuquerque.

Carelman, [Jacques]
    1971   Catalogue d'objets introuvables. 137 pp.
             Paris: André Balland. (American English
             edition published 1971 as Catalog of

fantastic things, 123 pp. New York: Ballantine Books.)

Carnap, Rudolf
1936-   Testability and meaning. Philosophy of Sci-
1937   ence 3.4:420-471; 4.1:1-40. Baltimore.

1939   Foundations of logic and mathematics.
           (International Encyclopedia of Unified Sci-
           ence 1.3.) 71 pp. Chicago: University of
           Chicago Press.

1942   Introduction to semantics. xii, 263 pp.
           Cambridge: Harvard University Press.

1954   Testability and meaning. 40 pp. New Haven:
           Graduate Philosophy Club of Yale University.

1955   Meaning and synonomy in natural languages.
           Philosophical Studies 6:33-47. Minneapolis.

1956a   Meaning and necessity: a study in semantics
(1947)   and modal logic. 2d edition. x, 258 pp.
           Chicago: University of Chicago Press.

1956b   The methodological character of theoretical
           concepts. Pp. 38-76 in Vol. 1 of Minnesota
           studies in the philosophy of science, edited
           by H. Feigl and M. Scriven. Minneapolis:
           University of Minnesota Press.

1959   Introduction to semantics and formalization
           of logic. 441 pp. Cambridge: Harvard
           University Press.

Carroll, John B.
1964a   Language and thought. x, 118 pp. Englewood
           Cliffs, N. J.: Prentice-Hall.

1964b   Words, meanings and concepts. Harvard Educa-
           tional Review 34.2:178-202. Montpelier, Vt.

Carroll, John B., editor
1956   Language, thought, and reality. Selected
           writings of Benjamin Lee Whorf. Foreword by
           Stuart Chase. 278 pp., bibliography of Whorf.
           Cambridge: MIT Press; New York: John Wiley.

Carroll, John B. and Joseph B. Casagrande
1958   The function of language classifications in
           behavior. Pp. 18-31 in Readings in social
           psychology, edited by E. Maccoby et al.
           New York: Holt.

Carroll, John B., Peter Davies, and Barry Richman
1971   The American Heritage word frequency book.
        liv, 856 pp. Boston: Houghton Mifflin;
        New York: American Heritage.

Carvell, H. T. and Jan Svartvik
1969   Computational experiments in grammatical
        classification. (Janua Linguarum, Series
        Minor 61.) 271 pp. The Hague and Paris:
        Mouton.

Casagrande, Joseph B.
1954   The ends of translation. International
        Journal of American Linguistics 20.4:335-
        340. Baltimore.

Casagrande, Joseph B. and Kenneth L. Hale
1960   The Southwest Project in Comparative Psycho-
        linguistics: a preliminary report. Pp. 777-
        782 in Men and cultures, (Selected papers of
        the Fifth International Congress of Anthro-
        pological and Ethnological Sciences, Phila-
        delphia, 1956), edited by A. F. C. Wallace.
        Philadelphia: University of Pennsylvania
        Press.

1967   Semantic relations in Papago folk-definitions.
        Pp. 165-196 in Studies in southwestern ethno-
        linguistics, edited by D. H. Hymes and W. E.
        Bittle. The Hague and Paris: Mouton.

Cassirer, Ernst
1923   Die Sprache. (Philosophie der symbolischen
        Formen, Vol. 1.) xii, 293 pp. Berlin:
        Bruno Cassirer. (Translated 1953 by Ralph
        Mannheim as Language, [Philosophy of symbolic
        forms, Vol. 1], xiv, 328 pp. New Haven:
        Yale University Press.)

Catford, J. C.
1959   English as a foreign language. Pp. 164-189
        in The teaching of English, edited by R.
        Quirk and A. H. Smith. London: Secker and
        Warburg.

1965   A linguistic theory of translation: an essay
        in applied linguistics. viii, 103 pp.
        London: Oxford University Press.

Cattell, Raymond B. and Malcolm A. Coulter
1966   Principles of behavioural taxonomy and the
        mathematical basis of the taxonomic computer

program. British Journal of Mathematical and Statistical Psychology 19.2:237-269. London.

Cazacu, Titiana
1956 Le Principe de l'adaptation au contexte. Revue de Linguistique 1:79-118. Bucharest.

Ceccata, Silvio, editor
1960 Linguistic analysis and programming for mechanical translation. 242 pp. Milan: Feltrinelli.

Chafe, Wallace L.
1962 Phonetics, semantics, and language. Language 38.4:335-344. Baltimore.

1963 Handbook of the Seneca language. (New York State Museum and Science Service Bulletin No. 388.) iv, 71 pp. Albany: University of the State of New York, State Education Department.

1965 Meaning in language. Pp. 23-36 in Formal semantic analysis, (American Anthropologist 67.5[Part 2], Special Publication), edited by E. A. Hammel. Menasha.

1967 Language as symbolization. Language 43.1: 57-91. Baltimore.

1970a Meaning and the structure of language. viii, 360 pp. Chicago and London: University of Chicago Press.

1970b A semantically based sketch of Onondaga. (Memoir 25; Supplement to International Journal of American Linguistics 36.2[Part 2].) 91 pp. Baltimore.

Chamberlain, Alexander F.
1903 Primitive theories of knowledge: a study in linguistic psychology. Monist 13:295-302. Chicago.

Chao, Yuen Ren
1956 Chinese terms of address. Language 32.1: 217-244. Baltimore.

Cheetham, Alan H. and Joseph E. Hazel
1969 Binary (presence-absence) similarity coefficients. Journal of Paleontology 43.5:1130-1136. Menasha.

Chevalier, Auguste
1923   L'Oeuvre d'Alexis Jordan et la notion
        actuelle d'espèce en systématique. Revue
        de Botanique Appliquée et d'Agriculture
        Coloniale 3:441-459. Paris.

Chiri, Mashio
1953-   Bunrui Ainugo jiten. (Classified dictionar-
1962   ies of the Ainu language.) 3 vols. Vol. 1,
        Plants, 1953; Vol. 2, Animals, 1962; Vol. 3,
        Humans, 1954. Tokyo: Nihon Jomin Bunka
        Kenkyusho.

Chomsky, A. Noam
1955   Semantic considerations in grammar. George-
        town University Monograph Series on Language
        and Linguistics, No. 8:141-150. Washington.

1957   Syntactic structures. (Janua Linguarum,
        Series Minor 4.) 116 pp. The Hague: Mouton.

1959a   Review of Essays, by J. H. Greenberg. Word
        15.1:202-218. New York.

1959b   Review of Verbal behavior, by B. F. Skinner.
        Language 35.1:26-58. Baltimore.

1961   On the notion "rule of grammar." Proceedings
        of Symposia in Applied Mathematics 12:6-24.
        Providence.

1962   Explanatory models in linguistics. In Pro-
        ceedings of the International Conference on
        Logic, Methodology, and Philosophy of Sci-
        ence. Stanford: Stanford University Press.

1965a   Aspects of the theory of syntax. 251 pp.
        Cambridge: MIT Press.

1965b   Persistent topics in linguistic theory.
        Diogenes 51:13-20. Montreal.

1966   Topics in the theory of generative grammar.
        (Janua Linguarum, Series Minor 56.) 95 pp.
        The Hague: Mouton.

1968   The sound pattern of English. xiv, 470 pp.
        New York: Harper and Row.

1970a   Some observations on the problems of semantic
        analysis in natural languages. Pp. 256-260
        in Sign·language·culture, (Janua Linguarum,

Series Maior 1), edited by A. J. Greimas
et al. The Hague and Paris: Mouton.

1970b   Deep structure, surface structure, and
semantic interpretation. Pp. 52-91 in
Studies in general and Oriental linguistics;
presented to Shirô Hattori on the occasion
of his sixtieth birthday, edited by R. Jakobson and S. Kawamoto. Tokyo: TEC Company.

Christensen, Bjarne Westring
1967   Glossématique, linguistique fonctionnelle,
grammaire générative et stratification du
langage. Word 23.1-2-3(Part 1):57-73.
New York.

Cicourel, Aaron Victor
1964   Method and measurement in sociology. viii,
247 pp. Glencoe, Ill.: Free Press.

Clarke, David L.
1968   Analytical archaeology. xx, 684 pp. London:
Methuen.

Cleverdon, Cyril
1967   The Cranfield tests on index language devices.
Aslib Proceedings 19.6:173-194. London.

Cofer, Charles N., editor
1961   Verbal learning and verbal behavior. Proceedings of a conference sponsored by the
Office of Naval Research and New York University. vi, 241 pp. New York: McGraw-Hill.

Cohen, B. H., W. A. Bousfield and G. A. Whitmarsh
1957   Cultural norms for verbal items in 43 categories. (Technical Report No. 22, Studies
on the mediation of verbal behavior.) iv,
41, V pp. Storrs, Conn.: Department of
Psychology, University of Connecticut.

Cohen, Morris and Ernest Nagel
1934   An introduction to logic and scientific
method. xii, 467 pp. New York: Harcourt,
Brace.

Cohn, Robert
1961   Language and behavior. American Scientist
49.4:502-508. New Haven.

Colby, Benjamin N.
1964   Folk science studies. El Palacio 70.4:5-14.
Santa Fe.

Colby, Benjamin N. (cont.)
1966   Ethnographic semantics: a preliminary sur-
        vey. Current Anthropology 7.1:3-32. Utrecht.

Cole, A. J., editor
1969   Numerical taxonomy. 324 pp. London and
        New York: Academic Press.

Cole, Michael, John Gay, Joseph A. Glick, Donald W.
        Sharp, et al.
1971   The cultural context of learning and think-
        ing, an exploration in experimental anthro-
        pology. 304 pp. New York: Basic Books.

Colless, Donald H.
1967a   An examination of certain concepts in
        phenetic taxonomy. Systematic Zoology 16.1:
        6-27. Lawrence, Kans.

1967b   The phylogenetic fallacy. Systematic Zoology
        16.4:289-295. Lawrence, Kans.

1969a   The phylogenetic fallacy revisited. System-
        atic Zoology 18.1:115-126. Lawrence, Kans.

1969b   The interpretation of Hennig's "Phylogenetic
        systematics"--a reply to Dr. Schlee. System-
        atic Zoology 18.1:134-155. Lawrence, Kans.

1969c   A note on the equivalence of characters and
        numbers of characters needed. Systematic
        Zoology 18.4:455-456. Lawrence, Kans.

1969d   Phylogenetic inference: a reply to Dr.
        Ghiselin. Systematic Zoology 18.4:462-466.
        Lawrence, Kans.

1970a   Type-specimens: their status and use. Sys-
        tematic Zoology 19.2:251-253. Lawrence, Kans.

1970b   The phenogram as an estimate of phylogeny.
        Systematic Zoology 19.4:352-262. Lawrence,
        Kans.

Collinson, William Edward
1961   Indication: a study of demonstratives,
(1937) articles, and other "indicaters." Edited
        by Alice V. Morris. 128 pp. Baltimore:
        Waverly Press. (Originally published 1937,
        Language Monographs No. 17. 128 pp. Balti-
        more.)

Collis, D. R. F.
1969-   On the establishment of visual parameters
1970   for the formalization of Eskimo semantics.
        Folk Nos. 11-12:309-328. Copenhagen.

Collitz, Klara H.
1931   Verbs of motion in their semantic divergence.
        (Supplement to Language, Language Monograph
        No. 8.) 112 pp. Philadelphia.

Conant, Francis P.
1961   Jarawa kin systems of reference and address:
        a componential comparison. Anthropological
        Linguistics 3.2:19-33. Bloomington, Ind.

Condon, John C., Jr.
1966   Semantics and communication. 115 pp. New
        York: Macmillan; London: Collier-Macmillan.

Conklin, Harold C.
1954   The relation of Hanunóo culture to the plant
        world. 471 pp. Ph.D. dissertation in
        anthropology, Yale University, New Haven.
        (Published by University Microfilms, Ann
        Arbor, Mich., 1967, [no. 67-4119].)

1955   Hanunóo color categories. Southwestern
        Journal of Anthropology 11.4:339-344.
        Albuquerque. (Reprinted 1964, pp. 189-192
        in Language in culture and society, edited
        by D. H. Hymes. New York: Harper and Row.)

1959   Linguistic play in its cultural context.
        Language 35.4:631-636. Baltimore. (Reprint-
        ed 1964, pp. 295-299 in Language, culture
        and society, edited by D. H. Hymes. New
        York: Harper and Row.)

1962a   Ethnobotanical problems in the comparative
        study of folk taxonomy. Proceedings of the
        Ninth Pacific Science Congress of the Pacific
        Science Association, 1957, 4:299-301.
        Bangkok.

1962b   Lexicographical treatment of folk taxonomies.
        Pp. 119-141 in Problems in lexicography:
        report of the Conference on Lexicography
        held at Indiana University, November 11-12,
        1960 (International Journal of American
        Linguistics 28.2[Part 4]; Publication 21,
        Indiana University Research Center in Anthro-
        pology, Folklore, and Linguistics), edited

by F. W. Householder and S. Saporta. Bloomington. (Volume reprinted with additions and corrections 1967.)

Conklin, Harold C. (cont.)
1962c   Comment [on C. O. Frake's "The ethnographic study of cognitive systems"]. Pp. 86-91 in Anthropology and human behavior, edited by T. Gladwin and W. C. Sturtevant. Washington: Anthropological Society of Washington. (Reprinted with corrections 1968, in Vol. 2 of Readings in anthropology, 2d edition, edited by M. H. Fried, New York: Crowell.)

1964   Ethnogenealogical method. Pp. 25-55 in Explorations in cultural anthropology: essays in honor of George Peter Murdock, edited by W. H. Goodenough. New York: McGraw-Hill. (Reprinted 1969, pp. 93-122 in Cognitive anthropology, edited by S. A. Tyler, New York: Holt, Rinehart, and Winston.)

1967a   Ifugao ethnobotany 1905-1965; the 1911 Beyer-Merrill report in perspective. Pp. 204-262 in Studies in Philippine anthropology, in honor of H. Otley Beyer, edited by M. D. Zamora. Quezon City: Alemar Phoenix. (Reprinted 1967 with minor changes, Economic Botany 21.3:243-273. Baltimore.)

1967b   Some aspects of ethnographic research in Ifugao. Transactions of the New York Academy of Sciences, Series 2, 30.1:99-121. New York.

Cooke, Charles A.
1952   Iroquois personal names--their classification. Proceedings of the American Philosophical Society 6.4:427-438. Philadelphia.

Cooper, John M.
1935   Magic and science. Thought 10.3:357-373. New York.

Copi, Irving M.
1954   Symbolic logic. 355 pp. New York: Macmillan.

Copley, James
1961   Shift of meaning. 166 pp. London: Oxford University Press.

Couffignal, Louis
1958   Le Symposium de Zürich et les concepts de
        base de la cybernétique. Cybernetica 1.1:
        15-31. Namur, Belgium.

Coult, Allan D.
1966   On the justification of untested componential
        analyses. American Anthropologist 68.4:1014-
        1015. Menasha.

1967   Lineage solidarity, transformational analysis,
        and the meaning of kinship terminologies.
        Man (n.s.)2.1:26-47. London.

Courrège, Philippe
1965   Un modèle mathématique des structures
        élémentaires de parenté. L'Homme 5.3-4:248-
        290. Paris.

Cowan, H. K. J.
1954   Ethno-linguistics and 'Papuan' etymology.
        Oceania 25.1:54-60. Sydney.

1963   Statistical determination of linguistic
        relationship. Studia Linguistica 16.2:57-
        96. Lund.

Cracraft, Joel
1967   Comments on homology and analogy. Systematic
        Zoology 16.4:355-359. Lawrence, Kans.

Cramer, Phebe
1968   Word association. ix, 274 pp. New York and
        London: Academic Press.

Crovello, Theodore J. and W. Wayne Moss
1971   A bibliography on classification in diverse
        disciplines. Classification Society Bulle-
        tin 2.3:29-45. Leicester, England.

Crowson, Roy A.
1970   Classification and biology. ix, 350 pp.
        New York: Atherton Press.

Cuisenier, J. and A. Miguel
1965   La Terminologie arabe de la parenté:
        analyse sémantique et analyse componentielle.
        L'Homme 5.3-4:17-59. Paris.

Čulík, Karel
1966   On mathematical models and the role of the
        mathematics in knowledge of reality. Kyber-
        netika 2.1:1-13. Prague.

Curtuis, Ernst Robert
1948   Europäische Literatur und lateinisches
        Mittelalter. 601 pp. Bern: A. Francke.

Dagnelie, P.
1966   A propos des différentes méthodes de classi-
        fication numérique. Revue de Statistique
        Appliqué 14.3:55-75. Paris.

Dalby, David
1964   The noun gàrii in Hausa: a semantic study.
        Journal of African Language 3(Part 3):273-
        305. London.

Dance, Frank E. X., editor
1967   Human communication theory: original essays.
        x, 332 pp. New York: Holt, Rinehart, and
        Winston.

D'Andrade, Roy G.
1965   Trait psychology and componential analysis.
        Pp. 215-228 in Formal semantic analysis,
        (American Anthropologist 67.5[Part 2],
        Special Publication), edited by E. A. Hammel.
        Menasha.

1970   Structure and syntax in the semantic analysis
        of kinship terminologies. Pp. 87-143 in
        Cognition: a multiple view, edited by P. L.
        Garvin. New York: Spartan Books.

Darlington, P. J., Jr.
1970   A practical criticism of Hennig-Brundin
        "phylogenetic systematics" and Antarctic
        biogeography. Systematic Zoology 19.1:1-18.
        Lawrence, Kans.

Davidson, R. A.
1967   A cybernetic approach to classification:
        preliminaries. Taxon 16.1:3-7. Utrecht.

Davies, Peter
1971   New views of lexicon. Pp. xli-liv in The
        American Heritage word frequency book, by
        J. B. Carroll, P. Davies, and B. Richman.
        Boston: Houghton Mifflin; New York:
        American Heritage.

Deese, James
1965   The structure of associations in language
        and thought. xiii, 216 pp. Baltimore:
        Johns Hopkins Press.

Delattre, Pierre
    1967   Acoustic or articulatory invariance?
            Glossa 1.1:3-25. Burnaby, B. C.

De Mauro, Tullio
    1967   Ludwig Wittgenstein: his place in the
            development of semantics. ix, 62 pp.
            Dordrecht: Reidel.

Deregowski, J. B.
    1966   Investigation into perception. Bulletin,
            Institute for Social Research, University
            of Zambia 1:27-30. Lusaka.

Descles, Jean-Pierre and Catherine Fuchs
    1969   Linguistique et mathématique. L'Homme 9.3:
            93-99. Paris.

Dettering, Richard
    1955   What phonetic writing did to meaning.
            Etc. 12:121-135. Bloomington, Ill.

Deutsch, Karl
    1966   On theories, taxonomies, and models as
            communication codes for organizing informa-
            tion. Behavioral Science 11.1:1-17. Ann
            Arbor.

Dewey, John
    1946   Peirce's theory of linguistic signs, thought,
            and meaning. Journal of Philosophy 43.4:
            85-95. New York.

Diemer, Alwin, editor
    1968   System und Klassifikation in Wissenschaft
            und Dokumentation. (Studien zur Wissen-
            schaftstheorie, Vol. 2.) 183 pp.
            Meisenheim am Glau: A. Hain.

Dijk, T. A. van
    1970   Sémantique structurale et analyse thématique.
            Un essai de lecture: André du Bouchet:
            'Du bord de la faux.' Lingua 23.1:28-54.
            Amsterdam.

Dixon, R. M. W.
    1964   On formal and contextual meaning. Acta
            Linguistica 14.1-2:23-45. Budapest.

    1971   A method of semantic description. Pp. 436-

471 in Semantics, an interdisciplinary
reader in philosophy, linguistics and
psychology, edited by D. D. Steinberg and
L. A. Jakobovits. Cambridge: Cambridge
University Press.

Dodd, Stuart Carter
    1968   Introducing "systemmetrics" for evaluating
        symbolic systems: 24 criteria for the
        excellence of scientific theories. System-
        atics 6.1:27-49. London.

Driver, Harold E.
    1965   Survey of numerical classification.
        Pp. 301-344 in The use of computers in
        anthropology, edited by D. Hymes. The
        Hague: Mouton.

Drozen, Vladimír and Stanislav Langer
    1966   A statistical evaluation of semantic
        information. Kybernetika 2.3:259-263.
        Prague.

Ducrot, Oswald
    1966   Logique et linguistique. Langages 2:3-30.
        Paris.

    1968   La Description sémantique des énoncés fran-
        çais et la notion de présupposition.
        L'Homme 8.1:37-53. Paris.

Duden   (Bibliographisches Institut, Mannheim)
    1956-   Der grosse Duden. (In 10 vols., compiled
    1970   by Paul Grebe, Rudolph Köster, Wolfgang
        Müller et al.) Vol. 1: Rechtschreibung,
        794 pp.; Vol. 2: Stilwörterbuch, 800 pp.;
        Vol. 3: Bildwörterbuch, [cf. The English
        Duden, etc.] 792 pp.; Vol. 4: Grammatik,
        699 pp.; Vol. 5: Fremdwörterbuch, 704 pp.;
        Vol. 6: Aussprachewörterbuch, 827 pp.;
        Vol. 7: Etymologie, 816 pp.; Vol. 8:
        Vergleichendes Synonymwörterbuch, ca. 750
        pp.; Vol. 9: Sprachliche Zweifelsfälle,
        760 pp.; Vol. 10: Bedeutungswörterbuch,
        800 pp. Mannheim: Bibliographisches
        Institut (Dudenverlag).

Duden (Bibliographisches Institut, Mannheim, and the
        Modern Languages Department of George S.
        Harrap and Co., Ltd., London)
    1960   The English Duden: a pictorial dictionary
        with English and German indexes. 672 pp.

Mannheim: Bibliographisches Institut
(Dudenverlag).

1962   Duden Français: Dictionnaire en images.
928 pp., illus., indices in French and
English. Mannheim: Bibliographisches
Institut (Dudenverlag).

1963   Duden Español: Diccionario por la imagen.
912 pp., illus., indices in Spanish and
English. Mannheim: Bibliographisches
Institut (Dudenverlag).

1964   Duden Italiano. Dizionario figurato. 896
pp., 368 picture plates, 8 plates in color.
Italian and German index with 25,000 entries.
Mannheim: Bibliographisches Institut
(Dudenverlag).

Dunnell, Robert C.
1971   Systematics in prehistory. x, 214 pp.
New York: Free Press; London: Collier-
Macmillan.

Durbin, Marshall E.
1966   The goals of ethnoscience. Anthropological
Linguistics 8.8:22-41. Bloomington, Ind.

Du Rietz, G. Einar
1930   The fundamental units of biological taxonomy.
Svensk Botanisk Tidskrift 24:333-428.
Uppsala.

Dutch, Robert A., editor
1962   Roget's thesaurus of English words and
phrases. New edition completely revised.
lii, 1309 pp. New York: St. Martin's Press.

Du Toit, Brian M.
1965   Pictorial depth perception and linguistic
relativity. Psychologica Africana 11.2:
51-63. Johannesburg.

Dyen, Isidore
1965   A lexicostatistical classification of the
Austronesian languages. (Supplement to
International Journal of American Linguistics 31.1; Memoir 19.) 64 pp. Baltimore.

Dyen, I., A. T. James and J. W. L. Cole
1967   Language divergence and estimated word
retention rate. Language 43.1:150-171.
Baltimore.

[0:34]

Eades, David C.
    1970   Theoretical and procedural aspects of numeri-
            cal taxonomy. Systematic Zoology 19.2:142-
            171. Lawrence, Kansas.

Ebeling, C. L.
    1955   On the meaning of the Russian cases. Pp.
            207-223 in Analecta Slavica, a Slavonic
            miscellany presented for his seventieth
            birthday to Bruno Becker... Amsterdam:
            De Bezige bij.

    1960   Linguistic units. (Janua Linguarum, Series
            Minor 12.) 143 pp. The Hague: Mouton.

    1962   A semantic analysis of the Dutch tenses.
            Lingua 11:86-99. Amsterdam.

Ehrmann, Jacques, editor
    1970   Structuralism. 264 pp. Garden City, N. Y.:
    (1966) Anchor Books. (Originally printed 1966,
            Yale French Studies 36-37, New Haven.)

Ellis, J. O.
    1966   On contextual meaning. Pp. 79-95 in In
            memory of J. R. Firth, edited by C. E.
            Bazell et al. London: Longmans.

Ellis, Jeffrey
    1966   Review of Structural semantics: an analysis
            of part of the vocabulary of Plato, by J.
            Lyons. Linguistics 24:85-115. The Hague.

Empson, W.
    1951   The structure of complex words. 449 pp.
            New York: New Directions.

Epling, P. J.
    1961   A note on Njamal kin-term usage. Man 61:
            152-159 (Art. 184). London.

Ervin, Susan M.
    1961   Semantic shift in bilingualism. American
            Journal of Psychology 74.2:233-241. Austin,
            Texas.

    1962   The connotations of gender. Word 18.3:249-
            261. New York.

Ervin-Tripp, Susan
    1964   An analysis of the interaction of language,
            topic, and listener. American Anthropologist

66.6(Part 2):86-102. Menasha.

Estabrook, George F.
1966   A mathematical model in graph theory for
          biological classification. Journal of
          Theoretical Biology 12.3:297-310. New York
          and London.

Estabrook, George F. and David J. Rogers
1966   A general method of taxonomic description
          for a computed similarity measure. Bio-
          science 16.11:789-793. Washington.

Evans, Bergen
1963   Couth to uncouth and vice versa. New York
          Times Magazine, November 10, pp. 22, 76,
          78, 80. New York.

Fabian, Johannes
1965   !Kung Bushman kinship: componential
          analysis and alternative interpretations.
          Anthropos 60.1-6:663-718. Fribourg.

Fant, Gunnar
1967   The nature of distinctive features. Pp.
          634-642 in To honor Roman Jakobson, essays
          on the occasion of his seventieth birthday,
          (Janua Linguarum, Series Maior 31). The
          Hague and Paris: Mouton.

Faris, James C.
1968   Validation in ethnographical description:
          the lexicon of 'occasions' in Cat Harbour.
          Man (n.s.)3.1:112-124. London.

Farradene, J. F. L.
1952   A scientific theory of classification and
          indexing: further consideration. Journal
          of Documentation 8.2:73-92. London.

Farris, James S.
1967a   The meaning of relationship and taxonomic
          procedure. Systematic Zoology 16.1:44-51.
          Lawrence, Kans.

1967b   Definitions of taxa. Systematic Zoology
          16.2:174-175. Lawrence, Kans.

1967c   Comment on psychologism. Systematic Zoology
          16.4:345-347. Lawrence, Kans.

1970   Methods for computing Wagner trees. System-
          atic Zoology 19.1:83-92. Lawrence, Kans.

[0:36]

Farris, James S., Arnold G. Kluge, and Michael J.
    Eckardt
  1970   A numerical approach to phylogenetic system-
          atics. Systematic Zoology 19.2:172-189.
          Lawrence, Kans.

Feibleman, James K.
  1967   Types of empirical discoveries. Systematics
          5.1:37-56. London.
Fel'dman, N. I.
  1957   Okkazional' nye slova v leksikografii.
          Voprosy jazykoznanija, No. 4:64-73. Moscow.

Ferguson, Charles A.
  1959   Diglossia. Word 15.2:325-340. New York.

Ferry, M.-P.
  1970   Sapir et l'ethnolinguistique. Langages
          18:12-21. Paris.

Feuer, Lewis S.
  1953   Sociological aspects of the relation between
          language and philosophy. Philosophy of
          Science 20.2:85-100. Baltimore.

Fillenbaum, Samuel and Amnon Rapoport
  1971   Structures in the subjective lexicon. viii,
          266 pp. New York and London: Academic
          Press.

Fillmore, Charles J.
  1966   Deictic categories in the semantics of
          'come.' Foundations of Language 2.3:219-227.
          Dordrecht.

  1967   On the syntax of preverbs. Glossa 1.2:91-
          125. Burnaby, B. C.

  1968a   Lexical entries for verbs. Foundations of
          Language 4.4:373-393. Dordrecht.

  1968b   The case for case. Pp. 1-88 in Universals
          in linguistic theory, edited by E. Bach and
          R. T. Harms. New York: Holt, Rinehart and
          Winston.

Fillmore, Charles J. and D. Terence Langendoen, editors
  1971   Studies in linguistic semantics. viii, 299
          pp. New York: Holt, Rinehart and Winston.

Findler, Nicholas V. and Wiley R. McKinzie
  1969   On a computer program that generates and

queries kinship structures. Behavioral
Science 14.4:334-340. Ann Arbor.

Firth, John Rupert
1935   The technique of semantics. Transactions
        of the Philological Society, 1935, pp. 36-
        72. London. (Reprinted, pp. 7-35 in
        Firth 1958.)

1948   The semantics of linguistic science. Lingua
        1.4:393-404. Haarlem.

1956   Linguistic analysis and translation. Pp.
        133-139 in For Roman Jakobson, edited by
        Morris Halle et al. The Hague: Mouton.

1957a   Ethnographic analysis and language with
        reference to Malinowski's views. Pp. 93-
        118 in Man and culture: an evaluation of
        the work of Bronislaw Malinowski, edited
        by Raymond Firth. London: Routledge and
        Kegan Paul.

1957b   A synopsis of linguistic theory, 1930-55.
        Pp. 1-32 in Studies in linguistic analysis,
        (Special Volume of the Philological Society).
        Oxford: Basel Blackwell.

1958   Papers on linguistics 1934-1951. xii, 233
        pp. London: Oxford University Press.

Fischer, John L.
1958   Social influences on the choice of a lin-
        guistic variant. Word 14.1:47-56. New
        York.

1966   The basic semantic variables of kinship
        terminology. Human Mosaic 1.2:68-77.
        New Orleans.

1967   Some analogies between word morphology and
        semantic structure. Anthropological
        Linguistics 9.3:1-5. Bloomington, Ind.

Fisher, Ann, editor
1970   Current directions in anthropology. (A
        special issue, Bulletins of the American
        Anthropological Association 3.3[Part 2].)
        vi, 138 pp. Washington.

Fiskus, Maurice
1962   Review of Semantic analysis, by Paul Ziff.
        L'Homme 2.1:141-143. Paris.

[0:38]

Flament, Claude
    1963   Applications of graph theory to group
              structure. 142 pp. Englewood Cliffs, N. J.:
              Prentice-Hall.

Flavell, John H.
    1963   The developmental psychology of Jean Piaget.
              xvi, 472 pp. Princeton: Von Nostrand.

Flegg, H. Graham
    1964   Boolean algebra and its application; includ-
              ing Boolean matrix algebra. 261 pp. New
              York: John Wiley.

Flint, Robert
    1904   Philosophy as scientia scientiarum, and A
              history of classifications of the sciences.
              x, 340 pp. New York: Scribner.

Fodor, István
    1959   The origin of grammatical gender, I and II.
              Lingua 8.1:1-41; 8.2:186-214. Amsterdam.

    1966   The problems in the classification of the
              African languages: methodological and
              theoretical conclusions concerning the
              classification system of Joseph H. Green-
              berg. 158 pp. Budapest: Center for
              Afro-Asian Research of the Hungarian Academy
              of Sciences.

Fogelson, Raymond D.
    1962   Ethno-ethnology. In Bulletin of the Phila-
              delphia Anthropological Society. Philadel-
              phia.

Fosberg, F. R.
    1967   The cult of the expert and numerical taxono-
              my. Taxon 16.5:369-370. Utrecht.

Foskett, Douglas John
    1963   Classification and indexing in the social
              sciences. x, 190 pp. Washington and Lon-
              don: Butterworths.

    1968   Some historical aspects of the classification
              of knowledge. Classification Society Bulle-
              tin 1.4:2-11. Leicester, England.

    1970a   Classification for a general index language:
              a review of recent research by the Classifi-
              cation Research Group. (Library Association

Research Publication No. 2.) 48 pp. London.

1970b   Classification and indexing in the social
         sciences. Aslib Proceedings 22.3:90-101.
         London.

1971   Problems of indexing and classification in
         the social sciences. International Social
         Science Journal 23.2:244-255. Paris.

Foster, Mary LeCron
1968   Componential analysis of grammar: the
         Tarascan verb. International Journal of
         American Linguistics 34.4:259-268.
         Baltimore.

Fowler, Roger
1963   "Meaning" and the theory of the morpheme.
         Lingua 12.2:165-176. Amsterdam.

Fox, James F.
1971   Semantic parallelism in Rotinese ritual
         language. Bijdragen tot de Taal-, Land-
         en Volkenkunde 127.2:215-255. 's-Graven-
         hage.

Frake, Charles O.
1961a   The diagnosis of disease among the Subanun.
         American Anthropologist 63.1:113-132.
         Menasha.

1961b   Review of Semantic analysis, by Paul Ziff.
         American Anthropologist 63.6:1386-1389.
         Menasha.

1962a   The ethnographic study of cognitive systems
         [with "Comment" by Harold C. Conklin]. Pp.
         72-93 in Anthropology and human behavior,
         edited by T. Gladwin and W. C. Sturtevant.
         Washington: Anthropological Society of
         Washington.

1962b   Cultural ecology and ethnography. American
         Anthropologist 64.1:53-59. Menasha.

1964a   Notes on queries in ethnography. Pp. 79-98
         in Transcultural studies in cognition,
         (American Anthropologist 66.3[Part 2],
         Special Publication), edited by A. K. Rom-
         ney and R. G. D'Andrade. Menasha.

1964b   A structural description of Subanun religious

behavior. Pp. 111-129 in Explorations in cultural anthropology: essays in honor of George Peter Murdock, edited by W. H. Goodenough. New York: McGraw-Hill.

Frake, Charles O. (cont.)
1964c   Further discussion of Burling. American Anthropologist 66.1:119. Menasha.

1969   Struck by speech: the Yakan concept of litigation. Pp. 147-167 in Law in culture and society, edited by L. Nader. Chicago: Aldine.

French, David H.
1957   An exploration of Wasco ethnoscience. Yearbook of the American Philosophical Society, 1956, pp. 224-227. Philadelphia.

1963   The relationship of anthropology to studies in perception and cognition. Pp. 388-428 in Vol. 6 of Psychology: a study of science, edited by S. Koch. New York: McGraw-Hill.

Freudenthal, Hans
1966   The language of logic. 105 pp. New York and London: Elsevier.

Friedrich, Paul
1963   An evolutionary sketch of Russian kinship. Pp. 1-26 in Symposium on language and culture, (Proceedings of the 1962 Annual Spring Meeting of the American Ethnological Society), edited by V. E. Garfield and W. L. Chafe. Seattle: University of Washington Press.

1964   Semantic structure and social structure: an instance from Russian. Pp. 131-166 in Explorations in cultural anthropology: essays in honor of George Peter Murdock, edited by W. H. Goodenough. New York: McGraw-Hill.

1966   Structural implications of Russian pronominal usage. Pp. 214-259 in Sociolinguistics, (Janua Linguarum, Series Maior 20), edited by W. Bright. Paris and the Hague: Mouton.

1969   Metaphor-like relations between referential subsets. Lingua 24.1:1-10. Amsterdam.

1970   Shape in grammar. Language 46.2(Part 1):
        379-407. Baltimore.

1971   Anthropological linguistics: recent research
        and immediate prospects. Georgetown Univer-
        sity Monograph Series on Languages and Lin-
        guistics, No. 24:167-184. Washington.

Gardin, Jean-Claude
1958   On the coding of geometrical shapes and
        other representations, with reference to
        archaeological documents. Pp. 889-901 in
        Vol. 2 of Proceedings of the International
        Conference on Scientific Information.
        Washington: National Academy of Sciences,
        National Research Council.

1970   Procédures d'analyse sémantique dans les
        sciences humaines. Pp. 628-657 in Échanges
        et communications; mélanges offerts à Claude
        Lévi-Strauss à l'occasion de son 60ème
        anniversaire, edited by J. Pouillon and
        P. Maranda. The Hague and Paris: Mouton.

Gardin, Jean-Claude et al.
1970   Archéologie et calculateurs: problèmes
        sémiologiques et mathématiques: Marseille
        7-12 avril 1969. 371 pp. Paris: Editions
        du Centre National de la Recherche Scien-
        tifique.

Gardiner, Alan
1954   The theory of proper names: a controversial
        essay. 2d edition. 77 pp. London: Oxford
        University Press.

Gardner, Riley, P. S. Holzman, G. S. Klein, H. Linton,
        and D. P. Spence
1959   Cognitive control: a study of individual
        consistencies in cognitive behavior. (Psy-
        chological Issues 1.4, Monograph 4.) 185
        pp. New York: International Universities
        Press.

Garfield, Viola and Wallace Chafe, editors
1963   Symposium on language and culture. (Pro-
        ceedings of the 1962 Annual Spring Meeting
        of the American Ethnological Society.)
        96 pp. Seattle: University of Washington
        Press.

Garfinkel, Harold
1967   Studies in ethnomethodology. xvi, 288 pp.

Englewood Cliffs, N. J.: Prentice-Hall.

Garner, Wendell R.
1962   Uncertainty and structure as psychological concepts. ix, 369 pp. New York: John Wiley.

Garvin, Paul
1944   Referential adjustment and linguistic structure. Acta Linguistica 4.2:53-60. Budapest.

1955   Problems in American Indian lexicography and text edition. Anais do 31 Congresso Internacional de Americanistas 2:1013-1028. São Paulo.

1958a   A descriptive technique for the treatment of meaning. Language 34.1:1-32. Baltimore.

1958b   Review of Language, thought, and reality: selected writings of Benjamin Lee Whorf, edited by J. B. Carroll. American Anthropologist 60.2:415-416. Menasha.

1960   On structuralist method. Georgetown University Monograph Series on Languages and Linguistics, No. 11:145-148. Washington.

1962   A study of inductive method in syntax. Word 18.1-2:107-120. New York.

Garvin, Paul L., editor
1970a   Cognition: a multiple view. xiv, 428 pp. New York and Washington: Spartan Books.

1970b   Method and theory in linguistics. (Janua Linguarum, Series Maior 40.) 325 pp. The Hague and Paris: Mouton.

Garvin, Paul L., Jocelyn Brewer, and Madeleine Mathiot
1967   Predication typing: a pilot study in semantic analysis. (Supplement to Language 43.2[Part 2]; Language Monograph 27.) 116 pp. Baltimore.

Gaster, Kathleen, compiler
1967   Thesaurus construction and use: a selective bibliography based on material in the Aslib Library in July 1967. Aslib Proceedings 19.9:310-317. London.

Gellner, Ernest A.
1957 Ideal language and kinship structure. Philosophy of Science 24.3:235-242. Baltimore.

1959 Words and things. A critical account of linguistic philosophy and a study of ideology. With an introduction by Bertrand Russell. 270 pp. London: Gollancz.

George, Frank H.
1964 Teach yourself semantics. 172 pp. London: English Universities Press.

1967 The development of semantic machines. Cybernetica 10.3:145-172. Namur, Belgium.

Ghiselin, Michael T.
1966a An application of the theory of definitions to systematic principles. Systematic Zoology 15.2:127-130. Lawrence, Kans.

1966b On psychologism in the logic of taxonomic controversies. Systematic Zoology 15.3: 207-215. Lawrence, Kans.

1967 Further comments on logical errors in systematic theory. Systematic Zoology 16.4:347-348. Lawrence, Kans.

1969a The distinction between similarity and homology. Systematic Zoology 18.1:148-149. Lawrence, Kans.

1969b Non-phenetic evidence in phylogeny. Systematic Zoology 18.4:460-462. Lawrence, Kans.

1969c An examination of Professor Blackwelder's philosophy. Systematic Zoology 18.4:472-475. Lawrence, Kans.

Gilchrist, Alan
1968 Further comments on the terminology of the analysis of library systems. Aslib Proceedings 20.10:408-412. London.

Gillie, Angelo C.
1965 Binary arithmetic and Boolean algebra. 248 pp. New York: McGraw-Hill.

Gilmartin, Amy Jean
1967 Numerical taxonomy--an eclectic view-point. Taxon 16.1:8-12. Utrecht.

Gilmour, J. S. L.
1940   Taxonomy and philosophy. Pp. 461-474 in
         The new systematics, edited by J. Huxley.
         London: Oxford University Press.

1951   The development of taxonomic theory since
         1851. Nature 168:400-402. London.

1958   The species: yesterday and tomorrow.
         Nature 181:379-380. London.

1961   Taxonomy. Pp. 27-45 in Contemporary botani-
         cal thought, edited by A. M. MacLeod and
         L. S. Cobley. Chicago: Quadrangle Books;
         Edinburgh: Oliver and Boyd.

Gilmour, J. S. L., compiler
1961   The mathematical assessment of taxonomic
         similarity, including the use of computers.
         Taxon 10.4:97-101. Utrecht.

Gilmour, J. S. L. and S. M. Walters
1964   Philosophy and classification. Pp. 1-22 in
         Recent researches in plant taxonomy, (Vistas
         in botany, Vol. 4), edited by W. B. Turrill.
         New York: Macmillan.

Gipper, Helmut
1956a   Die Kluft zwischen muttersprachlichem und
         physikalischem Weltbild. Physikalische
         Blätter 12.3:97-105, 12.6:284-287. Mosbach,
         Germany: Physik Verlag.

1956b   Muttersprachliches und wissenschaftliches
         Weltbild. Sprachforum 2:1-10. Köln.

Givón, Talmy
1970   Notes on the semantic structure of English
         adjectives. Language 46.4:816-837. Balti-
         more.

Galdwin, Thomas and William C. Sturtevant, editors
1962   Anthropology and human behavior. viii, 214
         pp. Washington: Anthropological Society
         of Washington.

Glasersfeld, Ernst von
1961a   Operational semantics: analysis of meaning
         in terms of operation. (CETIS [Centre de
         Traitment de l'Information Scientifique],
         No. 24.) Leiden: European Atomic Energy
         Community.

1961b   Translation and the structure of significa-
         tion. Pp. 508-516 (Paper 31) in The First
         International Conference on Machine Trans-
         lation, National Physical Laboratory,
         Teddington, England.

Gleason, Henry S., Jr.
1960   Review of The grammar of English nominaliza-
         tions, by Robert B. Lees. American Anthro-
         pologist 62.6:1110-1111. Menasha.

1961   An introduction to descriptive linguistics.
(1955)   Revised edition. 389 pp. New York: Henry
         Holt.

1964   The organization of language: a stratifica-
         tional view. Georgetown University Mono-
         graph Series on Languages and Linguistics,
         No. 17:75-95. Washington.

Gleitman, Lila R. and Henry Gleitman
1970   Phrase and paraphrase: some innovative
         uses of language. xii, 242 pp. New York:
         W. W. Norton.

Glick, Leonard B.
1964   Categories and relations in Gimi natural
         science. American Anthropologist 66.4(Part
         2):273-280. Menasha.

Gombrich, Ernst Hans Joseph
1960   Art and illustion, a study in the psychology
         of pictorial representation. xxxii, 466 pp.,
         319 illus. New York: Pantheon.

Good, I. J.
1964   Categorization of classification. Pp. 115-
         128 in Mathematics and computer science in
         biology and medicine; Proceedings of a
         conference held by the Medical Research
         Council...Oxford, 1964. London: Her
         Majesty's Stationery Office.

Goodenough, Ward H.
1951   Property, kin, and community on Truk.
         (Yale University Publications in Anthropol-
         ogy, No. 46.) 192 pp. New Haven.

1956   Componential analysis and the study of
         meaning. Language 32.2:195-216. Baltimore.

Goodenough, Ward H. (cont.)
1957   Cultural anthropology and linguistics.
(1956)   Georgetown University Monograph Series on
         Language and Linguistics, No. 9:167-173.
         Washington. (Pre-published 1956 in Bulletin
         of the Philadelphia Anthropological Society
         9.3:3-7, Philadelphia; reprinted 1964,
         pp. 36-39 in Language in culture and society,
         edited by D. Hymes, New York: Harper and
         Row.)

1965   Yankee kinship terminology: a problem in
         componential analysis. Pp. 259-287 in
         Formal semantic analysis, (American Anthro-
         pologist 67.5[Part 2], Special Publication),
         edited by E. A. Hammel. Menasha.

1967   Componential analysis. Science 156.3779:
         1203-1209. Washington.

1968   Componential analysis. International
         Encyclopedia of the Social Sciences 3:186-
         192. New York: Macmillan and Free Press.

1970   Description and comparison in cultural
         anthropology, xi, 173 pp. Chicago:
         Aldine.

1971   Culture, language, and society. 48 pp.
         Reading, Mass.: Addison-Wesley.

Goodenough, Ward H., editor
1964   Explorations in cultural anthropology:
         essays in honor of George Peter Murdock.
         xiii, 635 pp. New York: McGraw-Hill.

Goodman, Nelson
1949   On likeness of meaning. Analysis 10:1-7.
         Oxford. (Reprinted with note 1954, pp. 54-
         62 in Philosophy and analysis, edited by M.
         MacDonald, New York: Philosophical Library.)

1951   The structure of appearance. xv, 315 pp.
         Cambridge: Harvard University Press.

1953   On some differences about meaning. Analysis
         13:90-96. Oxford. (Reprinted with note
         1954, pp. 63-69 in Philosophy and analysis,
         edited by M. MacDonald, New York: Philo-
         sophical Library.)

Goodstein, Reuben Louis
1961   Recursive analysis. 138 pp. Amsterdam: North-Holland Publishing House.

Gorn, Saul
1968   The identification of the computer and information sciences: their fundamental semiotic concepts and relationships. Foundations of Language 4.4:339-372. Dordrecht.

Gould, Sydney W.
1954   Permanent numbers to supplement the binomial system of nomenclature. American Scientist 42.2:269-274. New Haven.

Gove, Philip B.
1961   Subject orientation within the definition. Georgetown University Monograph Series on Languages and Linguistics, No. 14:95-107. Washington.

Granger, Gilles-Gaston
1960   Pensée formelle et sciences de l'homme. 226 pp. Paris: Montaigne.

Gray, George W.
1948   The great ravelled knot. Scientific American 179.4:26-39. New York.

Gray, Jack C., editor
1963   Words, words, and words about dictionaries. xi, 207 pp. San Francisco: Chandler.

Grayson, T. J.
1967   Some aspects of industrial classification in the Soviet Union. Aslib Proceedings 19.5:129-145. London.

Greenberg, Joseph H.
1949   The logical analysis of kinship. Philosophy of Science 16.1:58-64. Baltimore.

1957a   The nature and uses of linguistic typologies. International Journal of American Linguistics 23.2:68-77. Baltimore.

1957b   Essays in linguistics. (Viking Fund Publications in Anthropology, No. 24.) xiii, 108 pp. New York: Wenner-Gren Foundation for Anthropological Research.

[0:48]

Greenberg, Joseph H. (cont.)
1960   A quantitative approach to the morphological
typology of languages. International Journal of American Linguistics 26.3:178-194.
Baltimore.

1963   The methodology of language classification.
Pp. 1-5 (Chapter 1) in The languages of
Africa, (International Journal of American
Linguistics 29.1[Part 2]; Indiana University
Research Center in Anthropology, Folklore
and Linguistics, Publication 25), by J. H.
Greenberg. Bloomington, Ind.

1966   Language universals. Pp. 61-112 in Vol. 3
of Current trends in linguistics, edited by
T. A. Sebeok. The Hague and Paris: Mouton.
(Published separately in 1966 with revisions
as Language universals: with special
reference to feature hierarchies. 89 pp.
The Hague and Paris: Mouton.)

1967   The first (and perhaps only) non-linguistic
distinctive feature analysis. Word 23.1-2-3
(Part 1):214-220. New York.

Greenberg, Joseph H., editor
1966   Universals of language. 2d edition.
(1963)   xxviii, 337 pp. Cambridge: MIT Press.

Gregg, John R.
1950   Taxonomy, language and reality. American
Naturalist 84.819:419-435. Lancaster, Pa.

1954   The language of taxonomy, an application of
symbolic logic to the study of classificatory systems. xii, 70 pp. New York:
Columbia University Press.

1967   Finite Linnaean structures. Bulletin of
Mathematical Biophysics 29.2:191-206.
London.

1968   Buck and Hull: a critical rejoinder.
Systematic Zoology 17.3:342-344. Lawrence,
Kans.

Greimas, A. J.
1964   La Structure élémentaire de la signification
en linguistique. L'Homme 4.3:5-17. Paris.

1966   Sémantique structurale. Recherche de

méthode. 262 pp. Paris: Larousse.

1968   Conditions d'une sémiotique du monde
naturel. Langages 10:3-35. Paris.

1970   Sémantique, sémiotiques et sémiologies.
Pp. 13-27 in Sign·language·culture, (Janua
Linguarum, Series Maior 1), edited by
A. J. Greimas et al. The Hague and Paris:
Mouton.

Greimas, A. J. et al., editors
1970   Sign·language·culture. (Janua Linguarum,
Series Maior 1.) xx, 723 pp. The Hague
and Paris: Mouton.

Greimas, A. J. and F. Fastier
1968   The interaction of semiotic constraints.
Yale French Studies 41:86-105. New Haven.

Grice, H. P.
1968   Utterer's meaning, sentence-meaning, and
word-meaning. Foundations of Language 4.3:
225-242. Dordrecht.

Grigg, David
1965   The logic of regional systems. Annals of
the Association of American Geographers
55.3:465-491. Albany.

Grimes, Joseph E. and Barbara F. Grimes
1962   Semantic distinctions in Huichol (Uto-
Aztecan) kinship. American Anthropologist
64.1:104-114. Menasha.

Grolier, Eric de
1962   A study of general categories applicable to
classification and coding in documentation.
248 pp. Paris: UNESCO.

Groot, Albert W. de
1948   Structural linguistics and word classes.
Lingua 1.4:427-500. Haarlem.

1957   Classification of word-groups. Lingua
6.2:113-157. Amsterdam.

Guilleminet, Paul, with the collaboration of Jules
Alberty
1959,   Dictionnaire: Bahnar-Français. 2 vols.
1963   Vol. 40, A-K, 494 pp.; Vol. 40, L-U, pp.
495-991. Paris: École Français d'Exreme-
Orient.

[0:50]

Guiraud, Pierre
1955   Le Sémantique. 118 pp. Paris: Presses
          Universitaires de France.

1964   Diacritical and statistical models in lin-
          guistics. Pp. 235-254 in The use of com-
          puters in anthropology, edited by D. H.
          Hymes. The Hague: Mouton.

1966   Sens et information. Pp. 51-54 in Statis-
          tique et analyse linguistique. Paris:
          Presses Universitaires de France.

1967   Structures étymologiques du lexique
          français. 211 pp. Paris: Larousse.

1968   The semic matrices of meaning. Information
          sur les Sciences Sociales 7.2:131-139.
          Paris.

Gukhman, M. M.
1961   Lingvisticheskaja teorija L. Vejsgerbera.
          Pp. 123-162 in Voprosy teorii jazyka v
          sovremennoj zarubezhnoj lingvistike, edited
          by R. A. Budagov and M. M. Gukhman. Moscow:
          USSR Academy of Sciences.

Gumperz, John J. and Dell H. Hymes, editors
1964   The ethnography of communication. (American
          Anthropologist 66.6[Part 2], Special Publi-
          cation.) 186 pp. Menasha.

Haas, Mary R.
1948   Classificatory verbs in Muskogee. Inter-
          national Journal of American Linguistics
          14.4:244-246. Baltimore.

1967   Language and taxonomy in northwestern
          California. American Anthropologist 69.3-4:
          358-362. Menasha.

Hale, Kenneth
1965   On the use of informants in field-work.
          Canadian Journal of Linguistics 10.2-3:
          108-119. Toronto.

Hall, A. V.
1969   Automatic grouping programs: the treatment
          of certain kinds of properties. Biological
          Journal of the Linnean Society 1.3:321-325.
          London.

Halle, Morris
    1964   On the bases of phonology. Pp. 324-333 in
            The structure of language, edited by J. A.
            Fodor and J. J. Katz. Englewood Cliffs,
            N. J.: Prentice-Hall.

Halle, Morris, Horace G. Lunt, Hugh McLean, and C. H.
            van Schooneveld, editors
    1956   For Roman Jakobson: essays on the occasion
            of his sixtieth birthday. 693 pp. The
            Hague: Mouton.

Halliday, Michael A. K.
    1961   Categories of the theory of grammar. Word
            17.3:241-292. New York.

    1963   Class in relation to the axes of chain and
            choice in language. Linguistics 2:5-15.
            The Hague.

    1966   Lexis as a linguistic level. Pp. 148-162
            in In memory of J. R. Firth, edited by
            C. E. Bazell et al. London: Longmans.

Hallig, Rudolf and Walther von Wartburg
    1952   Begriffssystem als Grundlage für die Lexi-
            kographie; Versuch eines Ordnungsschemas.
            (Abhandlungen der deutschen Akademie der
            Wissenschaften zu Berlin, No. 4.) xxxv,
            140 pp. Berlin: Akademie-Verlag. (New
            revised edition, 1963; also in French.)

Halmos, Paul R.
    1960   Naive set theory. vii, 104 pp. (University
            Series in Undergraduate Mathematics.)
            Princeton: Van Nostrand.

Hammel, Eugene A.
    1964   Further comments on componential analysis.
            American Anthropologist 66.2:1167-1171.
            Menasha.

    1966   A factor theory for Arunta kinship terminol-
            ogy. (University of California Anthro-
            pological Records, Vol. 24.) 19 pp. Berke-
            ley and Los Angeles.

Hammel, Eugene A., editor
    1965   Formal semantic analysis. (American Anthro-
            pologist 67.5[Part 2], Special Publication.)
            316 pp. Menasha.

Hammer, Muriel
1966   Some comments on formal analysis of gram-
        matical and semantic systems. American
        Anthropologist 68.2:362-373. Menasha.

Hamp, Eric
1959   Proper names in Scottish Gaelic. Names
        7.1:57-59. Berkeley.

Hanson, F. Allan
1970   The Rapan theory of conception. American
        Anthropologist 72.6:1444-1447. Menasha.

Hanson, Norwood Russell
1962   Scientists and logicians: a confrontation.
        Science 138.3547:1311-1314. Washington.

Harary, Frank
1964   Combinatorial problems in graphical enumer-
        ation. Pp. 185-216 (Chapter 6) in Applied
        combinatorial mathematics, edited by E. F.
        Beckenbach. New York: John Wiley.

Harary, Frank and Robert Z. Norman
1953   Graph theory as a mathematical model in
        social science. v, 45 pp. Ann Arbor:
        University of Michigan Institute for Social
        Research.

Harary, Frank, Robert Z. Norman, and Dorwin Cartwright
1965   Structural models: an introduction to the
        theory of directed graphs. 415 pp. New
        York: John Wiley.

Harper, Robert J., editor
1964   The cognitive process. vii, 717 pp.
        Englewood Cliffs, N. J.: Prentice-Hall.

Harris, Zellig S.
1942   Morpheme alternants in linguistic analysis.
        Language 18.3:169-180. Baltimore. (Re-
        printed 1957 in Readings in linguistics,
        edited by M. Joos. New York: ACLS.)

1944   Simultaneous components in phonology.
        Language 20.4:181-205. Baltimore.

1948   Componential analysis of a Hebrew paradigm.
        Language 24.1:87-91. Baltimore.

Hartman, R. R. K.
1969   Linguistics and translation. Aslib Proceed-
        ings 21.5:190-194. London.

Hartnack, Justus
1965   Wittgenstein and modern philosophy. Translated by Maurice Cranston. 142 pp. Garden City, N. Y.: Doubleday Anchor Books.

Harweg, Roland
1968   Language and music--an immanent and sign theoretical approach. Some preliminary remarks. Foundations of Language 4.3:270-281. Dordrecht.

Hattori, Shirô
1967   The sense of sentence and the meaning of utterance. Pp. 850-854 in To honor Roman Jakobson, essays on the occasion of his seventieth birthday, (Janua Linguarum, Series Maior 31). The Hague and Paris: Mouton.

Haudricourt, André G.
1968   Linguistique et ethnologie. Pp. 288-316 in Ethnologie générale, edited by Jean Poirer. Paris: Gallimard.

Haugen, Einar
1957   The semantics of Icelandic orientation. Word 13.3:447-459. New York.

Hayes, John R., editor
1970   Cognition and the development of language. (Annual Series of Symposia in the Areas of Cognition, 4.) x, 370 pp. New York and London: John Wiley.

Hays, David G.
1966   Readings in automatic language processing. 202 pp. Essex, England: Elsevier.

Heerdegen, Ferdinand von
1890   Grundzüge der Bedeutungslehre. In Part 2 of Vorlesungen über lateinische Sprachwerke, by Christian Karl Reisig. Berlin: S. Calvary.

Heidbreder, Edna
1958   Woodworth and Whorf on the role of language in thinking. Pp. 86-110 in Current psychological issues: essays in honor of Robert S. Woodworth, edited by G. S. Seward and J. P. Seward. New York: Henry Holt.

Heise, Helen and Mortimer P. Starr
1968   Nomenifers: are they christened or

classified? Systematic Zoology 17.4:458-467. Lawrence, Kans.

Heise, Helen and Mortimer P. Starr (cont.)
1969   A reply to Buchanan's critique. Systematic Zoology 18.3:345-347. Lawrence, Kans.

Heizer, Charles B., Jr.
1966   Methods in systematic research. Bioscience 16.1:31-34. Washington.

Helm, June, editor
1967   Essays on the verbal and visual arts. (Proceedings of the 1966 Annual Spring Meeting of the American Ethnological Society.) 215 pp. Seattle and London: University of Washington Press.

Hempel, Carl Gustav
1952   Fundamentals of concept formation in empirical science. 93 pp. Chicago: University of Chicago Press.

Hempel, Carl Gustav and Paul Oppenheim
1936   Der Typusbegriff im Lichte der neuen Logik Wissenschraftstheoretische Untersuchungen zur Konstitutionsforschung und Psychologie. vii, 130 pp. Leiden: A. W. Sijthoff.

Henle, Paul, editor
1958   Language, thought, and culture. vi, 273 pp. Ann Arbor: University of Michigan Press.

Henry, Jules
1936   The linguistic expression of emotion. American Anthropologist 38.2:250-256. Menasha.

Herdan, Gustav
1960   Type-token mathematics. 448 pp. The Hague: Mouton.

Heywood, Vernon Hilton
1970   Infraspecific categories: summary of discussion. Biological Journal of the Linnean Society 2.3:257-258. London.

Heywood, V. H. and J. McNeill, editors
1964   Phenetic and phylogenetic classification. (Systematics Association Publication No. 6.) 164 pp. London.

Hickerson, N. P.
1953   Ethnolinguistic notes from lexicons of
         Lokono (Arawak). International Journal
         of American Linguistics 19.3:181-190.
         Baltimore.

Hill, Archibald A.
1952   A note on primitive languages. International
         Journal of American Linguistics 18.3:172-177.
         Baltimore.

1966   Non-grammatical prerequisites. Foundations
         of Language 2.4:319-337. Dordrecht.

1970   Laymen, lexicographers, and linguists.
         Language 46.2:245-258. Baltimore.

Hincha, Georg
1961   Endocentric vs. exocentric constructions.
         Lingua 10.3:267-274. Amsterdam.

Hiorth, Finngeir
1955a   Arrangement of meanings in lexicography.
         Lingua 4.4:413-424. Amsterdam.

1955b   On the subject matter of lexicography.
         Studia Linguistica 9.1:57-65. Lund.

1956   On the relation between field research and
         lexicography. Studia Linguistica 10:57-66.
         Lund.

1957   On the foundations of lexicography. Studia
         Linguistica 11:8-27. Lund.

1959   Origin and control of meaning hypotheses.
         Lingua 8.3:294-305. Amsterdam.

1960   Zur Ordnung des Wortschatzes. Studia
         Linguistica 14:65-84. Lund.

Hiź, Henry
1970   Disambiguation. Pp. 124-134 in Sign·
         language·culture, (Janua Linguarum, Series
         Maior 1), edited by A. J. Greimas et al.
         The Hague and Paris: Mouton.

Hjelmslev, Louis
1935,   La Catégorie des cas: étude de grammaire
1937   générale. Acta Jutlandica 7.1:i-xii, 1-
         184; 9.2:vii, 1-77. Aarhus.

Hjelmslev, Louis (cont.)
  1958   Dans quelle mesure les significations des
          mots peuvent-elles être considérées comme
          formant une structure? Pp. 636-654 in
          Proceedings of the Eighth International
          Congress of Linguists. Oslo: Oslo Univer-
          sity Press.

  1961   Prolegomena to a theory of language. Revised
  (1953) English edition, translated from 1943 Danish
          edition by Francis J. Whitfield. v, 144 pp.
          Madison: University of Wisconsin Press.
          (First translation published in 1953,
          International Journal of American Linguis-
          tics, Memoir 7, Baltimore.)

  1970   Language: an introduction. Translated by
  (1963) Francis J. Whitfield. xiii, 144 pp.
          (First English edition of Sproget: en
          introduktion, 1963.) Madison and London:
          University of Wisconsin Press.

Hockett, Charles F.
  1947   Problems of morphemic analysis. Language
          23.4:321-343. Baltimore. (Reprinted 1957,
          pp. 229-242 in Readings in linguistics,
          edited by M. Joos. New York: American
          Council of Learned Societies.)

  1954   Chinese versus English: an exploration of
          the Whorfian thesis. Pp. 106-123 in Lan-
          guage in culture, (American Anthropologist
          56.6[Part 2], Memoir No. 79; Comparative
          Studies of Cultures and Civilizations, No.
          3), edited by H. Hoijer. Menasha.

  1956   Idiom formation. Pp. 222-229 in For Roman
          Jakobson, edited by Morris Halle et al.
          The Hague: Mouton.

  1958a   A course in modern linguistics. 621 pp.
          New York: Macmillan.

  1958b   Ethnolinguistic implications of studies in
          linguistics and psychiatry. Georgetown
          University Monograph Series on Languages
          and Linguistics, No. 11:175-193. Washington.

  1961   Linguistic elements and their relations.
          Language 37.1:29-53. Baltimore.

  1964   Scheduling. Pp. 125-144 in Cross-cultural

understanding: epistemology in anthropology, edited by F. S. C. Northrop and H. H. Livingston. New York: Harper and Row.

1966   Language, mathematics, and linguistics. Pp. 155-304 in Vol. 3 of Current trends in linguistics, edited by T. A. Sebeok. The Hague and Paris: Mouton.

1967   Language, mathematics, and linguistics. 243 pp. The Hague and Paris: Mouton; New York: Humanities Press.

Hockett, Charles F., Robert E. Pittenger, and John J. Danehy
1960   The first five minutes: a sample of microscopic interview analysis. ix, 264 pp. Ithaca: Paul Martineau.

Hoenigswald, Henry M.
1960   Language change and linguistic reconstruction. 168 pp. Chicago: University of Chicago Press.

1966   A proposal for the study of folk-linguistics. Pp. 16-26 in Sociolinguistics, (Janua Linguarum, Series Maior 20), edited by W. Bright. The Hague and Paris: Mouton.

Hoijer, Harry
1954   The Sapir-Whorf hypothesis. Pp. 92-105 in Language in culture, (American Anthropologist 56.6[Part 2], Memoir No. 79; Comparative Studies of Cultures and Civilizations, No. 3), edited by H. Hoijer. Menasha.

Hoijer, Harry, editor
1954   Language in culture. (American Anthropologist 56.6[Part 2], Memoir No. 79; Comparative Studies of Cultures and Civilizations, No. 3.) xi, 286 pp. Menasha.

Hollyman, K. J.
1970   Nomenclature scientifique et lexique populaire. Pp. 84-91 in Mélanges Marcel Cohen, (Janua Linguarum, Series Maior 27), edited by David Cohen. The Hague and Paris: Mouton.

Holmer, N. M.
1953   Comparative semantics: a new aspect of linguistics. International Anthropological

and Linguistic Review 1.1:97-106. Miami,
Fla.

Hopkins, Nicholas S.
1963   Dogon classificatory systems. Anthropology
          Tomorrow 9.1:48-54. Chicago.

Householder, Fred W., Jr.
1959   On linguistic primes. Word 15.2:231-239.
          New York.

1961   On linguistic terms. Pp. 15-25 in Psycho-
          linguistics, edited by S. Saporta. New
          York: Holt, Rinehart and Winston.

1962   On the uniqueness of semantic mapping.
          Word 18.1-2:173-185. New York.

Householder, Fred W. and Sol Saporta, editors
1962   Problems in lexicography: report of the
          Conference on Lexicography held at Indiana
          University, November 11-12, 1960. (Inter-
          national Journal of American Linguistics
          28.2[Part 4]; Publication 21, Indiana
          University Research Center in Anthropology,
          Folklore, and Linguistics.) viii, 286 pp.
          Bloomington: Indiana University Research
          Center in Anthropology, Folklore, and Lin-
          guistics. (Volume reprinted with additions
          and corrections as second edition 1967.
          Bloomington: Indiana University; The Hague:
          Mouton.)

Hruška, Jozef
1967   On a classification of context-free languages.
          Kybernetika 3.1:22-29. Prague.

Hull, David L.
1965   The effect of existentialism on taxonomy:
          two thousand years of stasis. British
          Journal for the Philosophy of Science 15.60:
          314-326; 16.61:1-18. Edinburgh and London.

1966   Phylogenetic numericlature. Systematic
          Zoology 15.1:14-17. Lawrence, Kans.

1968a   The operational imperative: sense and
          nonsense in operationalism. Systematic
          Zoology 17.4:438-457. Lawrence, Kans.

1968b   The syntax of numericlature. Systematic
          Zoology 17.4:472-474. Lawrence, Kans.

1970 Contemporary systematic philosophies.
Annual Review of Ecology and Systematics
1:19-54. Palo Alto.

Hull, David L. and Roger Buck
1967 Definitions of taxa. Systematic Zoology
16.4:349. Lawrence, Kans.

Hull, David L. and D. Paul Snyder
1969 Contemporary logic and evolutionary taxonomy:
a reply to Gregg. Systematic Zoology 18.3:
347-354. Lawrence, Kans.

Humboldt, Wilhelm von
1836 Ueber die Verschiedenheit des menschlichen
Sprachbaues und ihren Einfluss auf die
geistige Entwicklung des Menschengeschlechts.
xi, 511 pp. Berlin: F. Dümmler.

Hunt, Earl B.
1962 Concept learning: an information processing
problem. 286 pp. New York: John Wiley.

Hunt, Earl B., Janet Marin, and Philip J. Stone
1966 Experiments in induction. xi, 247 pp.
New York: Academic Press.

Huxley, Julian S., editor
1940 The new systematics. 583 pp. Oxford:
Clarendon.

Hymes, Dell H.
1960 Discussion of the symposium on translation
between language and culture. Anthropological Linguistics 2.2:81-84. Bloomington, Ind.

1962 The ethnography of speaking. Pp. 13-53 in
Anthropology and human behavior, edited by
T. Gladwin and W. C. Sturtevant. Washington:
Anthropological Society of Washington.

1963 Toward a history of linguistic anthropology.
Anthropological Linguistics 5.1:59-103.
Bloomington, Ind.

1964a Discussion of Burling's paper "Cognition
and componential analysis: God's truth or
hocus-pocus?" American Anthropologist 66.1:
116-119. Menasha.

1964b Introduction: toward ethnographies of
communication. American Anthropologist 66.6
(Part 2):1-34. Menasha.

Hymes, Dell H. (cont.)
1964c   A perspective for linguistic anthropology.
         Pp. 92-107 in Horizons of anthropology,
         edited by S. Tax. Chicago: Aldine.

1966   Two types of linguistic relativity (with
         examples from Amerindian ethnography).
         Pp. 114-167 in Sociolinguistics, (Janua
         Linguarum, Series Maior 20), edited by W.
         Bright. Paris and The Hague: Mouton.

1967   The anthropology of communication. Pp. 1-
         39 in Human communication theory, edited by
         F. E. X. Dance. New York: Holt, Rinehart,
         and Winston.

1970a   Comments on Analytical archaeology by D. L.
         Clarke. Norwegian Archaeological Review
         3:16-21. Oslo.

1970b   Linguistic models in archaeology. Pp. 91-118
         in Archéologie et calculateurs. by J.-C.
         Gardin et al. Paris: Éditions du Centre
         National de la Recherche Scientifique.

1970c   Linguistic method in ethnography: its
         development in the United States. Pp. 249-
         325 in Method and theory in linguistics,
         edited by P. L. Garvin. Paris: Mouton.

Hymes, Dell H., editor
1964   Language in culture and society: a reader
         in linguistics and anthropology. 764 pp.
         New York: Harper and Row.

1965   The use of computers in anthropology. 558
         pp. The Hague: Mouton.

Hymes, Dell H. and William E. Bittle
1967   Studies in southwestern ethnolinguistics:
         meaning and history in the languages of the
         American Southwest. ix, 464 pp. The Hague
         and Paris: Mouton.

Ihm, Peter
1965   Automatic classification in anthropology.
         Pp. 357-376 in The use of computers in
         anthropology, edited by D. Hymes. The
         Hague: Mouton.

1970   Distance et similitude en taxométrie. Pp.
         309-316 in Archéologie et calculateurs, by

J.-C. Gardin et al. Paris: Éditions du
Centre National de la Recherche Scientifique.

Ikegami, Yoshihiko
1967   Structural semantics: a survey and problems.
Linguistics 33:49-67. The Hague.

1970   The semological structure of the English
verbs of motion: a stratificational
approach. Tokyo: Sanseido.

Inger, Robert F.
1958   Comments on the definition of genera.
Evolution 12.3:370-384. Lancaster, Pa.

Inglis, William Grant
1966   The observational basis of homology. Systematic Zoology 15.3:219-228. Lawrence, Kans.

1970a   Similarity and homology. Systematic Zoology
19.1:93. Lawrence, Kans.

1970b   The purpose and judgments of biological
classifications. Systematic Zoology 19.3:
240-253. Lawrence, Kans.

Institut Jazykoznanija
1957-   Leksikograficheski sbornik. Vols. 1-3.
1958   186, 212, 191 pp. Moscow: USSR Academy of
Sciences.

Ivanov, Vjacheslav V.
1956   Die genealogische Klassifikation der Sprachen
und der Begriff der Sprachverwandtschaft.
Translated into German by K. A. Paffen.
77 pp. Halle: M. Niemeyer.

Ivanov, Vjacheslav V. and Vladimir N. Toporov
1965   Slavjanskie jazykovye modelirujushchie
semioticheskie sistemy. 245 pp. Moscow:
Nauka.

Izutsu, Toshihiko
1956   Language and magic: studies in the magical
function of speech. (Keio University Studies
in the Humanities and Social Relations, Vol.
1.) 140 pp. Tokyo: Keio University Institute of Philological Studies.

1966   Ethico-religious concepts in the Qur'ān. Re-
(1959)   vised edition. (McGill Islamic Studies, I.)
284 pp. Montreal: McGill University.

Press. (First published 1959 as The structure of the ethical terms in the Koran: a
study in semantics. [Keio University Studies
in the Humanities and Social Relations,
Vol. 2.] 275 pp. Tokyo.)

Jakobovits, Leon A.
1966   Comparative psycholinguistics in the study
        of cultures. International Journal of Psy-
        chology 1.1:15-38. Paris.

Jakobovits, Leon A. and Murray S. Miron, editors
1967   Readings in the psychology of language.
        xi, 636 pp. Englewood Cliffs, N. J.:
        Prentice-Hall.

Jakobson, Roman
1936   Beitrag zur allgemeinen Kasuslehre;
        Gesamtbedeutungun der russischen Kasus.
        Travaux du Cercle Linguistique de Prague
        6:240-288. Prague.

1957   Shifters, verbal categories, and the Russian
        verb. 14 pp. Cambridge: Russian Language
        Project, Department of Slavic Languages and
        Literatures, Harvard University.

1959a   Boas' view of grammatical meaning. Pp. 139-
        146 in The anthropology of Franz Boas:
        essays on the centennial of his birth,
        (American Anthropological Association,
        Memoir No. 89), edited by W. Goldschmidt.
        San Francisco: Howard Chandler.

1959b   On linguistic aspects of translation. Pp.
        232-239 in On translation, edited by R. A.
        Brower. Cambridge: Harvard University
        Press.

1965   Quest for the essence of language. Diogenes
        51:21-37. Montreal.

1971   Word and language. (Selected writings, Vol.
        2.) xii, 752 pp. The Hague and Paris:
        Mouton.

Jakobson, Roman, editor
1961   Structure of language and its mathematical
        aspects. (Proceedings of Symposia in Applied
        Mathematics, Vol. 12.) vi, 279 pp.
        Providence.

Jakobson, Roman, C. Gunnar, M. Fant, and Morris Halle
1963   Preliminaries to speech analysis: the
(1952)   distinctive features and their correlates.
          xiii, 64 pp., supplement. Cambridge:
          MIT Press. (Original edition 1952.)

Jakobson, Roman and Morris Halle
1956   Fundamentals of language. 87 pp. The
          Hague: Mouton.

Jaquith, James R.
1967   Toward a typology of formal communicative
          behaviors: glossolalia. Anthropological
          Linguistics 9.8:1-8. Bloomington, Ind.

Jardine, Nicholas
1969a   What is biological homology? Classification
          Society Bulletin 2.1:2-4. Leicester,
          England.

1969b   A logical basis for biological classifica-
          tion. Systematic Zoology 18.1:37-52.
          Lawrence, Kans.

Jardine, N. and C. J. Jardine
1969   Is there a concept of homology common to
          several sciences? Classification Society
          Bulletin 2.1:12-18. Leicester, England.

Jardine, N. and R. Sibson
1968   A model for taxonomy. Mathematical Bio-
          sciences 2.3-4:465-482. New York.

Jaulin, B.
1970   Mesure de la ressemblance en archéologie.
          Pp. 343-355 in Archéologie et calculateurs,
          by J.-C. Gardin et al. Paris: Éditions du
          Centre National de la Recherche Scientifique.

Jespersen, Jens Otto Henry
1964   Language; its nature, development, and
(1922)   origin. 448 pp. New York: W. W. Norton.

Johansen, Svend
1950   Glossematics and logistics. Acta Linguistica
          6:17. Budapest.

Johnson, L. A. S.
1967   Rainbow's end: the quest for an optimal
          taxonomy. Proceedings of the Linnaean
          Society of New South Wales 93.1:8-45.
          Sydney. (Reprinted 1970, Systematic Zoology
          19.3:203-239. Lawrence, Kans.)

[0:64]

Johnson, Stephen C.
   1967   Hierarchical clustering schemes. Psycho-
          metrika 32.3:241-254. Richmond, Va.

Johnson, William Ernest
   1921   Logic, Part 1. xl, 255 pp. Cambridge:
          Cambridge University Press; New York:
          Macmillan.

Jolley, J. L.
   1967a The pattern of meaning: a study in the
          classification of ideas. Classification
          Society Bulletin 1.3:2-13. Leicester,
          England.

   1967b The logic of co-ordinate indexing. Aslib
          Proceedings 19.9:295-309. London.

Jones, K. P.
   1967   The use of links and roles on a pre-co-
          ordination basis in optical coincidence
          systems. Aslib Proceedings 19.6:195-199.
          London.

Jones, Karen Sparck
   1970   Automatic thesaurus construction and the
          relation of a thesaurus to indexing terms.
          Aslib Proceedings 22.5:226-228. London.

Jones, Lyle V. and L. L. Thurstone
   1955   The psychophysics of semantics: an experi-
          mental investigation. Journal of Applied
          Psychology 39.1:31-36. Lancaster, Pa.

Joos, Martin
   1936   Review of Psycho-Biology of language, by
          Paul Zipf. Language 12.3:196-210.
          Baltimore.

   1956   Review of Machine translation of languages:
          fourteen essays, edited by W. N. Locke and
          A. D. Booth. Language 32.2:293-298.
          Baltimore.

   1957   Meaning in relation to MT. Georgetown
          University Monograph Series on Languages
          and Linguistics, No. 10:13-18. Washington.

   1958   Semology: a linguistic theory of meaning.
          Studies in Linguistics 13:53-70. Buffalo.

   1962a Structure in meaning. Georgetown University

Monograph Series on Languages and Linguistics, No. 13:41-48. Washington.

Joos, Martin (cont.)
1962b   The five clocks. (International Journal of American Linguistics 28.2[Part 5].) 62 pp. Baltimore.

1964   A chapter of semology in the English verb. Georgetown University Monograph Series on Language and Linguistics, No. 17:59-72. Washington.

Joos, Martin, editor
1957   Readings in linguistics; the development of descriptive linguistics in America since 1925. 421 pp. Washington: American Council of Learned Societies.

Jordan, Alexis
1923   Remarques sur le fait de l'existence en
(1873)   société, à l'état sauvage, des espèces végétales affines, et sur d'autres faits relatifs à la question de l'espèce. Revue de Botanique Appliquée et d'Agriculture Coloniale 3:459-477. Paris. (Original edition 1873.)

Jorden, Eleanor Harz
1955   The syntax of modern colloquial Japanese. (Language 31.1[Part 3].) vi, 135 pp. Baltimore.

Joseph, Horace William Brindley
1916   An introduction to logic. xii, 608 pp. Oxford: Clarendon.

Jullien, Marc Antoine
1819   Esquisse d'un essai sur la philosophie des sciences, contenant un nouveau projet d'une division générale des connaissances humaines. iv, 63 pp. Paris: Baudouin frères.

Kamil, T. W.
1962   Binary semantic analysis. Archiv Orientální 30.4:632-633. Prague.

Kany, Charles E.
1960   American-Spanish semantics. xi, 352 pp. Berkeley and Los Angeles: University of California Press.

[0:66]

Kaplan, Abraham
  1955   An experimental study of ambiguity and
          context. Mechanical Translation 2:39-46.
          Cambridge, Mass.

Katz, Jerrold J.
  1964   Analyticity and contradiction in natural
          language. Pp. 519-543 in The structure of
          language, by J. A. Fodor and J. J. Katz.
          Englewood Cliffs, N. J.: Prentice-Hall.

  1967   Recent issues in semantic theory. Founda-
          tions of Language 3.2:124-194. Dordrecht.

  1970   Interpretative semantics vs. generative
          semantics. Foundations of Language 6.2:
          220-259. Dordrecht.

Katz, Jerrold and Jerry Fodor
  1963   The structure of a semantic theory.
          Language 39.2:170-210. Baltimore.

Katz, Jerrold J. and Paul M. Postal
  1963   Semantic interpretation of idioms and
          sentences containing them. MIT Research
          Laboratory of Electronics, Quarterly
          Progress Report No. 70:275-282. Cambridge.

  1964   An integrated theory of linguistic descrip-
          tions. (MIT Research Monograph No. 26.)
          Cambridge: MIT Press.

Kay, Paul
  1966   Comment on Ethnographic semantics: a pre-
          liminary survey, by B. N. Colby. Current
          Anthropology 7.1:20-23. Utrecht.

  1969   Comment on Colby. Pp. 78-90 in Cognitive
          anthropology, edited by S. A. Tyler. New
          York: Holt, Rinehart and Winston.

  1970   Some theoretical implications of ethnographic
          semantics. Bulletins of the American Anthro-
          pological Association 3.3(Part 2):19-31.
          Washington.

  1971a   Explorations in mathematical anthropology.
          xviii, 286 pp. Cambridge, Mass. and London:
          MIT Press.

  1971b   Taxonomy and semantic contrast. Language
          47.4:866-887. Baltimore.

Kay, Paul and A. Kimball Romney
    1967   On simple semantic spaces and semantic
            categories. (Working Paper No. 2.) 14 pp.
            Berkeley: Language-Behavior Research
            Laboratory, University of California.

Kecskemeti, Paul
    1952   Meaning, communication and value. 349 pp.
            Chicago: University of Chicago Press.

Keesing, Roger M.
    1966   Descriptive categories in the analysis of
            social organization: a rejoinder to Nelson.
            American Anthropologist 68.2(Part 1):474-
            477. Menasha.

    1968   Step kin, in-laws, and ethnoscience.
            Ethnology 7.1:59-70. Pittsburgh.

Kelkar, Ashok R.
    1965   Participant placement in Algonquian and
            Georgian. International Journal of American
            Linguistics 31.3:195-205. Baltimore.

Kelly, George A.
    1955   A theory of personality. (The psychology
            of personal constructs, Vol. 1.) xviii,
            566 pp. New York: W. W. Norton.

Kelly, Louis G.
    1970   Cultural consistency in translation. The
            Bible Translator 21.4:170-175. London.

Kemeny, John G., J. Laurie Snell, and Gerald L.
            Thompson
    1957   Introduction to finite mathematics. 372 pp.
            Englewood Cliffs, N. J.: Prentice-Hall.

Kendall, Maurice George
    1957   A course in multivariate analysis. 185 pp.
            London: Charles Griffin; New York: Hafner.

Kennedy, Kenneth A. R.
    1960   The phylogenetic tree: an analysis of its
            development in studies of human evolution.
            Kroeber Anthropological Society Papers 23:
            7-53. Berkeley.

Key, K. H. L.
    1967   Operational homology. Systematic Zoology
            16.3:275-276. Lawrence, Kans.

[0:68]

Key, Mary Ritchie
 1970   Preliminary remarks on paralanguage and
         kinesics in human communication. La Linguis-
         tique 6.2:17-36. Paris.

Keyser, Cassius
 1934   Mathematics and the science of semantics.
         Scripta Mathematica 2:247-260. New York.

Kiefer, Ferenc
 1966   Some semantic relations in natural language.
         Foundations of Language 2.3:228-240.
         Dordrecht.

Kiparsky, Paul and Carol Kiparsky
 1971   Fact. Pp. 345-369 in Semantics: an inter-
 (1970)   disciplinary reader in philosophy, linguis-
         tics and psychology, edited by D. D. Stein-
         berg and L. A. Jakobovits. Cambridge:
         Cambridge University Press. (Published
         1970 in Progress in linguistics, edited by
         M. Bierwisch and K. Heidolph. The Hague:
         Mouton.)

Kiriakoff, Sergius G.
 1966   Cladism and phylogeny. Systematic Zoology
         15.1:91-93. Lawrence, Kans.

Kluckhohn, Clyde
 1960a   The use of typology in anthropological
         theory. Pp. 134-140 in Men and cultures,
         (Selected Papers of the Fifth International
         Congress of Anthropological and Ethnological
         Sciences, Philadelphia, 1956), edited by
         A. F. C. Wallace. Philadelphia: University
         of Pennsylvania Press.

 1960b   Navaho categories. Pp. 65-98 in Culture
         and history, edited by S. Diamond. New
         York: Columbia University Press.

 1961   Notes on some anthropological aspects of
         communication. American Anthropologist
         63.5(Part 1):895-910. Menasha.

Knudsen, Trygve and Alf Sommerfelt
 1958   Principles of unilingual dictionary defini-
         tions. Pp. 92-101 in Proceedings of the
         Eighth International Congress of Linguists,
         edited by E. Sivertsen. Oslo: Oslo
         University Press.

Koffka, Kurt
1922   Perception: an introduction to the Gestalt-
        theorie. Psychological Bulletin 19.10:531-
        585. Princeton.

Kooij, J. G.
1968   Compounds and idioms. Lingua 21:250-268.
        Amsterdam.

Korn, F.
1969   An analysis of the use of the term 'model'
        in some of Lévi-Strauss's works. Bijdragen
        tot de Taal-, Land- en Volkenkunde 125.1:
        1-11.   's-Gravenhage.

Kovalevskaja, V. B.
1970   Recherches sur les systèmes sémiologiques
        en archéologie par les méthodes de la
        théorie de l'information. Pp. 187-190 in
        Archéologie et calculateurs, by J.-C.
        Gardin et al. Paris: Éditions du Centre
        National de la Recherche Scientifique.

Krauss, Michael E.
1968   Noun-classification systems in Athapaskan,
        Eyak, Tlingit and Haida verbs. International
        Journal of American Linguistics 34.3:194-
        203. Baltimore.

1969   On the classification in the Athapaskan,
        Eyak and Tlingit verb. Supplement to
        International Journal of American Linguistics
        35.4(Part 2):49-83; Memoir No. 24. Balti-
        more.

Kreps, Theodora Charlene
1964   Computer analysis of Uto-aztecan kinship
        systems. Ph.D. dissertation in Stanford
        University. 284 pp. Stanford.

Kroeber, A. L.
1909   Classificatory systems of relationship.
        Journal of the Royal Anthropological Insti-
        tute 39:77-84. London.

1960   Statistics, Indo-European, and taxonomy.
        Language 36.1:1-21. Baltimore.

Kronasser, Heinz
1952   Handbuch der Semasiologie. Kurze Einfuhrung
        in die Geschichte, Problematik und Terminolo-
        gie der Bedeutungslehre. 204 pp. Heidel-
        berg: C. Winter.

[0:70]

Krupa, Victor and G. Altmann
1961   Semantic analysis of the system of personal
pronouns in Indonesian language. Archiv
Orientální 29:620-625. Prague.

Kučera, Henry and W. Nelson Francis
1967   Computational analysis of present-day
American English. xxv, 424 pp. Providence:
Brown University Press.

Kuipers, Aert H.
1962   The Circassian nominal paradigm: a contribution to case-theory. Lingua 11:231-248.
Amsterdam.

1968   The categories verb-noun and transitive-
intransitive in English and Squamish.
Lingua 21:610-626. Amsterdam.

Kumata, Hideya and Wilbur Schramm
1956   A pilot study of cross-cultural meaning.
Public Opinion Quarterly 20:229-237. New
York.

Kunihiro, Tetsuya
1970   A contrastive study of vocabulary--with
special reference to English and Japanese.
Pp. 325-347 in Studies in general and
Oriental linguistics: presented to Shirô
Hattori on the occasion of his sixtieth
birthday, edited by R. Jakobson and S.
Kawamoto. Tokyo: TEC Company.

Kunjunni Raja K.
1963   Indian theories of meaning. (Adjar Library
Series, Vol. 91.) xv, 360 pp. Adjar,
Madras: Adjar Library and Research Center.

Kurath, Hans
1961   The semantic patterning of words. Georgetown University Monograph Series on Languages and Linguistics, No. 14:91-94.
Washington.

Kurylowicz, Jerzy
1970   Metaphor and metonymy in linguistics.
Pp. 135-136 in Sign·language·culture,
(Janua Linguarum, Series Maior 1), edited
by A. J. Greimas et al. The Hague and Paris:
Mouton.

La Barre, Weston
1942   Folk medicine and folk science. Journal

of American Folklore 55.218:197-203.
Philadelphia.

1947   Kiowa folk sciences. Journal of American
        Folklore 60.236:105-114. Philadelphia.

Ladefoged, Peter
    1955   The classification of vowels. Lingua 5.2:
            113-128. Amsterdam.

Laffal, Julius
    1964a   Linguistic field theory and studies of word
            association. Journal of General Psychology
            71:145-155. Provincetown, Mass.

    1964b   Psycholinguistics and the psychology of
            language: comments. American Psychologist
            19.10:813-815. Lancaster, Pa.

Laird, Charlton
    1971   Webster's new world thesaurus. ix, 678 pp.
            New York and Cleveland: World.

Lam, H. J.
    1936   Phylogenetic symbols, past and present.
            Acta Biotheoretica 2:153-193. Leiden.

    1948   Classification and the new morphology.
            Acta Biotheoretica 8:107-154. Leiden.

    1957   What is a taxon? Taxon 6.8:213-215.
            Utrecht.

Lamb, Sydney M.
    1959   Some proposals for linguistic taxonomy.
            Anthropological Linguistics 1.2:33-49.
            Bloomington, Ind.

    1964a   On alternation, transformation, realization,
            and stratification. Georgetown University
            Monograph Series on Languages and Linguis-
            tics, No. 15:105-122. Washington.

    1964b   The sememic approach to structural semantics.
            Pp. 57-78 in Transcultural studies in cogni-
            tion, (American Anthropologist 66.3[Part 2],
            Special Publication), edited by A. K.
            Romney and R. G. D'Andrade. Menasha.

    1965   Kinship terminology and linguistic structure.
            Pp. 37-64 in Formal semantic analysis,
            (American Anthropologist 67.5[Part 2],

Special Publication), edited by E. A. Hammel. Menasha.

Lamb, Sydney M. (cont.)
1966a   Outline of stratificational grammar, with an appendix by Leonard E. Newell. 109 pp. Washington: Georgetown University Press.

1966b   Prolegomena to a theory of phonology. Language 42.2:536-573. Baltimore.

1966c   Epilegomena to a theory of language. Romance Philology 19.4:531-573. Berkeley.

1966d   L'Utilisation de l'information sémantique pour la résolution des ambiguïtés syntaxiques. Pp. 13-36 in Actes du Premier Colloque International de Linguistique Appliquée. Nancy.

1970   Linguistic and cognitive networks. Pp. 195-222 in Cognition: a multiple view, edited by P. L. Garvin. New York: Spartan Books.

Lance, G. N. and W. T. Williams
1965   Computer programs for monothetic classification ("association analysis"). Computer Journal 8.3:246-249. London.

1967   Mixed data classificatory programs. 1. Agglomerative systems. Australian Computer Journal 1.1:15-20. Chippendale.

Landar, Herbert J.
1960   A note on accepted and rejected arrangements of Navaho words. International Journal of American Linguistics 26.4:351-354. Baltimore.

1964   Seven Navaho verbs of eating. International Journal of American Linguistics 30.1:94-98. Baltimore.

1966   Language and culture. 274 pp. New York: Oxford University Press.

Lane, Harlan
1967   Identification, discrimination, translation: the effects of mapping ranges of physical continua onto phoneme and sememe categories. Pp. 155-170 in Applied linguistics and the teaching of French, Linguistique appliquée

et enseignement du français, edited by P. R. Leon. Montréal: Centre Éducatif et Culturel.

Lang, Ranier
1970   Enga questions: structural and semantic studies. 237 pp. Ph.D. thesis in the Australian National University, Canberra.

Lange, R. T., N. S. Stenhouse, and C. E. Offler
1965   Experimental appraisal of certain procedures for classification of data. Australian Journal of Biological Science 18.6:1189-1205. Sydney.

Langer, Susanne K.
1953   An introduction to symbolic logic. 2d
(1937) revised edition. 368 pp. New York: Dover.

1956   Philosophy in a new key: a study in the
(1942) symbolism of reason, rite, and art. 3d edition. xx, 313 pp. Cambridge: Harvard University Press.

Lanyon, W. E. and W. N. Tavolga
1960   Animal sounds and communication. (AIBS Publication 7.). xiii, 443 pp. Washington: American Institute of Biological Sciences.

Lauriault, James
1951   Lexical problems in Shipibo Mark. The Bible Translator 2.1:56-66. London.

1957   Some problems in translating paragraphs idiomatically. The Bible Translator 8.4: 166-169. London.

1958   On handling meanings in the vernacular. The Bible Translator 9.4:145-150. London.

Law, Howard W.
1966   Grammatical equivalences in Bible translating. The Bible Translator 17.3:123-128. London.

Lawrence, George H. M.
1951   Taxonomy of vascular plants. 823 pp. New York: Macmillan.

Lazarsfeld, Paul F.
1937   Some remarks on the typological procedures in social research. Zeitschrift für Sozial-forschung 6:119-139. Leipzig.

Lazarsfeld, Paul F. (cont.)
   1960   Latent structure analyses. Pp. 477-543 in
           Vol. 3 of Psychology: a study of a science,
           edited by S. Koch. New York: McGraw-Hill.

   1961   The algebra of dichotomous systems. Pp. 111-
           157 in Studies in item analysis and predic-
           tion, edited by H. Solomon. Stanford:
           Stanford University Press.

Lazarsfeld, Paul F. and A. H. Barton
   1951   Qualitative measurement in the social
           sciences: classification, typologies, and
           indices. Pp. 155-192 in The policy sciences,
           edited by D. Lerner and H. Lasswell.
           Stanford: Stanford University Press.

Leach, Edmund R.
   1964a   Telstar et les aborigènes ou "La Pensée
           sauvage." Annales: Economies-Sociétés-
           Civilisations 19.6:1000-1116. Paris.

   1964b   Anthropological aspects of language:
           animal categories and verbal abuse. Pp.
           23-63 in New directions in the study of
           language, edited by E. Lenneberg. Cambridge:
           MIT Press.

   1966a   The legitimacy of Solomon: some structural
           aspects of Old Testament history. Archives
           Europeennes de Sociologie, European Journal
           of Sociology 7:58-101. Paris.

   1966b   Twins, birds, and vegetables. Man (n.s.)
           1.4:557-558. London.

   1966c   Classification in social and cultural
           anthropology, and prehistoric archaeology,
           a select bibliography. Classification
           Society Bulletin 1.2:19-26. Leicester,
           England.

   1970   Lévi-Strauss. 127 pp. (Fontana Modern
           Masters Series.) London: Wm. Collins.

Lee, D. Demetracopoulou
   1938   Conceptual implications of an Indian lan-
           guage. Philosophy of Science 5.1:89-102.
           Baltimore.

   1944a   Categories of the generic and particular in
           Wintu'. American Anthropologist 46.3:362-
           369. Menasha.

1944b   Linguistic reflection of Wintu·' thought.
         International Journal of American Linguis-
         tics 10.4:181-187. Baltimore.

1950   Lineal and nonlineal codifications of
         reality. Etc. 8:13-26. Bloomington, Ill.

Leech, Geoffrey N.
1969   Towards a semantic description of English.
         xiii, 277 pp. London: Longmans, Green.

1970   On the theory and practice of semantic
         testing. Lingua 24.4:343-364. Amsterdam.

Lees, Robert B.
1959   Review of Logique, langage et théorie de
         l'information, by Léo Apostel, Benoit
         Mandelbrot and Albert Morf, with an intro-
         duction by Jean Piaget. Language 35.2(Part
         1):271-301. Baltimore.

1960   The grammar of English nominalizations.
         (International Journal of American Linguis-
         tics 26.3[Part 2].) xxvi, 205 pp.
         Baltimore.

1964   On the so-called 'substitution in frames'
         technique. General Linguistics 6.1:11-20.
         Lexington, Ky.

Legendre, P. and P. Vaillancourt
1969   A mathematical model for the entities
         species and genus. Taxon 18.3:245-252.
         Utrecht.

Lehrer, Adrienne
1970a   Indeterminacy in semantic description.
         Glossa 4.1:87-110. Burnaby, B. C.

1970b   Meaning in linguistics. Pp. 9-16 in Theory
         of meaning, edited by Adrienne and Keith
         Lehrer. Englewood Cliffs, N. J.: Prentice-
         Hall.

Leisi, Ernst
1961   Der Wortinhalt: seine Strucktur im Deutsch-
         en und Englischen. Enlarged edition. 130
         pp. Heidelberg: Quelle and Meyer.

Lenneberg, Eric H.
1953   Cognition in ethnolinguistics. Language
         29.4:463-471. Baltimore.

Lenneberg, Eric H. (cont.)
  1955   A note on Cassirer's philosophy of language.
          Philosophy and Phenomenological Research
          15:512-522. Buffalo.

  1964   New directions in the study of language.
          194 pp. Cambridge: MIT Press.

Lerman, I. C.
  1970   H-classificabilité. Pp. 319-326 in
          Archéologie et calculateurs, by J.-C.
          Gardin et al. Paris: Éditions du Centre
          National de la Recherche Scientifique.

Lerner, Daniel and Harold D. Lasswell
  1951   The policy sciences, recent developments in
          scope and method. xiv, 344 pp. Stanford:
          Stanford University Press.

Leroy, Jean F.
  1958   Taxon, taxonomie...querelle de mots?
          querelle de fond! Journal d'Agriculture
          Tropicale et de Botanique Appliquée
          5.1-2-3:173-176. Paris.

Lévi-Strauss, Claude
  1962   La Pensée sauvage. 395 pp. Paris: Plon.
          (Translated 1966 as The savage mind. xii,
          290 pp. London: Wiedenfeld and Nicolson.)

Lévi-Strauss, Claude, Roman Jakobson, Charles F.
          Voegelin, and Thomas A. Sebeok
  1953   Results of the conference of anthropologists
          and linguists. (Indiana University Publica-
          tion in Anthropology and Linguistics;
          International Journal of American Linguis-
          tics, Memoir No. 8.) vi, 67 pp. Blooming-
          ton, Ind.

Lévy, F.
  1967   On the relative nature of relational factors
          in classifications. Information Storage
          and Retrieval 3:315-324. Oxford.

Lévy-Bruhl, Lucien
  1910   Les Fonctions mentales dans les sociétés
          inférieures. 461 pp. Paris: Félix Alcan.
          (Translated 1926 by Lilian A. Clare as
          How natives think, 392 pp., London: Allen
          and Unwin. Reprinted 1966, xxv, 355 pp.
          New York: Washington Square Press.)

Liberman, Alvin M. et al.
1957   The discrimination of speech sounds within
        and across phoneme boundaries. Journal of
        Experimental Psychology 54.5:358-368.
        Lancaster, Pa.

1967   Perception of the speech code. Psychologi-
        cal Review 74.6:431-461. Lancaster, Pa.

Library Association, Classification Research Group
1969   Classification and information control.
        Papers from the Classification Research
        Group, 1960-1968. (Library Association
        Research Publication No. 1.) 130 pp.
        London.

Lindekens, R.
1968   Essai de description d'un espace sémantique.
        Cahiers de Lexicologie 12.1:15-36. Paris.

Lindenfeld, Jacqueline
1971   Semantic categorization as a deterrent to
        grammatical borrowing: a Yaqui example.
        International Journal of American Linguis-
        tics 37.1:6-14. Baltimore.

Linnaeus, Carolus
1935   Systema naturae. 1st edition. 13 pp.
        Leiden: Haak.

Linsky, Leonard, editor
1952   Semantics and the philosophy of language:
        a collection of readings. 289 pp. Urbana:
        University of Illinois Press.

Locke, John
1700   Of words. In Book 3 of Essay concerning
(1690) human understanding. London: A. and J.
        Churchill.

Loewen, Jacob A.
1966   Lengua Indians and their "innermost."
        Practical Anthropology 13.6:252-272.
        Tarrytown, N. Y.

1967   Matrices for eliciting translation vocabu-
        lary. The Bible Translator 18.4:184-191.
        London.

Longacre, Robert
1958   Items in context: their bearing on transla-
        tion theory. Language 34.4:482-491.
        Baltimore.

Longacre, Robert   (cont.)
1964   Prolegomena to lexical structure. Linguis-
           tics 5:5-24. The Hague.

Lotz, John
1949   The semantic analysis of the nominal bases
           in Hungarian. Travaux du Cercle Linguis-
           tique de Copenhague 5:185-197. Copenhagen.

1955   On language and culture. International
           Journal of American Linguistics 21.2:187-
           189. Baltimore.

1962   Semantic analysis of the tenses in Hungarian.
           Lingua 11:256-262. Amsterdam.

1966   Productive inflectional morphophonemic
           selection in English. Anthropological
           Linguistics 8.9:27-31. Bloomington, Ind.

1967   Numerical properties of linguistic struc-
           tures. Anthropological Linguistics 9.4:
           1-4. Bloomington, Ind.

Lounsbury, Floyd G.
1954   Meanings of 'meaning.' Pp. 171-177 in
           Psycholinguistics: a survey of theory and
           research problems, (International Journal
           of American Linguistics, Memoir No. 10),
           edited by C. E. Osgood. Baltimore.

1955   The varieties of meaning. Georgetown
           University Monograph Series on Languages
           and Linguistics, No. 8:158-164. Washington.

1956   A semantic analysis of the Pawnee kinship
           usage. Language 32.1:158-194. Baltimore.

1960   Similarity and contiguity relations in
           language and culture. Georgetown University
           Monograph Series on Languages and Linguis-
           tics, No. 12:123-128. Washington.

1963   Linguistics and psychology. Pp. 551-582 in
           Vol. 6 of Psychology: a study of a science,
           edited by S. Koch. New York: McGraw-Hill.

1964a   A formal analysis of the Crow and Omaha-
           type kinship terminologies. Pp. 351-393
           in Explorations in cultural anthropology:
           essays in honor of George Peter Murdock,
           edited by W. H. Goodenough. New York:
           McGraw-Hill.

1964b   The structural analysis of kinship semantics.
         Pp. 1073-1093 in Proceedings of the Ninth
         International Congress of Linguists. The
         Hague: Mouton.

1965   Another view of the Trobriand kinship
         categories. Pp. 142-185 in Formal semantic
         analysis, (American Anthropologist 67.5
         [Part 2], Special Publication), edited by
         E. A. Hammel. Menasha.

1968   One hundred years of anthropological lin-
         guistics. Pp. 150-225, 256-264, in One
         hundred years of anthropology, edited by
         J. O. Brew. Cambridge: Harvard University
         Press.

1969   Language and culture. Pp. 3-29 in Language
         and philosophy, edited by S. Hook. New
         York: New York University Press.

Luria, A. R. and O. S. Vingradova
1959   An objective investigation of the dynamics
         of semantic systems. British Journal of
         Psychology 50.2:89-105. Cambridge.

Lyons, John
1963   Structural semantics: an analysis of part
         of the vocabulary of Plato. (Publications
         of the Philological Society, No. 20.)
         237 pp. Oxford: Basil Blackwell.

1968   Introduction to theoretical linguistics.
         x, 519 pp. Cambridge: Cambridge University
         Press.

1970   The meaning of meaning. Times Literary
         Supplement No. 3569 (23 July):795-797.
         London.

Lyons, John, editor
1970   New horizons in linguistics. 367 pp.
         Baltimore: Penguin Books.

Lyons, J. and R. J. Wales, editors
1966   Psycholinguistics papers: the proceedings
         of the 1966 Edinburgh Conference. 243 pp.
         Edinburgh: Edinburgh University Press.

McClelland, R. M. A. and W. W. Mapleson
1966   Construction and usage of classified
         schedules and generic features in

[0:80]

co-ordinate indexing. With discussion.
Aslib Proceedings 18.10:290-302. London.

McIntosh, Angus
1961   Patterns and ranges. Language 37.3:325-337.
        Baltimore.

McKaughan, Howard
1959   Semantic components of pronoun systems:
        Maranao. Word 15.1:101-102. New York.

MacKaye, James
1939   The logic of language. 303 pp. Hanover:
        Dartmouth College Publications.

Maclay, Howard and Mary D. Sleator
1960   Responses to language: judgments of
        grammaticalness. International Journal of
        American Linguistics 26.4:275-282. Balti-
        more.

Macnamara, John
1971   Parsimony and the lexicon. Language 47.2:
        389-374. Baltimore.

MacNaughton-Smith, P.
1965   Some statistical and other numerical tech-
        niques for classifying individuals.
        (Research Unit Report No. 6.) v, 33 pp.
        London: Her Majesty's Stationery Office.

MacQueen, J. B.
1967   Some methods for classification and analysis
        of multivariate observations. Proceedings
        5th Berkeley Symposium on Mathematical
        Statistics and Probability 1:281-297.
        Berkeley.

Makkai, Adam
1966   Idiom structure in English. v, 219 pp.
        Ph.D dissertation in Yale University.
        New Haven. (Published by University Micro-
        films, Ann Arbor, Mich.)

Malinowski, Bronislaw
1935   The language of magic and gardening. (Coral
        gardens and their magic, Vol. 2.) xxxiii,
        350 pp. London: Allen and Unwin; New York:
        American Book. (Republished 1965, 384 pp.
        Bloomington: Indiana University Press.)

1962   The language of magic. Pp. 72-90 in The

importance of language, edited by M. Black. Englewood Cliffs, N. J.: Prentice-Hall.

Malkiel, Yakov
1959   Studies in irreversible binomials. Lingua 8.2:113-160. Amsterdam.

1967   Each word has a history of its own. Glossa 1.2:137-149. Burnaby, B. C.

Mandelbaum, David G., editor
1949   Selected writings of Edward Sapir in language, culture and personality. 617 pp. Berkeley and Los Angeles: University of California Press.

Mandelbrot, Benoit
1956a   La Distribution de Willis-Yule, relative aux nombres de l'espèce dans les genres biologiques. Comptes Rendus des Séances de l'Académie des Sciences 242:2223-2226. Paris.

1956b   On the language of taxonomy: an outline of a 'thermostatistical' theory of systems of categories with Willis (natural) structure. Pp. 135-145 (Chapter 15) in Information theory, edited by C. Cherry. London: Butterworths.

Maquet, Charles
1936   Dictionnaire analogique. vii, 591 pp. Paris: Larousse.

Maranda, Pierre
1964   Kinship semantics. Anthropos 59.3-4:517-528. Fribourg.

1967   Formal analysis and inter-cultural studies. Information sur les Sciences Sociales 6.4: 7-36. Paris.

1968   Analyse quantitative et qualitative de mythes sur ordinateur. Pp. 79-86 in Calcul et formalisation dans les sciences de l'homme, edited by B. Jaulin and J.-C. Gardin. Paris: Éditions du Centre National de la Recherche Scientifique.

Marchand, Hans
1969   The categories and types of present-day English word-formation. xxvi, 545 pp. Munich: Beck.

Margolis, Joseph
 1968   Quine on observationality and translation.
          Foundations of Language 4.2:128-137.
          Dordrecht.

Margulis, Lynn and T. N. Margulis
 1968   A note on the equivalence of characters:
          pheneticist vs. phylogeneticist. Systematic
          Zoology 17.4:477-479. Lawrence, Kans.

Mariétan, Joseph
 1901   Problème de la classification des sciences
          d'Aristote à St. Thomas. 203 pp. St.
          Maurice: Imprimerie St. Augustin; Paris:
          Felix Alcan.

Markel, Norman N. and Eric P. Hamp
 1961   Connotative meanings of certain phoneme
          sequences. Studies in Linguistics 15.3-4:
          47-61. Buffalo.

Marouzeau, J.
 1923   Le Rôle de l'interlocuteur dans l'expression
          de la pensée. Journal de Psychologie 10:
          12-18. Paris.

Martin, Richard Milton
 1959   Toward a systematic pragmatics. 107 pp.
          Amsterdam: North-Holland Publishing Co.

 1963   Intension and decision: a philosophical
          study. 159 pp. Englewood Cliffs, N. J.:
          Prentice-Hall.

Martinet, André
 1965   The word. Diogenes 51:38-54. Montreal.

Marty, Anton
 1950   Ueber Wert und Methode einer allgemeinen
          beschreibenden Bedeutungslehre. 111 pp.
          Berne: O. Funke.

Maruyama, Magoroh
 1963a   The second cybernetics: deviation-
          amplifying mutual causal processes.
          Cybernetica 6.1:5-23. Namur, Belgium.
          (Reprinted from American Scientist 51.2:
          164-179. New Haven.)

 1963b   Basic elements in misunderstandings.
          Cybernetica 6.3:111-132. Namur, Belgium.

1965   Metaorganization of information: information
          in classificational universe, relational
          universe and relevantial universe. Cyber-
          netica 8.3:224-236. Namur, Belgium.

Mason, Herbert L.
1950   Taxonomy, systematic botany and biosystemat-
          ics. Madroño 10:193-208. Berkeley.

Mason, Herbert L. and Jean H. Langenheim
1957   Language analysis and concept environment.
          Ecology 38.2:325-340. Durham.

Mates, Benson
1952   Synonymity. Pp. 111-136 in Semantics and
          the philosophy of language, edited by L.
          Linsky. Urbana: University of Illinois
          Press.

Mathiot, Madeleine
1962   Noun classes and folk taxonomy in Papago.
          American Anthropologist 64.2:340-350. Menasha.

1967a   The cognitive significance of the category
          of the nominal number in Papago. Pp. 197-
          237 in Studies in southwestern ethnolinguis-
          tics, edited by D. H. Hymes and W. E. Bittle.
          The Hague: Mouton.

1967b   The place of the dictionary in linguistic
          description. Language 43.3:703-724.
          Baltimore.

1968   An approach to the cognitive study of
          language. (International Journal of Ameri-
          can Linguistics 34.1[Part 2]; Publication
          45, Indiana University Research Center in
          Anthropology, Folklore, and Linguistics.)
          224 pp. Bloomington, Ind.

Mauss, Marcel
1964   On language and primitive forms of classifi-
(1923)   cation. Pp. 124-217 in Language in culture
          and society, edited by D. Hymes. New York:
          Harper and Row. (Originally published in
          French in 1923, in Journal de Psychologie:
          Normale et pathologique 20:944-947. Paris.)

Mayne, Alan J.
1968   Some modern approaches to the classification
          of knowledge. Classification Society Bulle-
          tin 1.4:12-17. Leicester, England.

[O:84]

Mayr, Ernst
1946   The naturalist in Leidy's time and today.
         Proceedings of the Academy of Natural
         Science 98:271-276. Philadelphia.

1949   The species concept: semantics versus
         semantics. Evolution 3:371-372. Lancaster,
         Pa.

1954   Notes on nomenclature and classification.
         Systematic Zoology 3.2:86-89. Baltimore.

1955   The species as a systematic and as a bio-
         logical problem. Pp. 3-12 in Biological
         systematics, 16th Annual Biological
         Colloquium, edited by E. Mayr. Corvallis:
         Oregon State College.

1957a   Species concepts and definitions. Pp. 1-22
         in The species problem, (AAAS Publication
         No. 50), edited by E. Mayr. Washington:
         American Association for the Advancement
         of Science.

1957b   Difficulties and importance of the biologi-
         cal species concept. Pp. 371-388 in The
         species problem, (AAAS Publication No. 50),
         edited by E. Mayr. Washington: American
         Association for the Advancement of Science.

1966   The proper spelling of taxonomy. Systematic
         Zoology 15.1:88. Lawrence, Kans.

1968   Theory of biological classification. Nature
         220.5167:545-548. London.

1969a   The biological meaning of species. Biologi-
         cal Journal of the Linnean Society 1.3:311-
         320. London.

1969b   Principles of systematic zoology. xi, 428
         pp. New York: McGraw-Hill.

Mayr, Ernst, editor
1955   Biological systematics, 16th Annual Bio-
         logical Colloquium. iv, 51 pp. Corvallis:
         Oregon State College.

1957   The species problem: a symposium presented
         at the Atlanta meeting of the American
         Association for the Advancement of Science,
         1955. (AAAS Publication No. 50.) x, 395 pp.

[0:85]

Washington: American Association for the Advancement of Science.

Mayr, Ernst, E. Gorton Linsley, and Robert Usinger
1953   Methods and principles of systematic zoology. 328 pp. New York: McGraw-Hill.

Maze, Jack
1966   A conceptual framework for taxonomy, and numerical taxonomy--a brief comment. Systematic Zoology 15.3:249-250. Lawrence, Kans.

Mbaga, K. and W. H. Whiteley
1961   Formality and informality in Yao speech. Africa 31:135-146. London.

Medical Research Council, Microbial Systematics Research Unit
1966   Classification Programs Newsletter. 49 mimeographed pp. Leicester, England: University of Leicester.

Menner, Robert J.
1945   Multiple meaning and change of meaning in English. Language 21.2:59-76. Baltimore.

Meredith, G. P., Stephen Ullmann, and Russell Brain
1956   Semantics: a symposium. Archivum Linguisticum 8:1-27. Glasgow.

Metcalf, Z. P.
1954   The construction of keys. Systematic Zoology 3.1:38-45. Baltimore.

Metzger, Duane G. and G. E. Williams
1966   Some procedures and results in the study of native categories: Tzeltal "firewood." American Anthropologist 68.2(Part 1):389-407. Menasha.

Meyer, R. M.
1910   Bedeutungssysteme. Zeitschrift für vergleichende Sprachforschung 43:352-368. Göttingen.

Michener, Charles D. and Robert R. Sokal
1957   A quantitative approach to a problem in classification. Evolution 11.2:130-162. Lancaster, Pa.

Mill, John Stuart
1846   A system of logic. xii, 593 pp. New York:

103

Harper. (8th edition, 1959, xvi, 622 pp. London: Longmans, Green.)

Miller, George A.
1951   Language and communication. 298 pp. New York: McGraw-Hill.

1953   What is information measurement? American Psychologist 8.1:3-11. Lancaster, Pa.

1956a   Human memory and the storage of information. I.R.E. Transactions on Information Theory IT-2.3:129-137. New York.

1956b   The magical number seven, plus or minus two: some limits on our capacity for processing information. Psychological Review 63.2: 81-97. Lancaster, Pa.

1969   The organization of lexical memory: are word associations sufficient? Pp. 223-236 in The pathology of memory, edited by G. A. Talland and N. C. Waugh. New York: Academic Press.

Miller, George A., Eugene Galanter, and Karl H. Pribram
1960   Plans and the structure of behavior. x, 266 pp. New York: Henry Holt.

Miller, George A. and David McNeill
1968   Psycholinguistics. Pp. 666-794 in Vol. 3 of The handbook of social psychology, 2d edition, edited by G. Lindzey and E. Aronson. Reading, Mass.: Addison-Wesley.

Millier, C. and R. E. Tomassone
1970   Méthodes d'ordination et de classification: leur efficacité et leurs limites. Pp. 207-226 in Archéologie et calculateurs, edited by J.-C. Gardin et al. Paris: Éditions du Centre National de la Recherche Scientifique.

Mills, C. Wright
1938   Language, logic and culture. American Sociological Review 4.5:670-680. Menasha.

1940   Situated actions and vocabularies of motive. American Sociological Review 5.6:904-913. Menasha. (Reprinted 1963, pp. 439-452 in Power, politics and people: the collected essays of C. Wright Mills, edited by I. L. Horowitz. New York: Oxford University Press; available as paperback, Ballantine Books.)

Mills, J.
1968   Some current problems of classification for
        information retrieval. Classification
        Society Bulletin 1.4:18-27. Leicester,
        England.

Milner, George B.
1969   De l'armature des locutions proverbiales.
        Essai de taxonomie sémantique. L'Homme
        9.3:49-70. Paris.

Minsky, Marvin Lee, editor
1968   Semantic information processing. vii, 440
        pp. Cambridge: MIT Press.

Möller, F.
1962   Quantitative methods in the systematics of
        Actinomycetales IV: the theory and applica-
        tion of a probabilistic identification key.
        Giornale di Microbiologia 10.1:29-47.
        Milan.

Moravcsik, J. M. E.
1970   Subcategorization and abstract terms.
        Foundations in Language 6.4:473-487.
        Dordrecht.

Morazé, Charles
1970   Pensée sauvage et logique géométrique.
        Pp. 964-980 in Échanges et communications;
        mélanges offerts à Claude Lévi-Strauss à
        l'occasion de son 60ème anniversaire,
        edited by J. Pouillon and P. Maranda.
        The Hague and Paris: Mouton.

Morris, Charles W.
1938   Foundations of the theory of signs. (Inter-
        national Encyclopedia of Unified Science,
        1.2.) 59 pp. Chicago: University of
        Chicago Press.

1946   Signs, language and behavior. 365 pp.
        New York: Prentice-Hall.

1964   Signification and significance: a study
        of the relations of signs and values. 99 pp.
        Cambridge: MIT Press.

Morse, Larry E.
1971   Specimen identification and key construction
        with time-sharing computers. Taxon 20.2-3:
        269-282. Utrecht.

[0:88]

Morton, C. V.
1957   The misuse of the term taxon. Taxon 6.5:
        155. Utrecht. (Reprinted 1957, Rhodora
        59:43-44. Boston.)

Mounin, Georges
1963   Les Problèmes théoriques de la traduction.
        Bibliothèque des idées. xii, 296 pp.
        Paris: Gallimard.

1965   Un champ sémantique: la dénomination des
        animaux domestiques. La Linguistique 1.1:
        31-54. Paris.

1968   Travaux récents de sémantique. La Linguis-
        tique 4.1:131-140. Paris.

1970   Sémiologie et linguistique: l'exemple du
        blason. La Linguistique 6.2:5-16. Paris.

Mowrer, O. Hobart
1960   Learning theory and the symbolic processes.
        xiii, 473 pp. New York: John Wiley.

Mueller, Hugo J.
1960   Review of Semantische Studien im Sinnbereich
        der Schenelligkeit..., by E. Oskaar.
        Language 36.1:162-165. Baltimore.

Müller, Walter
1960   Englische Idiomatik nach Sinngruppen: eine
        systematische Einführung in die heutige
        Umgangssprache. xi, 322 pp. Berlin:
        Walter de Gruyter.

Naert, Pierre
1967   L'"Arbitraire" du signe. Word 23.1-2-3(Part
        1):422-427. New York.

Naess, Arne
1953   Interpretation and preciseness, a contribu-
        tion to the theory of communication. xiv,
        450 pp. Oslo: Jocob Dybwad.

1957   Synonymity as revealed by intuition.
        Philosophical Review 66:87-93. Ithaca.

Nagel, Ernest
1961   The structure of science: problems in the
        logic of scientific explanation. xiii,
        618 pp. New York: Harcourt, Brace and
        World.

National Institute of Sciences of India
1967   Proceedings of Symposium on Newer Trends in
        Taxonomy. (Bulletin of the National Insti-
        tute of Sciences of India, 34.) vi, 409 pp.
        New Delhi.

Needham, Rodney
1960   Descent systems and ideal language. Philoso-
        phy of Science 27:96-101. Baltimore.

1963   Introduction. Pp. xii-xlvii in Primitive
        classification, by É. Durkheim and M. Mauss,
        translated and edited by R. Needham.
        Chicago: University of Chicago Press.

Needham, Roger M.
1965   Computer methods for classification and
        grouping. Pp. 345-356 in The use of comput-
        ers in anthropology, edited by D. Hymes.
        The Hague: Mouton.

Needham, Roger M. and K. Sparck Jones
1964   Key words and clumps. Journal of Documenta-
        tion 20.1:5-15. London.

Neisser, Ulric
1967   Cognitive psychology. xi, 351 pp. New York:
        Appleton-Century-Crofts.

Nelson, Gareth J.
1970   Outline of a theory of comparative biology.
        Systematic Zoology 19.4:373-384. Lawrence,
        Kans.

Newell, Allen, editor
1961   Information processing language--V manual.
        xii, 244 pp. Englewood Cliffs, N. J.:
        Prentice-Hall.

Newell, Leonard E.
1971   Semantic theory and lexicography. Philip-
        pine Journal of Linguistics. 1.2:106-111.
        Manila.

Newman, Stanley
1954   Semantic problems in grammatical systems
        and lexemes: a search for method. Pp. 82-
        91 in Language in culture, (American Anthro-
        pologist 56.6[Part 2], Memoir No. 79;
        Comparative Studies of Cultures and Civiliza-
        tions, No. 3), edited by H. Hoijer. Menasha.

[0:90]

Newmark, Leonard
1962   An Albanian case system. Lingua 11:313-321.
        Amsterdam.

Nida, Eugene A.
1945   Linguistics and ethnology in translation
        problems. Word 1.2:194-208. New York.

1947   Bible translating: an analysis of principles
        and procedures with special reference to
        aboriginal languages. vii, 362 pp. New
        York: American Bible Society.

1949   Morphology: the descriptive analysis of
        words. 2d edition. 342 pp. Ann Arbor:
        University of Michigan Press.

1951   A system for the description of semantic
        elements. Word 7.1:1-14. New York.

1954   What is a primitive language? The Bible
        Translator 5.3:106-112. London.

1957   Meaning and translation. The Bible Trans-
        lator 8.3:97-108. London.

1958   Analysis of meaning and dictionary making.
        International Journal of American Linguis-
        tics 24.4:279-292. Baltimore.

1959   Principles of translation as exemplified by
        Bible translating. Pp. 11-31 in On trans-
        lation, edited by R. A. Brower. Cambridge:
        Harvard University Press. (Also 1959, The
        Bible Translator 10.4:148-164. London.)

1961   Some problems of semantic structure and
        translational equivalence. Pp. 313-325 in
        A William Cameron Townsend en el vigesimo-
        quinto aniversario del Instituto Linguís-
        tico de Verano, edited by B. Elson. Mexico
        City: Summer Institute of Linguistics.

1964   Toward a science of translating; with special
        reference to principles and procedures
        involved in Bible translating. x, 331 pp.,
        bibliography. Leiden: Brill.

1969   Science of translation. Language 45.3:
        483-498. Baltimore.

1970   Formal correspondence in translation. The
        Bible Translator 21.3:105-113. London.

Nida, Eugene A. and Charles R. Taber
1969   The theory and practice of translation with
        special reference to Bible translating.
        viii, 220 pp. Leiden: Brill.

Nidditch, Peter Herold
1960   Elementary logic of science and mathematics.
        vii, 371 pp. Glencoe, Ill.: Free Press.

Nilsson, N. J.
1969   Survey of pattern recognition. Annals of
        the New York Academy of Sciences 161.2:380-
        401. New York.

Northrop, F. S. C.
1966   The logic of the sciences and humanities.
(1931) 402 pp. (Meridan Books M 71.) Cleveland
        and New York: World.

Nutini, Hugo C.
1970   Lévi-Strauss' conception of science. Pp. 543-
        570 in Échanges et communications; mélanges
        offerts à Claude Lévi-Strauss à l'occasion
        de son 60ème anniversaire, edited by J.
        Pouillon and P. Maranda. The Hague and Paris:
        Mouton.

Ogden, Charles Kay
1932   Opposition: a linguistic and psychological
        analysis. 104 pp. London: Kegan Paul,
        Trench, Trubner.

Ogden, C. K. and I. A. Richards
1948   The meaning of meaning: a study of the
(1923) influence of language upon thought and of
        the science of symbolism. 8th edition.
        New York: Harcourt, Brace and World;
        London: Routledge and Kegan Paul.

Öhman, S.
1951   Wortinhalt und Weltbild. Vergleichende und
        methodologische Studien zu Bedeutungslehre
        und Wortfeldtheorie. Stockholm: University
        of Stockholm.

1953   Theories of the linguistic field. Word
        9.2:123-134. New York.

Olds, M. E.
1956   Synonymity: extensional isomorphism.
        Mind 65.260:473-488. Edinburgh.

Olmsted, David L.
    1950   Ethnolinguistics so far. (Studies in Lin-
            guistics, Occasional Papers No. 2.) 16 pp.
            Norman: Battenburg Press.

    1954   Toward a cultural theory of lexical innova-
            tion: a research design. Georgetown Uni-
            versity Monograph Series on Languages and
            Linguistics, No. 7:105-117. Washington.

O'Neil, W. M.
    1958   Basic issues in perceptual theory. Psycho-
            logical Review 65.6:348-361. Lancaster, Pa.

Ore, Oystein
    1962   Theory of graphs. (American Mathematical
            Society Colloquium Publications, Vol. 38.)
            270 pp. Providence.

    1963   Graphs and their uses. (New Mathematics
            Library 0.10.) viii, 131 pp. New York:
            Random House.

Orloci, L.
    1966   Geometric models in ecology. 1. The theory
            and application of some ordination methods.
            Journal of Ecology 54.1:193-215. Oxford.

Osgood, Charles E.
    1952   The nature and measurement of meaning.
            Psychological Bulletin 49.3:197-237.
            Lancaster, Pa.

Osgood, Charles E. and Thomas A. Sebeok, editors
    1965   Psycholinguistics: a survey of theory and
            research problems. Report of the 1953
            summer seminar sponsored by the Committee
            on Linguistics and Psychology of the Social
            Science Research Council. (Indiana Univer-
            sity Publications in Anthropology and
            Linguistics, Memoir No. 10.) xi, 203 pp.
            Baltimore: Waverly Press.

Osgood, Charles E., Thomas A. Sebeok, and Richard
            Diebold, Jr.
    1965   Psycholinguistics: a survey of theory and
            research problems; a survey of psycholin-
            guistic research, 1954-1964. 307 pp.
            Bloomington: Indiana University Press.

Osgood, Charles E., George J. Suci, and Percy H.
            Tannenbaum
    1957   The measurement of meaning. vii, 342 pp.

Urbana: University of Illinois Press.

Oskaar, Els
1958   Semantische Studien im Sinnbereich der
          Schnelligkeit: plötzlich, schnell und ihre
          Synonymik in Deutsch der Gegenwart und der
          Früh-, Hoch- und Spätmittelalters. Acta
          Universitatis Stockholmiensis, Stockholmer
          germanistische Forschungen, No. 2. Stock-
          holm.

Oyelaran, Olasope O.
1967   Aspects of linguistic theory in Firthian
          linguistics. Word 23.1-2-3(Part 1):428-452.
          New York.

Pagès, Robert
1967   Relational aspects of conceptualization in
          message analysis. Information Storage and
          Retrieval 3.4:351-372. Oxford.

Palmer, F. R.
1957-   Linguistic hierarchy. Lingua 7.3:225-241.
1958   Amsterdam.

Panoff, Michel
1965   La Terminologie de la parenté en Polynésie:
          essai d'analyse formelle. L'Homme 4.3-4:
          60-87. Paris.

Pap, Arthur
1957   Mathematics, abstract entities, and modern
          semantics. Scientific Monthly 85:29-40.
          Washington.

Park, Roswell
1841   Pantology; or, A systematic survey of human
          knowledge. 587 pp. Philadelphia: Hogan
          and Thompson.

Parker-Rhodes, A. F.
1957   Review of The language of taxonomy: an
          application of symbolic logic to the study
          of classificatory systems, by John R. Gregg.
          Philosophical Review 66.1:124-125. Ithaca.

Parkes, Kenneth C.
1967   A qualified defense of traditional nomencla-
          ture. Systematic Zoology 16.3:268-273.
          Lawrence, Kans.

Parsons, Terence
1970   An analysis of mass terms and amount terms.

Foundations of Language 6.3:362-388.
Dordrecht.

Partee, Barbara Hall
1970   Negation, conjunction, and quantifiers:
syntax vs. semantics. Foundations of
Language 6.2:153-165. Dordrecht.

Passin, Herbert
1966   Intra-familial linguistic usage in Japan.
Monumenta Nipponica 21.1-2:97-113. Tokyo.

Pawley, Andrew
1970   Are emic dictionaries possible? Kivung
3.1:8-16. Boroko, T.P.N.G.

Peirce, Charles Santiago Sanders
1931-   Elements of logic. Vol. 2 of Collected
1938   papers, edited by Charles Hartshorne and
Paul Weiss. Cambridge: Harvard University
Press.

1955   Logic as semiotic: the theory of signs.
Pp. 98-119 in Philosophical writings of
Peirce, edited by J. Buchler. New York:
Dover.

Pelc, Jerzy
1970   A functional approach to the logical
semiotics of natural language. Pp. 89-112
in Sign·language·culture, (Janua Linguarum,
Series Maior 1), edited by A. J. Griemas et
al. The Hague and Paris: Mouton.

Perchonock, Norma and Oswald Werner
1969   Navaho systems of classification: some
implications for ethnoscience. Ethnology
8.3:229-242. Pittsburgh.

Percival, Keith
1966   A reconsideration of Whorf's hypothesis.
Anthropological Linguistics 8.8:1-12.
Bloomington, Ind.

Phillips, Frank Coles
1963   An introduction to crystallography.
3d edition. x, 340 pp. London: Longmans.

Phillips, H. P.
1959   Problems of translation and meaning in
fieldwork. Human Organization 18:184-192.
New York.

Piaget, Jean
1968   Le Structuralisme. 124 pp. Paris: Presses
        Universitaires de France.

Pike, Kenneth L.
1954-   Language in relation to a unified theory
1960   of the structure of human behavior. Prelim-
        inary edition. Part 1, 170 pp., 1954;
        Part 2, 85 pp., 1955; Part 3, 146 pp.,
        1960. Glendale, California: Summer Insti-
        tute of Linguistics. (See combined edition
        1967.)

1956   Towards a theory of the structure of human
        behavior. Pp. 659-671 in Estudios antro-
        pológicos publicados en homenaje al doctor
        Manuel Gamio. Mexico City: Universidad
        Nacional Autónoma.

1959   Language as particle, wave and field.
        Texas Quarterly 2.2:37-54. Austin.

1964   Name fusions as high-level particles in
        matrix theory. Linguistics 6:83-91.
        The Hague.

1967   Language in relation to a unified theory of
        the structure of human behavior. 762 pp.
        New York: Humanities Press; The Hague:
        Mouton.

Pilcher, William W.
1967   Some comments on the folk taxonomy of the
        Papago. American Anthropologist 69.2:204-
        208. Menasha.

Pilling, A. R.
1962   Statistics, sorcery, and justice. American
        Anthropologist 64.5:1057-1059. Menasha.

Pollio, Howard R.
1966   The structural basis of word association
        behavior. 95 pp. The Hague: Mouton.

Pos, H. J.
1948   The foundation of word meanings. Lingua
        1.3:281-292. Haarlem.

Pospisil, Leopold
1965a   A formal analysis of substantive law:
        Kapauku Papuan laws of inheritance. Pp. 166-
        185 in The ethnography of law, (American

[0:96]

Anthropologist 67.6[Part 2], Special Publication), edited by L. Nader. Menasha.

Pospisil, Leopold (cont.)
1965b   A formal analysis of substantive law:
Kapauku Papuan laws of land tenure. Pp. 186-214 in Formal semantic analysis, (American Anthropologist 67.5[Part 2], Special Publication), edited by E. A. Hammel. Menasha.

Postal, Paul
1964   Constituent structure: a study of contemporary models of syntactic description. (International Journal of American Linguistics 31.1[Part 3].) 122 pp. Baltimore.

Pottier, Bernard, editor
1970   L'Ethnolinguistique. (Languages, 18.) 130 pp. Paris.

Pouillon, Jean and Pierre Maranda, editors
1970   Échanges et communications; mélanges offerts à Claude Lévi-Strauss à l'occasion de son 60ème anniversaire. 2 vols. 1452 pp. The Hague and Paris: Mouton.

Pribram, Karl H.
1971   What makes man human. (39th James Arthur Lecture on the evolution of the human brain.) 38 pp. New York: American Museum of Natural History.

Price, P. David
1967   Two types of taxonomy: a Huichol ethnobotanical example. Anthropological Linguistics 9.7:1-28. Bloomington, Ind.

Price-Williams, D. R.
1961   A study concerning concepts of conservation of quantities among primitive children. Acta Psychologica 18.4:297-305. Amsterdam.

1962   Abstract and concrete modes of classification in a primitive society. British Journal of Educational Psychology 32:50-61. Birmingham, England.

Procaccini, Donald J.
1969   Concerning "the phylogenetic fallacy"--a basic concept. Systematic Zoology 18.1: 144-145. Lawrence, Kans.

Proctor, Jean R.
1966   Some processes of numerical taxonomy in
        terms of distance. Systematic Zoology 15.2:
        131-140. Lawrence, Kans.

Proskauer, J.
1968   On nomenclatural dialectics, or two blatantly
        different names are not the same. Taxon
        17.5:502-503. Utrecht.

Puhvel, Jaan, editor
1969   Substance and structure of language. viii,
        223 pp. Berkeley and Los Angeles: Univer-
        sity of California Press.

Pulgram, Ernst
1954   Theory of names. Beiträge zur Namenforschung
        5.2:149-196. Heidelberg. (Also available
        paperbound, Berkeley: American Name Society.)

Putnam, Hilary
1962   The analytic and the synthetic. Pp. 358-397
        in Scientific explanation, space, and time,
        (Minnesota Studies in the Philosophy of
        Science, Vol. 3), edited by H. Feigl and
        G. Maxwell. Minneapolis: University of
        Minnesota Press.

Quillian, M. Ross
1966   Semantic memory. 222 pp. Cambridge: Bolt
        Baranek and Newman.

1967   Word concepts: a theory simulation of some
        basic semantic capabilities. Behavioral
        Science 12.5:410-430. Ann Arbor.

Quine, Willard Van Orman
1950   Methods of logic. xix, 264 pp. New York:
        Henry Holt.

1953   The problem of meaning in linguistics.
        Pp. 47-64 (Chapter 3) in From a logical
        point of view, by W. V. Quine. Cambridge:
        Harvard University Press.

1958   Speaking of objects. Proceedings and
        Addresses of the American Philosophical
        Association, 1957-1958, 31:5-22. Yellow
        Springs, Ohio.

1959   Meaning and translation. Pp. 148-172 in
        On Translation, edited by R. A. Brower.

Cambridge: Harvard University Press.

Quine, Willard Van Orman (cont.)
1960   Word and object. 294 pp. New York: John
        Wiley. Cambridge: MIT Press.

1969   Natural kinds. Pp. 5-23 in Essays in honor
        of Carl G. Hempel, edited by N. Rescher.
        Dordrecht: Reidel.

Quirk, Randolf
1965   Descriptive statement and serial relation-
        ship. Language 41.2:205-217. Baltimore.

Randal, J. M. and G. H. Scott
1967   Linnaean nomenclature: an aid to data
        processing. Systematic Zoology 16.3:278-
        281. Lawrence, Kans.

1969   Has nomenclature a syntax? Systematic
        Zoology 18.4:466-468. Lawrence, Kans.

Ranganathan, Shiyali Ramamritha
1957   Prolegomena to library classification.
        487 pp. London: Library Association.

Ranken, Howard B.
1963   Language and thinking: positive and nega-
        tive effects of naming. Science 141.3575:
        48-50. Washington.

Rankin, Bunyan Kirk, III
1965   A linguistic study of the formation of
        Chinese characters. xviii, 219 pp. Ph.D.
        dissertation in linguistics, University of
        Pennsylvania. (Published by University
        Microfilms, Ann Arbor, Mich.)

Rapoport, Anatol
1952   What is semantics? American Scientist 40.1:
        123-135. New Haven.

Rapoport, Anatol, Amnon Rapoport, William P. Livant,
        and John Boyd
1966   A study of lexical graphs, I.
        Foundations of Language 2.4:338-376.
        Dordrecht.

Rapoport, Anatol, R. J. Albers, W. P. Livant, and
        P. H. Roosen-Runge
1969   A study of lexical graphs, II. Foundations
        of Language 5.3:349-385. Dordrecht.

116

Raven, Peter H. and Richard W. Holm
1967   Systematics and the levels-of-organization
        approach. Systematic Zoology 16.1:1-5.
        Lawrence, Kans.

Regnéll, Hans
1958   Semantik. 187 pp. Stockholm: Svenska
        bokförlaget.

Régnier, Andre
1971   Formalisme et analyse de contenu. L'Homme
        et la Société 18.1:271-290. Paris.

Régnier, Simon
1970   Non-fécondité du modèle statistique général
        de la classification automatique. Pp. 301-
        307 in Archéologie et calculateurs, by
        J.-C. Gardin et al. Paris: Éditions du
        Centre National de la Recherche Scientifique.

Reichenbach, Hans
1947   Elements of symbolic logic. xiii, 444 pp.
        New York: Macmillan. (Reprinted 1966 in
        paperback, New York: Free Press.)

Reifler, Erwin
1953   Linguistic analysis, meaning and comparative
        semantics. Lingua 3.4:371-390. Haarlem.

Reitman, Walter R.
1965   Cognition and thought: an information-
        processing approach. xiii, 312 pp.
        New York: John Wiley.

Reuning, Karl
1941   Joy and Freude: a comparative study of the
        linguistic fields of pleasurable emotions
        in English and German. ix, 141 pp.
        Swarthmore, Pa.: Swarthmore College
        Bookstore.

Révész, G.
1955   The psychogenetic foundation of language.
        Lingua 4.3:318-332. Amsterdam.

Rey, Alain
1965   Les Dictionnaires: forme et contenu.
        Cahiers de Lexicologie 7.2:65-102. Paris.

1970   Typologie génétique des dictionnaires.
        Langages 19:48-68. Paris.

[0:100]

Rey-Debove, Josette
    1967   Autonymie et métalangue. Cahiers de
            Lexicologie 11.2:15-27. Paris.

Rey-Debove, Josette, editor
    1970   La Lexicographie. (Langages, 19.) 120 pp.
            Paris.

Richardson, Ernest Cushing
    1901   Classification, theoretical and practical:
            together with an appendix containing an
            essay towards a bibliographical history of
            the systems of classification. 248 pp.
            New York: Scribner. (3d edition, 1930,
            New York: Wilson.)

Rickett, H. W.
    1958   So what is a taxon? Taxon 7.2:37-38.
            Utrecht.

Rickman, H. P.
    1960   Philosophical anthropology and the problem
            of meaning. Philosophical Quarterly 10.38:
            12-20. St. Andrews.

Riegel, Klaus F. and Ruth M. Riegel
    1963   An investigation into denotative aspects of
            word-meaning. Language and Speech 6(Part
            1):5-21. Teddington, England.

Rignano, Eugenio
    1923   The psychology of reasoning. viii, 395 pp.
            London: Kegan Paul, Trench, Trubner.

Roberts, M. H.
    1944   The science of idiom. Publications of the
            Modern Languages Association 49:291-306.
            Menasha.

Robins. R. H.
    1952   A problem in the statement of meanings.
            Lingua 3.2:121-137. Haarlem.

    1966   The development of the word class-system of
            the European grammatical tradition. Founda-
            tions of Language 2.1:3-19. Dordrecht.

Robinson, Richard
    1965   Definition. viii, 200 pp. Oxford:
            Clarendon.

Rogers, David J.
    1963   Taximetrics--new name, old concept.

118

Brittonia 15.4:285-290. New York.

Roget, Peter Mark
1852   Thesaurus of English words and phrases;
         classified and arranged so as to facilitate
         the expression of ideas and assist in
         literary composition. 1st edition.
         xxxviii, 418 pp. London: Longman, Brown,
         Green and Longmans.

1962   (See Dutch, R. A., editor.)

Rollins, Reed C.
1965   On the bases of biological classification.
         Taxon 14.1:1-16. Utrecht.

Romney, A. Kimball
1965   Kalmuk Mongol and the classification of
         lineal kinship terminologies. Pp. 127-141
         in Formal semantic analysis, (American
         Anthropologist 67.5[Part 2], Special Publi-
         cation), edited by E. A. Hammel. Menasha.

Romney, A. Kimball and Roy G. D'Andrade, editors
1964   Transcultural studies in cognition. (Ameri-
         can Anthropologist 66.3[Part 2], Special
         Publication.) 253 pp. Menasha.

Rose, Edward
1960   The English record of a natural sociology.
         American Sociological Review 25.2:193-208.
         Albany.

Rosen, Charles A.
1967   Pattern classification by adaptive machines.
         Science 156.3771:38-44. Washington.

Ross, R.
1958   What is a "new taxon?" Taxon 7.3:65-68.
         Utrecht.

Rostron, R. M.
1968   The construction of a thesaurus. Aslib
         Proceedings 20.3:181-187. London.

Rowe, John Howland
1950   Thoughts on knowledge and ignorance. Kroeber
         Anthropological Society Papers 2:6-8.
         Berkeley.

Royce, Joseph R.
1959   The search for meaning. American Scientist
         47.4:515-535. New Haven.

[0:102]

Royen, Gerlach
1929   Die nominale Klassifikations-System in den
        Sprachen der Erde. xvi, 1030 pp. Mödling
        bei Wien, Austria.

Rubin, Jerrold
1966   An approach to organizing data into homo-
        genous groups. Systematic Zoology 15.3:
        169-182. Lawrence, Kans.

Ruhemann, Barbara
1967   Purpose and mathematics--a problem in the
        analysis of classificatory kinship systems.
        Bijdragen tot de Taal-, Land- en Volkenkunde
        123.1:83-124. 's-Gravenhage.

Russell, Bertrand
1940   An inquiry into meaning and truth. 445 pp.
        New York: W. W. Norton.

Ryan, D'Arcy
1958   Names and naming in Mendi. Oceania 29.2:
        109-116. Sydney.

Ryle, Gilbert
1953   Ordinary language. Philosophical Review
        62.2:167-186. Ithaca.

1961   Categories. Pp. 79-80 in Logic and language,
        2d series, edited by J. L. Austin et al.
        Oxford: Basil Blackwell.

1962   The theory of meaning. Pp. 147-170 in The
        importance of language, edited by M. Black.
        Englewood Cliffs, N. J.: Prentice-Hall.

Salomon, Louis B.
1966   Semantics and common sense. 180 pp. New
        York: Holt, Rinehart, and Winston.

Salzmann, Zdenek
1960   Cultures, languages, and translations.
        Anthropological Linguistics 2.2:43-47.
        Bloomington, Ind.

Samarin, William J.
1965a   Language of silence. Practical Anthropology
        12.3:115-122. Tarrytown, N. Y.

1965b   Perspective on African ideophones. African
        Studies 24.2:117-121. Witwatersrand,
        So. Africa.

1967a   Determining the meanings of ideophones.
         Journal of West African Languages 4.2:35-41.
         London.

1967b   Field linguistics: a guide to linguistic
         field work. viii, 246 pp. New York: Holt,
         Rinehart, and Winston.

1969   Forms and functions of nonsense language.
         Linguistics 50:70-74. The Hague.

Sapir, Edward
1921   Language, and introduction to the study of
         speech. vii, 258 pp. New York: Harcourt,
         Brace.

1931   Conceptual categories in primitive languages.
         Science 74.1927:578. Washington.

1944   Grading, a study in semantics. Philosophy
         of Science 11.2:93-116. Baltimore.
         (Reprinted 1949 in Selected writings of
         Edward Sapir in language, culture and
         personality, edited by D. Mandelbaum.
         Berkeley and Los Angeles: University of
         California Press.)

Saporta, Sol, editor
1961   Psycholinguistics: a book of readings.
         xv, 551 pp. New York: Holt, Rinehart,
         and Winston.

Sarles, Harvey B.
1966a   The dynamic study of interaction as ethno-
         scientific strategy. Anthropological
         Linguistics 8.8:66-70. Bloomington, Ind.

1966b   New approaches to the study of human communi-
         cation. Anthropological Linguistics 8.9:
         20-26. Bloomington, Ind.

Sastri, Madugula I.
1967   Complements: a semantic classification.
         Linguistics 34:69-72. The Hague.

1968   Prepositions in Chemical Abstracts: a
         sememic study. Linguistics 38:42-51.
         The Hague.

Saumjan, S. K.
1970   Semiotics and the theory of generative
         grammars. Pp. 244-255 in Sign·language·

[0:104]

culture, (Janua Linguarum, Series Maior 1),
edited by A. J. Greimas et al. The Hague
and Paris: Mouton.

Saussure, Ferdinand de
1959   Course in general linguistics, edited by
(1915)   C. Bally and A. Sechehaye. Translated from
         the French by Wade Baskin. xvi, 240 pp.
         New York: Philosophical Library. (1st,
         edition 1915, Cours de linguistique générale.)

Sayers, William Charles Berwick
1955   Manual of classification for librarians and
(1926)   bibliographers. 3d edition, revised.
         xviii, 346 pp. London: Grafton. (1st
         edition 1926.)

Schaff, Adam
1962   Introduction to semantics. Translated from
         Polish by Olgierd Wojtasiewicz. 395 pp.
         New York: Macmillan. (Translated 1968 by
         Georges Lisowski as Introduction à la
         sémantique. x, 336 pp. Paris: Éditions
         Anthropos.)

Scheffler, Harold W. and Floyd G. Lounsbury
1971   A study in structural semantics, the Siriono
         kinship system. 260 pp. Englewood Cliffs,
         N. J.: Prentice-Hall.

Scheffler, Israel
1963   The anatomy of inquiry: philosophical
         studies in the theory of science. xii,
         332 pp. New York: Knopf.

Schenk, Edward T. and John H. McMasters
1956   Procedure in taxonomy. 3d edition, revised
         by A. M. Keen and S. W. Muller. vii, 119
         pp. Stanford: Stanford University Press.

Schlee, Dieter
1969   Hennig's principle of phylogenetic system-
         atics, an "intuitive, statistico-phenetic
         taxonomy?" Systematic Zoology 18.1:127-134.
         Lawrence, Kans.

Schneider, David M.
1965   American kin terms and terms for kinsmen:
         a critique of Goodenough's componential
         analysis of Yankee kinship terminology.
         Pp. 288-308 in Formal semantic analysis,
         (American Anthropologist 67.5[Part 2],

Special Publication), edited by E. A. Hammel. Menasha.

Schneider, John H.
1971   Selective dissemination and indexing of scientific information. Science 173.3994: 300-308. Washington.

Schutz, Alfred
1962-   Collected papers. 3 vols. Vol. 1, The
1966   problem of social reality, xlvii, 361 pp., 1962; Vol. 2, Studies in social theory, 300 pp., 1964; Vol. 3, Studies in phenomenological philosophy, xxxi, 191 pp., 1966. The Hague: Martinus Nijhoff.

Scipio, L. Albert, II
1959   On the design of structural models to study the thermal stress phenomenon. Annals of the New York Academy of Sciences 79.5:143-156. New York.

Searle, John
1969   Speech acts: an essay in the philosophy of language. vi, 203 pp. Cambridge: Cambridge University Press.

Sebeok, Thomas A.
1946   Finnish and Hungarian case systems: their form and function. (Acta Instituti Hungarici Universitatis Holmiensis, Series B, Linguistica 3.) 32 pp. Stockholm.

1962   Materials for a typology of dictionaries. Lingua 11:363-374. Amsterdam.

1965   Zoosemiotics: juncture of semiotics and the biological study of behavior. Science 147.3657:492-493. Washington.

1968a   Zoosemiotics: a guide to its literature. Language Sciences 3:7-14. Bloomington, Ind. (See also: A selected and annotated guide to the literature of zoosemiotics and its background, Social Science Information 7.5:103-117, [1968], Paris.)

1968b   Animal communication: techniques of study and results of research. xvii, 686 pp. Bloomington: University of Indiana Press.

1970   Is a comparative semiotics possible? Pp. 614-657 in Échanges et communications;

mélanges offerts à Claude Lévi-Strauss à
l'occasion de son 60ème anniversaire,
edited by J. Pouillon and P. Maranda.
The Hague and Paris: Mouton.

Sebeok, Thomas A., editor
1960   Style in language. xvii, 470 pp. New
        York: John Wiley; Cambridge: MIT Press.

1966   Current trends in linguistics. Vol. 3,
        Theoretical foundations. 537 pp. The
        Hague and Paris: Mouton.

Sebeok, Thomas A., Alfred S. Hayes, and Mary Catherine
        Bateson, editors
1964   Approaches to semiotics. Transactions of
        the Indiana University Conference on
        Paralinguistics and Kinesics. 294 pp.
        The Hague: Mouton.

Sebestyen, G. S.
1962   Decision-making processes in pattern
        recognition. viii, 162 pp. New York and
        London: Macmillan.

Segall, Marshall H., Donald T. Campbell, and Melville
        J. Herskovits
1963   Cultural differences in the perception of
        geometric illustions. Science 139.3556:
        769-771. Washington.

Seiler, Hansjakob
1967   Toward an exploration of the lexical field.
        Pp. 1783-1798 in To honor Roman Jakobson,
        essays on the occasion of his seventieth
        birthday, (Janua Linguarum, Series Maior
        31). The Hague and Paris: Mouton.

Shapiro, A. B.
1955   Nekotorye voprosy teorii sinonimov.
        Akademija Nauk SSSR, Institut Jazykoznanija,
        Doklady i soobshchenija 8:69-87. Moscow.

Shcherba, L. V.
1940   Opyt obshchej teorii leksikografii (I).
        Akademija Nauk SSSR, Otdelenie litaratury
        i jazyka, Izvestija, No. 3:89-117. Moscow.

Sher, J. A.
1970   Un algorithme de classification typologique.
        Pp. 193-203 in Archéologie et calculateurs,
        by J.-C. Gardin et al. Paris: Éditions du

Centre National de la Recherche Scientifique.

Shrejder, Ju. A.
1965   On the semantic characteristics of information. Information Storage and Retrieval
2.4:221-233. Oxford.

Shwayder, D. S.
1963   Modes of referring and the problem of
universals: an essay in metaphysics.
164 pp. Berkeley and Los Angeles:
University of California Press.

Siertsema, B.
1969   Language and world view (semantics for
theologians). The Bible Translator 20.1:
3-21. London.

Silverman, Martin
1962   Numeral classifiers in the Gilbertese
language. Anthropology Tomorrow 8:41-58.
Chicago.

Simon, Herbert A.
1969   The sciences of the artificial. xii, 123
pp. Cambridge: MIT Press.

Simpson, George Gaylord
1945   The principles of classification and a
classification of mammals. (Bulletin of
the American Museum of Natural History
85.) 350 pp. New York.

1952   How many species? Evolution 6.3:342.
Lancaster, Pa.

1959   Anatomy and morphology: classification
and evolution: 1859 and 1959. Proceedings
of the American Philosophical Society
103.2:286-306. Philadelphia.

1961   Principles of animal taxonomy. xii, 247 pp.
New York: Columbia University Press.

1963   The meaning of taxonomic statements. Pp. 1-
31 in Classification and human evolution,
(Viking Fund Publications in Anthropology,
No. 37), edited by S. Washburn. New York:
Wenner-Gren Foundation for Anthropological
Research.

[0:108]

Skinner, B. F.
1957   Verbal behavior. x, 478 pp. New York:
        Appleton-Century-Crofts.

Sklar, Abe
1964   On category overlapping in taxonomy. Pp.
        395-401 in Form and strategy in science,
        edited by J. R. Gregg and F. T. C. Harris.
        Dordrecht: Reidel.

Slama-Cazacu, T.
1961   Langage et contexte, le problème du langage
        dans le conception de l'expression et de
        l'interprétation par les organisations
        contextuelles. (Janua Linguarum, Series
        Maior 6.) 251 pp. The Hague and Paris:
        Mouton.

Sledd, James and Wilma R. Ebbitt
1962   Dictionaries and that dictionary: a case-
        book on the aims of lexicographers and the
        targets of reviewers. xi, 273 pp.
        Chicago: Scott, Foreman.

Slobin, Dan I., editor
1967   A field manual for cross-cultural study of
        the acquisition of communicative competence.
        2d version. xv, 248 pp. Berkeley:
        University of California.

Slobodkin, L. B.
1965   On the present incompleteness of mathemati-
        cal ecology. American Scientist 53.3:347-
        357. New Haven.

Smirnov, Eugen
1925   The theory of type and the natural system.
        Zeitschrift für Induktive Abstammungs-
        und Vererbungslehre 37:28-66. Leipzig.

Smith, Albert C.
1969   Systematics and appreciation of reality.
        Taxon 18.1:5-13. Utrecht.

Smith, Alfred Goud
1966   Communication and culture: readings in the
        codes of human interaction. 626 pp. New
        York: Holt, Rinehart and Winston.

Smith, Henry Lee, Jr.
1963   Syntax and semology. Georgetown University
        Monograph Series on Languages and Linguis-
        tics, No. 16:91-111. Washington.

Smith, Hobart M.
1967   Classification of non-nomenclatural ranges
        of biological variation. Systematic Zoolo-
        gy 16.2:171. Lawrence, Kans.

1969   Parapatry: sympatry or allopatry? System-
        atic Zoology 18.2:254-259. Lawrence, Kans.

1970   Nomina and taxa dubia. Systematic Zoology
        19.1:94. Lawrence, Kans.

Sneath, P. H. A.
1957   The application of computers to taxonomy.
        Journal of General Microbiology 17.1:201-
        226. London.

1962a   The construction of taxonomic groups.
        Symposium of the Society for General
        Microbiology 12:281-332. Cambridge,
        England.

1962b   Numerical taxonomy. Nature 193.4818:855-
        860. London.

1966   A comparison of different clustering methods.
        Classification Society Bulletin 1.2:2-18.
        Leicester, England.

1967   Numerical taxonomy; steps in preparing
        taxonomic data for the computer. Classifi-
        cation Society Bulletin 1.3:14-18.
        Leicester, England.

1968   Goodness of intuitive arrangements into
        time trends based on complex pattern.
        Systematic Zoology 17.3:256-260. Lawrence,
        Kans.

1969a   Problems of homology in geology and related
        fields. Classification Society Bulletin
        2.1:5-11. Leicester, England.

1969b   Recent trends in numerical taxonomy. Taxon
        18.1:14-20. Utrecht.

[Sneath, P. H. A., editor]
1969   Report of a meeting on classification in
        linguistics and archaeology. Classification
        Society Bulletin 2.1:22-28. Leicester,
        England.

Soergel, Dagobert
1967   Some remarks on information languages,

[0:110]

their analysis and comparison. Information
Storage and Retrieval 3.4:219-292. Oxford.

Sokal, Robert R.
1962   Typology and empiricism in taxonomy.
        Journal of Theoretical Biology 3.2:230-267.
        New York and London.

1965   Statistical methods in systematics.
        Biological Review 40.3:337-391. London and
        New York.

1966   Numerical taxonomy. Scientific American
        215.6:106-116. New York.

Sokal, Robert R. and J. H. Camin
1965   The two taxonomies: areas of agreement and
        conflict. Systematic Zoology 14.3:176-195.
        Lawrence, Kans.

Sokal, Robert R. and C. D. Michener
1958   A statistical method for evaluating system-
        atic relationships. University of Kansas
        Science Bulletin 38.2:1409-1438. Lawrence.

Sokal, Robert R. and F. James Rohlf
1962   The comparison of dendrograms by objective
        methods. Taxon 11.2:33-40. Utrecht.

1970   The intelligent ignoramus, an experiment in
        numerical taxonomy. Taxon 19.3:305-319.
        Utrecht.

Sokal, Robert R. and Peter H. A. Sneath
1963   Principles of numerical taxonomy. xii,
        359 pp. San Francisco and London: W. H.
        Freeman.

1966   Efficiency in taxonomy. Taxon 15.1:1-21.
        Utrecht.

Sommerfelt, Alf
1938   La Langue et la société, charactères sociaux
        d'une langue de type archaïque. (Institut-
        tet for Sammenlígnende Kulturforskning,
        Serie A: Forelesninger, 18.) 233 pp.
        Oslo: H. Aschehoug.

1954   Sémantique et lexicographie; remarques sur
        la tâche du lexicographe. Norsk Tidsskrift
        for Sprogvidenskap 17:485-489. Oslo.

128

Sørensen, Holger Steen
1958   Word-classes in modern English; with special
        reference to proper names; with an intro-
        ductory theory of grammar, meaning and
        reference. 188 pp. Copenhagen: G. E. C.
        Gads Forlag.

1961   An analysis of linguistic signs occurring
        in suppositio materialis or the meaning of
        quotation marks and their phonetic equiva-
        lents. Lingua 10.2:174-189. Amsterdam.

1967   Classes et relations. Langages 6:26-35.
        Paris.

Southworth, Franklin C.
1967   A model of semantic structure. Language
        43.1:342-361. Baltimore.

Spang-Hanssen, Henning
1954   Recent theories on the nature of the
        language sign. Travaux de Cercle Linguis-
        tique de Copenhague 9:13-142. Copenhagen.

1959   Probability and structural classification
        in language description. 231 pp. Copen-
        hagen: Rosenkilde and Bagger.

Spence, Donald P.
1968   The processing of meaning in psychotherapy:
        some links with psycholinguistics and
        information theory. Behavioral Science
        13.5:349-361. Ann Arbor.

Spencer, Herbert
1870   The classification of the sciences, 2d
        edition. 64 pp. New York: Appleton.

Spier, Leslie, A. Irving Hallowell, and Stanley S.
        Newman
1941   Language, culture and personality: essays
        in memory of Edward Sapir. xii, 298 pp.
        Menasha: Sapir Memorial Publication Fund.
        (Reprinted 1960, Salt Lake City: University
        of Utah Press.)

Spilerman, Seymour
1966   Structural analysis and the generation of
        sociograms. Behavioral Science 11.4:312-
        318. Ann Arbor.

Spiro, Melford E., editor
1965   Context and meaning in cultural anthropology.

xxii, 442 pp. New York: Free Press;
London: Collier-Macmillan.

Staal, J. F.
1966   Indian semantics, I. Journal of the American Oriental Society 86.3:304-310. New
Haven.

1968   Meaning, regular and irregular. Foundations
of Language 4.2:182-184. Dordrecht.

Stebbing, Lizzie Susan
1945   A modern introduction to logic. 4th edition.
525 pp. London: Methuen.

Stefflre, Volney
1965   Simulation of people's behavior toward new
objects and events. American Behavioral
Scientist 8.9:12-15. Princeton.

Stefflre, Volney and DeLee Lantz
1964   Language and cognition revisited. Journal
of Abnormal and Social Psychology 69.5:
472-481. Lancaster, Pa.

Steinberg, Danny D. and Leon A. Jakobovits
1971   Semantics: an interdisciplinary reader in
philosophy, linguistics and psychology.
Cambridge: Cambridge University Press.

Stern, Gustaf
1968   Meaning and change of meaning: with special
(1931) reference to the English language. xiii,
456 pp. Bloomington and London: Indiana
University Press.

Steyskal, George C.
1967   Another view of the future of taxonomy.
Systematic Zoology 16.3:265-268. Lawrence,
Kans.

1970   The language of zoological names. Systematic Zoology 19.1:94-97. Lawrence, Kans.

Stoll, Robert Roth
1961   Sets, logic and axiomatic theories. x,
206 pp. San Francisco and London: W. H.
Freeman.

Stuchlik, Milan
1970   Categorias de terrenos entre los Batakos
de Sumatra Central, un problema taxinomico.
Rehue 3:27-37. Concepcion, Chile.

Sturtevant, William C.
1964   Studies in ethnoscience. Pp. 99-113 in
        Transcultural studies in cognition, (American Anthropologist 66.3[Part 2], Special
        Publication), edited by A. K. Romney and
        R. G. D'Andrade. Menasha.

1968   Categories, percussion and physiology.
        Man (n.s.)3.1:133-134. London.

Suppes, Patrick
1960   Axiomatic set theory. xii, 256 pp.
        (University Series in Undergraduate Mathematics.) Princeton: Van Nostrand.

Svartivik, J. and H. T. Carvell
1964   Linguistic classification and numerical
        taxonomy. (Survey of English Usage,
        Working paper, Part 1.) London: University
        College.

Swadesh, Morris
1946   Chitimacha. Pp. 312-336 in Linguistic
        structures of native North America, by
        H. Hoijer et al. New York: Viking Fund.

1960   On the unit of translation. Anthropological
        Linguistics 2.2:39-42. Bloomington, Ind.

Swanson, Earl H., Jr.
1970   Languages and cultures of western North
        America: essays in honor of Sven S. Liljeblad. ix, 288 pp. Pocatello: Idaho State
        University Press.

Sylvester-Bradley, P. C.
1968   The science of diversity. Systematic
        Zoology 17.2:176-181. Lawrence, Kans.

Tajfel, Henri
1968   Social and cultural factors in perception.
        Pp. 315-393 in Vol. 3 of The handbook of
        social psychology, 2d edition, edited by
        G. Lindzey and E. Aronson. Reading, Mass.:
        Addison-Wesley.

Talbot, P. B.
1971   Principles of fungal taxonomy. 272 pp.
        New York: St. Martin's Press.

Tanimoto, T. T.
1958   An elementary mathematical theory of

[0:114]

classification and prediction. Pp. 30-39 in Part 3 of The IBM taxonomy application M̄ and A-6. White Plains, N. Y.: Program Information Department, IBM Data Processing Division.

Tarski, Alfred
1944 The semantic conception of truth. Philosophy and Phenomenological Research 4.3:341-375. Buffalo.

1956 Logic, semantics, metamathematics; papers form 1923 to 1938. 471 pp. Oxford: Clarendon.

Taylor, Donald W.
1968 Problem solving. International Encyclopedia of the Social Sciences 12:505-511. New York: Macmillan and Free Press.

Taylor, Douglas
1959 La Catégorie du genre en Caraïbe Insulaire: un cas d'interférence linguistique? Bulletin de la Société de Linguistique de Paris 54:201-207. Paris.

1970 Arawak grammatical categories and translation. International Journal of American Linguistics 36.3:199-204. Baltimore.

Tax, Sol
1950 Animistic and rational thought. Kroeber Anthropological Society Papers 2:1-5. Berkeley.

Thoday, J. M.
1952 Units of evolution and units of classification. Proceedings of the Leeds Philosophical and Literary Society 6(Part 1):61-64. Leeds.

Thomas, David
1955 Three analyses of the Ilocano pronoun system. Word 11.2:204-208. New York.

Thomas, P. A. and H. East
1968 Comments on the terminology of the analysis of library systems and the function of forms therein. Aslib Proceedings 20.8:340-344. London.

Thorndike, Edward L.
1947 Semantic changes. American Journal of

132

Psychology 60.4:588-597. Ithaca.

Thorndike, E. L. and I. Lorge
1952   The teacher's word book of 30,000 words.
        274 pp. New York: Teacher's College,
        Columbia University.

Tikhomirov, O. K.
1959   Review of Verbal behavior, by B. F. Skinner.
        Word 15.2:362-367. New York.

Timmermans, J. et al.
1963   La Classification dans les sciences.
        236 pp. Gembloux: J. Duculot.

Titone, Renzo
1964   La psicolinguistic oggi. 313 pp. Zürich:
        Pas-Verlag.

Todorov, Tzvetan
1966a   Recherches sémantiques. Langages 1:4-43.
        Paris.

1966b   Les Anomalies sémantiques. Langages 1:
        100-123. Paris.

1967   Connaissance de la parole. Word 23.1-2-3
        (Part 1):500-517. New York.

Tollenaere, F. de
1960   Alfabetische of ideologische Lexicografie?
        (Bijdragen tot de nederlandse Taal- en
        Letterkunde, No. 1.) vii, 44 pp. Leiden:
        Brill.

Tondl, Ladislav
1966   Antinomy of "liar" and antinomy of synony-
        mous names. Kybernetika 2.1:14-37. Prague.

1968   Semantics of the question in the problem-
        solving situation. Kybernetika 4.4:295-317.
        Prague.

Tortonese, Enrico
1967   Again about specific names. Systematic
        Zoology 16.3:278. Lawrence, Kans.

Trager, George L.
1958   Paralanguage: a first approximation.
        Studies in Linguistics 13:1-12. Buffalo.

1961   The typology of paralanguage. Anthropologi-
        cal Linguistics 3.1:17-21. Bloomington, Ind.

Trager, George L. (cont.)
1966   Review of Approaches to semiotics: cultural
        anthropology, education, linguistics, psy-
        chiatry, psychology, edited by Thomas A.
        Sebeok, Alfred S. Hayes, and Mary Catherine
        Bateson. American Anthropologist 68.1:296-
        297. Menasha.

1967   A componential morphemic analysis of English
        personal pronouns. Language 43.1:372-378.
        Baltimore.

Trager, George L. and Edward T. Hall, Jr.
1953   Culture and communication: a model and an
        analysis. Explorations 3:137-149. Toronto.

Trager, George L. and John G. Mutziger
1947   The linguistic structure of Mongolian place
  .   names. Journal of the American Oriental
        Society 67.3:184-195. New Haven.

Trier, Jost
1931   Der deutsche Worschatz im Sinnbezirk des
        Verstandes: die Geschichte eines sprachlich-
        en Feldes, Vol. 1. 347 pp. Heidelberg:
        C. Winter.

1967   Name und Technik. Beiträge zur Namenfor-
        schung II 2.2:131-145. Heidelberg.

Trnka, Bohumil
1967   Words, semantemes, and sememes. Pp. 2050-
        2054 in To honor Roman Jakobson, essays on
        the occasion of his seventieth birthday,
        (Janua Linguarum, Series Maior 31). The
        Hague and Paris: Mouton.

Tryon, Robert Choate and Daniel E. Bailey
1970   Cluster analysis. xviii, 347 pp. New York:
        McGraw-Hill.

Tukey, John W.
1965   Data analysis and the frontiers of geo-
        physics. Science 148.3675:1283-1289.
        Washington.

Turner, John R. G.
1967   Goddess changes sex, or the gender game.
        Systematic Zoology 16.4:349-350. Lawrence,
        Kans.

Turrill, W. B. et al.
1942   Differences in the systematics of plants and

animals and their dependence on differences
in structure, function, and behavior in the
two groups. Proceedings of the Linnean
Society of London 153:272-287. London.

Tyler, Stephen A.
1965   Koya language morphology and patterns of
        kinship behavior. American Anthropologist
        67.6:1428-1440. Menasha.

1969   The myth of P: epistemology and formal
        analysis. American Anthropologist 71.1:
        71-79. Menasha.

Tyler, Stephen A., editor
1969   Cognitive anthropology: readings. xiii,
        521 pp. New York: Holt, Rinehart and
        Winston.

Uhlenbeck, E. M.
1956   Verb structure in Javanese. Pp. 567-573 in
        For Roman Jakobson, edited by M. Halle
        et al. The Hague: Mouton.

Uldall, Hans J.
1957   General theory. Part 1 of Outline of
        glossematics, a study in the methodology of
        the humanities with special reference to
        linguistics. Travaux du Cercle Linguistique
        de Copenhague 10(Part 1):1-90. Copenhagen.

Ullmann, Stephen de
1946   Language and meaning. Word 2.2:113-126.
        New York.

1952   Précis de sémantique française. 334 pp.
        Berne: A. Francke.

1953   Descriptive semantics and linguistic
        typology. Word 9.3:225-240. New York.

1956   The concept of meaning in linguistics.
        Archivum Linguisticum 8:12-20. Glasgow.

1957   The principles of semantics. 2d edition.
        (Glasgow University Publication 84.)
        346 pp. New York: Philosophical Library.

1962   Semantics: an introduction to the science
        of meaning. 278 pp. Oxford: Basil
        Blackwell.

Ullmann, Stephen de   (cont.)
1963   Semantic universals. Pp. 172-207 in
          Universals of language, edited by J. H.
          Greenberg. Cambridge: MIT Press.

Utley, Francis Lee
1963   The linguistic component of onomastics.
          Names 11.3:145-176. Youngstown, Ohio.

Valen, Leigh van
1964   An analysis of some taxonomic concepts.
          Pp. 402-415 in Form and strategy in science,
          edited by J. R. Gregg and F. T. C. Harris.
          Dordrecht: Reidel.

Van Holk, Andre
1962   Referential and attitudinal constructions.
          Lingua 11:165-181. Amsterdam.

Vega, W. F. de la
1970   Quelques propriétés des hiérarchies de
          classification. Pp. 329-342 in Archéologie
          et calculateurs, by J.-C. Gardin et al.
          Paris: Éditions du Centre National de la
          Recherche Scientifique.

Venn, John
1907   The principles of empirical or inductive
          logic. 2d edition. xx, 604 pp. London:
          Macmillan.

Verguin, J.
1967   Prépositions, conjonctions, relatifs.
          Word 23.1-2-3(Part 1):573-577. New York.

Vickery, B. C.
1958   Classification and indexing in science.
          With an introduction by D. J. Foskett.
          xvii, 185 pp. London: Butterworths.
          (2d edition, enlarged, 1959, 235 pp.
          London: Butterworths.)

1960   Faceted classification: a guide to construc-
          tion and use of special schemes. iii, 70 pp.
          London: Aslib.

Videbeck, R. and J. Pia
1966   Plans for coping: an approach to ethno-
          science. Anthropological Linguistics
          8.8:71-77. Bloomington, Ind.

Vinay, Jean Paul and Jean Louis Darbelnet
1958   Stylistique comparée du français et de

l'anglais; méthode de traduction. (Bibliothèque de Stylistique Comparée I.) 331 pp.
Paris: Didier.

Vinogradov, V. V.
1947   Ob osnovnykh tipakh frazeologicheskikh
        edinic v russkom jazyke. Pp. 339-364 in
        Sbornik...A. A. Shakhmatov. Moscow.

1952   Slovoobrazovanie v ego otnoshenii k grammatike
        i leksikologii. Pp. 99-152 in Voprosy teorii
        i istorii jazyka v svete trudov I. V. Stalina
        po jazykoznaniju. Moscow.

1953   Osnovnye tipy leksicheskikh znachenij slova.
        Voprosy jazykoznanija, No. 5:3-29. Moscow.

1956   Iz istorii leksikologii. Akademija Nauk
        SSSR, Institut Jazykoznanija, Doklady i
        soobshchenija 10:3-29. Moscow.

Voegelin, Charles F.
1960   Subsystem typology in linguistics. Pp. 202-
        206 in Men and Cultures, (Selected Papers
        of the Fifth International Congress of
        Anthropological and Ethnological Sciences,
        Philadelphia, 1956), edited by A. F. C.
        Wallace. Philadelphia: University of
        Pennsylvania Press.

Voegelin, Charles F. and Florence M. Voegelin
1957   Hopi domains: a lexical approach to the
        problem of selection. (International
        Journal of American Linguistics, Memoir
        No. 14.) 82 pp. Baltimore.

1970a   Cross-cultural typologies and folk taxonomies.
        Pp. 1132-1147 in Échanges et communications;
        mélanges offerts à Claude Lévi-Strauss à
        l'occasion de son 60ème anniversaire, edited
        by J. Pouillon and P. Maranda. The Hague
        and Paris: Mouton.

1970b   Hopi names and no names. Pp. 47-53 in
        Languages and cultures of western North
        America: essays in honor of Sven S.
        Liljeblad, edited by E. H. Swanson, Jr.
        Pocatello: Idaho State University Press.

1970c   Our knowledge of semantics and how it is
        obtained. International Journal of American
        Linguistics 36.4:241-246. Baltimore.

[0:120]

Voegelin, Charles F. and Florence M. Voegelin (cont.)
1971   The autonomy of linguistics and the depend-
         ence of cognitive culture. Pp. 303-317 in
         Studies in American Indian languages,
         (University of California Publications in
         Linguistics, Vol. 65), edited by J. Sawyer.
         Berkeley.

Vygotsky, Lev Semenovich
1962   Thought and language. Edited and translated
         by Eugenia Hanfmann and Gertrude Vakar.
         Introduction by Jerome S. Bruner. xxi,
         168 pp. New York: John Wiley; Cambridge:
         MIT Press.

Walker, D. E., J. J. Jenkins, and T. A. Sebeok
1954   Language, cognition, and culture. Pp. 192-
         203 in Psycholinguistics: a survey of
         theory and research problems, (International
         Journal of American Linguistics, Memoir No.
         10), edited by C. E. Osgood. Baltimore.

Walker, Willard
1965   Taxonomic structure and the pursuit of
         meaning. Southwestern Journal of Anthro-
         pology 21.3:265-276. Albuquerque.

1966   Inflectional class and taxonomic structure
         in Zuni. International Journal of American
         Linguistics 32.3:217-227. Baltimore.

1968   Review of Componential analysis of general
         vocabulary, by Edward H. Bendix. Language
         44.2:427-431. Baltimore.

Wallace, Anthony F. C.
1960   Review of Plans and the structure of behav-
         ior, by G. A. Miller, E. Galanter, and
         K. H. Pribram. American Anthropologist
         62.6:1065-1067. Menasha.

1961   On being just complicated enough. Proceed-
         ings of the National Academy of Sciences
         47.4:458-464. Washington.

1962   Culture and cognition. Science 135.3501:
         351-357. Washington.

1965a   The problem of the psychological validity
         of componential analysis. Pp. 229-248 in
         Formal semantic analysis, (American Anthro-
         pologist 67.5[Part 2], Special Publication),
         edited by E. A. Hammel. Menasha.

138

Wallace, Anthony F. C.   (cont.)
 1965b   Driving to work. Pp. 277-292 in Context and
           meaning in cultural anthropology, edited by
           M. E. Spiro. New York: Free Press; London:
           Collier-Macmillan.

 1968   Cognitive theory. International Encyclo-
           pedia of the Social Sciences 2:536-540.
           New York: Macmillan and Free Press.

Wallace, Anthony F. C. and John Atkins
 1960   The meaning of kinship terms. American
           Anthropologist 62.1:58-80. Menasha.

Wallace, David L.
 1968   Clustering. International Encyclopedia of
           the Social Sciences 2:519-524. New York:
           Macmillan and Free Press.

Wallach, Michael A.
 1958   On psychological similarity. Psychological
           Review 65.2:103-116. Lancaster, Pa.

Warburton, Frederick E.
 1967   The purposes of classifications. Systematic
           Zoology 16.3:241-245. Lawrence, Kans.

Ward, Joe H., Jr.
 1963   Hierarchical grouping to optimize an objec-
           tive function. Journal of the American
           Statistical Association 58.301:236-244.
           Washington.

Waterman, J. T.
 1957   Benjamin Lee Whorf and linguistic field
           theory. Southwestern Journal of Anthro-
           pology 13.3:201-211. Albuquerque.

Watson, O. Michael and Theodore D. Graves
 1966   Quantitative research in proxemic behavior.
           American Anthropologist 68.4:971-985.
           Menasha.

Watt, William C.
 1966   Morphology of the Nevada cattlebrands and
           their blazons, Part I. 123 pp., appendices.
           Washington: U. S. Department of Commerce,
           National Bureau of Standards.

 1967a   Morphology of the Nevada cattlebrands and
           their blazons, Part II. iii, 57 pp.
           Pittsburgh: Department of Computer Science,
           Carnegie-Mellon University.

[0:122]

Watt, William C. (cont.)
1967b   Structural properties of the Nevada cattle-
         brands. Computer Science Research Review,
         No. 2:20-27. Pittsburgh.

Weigl, E.
1970   Neuropsychological studies of structure and
         dynamics of semantic fields with the
         deblocking method. Pp. 287-290 in Sign·
         language·culture, (Janua Linguarum, Series
         Maior 1), edited by A. J. Greimas et al.
         The Hague and Paris: Mouton.

Weinreich, Uriel
1958   Travels through semantic space. Word
         14.2-3:346-366. New York.

1959   A rejoinder [to Osgood's rejoinder to his
         book]. Word 15.1:200-201. New York.

1960   Mid-century linguistics: attainments and
         frustrations. Romance Philology 8.3:320-
         341. Berkeley.

1962   Lexicographic definition in descriptive
         semantics. Pp. 25-43 in Problems in lexi-
         cography: report of the Conference on
         Lexicography held at Indiana University,
         November 11-12, 1960. (International
         Journal of American Linguistics 28.2[Part
         4]; Publication 21, Indiana University
         Research Center in Anthropology, Folklore,
         and Linguistics), edited by F. W. House-
         holder and S. Saporta. Bloomington.
         (Volume reprinted with additions and
         corrections 1967.)

1963a   Lexicology. Pp. 60-93 in Vol. 1 of Current
         trends in linguistics, edited by T. A.
         Sebeok. The Hague and Paris: Mouton.

1963b   Review of Thought and language, by L. S.
         Vygotsky. American Anthropologist 65.6:
         1401-1404. Menasha.

1964   Webster's third: a critique of its semantics.
         International Journal of American Linguistics
         30.4:405-409. Baltimore.

1966a   Explorations in semantic theory. Pp. 395-
         478 in Vol. 3 of Current trends in linguis-
         tics, edited by T. A. Sebeok. The Hague
         and Paris: Mouton.

140

Weinreich, Uriel   (cont.)
  1966b On the semantic structure of language.
       Pp. 142-216 in Universals of language, 2d
       edition, edited by J. H. Greenberg.
       Cambridge: MIT Press.

  1968   Semantics and semiotics. International
       Encyclopedia of the Social Sciences 14:
       164-169. New York: Macmillan and Free
       Press.

  1969   Problems in the analysis of idioms. Pp. 23-
       81 in Substance and structure of language,
       edited by Jaan Puhvel. Berkeley: University
       of California Press.

Weisgerber, Leo
  1953-   Vom Weltbild der deutschen Sprache. 2 vols.
  1954   Vol. I, Die inhaltbezogene Grammatik;
       Vol. II, Die sprachliche Gestaltung der
       Welt. Düsseldorf: Schwann.

  1954   Die Sprachfelder in der geistigen Erschliess-
       ung der Welt. Pp. 34-49 in Festschrift
       für Jost Trier, edited by Benno von Weise
       and Karl Heinz Borck. Meisenheim: A. Hain.

Weiss, Paul and Arthur Burks
  1945   Peirce's sixty-six signs. Journal of Phil-
       osophy 42.14:383-388. Lancaster, Pa.

Wells, Rulon
  1954a   Archiving and language typology. Inter-
       national Journal of American Linguistics
       20.2:101-107. Baltimore.

  1954b   Meaning and use. Word 10.2-3:235-250.
       New York.

  1956   Acronymy. Pp. 662-667 in For Roman Jakobson,
       edited by Morris Halle et al. The Hague:
       Mouton.

  1957   A mathematical approach to meaning.
       Cahiers Ferdinand de Saussure 15:117-136.
       Geneva.

  1958   Is a structural treatment of meaning
       possible? Proceedings of the Eighth Inter-
       national Congress of Linguists, Oslo, 1957,
       pp. 654-666. Oslo.

[0:124]

Wells, Rulon (cont.)
    1962   What has linguistics done for philosophy?
             Journal of Philosophy 59.23:697-708. New
             York.

Wells, Rulon and Jay Keyser
    1961   The common feature method. (Interaction
             Laboratory Technical Report No. 12.)
             New Haven: Department of Sociology, Yale
             University.

Werner, Heinz
    1954   Change of meaning: a study of semantic
             processes through the experimental method.
             Journal of General Psychology 50.2:181-208.
             Provincetown, Mass.

Werner, Heinz and Bernard Kaplan
    1956   The developmental approach to cognition:
             its relevance to the psychological inter-
             pretation of anthropological and ethnolin-
             guistic data. American Anthropologist
             58.5:866-880. Menasha.

Werner, Oswald
    1966   Pragmatics and ethnoscience. Anthropologi-
             cal Linguistics 8.8:42-65. Bloomington,
             Ind.

    1967   Systematized lexicography or ethnoscience:
             the use of computer-made concordances.
             American Behavioral Scientist 10:5-8.
             Princeton.

Werner, Oswald and Donald T. Campbell
    1970   Translating, working through interpreters,
             and the problem of decentering. Pp. 398-
             420 in A handbook of method in cultural
             anthropology, edited by R. Naroll and R.
             Cohen. Garden City, N. Y.: Natural History
             Press.

Werner, Oswald and Joann Fenton
    1970   Method and theory in ethnoscience or ethno-
             epistemology. Pp. 537-578 in A handbook of
             method in cultural anthropology, edited by
             R. Naroll and R. Cohen. Garden City, N. Y.:
             Natural History Press.

Wheeler, Marcus
    1957   Meaning in bilingual dictionaries. Studia
             Linguistica 11:65-69. Lund.

Wheelwright, Philip
1967   On the semantics of poetry. Pp. 250-263 in
         Essays on the language of literature, edited
         by S. Chatman and S. R. Levin. Boston:
         Houghton Mifflin.

White, Colin
1952   The use of ranks in a test of significance
         for comparing two treatments. Biometrics
         8:33-41. Atlanta.

Whitehead, Alfred North and Bertrand Russell
1925-   Principia mathematica, 2d edition. 3 vols.
1927   Cambridge: Cambridge University Press.

Whiteley, Wilfred H.
1961   Political concepts and connotations; observa-
         tions on the use of some political terms in
         Swahili. Pp. 7-21 in St. Antony's Papers,
         Vol. 10 (African Affairs, 1), edited by
         K. Kirkwood. London: Chatto and Windus.

1966   Social anthropology, meaning and linguistics.
         Man 1.2:139-157. London.

Whorf, Benjamin Lee
1941   The relation of habitual thought and behav-
         ior to language. Pp. 75-93 in Language,
         culture, and personality: essays in memory
         of Edward Sapir, edited by L. Spier et al.
         Menasha: Sapir Memorial Publication Fund.

1945   Grammatical categories. Language 21.1:1-11.
         Baltimore.

1950a   Four articles on metalinguistics. 45 pp.
         Washington: Foreign Service Institute,
         Department of State.

1950b   An American Indian model of the universe.
         International Journal of American Linguistics
         16.2:67-72. Baltimore.

1956   (See Carroll, editor.)

Whyte, Lancelot Law, Albert G. Wilson, and Donna Wilson
1969   Hierarchical systems. xii, 322 pp. New
         York: American Elsevier.

Wilkins, John (Bishop)
1668   An essay towards a real character and a
(1968)   philosophical language. [24], 454, [154] pp.

[O:126]

London: Gellibrand. (Facsimile reprint, 1968, Menston: The Scholar Press.)

Williams, Gerald E.
1966   Linguistic reflections of cultural systems. Anthropological Linguistics 8.8:13-21. Bloomington, Ind.

Williams, Kenneth L.
1963   Checking translations for wrong meanings. Notes on Translation No. 8:1-4. Tlalpan, México, D. F.

Williams, W. T.
1969   The problem of attribute-weighting in numerical classification. Taxon 18.4:369-374. Utrecht.

Williams, W. T. and M. B. Dale
1965   Fundamental problems in numerical taxonomy. Advances in Botanical Research 2:35-68. London and New York.

Willis, John Christopher
1966   Dictionary of the flowering plants and
(1897) ferns. 7th edition, revised by H. K. Airy Shaw. xxii, 1214, liii pp. Cambridge: Cambridge University Press. (First published 1897 as A manual and dictionary of the flowering plants and ferns.)

Wils, J.
1935   De nominale klassifikatie in de Afrikaansche Negertalen. xv, 522 pp. Nijmegen: Uitgevers-Maatschappij "De Gelderlander."

Wilson, Kenneth G., R. H. Hendrickson, and Peter Alan Taylor
1963   Harbrace guide to dictionaries. xii, 208 pp. New York: Harcourt, Brace and World.

Wilson, Robert D.
1966   A criticism of distinctive features. Journal of Linguistics 2.2:195-206. London and New York.

Wissemann, H.
1958   Erlebte und abstrahierte Wortbedeutung. Pp. 195-202 in Sybaris, Festschrift Hans Krahe. Wiesbaden: Harrassowitz.

Wittgenstein, Ludwig
1958   The blue and brown books. 185 pp.

New York: Harper.

Wittgenstein, Ludwig   (cont.)
1966   Lectures and conversations on aesthetics,
          psychology, and religious belief, compiled
          from notes taken by Yorick Smythies, Rush
          Rhees and James Taylor. Edited by Cyril
          Barrett. 72 pp. Berkeley and Los Angeles:
          University of California Press.

Wójcik, Tadeusz
1970   The praxiological model of language. Pp.
          261-284 in Sign·language·culture, (Janua
          Linguarum, Series Maior 1), edited by
          A. J. Greimas et al. The Hague and Paris:
          Mouton.

Wonderly, William L.
1952   Semantic components in Kechua person
          morphemes. Language 28.3:366-376.
          Baltimore.

1968   Bible translations for popular use. (Helps
          for translators Vol. 7.) x, 216 pp. London:
          United Bible Societies.

Woodger, Joseph Henry
1937   The axiomatic method in biology. x, 174 pp.
          Cambridge: Cambridge University Press.

1948   Biological principles. 496 pp. London:
          Routledge and Kegan Paul.

1952   Biology and language, an introduction to
          the methodology of the biological sciences
          including medicine. xiv, 364 pp. Cambridge:
          Cambridge University Press.

1960-   Taxonomy and evolution. La Nuova Critica
1961   3.12:67-77. Rome.

Worth, D. S.
1960   Review of Leksikologija anglijskogo jazyka,
          by A. I. Smirnickij, (1956, Moscow:
          Izdatel'stvo Literatury na Inostrannykh
          Jazykakh). Word 16.2:277-284. New York.

Wren, F. Lynwood
1965   Basic mathematical concepts. 398 pp.
          New York: McGraw-Hill.

Wüster, E.
1959   Die Struktur der sprachlichen Begriffswelt

145

[0:128]

und ihre Darstellung in Wörterbüchern.
Studium Generale 12:615-627. Berlin.

Wyk, E. B. van
1968   Notes on word autonomy. Lingua 21:543-557.
        Amsterdam.

Yalman, Nur
1967   'The raw : the cooked : : nature : culture.'
        Pp. 71-89 in The structural study of myths
        and totemism, (Association of Social Anthro-
        pologists Monographs, 5), edited by E. R.
        Leach. London: Tavistock.

Yochelson, Ellis L.
1966   Nomenclature in the machine age. Systematic
        Zoology 15.1:88-91. Lawrence, Kans.

Yukawa, Yasutoshi
1970   Remarks on meaning. Pp. 680-694 in Studies
        in general and Oriental linguistics; pre-
        sented to Shirô Hattori on the occasion of
        his sixtieth birthday, edited by Roman
        Jakobson and Shigeo Kawamoto. Tokyo: TEC
        Company.

Zawadowski, Leon
1967   A classification of signs and semantic
        systems. Pp. 2333-2354 in To honor Roman
        Jakobson, essays on the occasion of his
        seventieth birthday, (Janua Linguarum,
        Series Maior 31). The Hague and Paris:
        Mouton. (Reprinted 1970, pp. 28-49 in
        Sign·language·culture, [Janua Linguarum,
        Series Maior 1], edited by A. J. Greimas
        et al. The Hague and Paris: Mouton.)

Zgusta, Ladislav et al.
1971   Manual of lexicography. (Janua Linguarum,
        Series Maior 39.) 360 pp. The Hague and
        Paris: Mouton.

Zierer, Ernesto
1970   The theory of graphs in linguistics. 62 pp.
        New York: Humanities Press.

Ziff, Paul
1960   Semantic analysis. x, 255 pp. Ithaca:
        Cornell University Press.

Zumthor, Paul
1955   Notes sur les champs sémantiques dans le

146

vocabulaire des idées. Neophilologus 39.3: 175-183. Groningen, Djakarta.

Zvegincev, Vladimir A.
1957   Semasiologija. 320 pp. Moscow: Izdatel'stvo Moskovskogo Universiteta.

Zwanenburg, W.
1970   La Classification des composés en français moderne. Lingua 25.2:128-141. Amsterdam.

Zwicky, Arnold M.
1971   In a manner of speaking. Linguistic Inquiry 2.2:223-236. Cambridge, Mass.

1. Kinship and Related Topics

[Including representative works on folk systems of kin categorization and similar ethnosociological classifications; cf. 3.]

Aaby, Peter S.
1970   The criterion of polarity. American Anthropologist 72.2:349-351. Menasha.

Aberle, David F.
1961   Matrilineal descent in cross-cultural perspective. Pp. 655-727 in Matrilineal kinship, edited by D. M. Schneider and K. Gough. Berkeley: University of California Press.

1967   A scale of alternate generation terminology. Southwestern Journal of Anthropology 23.2: 261-277. Albuquerque.

Aginsky, Burt Bernard W.
1935a   Kinship systems and the forms of marriage. (American Anthropologist 37.4(Part 2); Memoir No. 45.) 102 pp. Menasha.

1935b   The mechanics of kinship. American Anthropologist 37.3:450-457. Menasha.

Aoki, Haruo
1966   Nez Perce and Proto-Sahaptian kinship terms. International Journal of American Linguistics 32.4:357-368. Baltimore.

1970   Usage of referential kin terms in Nez Perce. Pp. 61-73 in Languages and cultures of western North America: essays in honor of Sven S. Liljeblad, edited by E. H. Swanson, Jr. Pocatello: Idaho State University Press.

Atkins, John R.
1959   The cardinality of a kin relationship. Bulletin of the Philadelphia Anthropological Society 31.1:7-10. Philadelphia.

Ayoub, Millicent
1964   Bipolarity in Arabic kinship terms. Pp. 1100-1106 in Proceedings of the Ninth International Congress of Linguistics, edited by H. G. Lunt. The Hague: Mouton.

Ballweg, John A.
1969   Extensions of meaning and use for kinship
        terms. American Anthropologist 71.1:84-87.
        Menasha.

Barnes, John Arundel
1961   Physical and social kinship. Philosophy of
        Science 28:269-299. Baltimore.

1967a   Inquest on the Murngin. (Royal Anthropolog-
        ical Institute of Great Britain and Ireland,
        Occasional Paper No. 26.) 50 pp. London.

1967b   Genealogies. Pp. 101-127 in The craft of
        social anthropology, edited by A. L. Epstein.
        London: Tavistock.

Basso, Ellen B.
1970   Xingu Carib kinship terminology and marriage:
        another view. Southwestern Journal of
        Anthropology 26.4:402-416. Albuquerque.

Beals, Ralph L.
1962   Kinship terminology and social structure.
        Kroeber Anthropological Society Papers 25:
        129-248. Berkeley.

Beattie, J. H. M.
1958   Nyoro kinship, marriage and affinity.
        (International African Institute, Memoir
        28.) London.

1964   Kinship and social anthropology. Man 64:
        101-103(Art. 130). London.

Befu, Harumi
1964   Eskimo systems of relationship terms:
        their diversity and uniformity. Arctic
        Anthropology 2.1:84-98. Madison, Wisc.

Beidelman, Thomas O.
1966   Utani: some Kaguru notions of death,
        sexuality, and affinity. Southwestern
        Journal of Anthropology 22.4:354-380.
        Albuquerque.

Bellah, Robert Neelly
1952   Apache kinship systems. 151 pp. Cambridge:
        Harvard University Press.

Benedict, Paul King
1942   Tibetan and Chinese kinship terms. Harvard

Journal of Asiatic Studies 6:313-337. Cambridge.

Benjamin, Geoffrey
1966   Temiar social groupings. Federation Museums Journal 11:1-25. Kuala Lumpur.

1967   Temiar kinship. Federation Museums Journal 12:1-25. Kuala Lumpur.

1968   Temiar personal names. Bijdragen tot de Taal-, Land- en Volkenkunde 124.1:99-134. 's-Gravenhage.

Benveniste, Émile
1965   Termes de parenté dans les langues indo-européennes. L'Homme 5.3-4:5-16. Paris.

1969   Le Vocabulaire des institutions indo-européennes. 1. Économie, parenté, société. 376 pp. Paris: Les Editions de Minuit.

Berndt, Ronald M.
1970   Two in one, and more in two. Pp. 1040-1068 in Échanges et communications; mélanges offerts a Claude Lévi-Strauss à l'occasion de son 60ème anniversaire, edited by J. Pouillon and P. Maranda. The Hague and Paris: Mouton.

Berthe, Louis
1965   Ainés et cadets: l'alliance et la hiérarchie chez les Baduj (Java occidental). L'Homme 5.3-4:189-223. Paris.

1970   Parenté, pouvoir et mode de production: éléments pour une typologie des sociétés agricoles de l'Indonésie. Pp. 707-738 in Échanges et communications; mélanges offerts a Claude Lévi-Strauss à l'occasion de son 60ème anniversaire, edited by J. Pouillon and P. Maranda. The Hague and Paris: Mouton.

Béteille, André
1967   Race and descent as social categories in India. Daedalus 96.2:444-463. Cambridge, Mass.

Bjerke, Robert
1969   A contrastive study of Old German and Old Norwegian kinship terms. (Supplement to

151

[1:4]

International Journal of American Linguistics
35.1(Part 2); Indiana University Publications
in Anthropology and Linguistics, Memoir 22.)
v, 172 pp. Baltimore.

Bloch, Maurice
1971   The moral and tactical meaning of kinship
        terms. Man 6.1:79-87. London.

Boas, Franz
1940   The relationship system of the Vandau.
        Pp. 386-396 in Race, language and culture,
        by F. Boas. New York: Macmillan.

Bock, Philip K.
1964   Social structure and language structure.
        Southwestern Journal of Anthropology 20.4:
        394-403. Albuquerque.

1968   Some generative rules for American kinship
        terminology. Anthropological Linguistics
        10.6:1-16. Bloomington, Ind.

Boyd, John Paul
1969   The algebra of group kinship. Journal of
        Mathematical Psychology 6.1:139-167. New
        York.

1971   Componential analysis and the substitution
        property. Pp. 50-59 in Explorations in
        mathematical anthropology, edited by P. Kay.
        Cambridge: MIT Press.

Brandenstein, Carl Georg von
1970   The meaning of section and section names.
        Oceania 41.1:39-49. Sydney.

Bright, William and Jan Minnick
1966   Reduction rules in Fox kinship. Southwest-
        ern Journal of Anthropology 22.4:381-388.
        Albuquerque.

Brito, Eduíno de
1955   Fula onomastics and degree of kinship.
        Boletim cultural de Guiné portuguesa
        10:599-616. Bissau.

Buchler, Ira R.
1964a   A formal account of the Hawaiian-and-Eskimo
        type kinship terminologies. Southwestern
        Journal of Anthropology 20.3:286-318.
        Albuquerque.

[1:5]

1964b   Measuring the development of kinship terminologies: scalogram and transformational accounts of Crow-type systems. American Anthropologist 66.4(Part 1):765-788. Menasha.

1964c   Cubical and tri-dimensional block models of Crow kinship structure. Man 64:6-8(Art. 3). London.

1965   Crow terminological scales: corrections. American Anthropologist 67.2:503-504. Menasha.

1966   Measuring the development of kinship terminologies: scalogram and transformational accounts of Omaha-type systems. Bijdragen tot de Taal-, Land- en Volkenkunde 122.1: 36-63. 's-Gravenhage.

1967   Analyse formelle des terminologies de parenté iroquoises. L'Homme 7.1:5-31. Paris.

Buchler, Ira R. and Hugo G. Nutini
1965   Structural changes in kinship terminology of San Bernardino Contla, a Nahuatl-speaking village of the central Mexican highlands. Anthropological Linguistics 7.3:67-75. Bloomington, Ind.

Buchler, Ira R. and Henry A. Selby
1968   Kinship and social organization; an introduction to theory and method. xii, 366 pp. New York: Macmillan.

1970   Animal, vegetable, or mineral? Pp. 213-234 in Échanges et communications; mélanges offerts à Claude Lévi-Strauss à l'occasion de son 60ème anniversaire, edited by J. Pouillon and P. Maranda. The Hague and Paris: Mouton.

Burling, Robbins
1962   A structural restatement of Njamal kinship terminology. Man 62:22-124(Art. 201). London.

1963   Garo kinship terms and the analysis of meaning. Ethnology 2.1:70-85. Pittsburgh.

1964a   Cognition and componential analysis: God's truth or hocus-pocus? American Anthropologist 66.1:20-28. Menasha.

153

Burling, Robbins (cont.)
  1964b   Burling's rejoinder. American Anthropologist
           66.1:120-122. Menasha.

  1965   Burmese kinship terminology. Pp. 106-117
           in Formal semantic analysis, (American
           Anthropologist 67.5[Part 2], Special Publi-
           cation), edited by E. A. Hammel. Menasha.

  1970a   American kinship terms once more. South-
           western Journal of Anthropology 26.1:15-24.
           Albuquerque.

  1970b   Man's many voices: language in its cultural
           context. xi, 222 pp. New York: Holt,
           Rinehart and Winston.

Bush, Archie
  1971   Latin kinship extensions. Ethnology 10.4:
           409-432. Pittsburgh.

Bush, Robert R.
  1963   An algebraic treatment of rules of marriage
           and descent. Appendix II in An anatomy of
           kinship, by H. C. White. Englewood Cliffs,
           N. J.: Prentice-Hall.

Chao, Yuen Ren
  1956   Chinese terms of address. Language 32.1:
           217-241. Baltimore.

Chock, Phyllis Pease
  1967   Kinship and culture: some problems in
           Ndembu kinship. Southwestern Journal of
           Anthropology 23.1:74-89. Albuquerque.

Conant, Francis P.
  1961   Jarawa kin systems of reference and address:
           a componential comparison. Anthropological
           Linguistics 3.2:19-33. Bloomington, Ind.

Condominas, Georges
  1960   The Mnong Gar of central Vietnam. Pp. 15-
           23 in Social structure in Southeast Asia,
           (Viking Fund Publications in Anthropology,
           No. 29.), edited by G. P. Murdock. New
           York: Wenner-Gren Foundation for Anthro-
           pological Research.

Conklin, Harold C.
  1964   Ethnogenealogical method. Pp. 25-55 in
           Explorations in cultural anthropology:

essays in honor of George Peter Murdock,
edited by W. H. Goodenough. New York:
McGraw-Hill. (Reprinted 1969, pp. 93-122
in Cognitive anthropology, edited by S. A.
Tyler. New York: Holt, Rinehart and
Winston.)

Cook, Edwin A.
1970   On the conversion of the non-agnates into
          agnates among the Manga, Jimi River, Western
          Highlands District, New Guinea. Southwestern
          Journal of Anthropology 26.2:190-196.
          Albuquerque.

Coult, Allan D.
1965   Terminological correlates of cross-cousin
          marriage. Bijdragen tot de Taal-, Land- en
          Volkenkunde 121.1:120-139. 's-Gravenhage.

1966a   On the justification of untested componential
          analyses. American Anthropologist 68.4:1014-
          1015. Menasha.

1966b   A simplified method for the transformational
          analysis of kinship terms. American Anthro-
          pologist 68.6:1476-1483. Menasha.

1967   Lineage solidarity, transformational analysis
          and the meaning of kinship terminologies.
          Man (n.s.) 2.1:26-47. London.

Courrège, Philippe
1965   Un modèle mathématique des structures
          élémentaires de parenté. L'Homme 5.3-4:
          248-290. Paris.

Cuisinier, Jeanne and Andro Miguel
1965   La Terminologie arabe de la parenté: analyse
          sémantique et analyse componentielle.
          L'Homme 5.3-4:17-59. Paris.

Cunningham, Clark E.
1966   Categories of descent groups in a Timor
          village. Oceania 37.1:13-21. Sydney.

1967   Atoni kin categories and conventional behav-
          ior. Bijdragen tot de Taal-, Land- en
          Volkenkunde 123.1:53-70. 's-Gravenhage.

Damas, David
1963   Igluligmiut kinship and local groupings:
          a structural approach. (National Museum
          of Canada Bulletin No. 196; Anthropological

Series No. 64.) 216 pp. Ottawa: Department of Northern Affairs and National
Resources.

Damas, David (cont.)
    1964   The patterning of the Iglulingmuit kinship
            system. Ethnology 3.4:377-388. Pittsburgh.

D'Andrade, Roy G.
    1970   Structure and syntax in the semantic analy-
            sis of kinship terminologies. Pp. 87-143
            in Cognition: a multiple view, edited by
            P. L. Garvin. New York: Spartan.

    1971   Procedures for prediction kinship terminolo-
            gies from features of social organization.
            Pp. 60-76 in Explorations in mathematical
            anthropology, edited by P. Kay. Cambridge:
            MIT Press.

Davies, Peter
    1971   New views of lexicon. Pp. xli-liv in The
            American Heritage word frequency book, by
            J. B. Carroll, P. Davies and B. Richman.
            Boston: Houghton Mifflin; New York: American
            Heritage.

David, Kingsley and W. Lloyd Warner
    1937   Structural analysis of kinship. American
            Anthropologist 39.2:291-313. Menasha.

Diebold, A. Richard, Jr.
    1966   The reflection of coresidence in Mareño
            kinship terminology. Ethnology 5.1:37-39.
            Pittsburgh.

Dole, Gertrude E.
    1960   The classification of Yankee nomenclature
            in the light of evolution in kinship. Pp.
            162-178 in Essays in the science of culture,
            edited by G. E. Dole and R. L. Carneiro.
            New York: Crowell.

    1965   The lineage pattern of kinship nomenclature:
            its significance and development. South-
            western Journal of Anthropology 21.1:36-62.
            Albuquerque.

    1969   Generation kinship nomenclature as an
            adaptation to endogamy. Southwestern
            Journal of Anthropology 25.2:105-123.
            Albuquerque.

Dozier, Edward P.
1960   A comparison of the eastern Keresan and
        Tewa kinship systems. Pp. 430-436 in Men
        and cultures, (Selected papers of the Fifth
        International Congress of Anthropological
        and Ethnological Sciences, Philadelphia,
        1956), edited by A. F. C. Wallace. Phila-
        delphia: University of Pennsylvania Press.

Dreyfus, Simone
1970   Alliances inter-tribales et systèmes de
        parenté du haut Xingu (Brésil central).
        Pp. 258-271 in Échanges et communications;
        mélanges offerts à Claude Lévi-Strauss à
        l'occasion de son 60ème anniversaire,
        edited by J. Pouillon and P. Maranda. The
        Hague and Paris: Mouton.

Dubois, J. and L. Irigary
1966   Les Structures linguistiques de la parenté.
        Cahiers de Lexicologie 8.1:47-69. Paris.

Dumont, Louis
1950   Kinship and alliance among the Pramalai
        Kallar. Eastern Anthropologist 4.1:3-26.
        Lucknow.

1953a   The Dravidian kinship terminology as an
        expression of marriage. Man 53:34-39(Art.
        54). London

1953b   Dravidian kinship terminology. Man 53:
        143(Art. 224). London.

1957   Hierarchy and marriage alliance in South
        Indian kinship. (Royal Anthropological
        Institute of Great Britain and Ireland,
        Occasional Paper No. 12.) 45 pp. London.

1962   Le Vocabulaire de parenté dans l'Inde du
        nord. L'Homme 2.2:5-48. Paris.

1966   Descent or intermarriage? A relational
        view of Australian section systems. South-
        western Journal of Anthropology 22.3:231-
        250. Albuquerque.

1968   Marriage alliance. International Encyclo-
        pedia of the Social Sciences 10:19-23.
        New York: Macmillan and Free Press.

1970   Sur le vocabulaire de parenté kariera.

Pp. 272-286 in Échanges et communications; mélanges offerts à Claude Lévi-Strauss à l'occasion de son 60ème anniversaire, edited by J. Pouillon and P. Maranda. The Hague and Paris: Mouton.

Durbin, Marshall and M. Saltarelli
1967   Patterns in kinship. Anthropological Linguistics 9.3:6-14. Bloomington, Ind.

Durkheim, Emile
1898   Review of Zur Urgeschichte der Ehe, by J. Kohler. Année Sociologique 1:306-319. Paris.

Durkheim, Emile and Marcel Mauss
1963   Primitive classification. Translated and edited, with an introduction by Rodney Needham. xlvii, 96 pp. Chicago: University of Chicago Press.

Edmonson, Monro S.
1957   Kinship terms and kinship concepts. American Anthropologist 59.3:393-433. Menasha.

1958   Status terminology and the social structure of North American Indians. 84 pp. Seattle: University of Washington Press.

Eggan, Fred
1950   Social organization of the western Pueblos. 373 pp. Chicago: University of Chicago Press.

1955   Social anthropology of North American tribes. 2d edition. 574 pp. Chicago: University of Chicago Press.

1960   The Sagada Igorots of northern Luzon. Pp. 24-50 in Social structure in Southeast Asia, (Viking Fund Publications in Anthropology, No. 29), edited by G. P. Murdock. New York: Wenner-Gren Foundation for Anthropological Research.

1966   The American Indian: perspectives for the study of social change. 193 pp. Chicago: Aldine.

1968   Kinship. International Encyclopedia of the Social Sciences 8:390-401. New York: Macmillan and Free Press.

Elkin, Adolphus Peter
　1954　The Australian aborigines; how to understand
　　　　them. 3d edition. 349 pp. London: Angus
　　　　Robertson.

Elkins, Richard E.
　1968　Three models of western Bukidnon Manobo
　　　　kinship. Ethnology 7.2:171-189. Pittsburgh.

Emeneau, Murray B.
　1941　Language and social forms: a study of Toda
　　　　kinship terms and dual descent. Pp. 158-
　　　　179 in Language, culture, and personality:
　　　　essays in memory of Edward Sapir, edited by
　　　　I. Hallowell, and S. Newman. Menasha:
　　　　Sapir Memorial Publication Fund.

Epling, Philip J.
　1961　A note on Njamal kin-term usage. Man 61:
　　　　152-159(Art. 184). London.

　1967　Lay perception of kinship: a Samoan case
　　　　study. Oceania 37.4:260-280. Sydney.

Etienne, P. and M. Etienne
　1967　Terminologie de la parenté et de l'alliance
　　　　chez les Baoulé. L'Homme 7.4:50-76. Paris.

Evans-Pritchard, E. E.
　1929　The study of kinship in primitive societies.
　　　　Man 29:190-193(Art. 148). London.

　1932　The nature of kinship extensions. Man 32:
　　　　12-15(Art. 7). London.

　1951　Kinship and marriage among the Nuer. xi,
　　　　183 pp. London: Oxford University Press.

Eyde, David and Paul Postal
　1961　Avunculocality and incest: the development
　　　　of unilateral cross-cousin marriage and
　　　　Crow-Omaha kinship systems. American
　　　　Anthropologist 63.4:747-771. Menasha.

　1963　Matrilineality versus matrilocality among
　　　　the Siriono: a reply to Needham. Bijdragen
　　　　tot de Taal-, Land- en Volkenkunde 119.3:
　　　　284-285. 's-Gravenhage.

Fabian, Johannes
　1965　!Kung Bushman kinship: componential analy-
　　　　sis and alternative interpretations. Anthro-
　　　　pos 60.1-6:663-718. Fribourg.

[1:12]

Fainberg, Leo A.
1967   On the question of the Eskimo kinship system.
        Arctic Anthropology 4.1:244-256. Madison,
        Wisc.

Falkenberg, Johannes
1962   Kin and totem. Group relations of Austral-
        ian aboriginals in the Port Keat District.
        Oslo: Oslo University Press; London:
        Allen and Unwin.

Farber, Bernard
1968   Comparative kinship systems: a method of
        analysis. 147 pp. New York: John Wiley.

1971   Kinship and class: a midwestern study.
        210 pp. New York and London: Basic Books.

Faris, James C.
1969a   Sibling terminology and cross-sex behavior:
        data from the south - eastern Nuba. American
        Anthropologist 71.3:482-488. Menasha.

1969b   Some cultural considerations of duo-lineal
        descent organization. Ethnology 8.3:243-
        254. Pittsburgh.

Festinger, Georges
1970a   Nouvelle analyse formelle de la terminologie
        de parenté seneca. L'Homme 10.1:77-93.
        Paris.

1970b   Conditions de symétrie des prohibitions
        lignagères de mariage: application au cas
        omaha. L'Homme 10.2:109-115. Paris.

Findler, Nicholas V. and Wiley R. McKinzie
1969   On a computer program that generates and
        queries kinship structures. Behavioral
        Science 14.4:334-340. Ann Arbor.

Firth, Raymond
1930   Marriage and the classificatory system of
        relationship. Journal of the Royal Anthro-
        pological Institute of Great Britain and
        Ireland 60.1:235-268. London.

1936   We, the Tikopia: a sociological study of
        kinship in primitive Polynesia. xxix,
        605 pp. London: Allen and Unwin.

1963   Bilateral descent groups. Pp. 22-37 in

160

Studies in kinship and marriage, edited by
I. Schapers. London: Royal Anthropological Institute.

1968   Rivers on Oceanic kinship. Pp. 17-36 in
Kinship and social organization, (London
School of Economics Monographs on Social
Anthropology, No. 34), edited by W. H. R.
Rivers. New York: Humanities Press.

Fischer, Henri Th.
1957   Some notes on kinship systems and relationship terms of Sumba, Manggarai and South
Timor. International Archives of Ethnography
48:1-31. Leiden.

Fischer, Henri Th. and H. C. Van Renselaar
1959   Over enkele Batakse verwantschapstermen.
Bijdragen tot de Taal-, Land- en Volkenkunde
115.1:40-55. 's-Gravenhage.

Fischer, J.
1958   The classification of residence in censuses.
American Anthropologist 60.3:508-517.
Menasha.

1959   A note on terminology for primary kin.
Southwestern Journal of Anthropology 15.4:
348-354. Albuquerque.

1960   Genealogical space. Oceania 30.3:181-187.
Sydney.

1966   The basic semantic variables of kinship
terminology. Human Mosaic 1.2:68-77. New
Orleans.

Fison, Lorimer
1880   Kamilaroi marriage, descent, and relationship. Pp. 23-96 in Kamilaroi and Kurnai,
by L. Fison and A. W. Howitt. Melbourne:
G. Robertson.

Forge, Anthony
1971   Marriage and exchange in the Sepik: comments on Francis Korn's analysis of Iatmul
society. Pp. 133-144 in Rethinking kinship
and marraige, (Association of Social Anthropologists Monographs, 11), edited by R.
Needham. London: Tavistock.

Fortes, Meyer
1945   The dynamics of clanship among the Tallensi.

xx, 270 pp. London: Oxford University Press.

Fortes, Meyer (cont.)
1949   The web of kinship among the Tallensi. xiv, 358 pp. London: Oxford University Press.

1950   Kinship and marriage among the Ashanti. Pp. 252-285 in African systems of kinship and marriage, edited by A. R. Radcliffe-Brown. London: Oxford University Press.

1959   Descent, filiation and affinity: a rejoinder to Dr. Leach. Man 59:193-197, 206-212. London.

1969   Kinship and social order, the legacy of Lewis Henry Morgan. ix, 347 pp. Chicago: Aldine.

Fox, James J.
1971   Sister's child as plant: metaphors in an idiom of consanguinity. Pp. 219-256 in Rethinking kinship and marriage, (Association of Social Anthropologists Monographs, 11), edited by R. Needham. London: Tavistock.

Fox, Robin
1965   Prolegomena to the study of British kinship. Pp. 128-143 in Penguin Survey of the Social Sciences 1965, edited by J. Gould. Baltimore: Penguin Books.

1967a   The Keresan bridge: a problem in Pueblo ethnology. (London School of Economics Monographs on Social Anthropology, No. 35.) xii, 216 pp. London: Althone.

1967b   Kinship and marriage: an anthropological perspective. 271 pp. Harmondsworth, England: Penguin Books.

Frake, Charles O.
1960   The Eastern Subanun of Mindanao. Pp. 51-64 in Explorations in cultural anthropology: essays in honor of George Peter Murdock, edited by W. H. Goddenough. New York: McGraw-Hill.

Freed, Stanley A. and Ruth S. Freed
1970   A note on regional variation in Navajo

kinship terminology. American Anthropologist
72.6:1439-1444. Menasha.

Friedrich, Paul
1963   An evolutionary sketch of Russian kinship.
        Pp. 1-26 in Symposium on Language and Cul-
        ture, (Proceedings of the 1962 Annual Spring
        Meeting of the American Ethnological Society),
        edited by V. A. Garfield and W. L. Chafe.
        Seattle: University of Washington Press.

1964   Semantic structure and social structure:
        an instance from Russia. Pp. 131-166 in
        Explorations in cultural anthropology:
        essays in honor of George Peter Murdock,
        edited by W. H. Goodenough. New York:
        McGraw-Hill.

1966a   Proto-Indo-European kinship. Ethnology
        5.1:1-36. Pittsburgh.

1966b   The linguistic reflex of social change:
        from Tsarist to Soviet Russian kinship.
        Sociological Inquiry 36.2:159-185. Haver-
        ford, Pa.

Frisch, Jack A.
1971   A formal analysis of Sinhalese kinship
        terms. Anthropological Linguistics 13.3:
        100-105. Bloomington, Ind.

Frisch, Jack A. and Noel W. Schutz
1967   Componential analysis and semantic recon-
        struction: the proto central Yuman kinship
        system. Ethnology 6.3:272-293. Pittsburgh.

Galton, Francis
1889   Note on Australian marriage systems. Jour-
        nal of the Royal Anthropological Institute
        of Great Britain and Ireland 18.1:70-72.
        London.

Gates, H. Phelps
1971   The kinship terminology of Homeric Greek.
        (Supplement to International Journal of
        American Linguistics 37.4[Part 2]; Indiana
        University Publications in Anthropology and
        Linguistics, Memoir 27.) 82 pp. Baltimore.

Gellner, Ernest A.
1957   Ideal language and kinship structure.
        Philosophy of Science 24:235-242. Baltimore.

163

[1:16]

Gifford, Edward Winslow
1916   Miwok moieties. University of California
        Publications in American Archaeology and
        Ethnology 12.4:139-194. Berkeley.

1922   California kinship terminologies. University
        of California Publications in American
        Archaeology and Ethnology 18:1-285.
        Berkeley.

1940   A problem in kinship terminology. American
        Anthropologist 42.2(Part 1):190-194.
        Menasha.

Glick, Leonard B.
1967   The role of choice in Gimi kinship. South-
        western Journal of Anthropology 23.4:371-
        382. Albuquerque.

Goitein, S. S.
1970   Nicknames as family names. Journal of the
        American Oriental Society 90.4:517-524.
        New Haven.

Goodenough, Ward H.
1951   Property, kin, and community on Truk. (Yale
        University Publications in Anthropology, No.
        46.) 192 pp. New Haven.

1956a   Residence rules. Southwestern Journal of
        Anthropology 12.1:22-37. Albuquerque.

1956b   Componential analysis and the study of
        meaning. Language 32.1:195-216. Baltimore.

1964   Componential analysis of Könkämä Lapp kin-
        ship terminology. Pp. 221-238 in Explora-
        tions in cultural anthropology: essays in
        honor of George Peter Murdock, edited by
        W. H. Goodenough. New York: McGraw-Hill.

1965   Yankee kinship terminology: a problem in
        componential analysis. American Anthropolo-
        gist 67.5(Part 2):258-287. Menasha.

1967   Componential analysis. Science 156.3779:
        1203-1209. Washington.

1968   Componential analysis. International
        Encyclopedia of the Social Sciences 1:186-
        192. New York: Macmillan and Free Press.

164

1970   Description and comparison in cultural anthropology. xi, 173 pp. Chicago: Aldine.

Goody, Jack
1961   The classification of double descent systems. Current Anthropology 2.1:3-25. Chicago.

1970   Cousin terms. Southwestern Journal of Anthropology 26.2:125-142. Albuquerque.

1971   The analysis of kin terms. Pp. 299-306 in Kinship, edited by Jack Goody. Harmondsworth, England: Penguin Books.

Goss, James A.
1967   Ute language of kin, myth and nature: a demonstration of a multi-dimensional folk taxonomy. Anthropological Linguistics 9.9:1-11. Bloomington, Ind.

Graburn, Nelson
1971   Readings in kinship and social structure. 451 pp. New York: Harper and Row.

Greenberg, Joseph H.
1949   The logical analysis of kinship. Philosophy of Science 16.1:58-64. Baltimore.

1966   Language universals. Pp. 61-112 in Vol. 3 of Current trends in linguistics, edited by T. A. Sebeok. The Hague: Mouton.

Grimes, Joseph E. and Barbara F.
1962   Semantic distinctions in Huichol (Uto-Aztecan) kinship. American Anthropologist 64.1:104-114. Menasha.

Guemple, D. Lee
1965   Saunik: name sharing as a factor governing Eskimo kinship terms. Ethnology 4.3:323-335. Pittsburgh.

1966   Kinship reckoning among the Belcher Island Eskimo. Ph.D. dissertation in the University of Chicago. Chicago.

1969   The Eskimo ritual sponsor: a problem in the fusion of semantic domains. Ethnology 8.4:468-483. Pittsburgh.

Guhr, Günter
1963   Heirat und Verwandtschaftssystem bei den

Aranda in Zentralaustralien, Kritik des sogenannten Aranda-typs von Radcliffe-Brown. vii, 194 pp. Berlin: Akademie Verlag.

Guilbaud, Georges
1970   Système parental et matrimonial au Nord Ambrym. Journal de la Société des Océanistes 26.26:9-32. Paris.

Haas, Mary R.
1969   Sibling terms as used by marriage partners. Southwestern Journal of Anthropology 25.3: 228-235. Albuquerque.

Hamilton, Annette
1971   The equivalence of siblings. Anthropological Forum 3.2:13-20. Perth.

Hammel, Eugene A.
1960   Some models for the analysis of marriage-section systems. Oceania 31.1:14-30. Sydney.

1964   Further comments of componential analysis. American Anthropologist 66.2:1167-1171. Menasha.

1965a   A transformational analysis of Comanche kinship terminology. Pp. 65-105 in Formal semantic analysis, (American Anthropologist 67.5[Part 2], Special Publication), edited by E. A. Hammel. Menasha.

1965b   An algorithm for Crow-Omaha solutions. Pp. 118-126 in Formal semantic analysis, (American Anthropologist 67.5[Part 2], Special Publication), edited by E. A. Hammel. Menasha.

1966a   A factor theory for Arunta kinship terminology. University of California Anthropological Records 24:1-19. Berkeley and Los Angeles.

1966b   Rejoinder to Coult. American Anthropologist 68.6:1483-1488. Menasha.

1971   Formal semantic analysis. Pp. 317-327 in Kinship, edited by Jack Goody. Harmondsworth, England: Penguin Books.

Hammer, Muriel
1966   Some comments on formal analysis of

grammatical and semantic systems. American
Anthropologist 68.2(Part 1):362-373. Menasha.

Handy, Edward Smith Craighill and Mary Kawena Pukui
1950   The Polynesian family system in Ka'u,
        Hawaii. Journal of the Polynesian Society
        59:232-240. Wellington.

Hara, Hiroko Sue
1970   Explicit and implicit structures of the
        Hare kinship. Japanese Journal of Ethnology
        35.3:165-176. Tokyo.

Harvey, John H. T. and Pin-Hsiung Liu
1967   Numerical kinship notation systems: mathe-
        matical model of genealogical space. Bulle-
        tin of the Institute of Ethnology, Academia
        Sinica No. 23:1-22. Nankang, Taipei, Taiwan.

Hattori, Takeshi
1963   Gilyak kinship terms. Anthropology Tomorrow
        9.1:1-12. Chicago.

Healey, Alan
1962   Linguistic aspects of Telefomin kinship
        terminology. Anthropological Linguistics
        4.7:14-28. Bloomington, Ind.

Heinrich, Albert C.
1960   Structural features of northwestern Alaskan
        Eskimo kinship. Southwestern Journal of
        Anthropology 16.1:110-126. Albuquerque.

Heinrich, Albert C. and Russell L. Anderson
1968   Co-affinal siblingship as a structural
        feature among some northern North American
        peoples. Ethnology 7.3:290-295. Pittsburgh.

1971   Some formal aspects of a kinship system.
        Current Anthropology 12.4-5:541-557. Glas-
        gow.

Henderson, Richard N.
1967   Onitsha Ibo kinship terminology: a formal
        analysis and its functional applications.
        Southwestern Journal of Anthropology 23.1:
        15-51. Albuquerque.

Hiatt, L. R.
1965   Kinship and conflict: a study of an aborig-
        inal community in northern Arnhem land.

xxi, 162 pp. Canberra: Australian National
University Press.

Himes, Ron
1971   Kinship, disease, property, and time in the
Tagalog area, Philippines: a study in
ethnoscience. Doctoral dissertation in
anthropology, University of Hawaii.
Honolulu.

Hocart, Arthur Maurice
1928   The Indo-European kinship system. Ceylon
Journal of Science (Section G) 1(Part 4):
179-204. Colombo.

1937   Kinship systems. Anthropos 32:345-351.
Vienna.

Hooper, Antony
1970   "Blood" and "belly." Tahitian concepts of
kinship and descent. Pp. 306-320 in
Échanges et communications; mélanges offerts
à Claude Lévi-Strauss à l'occasion de son
60ème anniversaire, edited by J. Pouillon
and P. Maranda. The Hague and Paris:
Mouton.

Hopkins, Nicholas A.
1969   A formal account of Chalchihuitán Tzozil
kinship terminology. Ethnology 8.1:85-102.
Pittsburgh.

Hsu, Francis Lang Kwang
1942   The differential functions of relationship
terms. American Anthropologist 44.2:248-
256. Menasha.

1947   On a technique for studying relationship
terms. American Anthropologist 49.4:618-
624. Menasha.

Hunt, Eva
1969   The meaning of kinship in San Juan:
genealogical and social models. Ethnology
8.1:37-53. Pittsburgh.

Huntsman, Judith W.
1971   Concepts of kinship and categories of
kinsmen in the Tokelau Islands. Journal
of the Polynesian Society 80:317-354.
Wellington.

Hymes, Dell H.
1964   Discussion of Burling's paper. American
        Anthropologist 66.1:116-119. Menasha.

1966   Reply to Coult. American Anthropologist
        68.4:1015. Menasha.

Ivanitsky, M.
1915   The system of kinship amongst the primitive
        peoples as determined by their mode of
        grouping. Man 15:163-165. London.

Josselin de Jong, Patrick Edward de
1952   Lévi-Strauss' theory of kinship and marriage.
        59 pp. Leiden: Brill.

1962   A new approach to kinship studies: being a
        discussion of F. G. G. Rose, Kin, age struc-
        ture and marriage. Bijdragen tot de Taal-,
        Land en Volkenkunde 118.1(Anthropologica
        III):42-67. 's-Gravenhage.

1966   Ambrym and other class systems: a further
        note on symmetry and asymmetry. Bijdragen
        tot de Taal-, Land- en Volkenkunde 122.1:
        64-81. 's-Gravenhage.

Kaut, Charles R.
1967   Bansag and apelyido: problems of comparison
        in changing Tagalog social organization.
        Pp. 397-418 in Studies in Philippine anthro-
        pology, edited by M. D. Zamora. Quezon City:
        Alemar-Phoenix.

Kay, Paul
1965   A generalization of the cross/parallel
        distinction. American Anthropologist 67.1:
        30-43. Menasha.

1966   Comment on B. N. Colby, Ethnographic seman-
        tics: a preliminary survey. Current
        Anthropology 7.1:20-23. Utrecht.

1967   On the multiplicity of cross/parallel
        distinctions. American Anthropologist 69.1:
        83-85. Menasha.

Keesing, Roger M.
1965   Mota kinship terminologies and marriage:
        a reexamination. Journal of the Polynesian
        Society 73.3:294-301. Wellington.

Keesing, Roger M. (cont.)
1966 Descriptive categories in the analysis of social organization: a rejoinder to Nelson. American Anthropologist 68.2(Part 1):474-476. Menasha.

1967 Statistical models and decision models of social structure: a Kwaio case. Ethnology 6.1:1-16. Pittsburgh.

1968a Step kin, in-laws, and ethnoscience. Ethnology 7.1:59-70. Pittsburgh.

1968b Nonunilineal descent and contextual definition of status: the Kwaio evidence. American Anthropologist 70.1:82-84. Menasha.

1969 On quibblings over squabblings of siblings: new perspectives on kin terms and role behavior. Southwestern Journal of Anthropology 25.3:207-227. Albuquerque.

1970 Shrines, ancestors and cognatic descent. American Anthropologist 72.4:755-775. Menasha.

1971 Descent, residence and cultural codes. Pp. 121-138 in Anthropology in Oceania, essays presented to Ian Hogbin, edited by L. R. Hiatt and C. Jayawardena. Sydney: Angus and Robertson.

Kernan, Keith T.
1965 A transformational analysis of the Kapauku kinship system. Kroeber Anthropology Society Papers 33:71-89. Berkeley.

Kernan, Keith T. and Allan D. Coult
1965 The cross generation relative age criterion of kinship terminology. Southwestern Journal of Anthropology 21.2:148-154. Albuquerque.

Köbben, André J. F.
1969 Classificatory kinship and classificatory status: the Cottica Djuka of Surinam. Man (n.s.)4.2:236-249. London.

Koch, Klaus-Friedrich
1970 Structure and variability in the Jale kinship terminology: a formal analysis. Ethnology 9.3:263-301. Pittsburgh.

Korn, Francis
1971a   Terminology and "structure": the Dieri case.
         Bijdragen tot de Taal-, Land- en Volkenkunde
         127.1:39-81. 's-Gravenhage.

1971b   A question of preferences: the Iatmul case.
         Pp. 99-132 in Rethinking kinship and marri-
         age, (Association of Social Anthropologists
         Monographs, 11), edited by R. Needham.
         London: Tavistock.

Korn, Francis and Rodney Needham
1970   Permutation models and prescriptive systems:
         the Taruau case. Man 5.3:393-420. London.

Kreps, Theodora Charlene
1964   Computer analysis of Uto-aztecan kinship
         systems. 284 pp. Ph.D. dissertation in
         Stanford University, Stanford, Calif.
         (Published by University Microfilms, Ann
         Arbor, Mich.)

Kroeber, A. L.
1909   Classificatory systems of relationship.
         Journal of the Royal Anthropological Insti-
         tute 39.77-84. London.

1917   California kinship systems. University of
         California Publications in American Archae-
         ology and Ethnology 12:339-396. Berkeley.

1919   Kinship in the Philippines. Anthropological
         Papers of the American Museum of Natural
         History 19(Part 3):73-84. New York.

1958   Miao and Chinese kin logic. Studies pre-
         sented to Yuen Ren Chao on his 65th birthday.
         Bulletin of the Institute of History and
         Philology, Academia Sinica 29:640-645.
         Nankang, Taipei, Taiwan.

Kunstadter, Peter
1966   Residential and social organization of the
         Lawa of northern Thailand. Southwestern
         Journal of Anthropology 22:61-84. Albuquer-
         que.

Lamb, Sydney M.
1964   The sememic approach to structural semantics.
         Pp. 57-78 in Transcultural studies in cogni-
         tion, (American Anthropologist 66.3[Part
         2], Special Publication), edited by A. K.
         Romney and R. G. D'Andrade. Menasha.

[1:24]

Lamb, Sydney M. (cont.)
1965   Kinship terminology and linguistic structure.
        Pp. 37-64 in Formal semantic analysis (Ameri-
        can Anthropologist 67.5[Part 2], Special
        Publication), edited by E. A. Hammel.
        Menasha.

Landar, Herbert Jay
1960   Semantic components of Tequistlatec kinship.
        International Journal of American Linguis-
        tics 26.1:72-75. Baltimore.

1962   Fluctuation of forms in Navaho kinship termi-
        nology. American Anthropologist 64.5(Part
        1):985-1000. Menasha.

Lang, Andrew
1903   Social origins. xviii, 207 pp. London:
        Longmans, Green.

Lang, János
1963   The term system of the Groote Eyelandt
        aborigines. Acta Ethnographica 12.(fasc.
        1-2):185-193. Budapest.

1966   A new trend in interpretation of classifica-
        tory systems. Acta Ethnographica 15:167-
        189. Budapest.

1968   Die australischen Terminsysteme. 200 pp.
        Budapest.

Lawrence, W. E.
1937   Alternating generations in Australia. Pp.
        319-354 in Studies in the science of society,
        edited by G. P. Murdock. New Haven: Yale
        University Press.

Leach, Edmund R.
1945   Jingphaw kinship terminology. Journal of
        the Royal Anthropological Institute of
        Great Britain and Ireland 75:59-72. London.
        (Reprinted, see Leach 1961.)

1951   The structural implications of matrilateral
        cross-cousin marriage. Journal of the Royal
        Anthropological Institute of Great Britain
        and Ireland 81.1:23-55. London. (Reprinted,
        see Leach 1961.)

1958   Concerning Trobriand clans and the kinship
        category "tabu." Pp. 120-145 in The develop-

mental cycle in domestic groups, (Cambridge Papers in Social Anthropology, No. 1), edited by J. Goody. Cambridge: Cambridge University Press.

1961   Rethinking anthropology. (London School of Economics Monographs on Social Anthropology, No. 22.) 143 pp. London: Athlone.

1963   Alliance and descent among the Lakher: a reconsideration. Ethnos 28.2-4:237-249. Stockholm.

1966   Classification in social and cultural anthropology, and prehistoric archaeology, a select bibliography. Classification Society Bulletin 1.2:19-26. Leicester, England.

1967   The language of Kachin kinship: reflections on a Tikopia model. Pp. 125-152 in Social organization: essays presented to Raymond Firth, edited by M. Freedman. London: Frank Cass.

1970   Lévi-Strauss. 127 pp. (Fontana Modern Masters Series.) London: Wm. Collins.

1971   More about 'mama' and 'papa.' Pp. 75-98 in Rethinking kinship and marriage, (Association of Social Anthropologists Monographs, 11), edited by R. Needham. London: Tavistock.

Leaf, Murray J.
1971   The Punjabi kinship terminology as a semantic system. American Anthropologist 73.3:545-554. Menasha.

Lehman, F. K.
1970   On Chin and Kachin marriage regulations. Man (n.s.)5.1:118-125. London.

Lévi-Strauss, Claude
1945   L'Analyse structurale en linguistique et en anthropologie. Word 1.1:33-53. New York. (Reprinted 1958 in Anthropologie structurale, by C. Lévi-Strauss. Paris: Plon.)

1949   Les Structures élémentaires de la parenté. Paris: Presses Universitaire de France. (Reprinted 1968, xxx, 591 pp., The Hague

and Paris: Mouton. Translated 1969 by
James Harle Bell and John Richard von
Sturmer, edited by R. Needham, as The
elementary structures of kinship. London:
Eyre and Spottiswoode; Boston: Beacon
Press.)

1951   Language and the analysis of social laws.
        American Anthropologist 53.2:155-163.
        Menasha. (Reprinted 1958 in Anthropologie
        structurale, by C. Lévi-Strauss. Paris:
        Plon.)

1965   The future of kinship studies: the Huxley
        Memorial Lecture, 1965. (Proceedings of the
        Royal Anthropological Institute of Great
        Britain and Ireland 1965.) 22 pp. London.

Liu, Pin-hsiung
    1968   Theory of groups of permutations, matrices
            and kinship: a critique of mathematical
            approaches to prescriptive marriage systems.
            Bulletin of the Institute of Ethnology,
            Academia Sinica 2:29-38. Nankang, Taipei,
            Taiwan.

    1969   Mathematical study of the Murngin system.
            Bulletin of the Institute of Ethnology,
            Academia Sinica 27:25-104. Nankang, Taipei,
            Taiwan.

    1970   Murngin: a mathematical solution. (Insti-
            tute of Ethnography, Academia Sinica, Mono-
            graph Series B, No. 2.) 140 pp. Nankang,
            Taipei, Taiwan.

Livingstone, Frank B.
    1959   A formal analysis of prescriptive marriage
            systems among the Australian aborigines.
            Southwestern Journal of Anthropology 15.4:
            361-372. Albuquerque.

    1965   Mathematical models of marriage systems.
            Man 65:149-152(Art. 146). London.

    1968   The application of structural models to
            marriage systems in anthropology. Pp. 235-
            251 in Game theory in the behavioral sci-
            ences, edited by I. R. Buchler and H. G.
            Nutini. Pittsburgh: University of Pitts-
            burgh Press.

Lizot, Jacques
1971   Remarques sur le vocabulaire de parenté
        yanõmani. L'Homme 11.2:25-38. Paris.

Löffler, Lorenz G.
1960   Patrilateral lineation in transition: the
        kinship system of the Lakher (Mara), Arakan.
        Ethnos 25.1-2:119-150. Stockholm.

1967   Kriterien symmetrischer und asymmetrischer
        allianz-systeme. Bijdragen tot de Taal-,
        Land- en Volkenkunde 123.1(Anthropologica
        IX):125-133. 's-Gravenhage.

Louis, Anne Sutherland
1971   Alliance or descent: the Trumaí Indians of
        Central Brazil. Man (n.s.)6.1:18-29.
        London.

Lounsbury, Floyd G.
1956   A semantic analysis of the Pawnee kinship
        usage. Language 32.1:158-194. Baltimore.

1962   Review of Structure and sentiment, by
        Rodney Needham. American Anthropologist
        64.6:1302-1310. Menasha.

1964a   The structural analysis of kinship semantics.
        Pp. 1073-1093 in Proceedings of the Ninth
        International Congress of Linguists, edited
        by H. G. Lunt. The Hague: Mouton.

1964b   A formal analysis of the Crow and Omaha-type
        kinship terminologies. Pp. 351-393 in
        Explorations in cultural anthropology:
        essays in honor of George Peter Murdock,
        edited by W. H. Goodenough. New York:
        McGraw-Hill.

1965   Another view of the Trobriand kinship cate-
        gories. Pp. 142-185 in Formal semantic
        analysis, (American Anthropologist 67.5
        [Part 2], Special Publication), edited by
        E. A. Hammel. Menasha.

1969   Language and culture. Pp. 3-29 in Language
        and philosophy, edited by S. Hook. New
        York: New York University Press.

Lowie, Robert H.
1928   A note on relationship terminologies.
        American Anthropologist 30:263-267. Menasha.

Lowie, Robert H. (cont.)
    1929   Relationship terms. Encyclopaedia Britan-
            nica, 14th edition, 19:84-89. Chicago.

    1934   The Omaha and Crow kinship terminologies.
            Proceedings of the 24th International
            Congress of Americanists, Hamburg, 1930,
            24:102-108. Hamburg.

Lubbock, John
    1885   On the customs of marriage and systems of
            relationship among the Australians. Jour-
            nal of the Royal Anthropological Institute
            of Great Britain and Ireland 14:292-300.
            London.

Lucich, Peter
    1968   The development of Omaha kinship terminolo-
            gies in three Australian aboriginal tribes
            of the Kimberley Division, Western Australia.
            (Australian Aboriginal Studies 15.) xvi,
            275 pp. Canberra: Australian Institute of
            Aboriginal Studies.

McElhanon, Kenneth A.
    1968   Selepet social organization and kinship.
            Ethnology 7.3:296-304. Pittsburgh.

    1969   Koba kinship terminology. Ethnology 8.3:
            273-277. Pittsburgh.

MacFarlane, Alfred
    1883   Analysis of relationships of consanguinity
            and affinity. Journal of the Royal Anthro-
            pological Institute of Great Britain and
            Ireland 12.1:46-63. London.

MacNeish, June Helm
    1960   Kin terms of Arctic drainage Dene: Hare,
            Slavey, Chipewyan. American Anthropologist
            62.2:279-295. Menasha.

Maddock, Kenneth
    1970   Rethinking the Murngin problem: a review
            article. Oceania 61.2:77-90. Sydney.

Malinowski, Bronislaw
    1929   Kinship. Encyclopaedia Britannica, 14th
            edition, 13:403-409. Chicago.
            (Reprinted 1962, pp. 132-164 in Sex, culture
            and myth, by B. Malinowski. New York:
            Harcourt, Brace, and World.)

1930   Kinship. Man 30:19-29(Art. 17). London.

1963   The family among the Australian aborigines:
(1913)   a sociological study. Introduction by J.
         A. Barnes. xxx, 322 pp. New York: Schock-
         en Books. (Originally published 1913,
         London: University of London Press.)

Maranda, Pierre
1963   Note sur l'élement de parenté. Anthropos
         58.5-6:810-828. Fribourg.

1964   Kinship semantics. Anthropos 59. 3-4:517-
         528. Fribourg.

Mark, Lindy Li
1967   Patrilateral cross-cousin marriage among the
         Magpie Miao: preferential or prescriptive.
         American Anthropologist 69.1:55-62. Menasha.

Marshall, L.
1957   The kin terminology of the !Kung Bushmen.
         Africa 27:1-55. London.

Matthews, G. Hubert
1959   Proto-Siouan kinship terminology. American
         Anthropologist 61.2:252-278. Menasha.

Maybury-Lewis, David
1960a   Parallel descent and the Apinayé anomaly.
         Southwestern Journal of Anthropology 16.2:
         191-216. Albuquerque.

1960b   The analysis of dual organizations: a
         methodological critique. Bijdragen tot de
         Taal-, Land- en Volkenkunde 116.1:17-44.
         's-Gravenhage.

1965a   Durkheim on relationship systems. Journal
         for the Scientific Study of Religion 4.2:
         253-260. Washington.

1965b   Prescriptive marriage systems. Southwestern
         Journal of Anthropology 21.3:207-230.
         Albuquerque.

1967   The Murngin moral. Transactions of the New
         York Academy of Sciences, Series 2, 29.24:
         482-494. New York.

Mayer, Iona
1965a   From kinship to common descent: four

generation genealogies among the Gusii.
Africa 35.4:366-384. London.

Mayer, Iona (cont.)
1965b The nature of kinship relations; the significance of the use of kinship terms among the
Gusii. (Rhodes-Livingstone Papers, No. 37.)
64 pp. Manchester: Manchester University
Press.

Mead, Margaret
1947 The Mountain Arapesh, III. Socio-economic
life. Anthropological Papers of the American Museum of Natural History 40.3:171-232.
New York.

Meggitt, Mervyn J.
1962 Desert people; a study of the Walbiri
aborigines of central Australia. xix, 348
pp. Sydney: Angus and Robertson.

Métais, Pierre
1956 Mariage et équilibre social dans les sociétés
primitives. (Travaux et Mémoires de l'Institut d'Ethnologie, 59.) xi, 545 pp. Paris.

1962 Quelques aspects d'une organisation matri-
moniale néocalédonienne. L'Année Sociologique, Séries III, 12:3-115. Paris.

Metzger, Duane and Gerald E. Williams
1963 A formal ethnographic analysis of Tenejapa
Ladino weddings. American Anthropologist
65.5:1076-1101. Menasha.

Michelson, Truman
1916 Terms of relationship and social organization. Proceedings of the National Academy
of Sciences 2:297-300. Washington.

1917 Remarks on terms of relationships. Journal
of the Washington Academy of Sciences 7:
182-184. Washington.

Miles, Douglas
1971 Ngadu kinship and social change on the
Upper Mentaya. Pp. 211-230 in Anthropology
in Oceania, essays presented to Ian Hogbin,
edited by L. R. Hiatt and C. Jayawardena.
Sydney: Angus and Robertson.

Moore, Sally Falk
1963 Oblique and asymmetrical cross-cousin

marriage and Crow-Omaha terminology.
American Anthropologist 65.2:296-311.
Menasha.

Morgan, Lewis Henry
1868   A conjectural solution of the origin of the
        classificatory system of relationship.
        Proceedings of the American Academy of Arts
        and Sciences 7:436-477. Washington.

1871   Systems of consanguinity and affinity of
        the human family. Smithsonian Contributions
        to Knowledge 17.218. Washington.

Murdock, George Peter
1947   Bifurcate merging, a test of five theories.
        American Anthropologist 49.1:56-69. Menasha.

1949   Social structure. xvii, 387 pp. New York:
        Macmillan.

1959   Cross-language parallels in parental kin
        terms. Anthropological Linguistics 1.9:
        1-5. Bloomington, Ind.

1968   Patterns of sibling terminology. Ethnology
        7.1:1-24. Pittsburgh.

1970   Kin term patterns and their distribution.
        Ethnology 9.2:165-207. Pittsburgh.

Murphy, Robert F.
1967   Tuareg kinship. American Anthropologist
        69.2:163-170. Menasha.

Nayacakalou, R. R.
1955,   The Fijian system of kinship and marriage,
1957   Parts I and II. Journal of the Polynesian
        Society 64:44-55; 66:44-59. Wellington.

Needham, Rodney
1958a   A structural analysis of Purum society.
        American Anthropologist 60.1:75-101.
        Menasha.

1958b   The formal analysis of prescriptive patri-
        lateral cross-cousin marriage. Southwestern
        Journal of Anthropology 14:199-219.
        Albuquerque.

1959   Mourning-terms. Bijdragen tot de Taal-,
        Land- en Volkenkunde 115.1:58-89.
        's-Gravenhage.

Needham, Rodney   (cont.)

1960a   A structural analysis of Aimol society.
Bijdragen tot de Taal-, Land- en Volkenkunde
116.1:81-108.   's-Gravenhage.

1960b   Alliance and classification among the Lamet.
Sociologus 10:97-119.   Berlin.

1960c   Lineal equations in a two-section system:
a problem in the social structure of the
Mota (Banks Islands).   Journal of the Polynesian Society 69.1:23-30.   Wellington.

1960d   Patrilateral prescriptive alliances and the
Ungarinyin.   Southwestern Journal of Anthropology 16.3:274-291.   Albuquerque.

1961   An analytical note on the structure of
Siriono society.   Southwestern Journal of
Anthropology 17.3:239-255.   Albuquerque.

1962a   Genealogy and category in Wikmunkan society.
Ethnology 1.2:223-264.   Pittsburgh.

1962b   Notes on comparative method and prescriptive
alliance.   Bijdragen tot de Taal-, Land en
Volkenkunde 118.1(Anthropologica III):160-
182.   's-Gravenhage.

1962c   Structure and sentiment.   134 pp.   Chicago:
University of Chicago Press.

1963   Introduction.   Pp. vii-xlvii in Primitive
classification, by E. Durkheim and M. Mauss,
translated and edited by R. Needham.   Chicago:
University of Chicago Press.

1964a   Descent, category and alliance in Siriono
society.   Southwestern Journal of Anthropology 20.3:229-240.   Albuquerque.

1964b   The Mota problem and its lessons.   Journal
of the Polynesian Society 73.3:302-314.
Wellington.

1964c   Explanatory notes on prescriptive alliance
and the Purum.   American Anthropologist
66.6(Part 1):1377-1386.   Menasha.

1964d   Death-names and solidarity in Penan society.
Bijdragen tot de Taal-, Land- en Volkenkunde
120.1:58-76.   's-Gravenhage.

1966a   Age, category, and descent. Bijdragen tot
         de Taal-, Land- en Volkenkunde 122.1:1-35.
         's-Gravenhage.

1966b   Comments on the analysis of Purum society.
         American Anthropologist 68.1:171-177.
         Menasha.

1966,   Terminology and alliance: I--Garo, Mang-
1967   garai. Sociologus 16.2:141-157. II--Mapuche;
         conclusions. Sociologus 17.1:39-53. Berlin.

1969   Gurage social classification: formal notes
         on an unusual system. Africa 39.2:153-166.
         London.

1970   Endeh II: test and confirmation. Bijdragen
         tot de Taal-, Land- en Volkenkunde 126:246-
         258. 's-Gravenhage.

Needham, Rodney, editor
1971   Rethinking kinship and marriage. (Associa-
         tion of Social Anthropologists Monographs,
         11.) xi, 276 pp. London: Tavistock.

Nelson, Donna
1966   Reply to Keesing. American Anthropologist
         68.2:476-477. Menasha.

Nerlove, Sara and A. Kimball Romney
1967   Sibling terminology and cross-sex behavior.
         American Anthropologist 69.2:179-187.
         Menasha.

Nimuendajú, Curt and Robert H. Lowie
1937   The dual organizations of the Ramkókamekra
         (Canella) of northern Brazil. American
         Anthropologist 39:565-582. Menasha.

Obayashi, Taryo
1955   The kinship system of the peoples on the
         mainland of Southeast Asia. (In Japanese.)
         440 pp. Tokyo: Tokyo Daigaku Toyo Bunka
         Kenkyosho.

Oberg, Kalervo
1955   Types of social structure among the lowland
         tribes of Central and South America.
         American Anthropologist 57.3(Part 1):472-
         487. Menasha.

Obeyesekere, Gananath
1968   Review of Under the Bo tree: studies in

[1:34]

caste, kinship and marriage in the interior of Ceylon, by Nur Yalman. American Anthropologist 70.4:790-793. Menasha.

Ogan, Eugene
   1966   Nasioi marriage: an essay in model-building. Southwestern Journal of Anthropology 22.2: 172-193. Albuquerque.

Ol'derogge, D. A.
   1961a   Osnovnye cherty èvoljucii sistemov rodstva (The principal traits of the evolution of kinship systems). Sovetskaja ètnografija 6:24-30. Moscow.

   1961b   Several problems in the study of kinship systems. Current Anthropology 2.2:103-107. Chicago.

Opler, Morris Edward
   1936   The kinship systems of the southern Athabaskan-speaking tribes. American Anthropologist 38.4:620-633. Menasha.

   1937   Apache data concerning the relation of kinship terminology to social classification. American Anthropologist 39.2:201-212. Menasha.

Panoff, Michel
   1965   La Terminologie de la parenté en Polynésie: essai d'analyse formelle. L'Homme 4.3-4: 60-87. Paris.

Parsons, Elsie Clews
   1932   The kinship nomenclature of the Pueblo Indians. American Anthropologist 34.3: 377-389. Menasha.

Paulme, Denise
   1970   Filiation et classes d'âge dans le sud de la Côte-d'Ivoire. Pp. 347-369 in Échanges et communications; mélanges offerts à Claude Lévi-Strauss à l'occasion de son 60ème anniversaire, edited by J. Pouillon and P. Maranda. The Hague and Paris: Mouton.

Pelto, Pertti J.
   1966   Cognitive aspects of American kin terms. American Anthropologist 68.1:198-202. Menasha.

182

Philipson, Jürn Jacob
1947   A note on the sociological interpretation
of some Tupí-Guaraní kinship terms. Acta
Americana 5:203-224. Mexico City.

Pospisil, Leopold
1960   The Kapauku Papuans and their kinship organization. Oceania 30.3:188-205. Sydney.

1961   Corrigenda. Oceania 32.1:71. Sydney.

Pospisil, Leopold J. and W. S. Laughlin
1963   Kinship terminology and kindred among the
Nunamuit Eskimo. Ethnology 2.2:180-189.
Pittsburgh.

Pouillon, Jean and Pierre Maranda, editors
1970   Échanges et communications: mélanges
offerts à Claude Lévi-Strauss à l'occasion
de son 60ème anniversaire. 2 vols. 1452 pp.
The Hague and Paris: Mouton.

Powell, H. A.
1969a   Genealogy, residence and kinship in Kiriwina. Man (n.s.)4.2:177-202. London.

1969b   Territory, hierarchy and kinship in Kiriwina. Man (n.s.)4.4:580-604. London.

Radcliffe-Brown, A. R.
1930   A system of notation for relationships.
Man 30:121-122(Art. 93). London.

1930-   The social organization of the Australian
1931   tribes. Oceania 1.1:34-63; 1.2:206-246;
1.3:322-341; 1.4:426-456. Sydney.

1935   Kinship terminologies in California.
American Anthropologist 37.3:530-535.
Menasha.

1941   The study of kinship systems. Journal of
the Royal Anthropological Institute of
Great Britain and Ireland 71.1:1-18.
London. (Reprinted, see Radcliffe-Brown
1952.)

1950   Introduction. Pp. 1-85 in African systems
of kinship and marriage, edited by A. R.
Radcliffe-Brown and D. Forde. London:
Oxford University Press.

1951   Murngin social organization. American

183

[1:36]

Anthropologist 53.1:37-55. Menasha.

Radcliffe-Brown, A. R. (cont.)
1952   Structure and function in primitive society.
        219 pp. Glencoe, Ill.: Free Press. (2d
        edition, 1965.)

1953   Dravidian kinship terminology. Man 53:112
        (Art. 169). London.

Raj, Hilda
1950   Some observations on the classificatory
        system as seen in North India and South
        India. Eastern Anthropologist 4.1:27-31.
        Lucknow.

Reid, Russell M.
1967   Marriage systems and algebraic theory: a
        critique of White's An anatomy of kinship.
        American Anthropologist 60.1:59-74.
        Menasha.

Richard, Philippe and Robert Jaulin, editors
1971   Anthropologie et calcul. 384 pp. Paris:
        Union Générale d'Éditions.

Ridington, Robin
1969   Kin categories versus kin groups: a two-
        section system without sections. Ethnology
        8.4:460-467. Pittsburgh.

Rigby, Peter
1966   Dual symbolic classification among the Gogo
        of central Tanzania. Africa 36.1:1-17.
        London.

1968   Joking relationships, kin categories, and
        clanship among the Gogo. Africa 38.2:133-
        155. London.

Rivère, Peter Gerard
1966   Age: a determinant of social classification.
        Southwestern Journal of Anthropology 22.1:
        43-60. Albuquerque.

Rivers, W. H. R.
1900   A genealogical method of collecting social
        and vital statistics. Journal of the Royal
        Anthropological Institute of Great Britain
        and Ireland 30:74-82. London.

1906   The Todas. xviii, 755 pp. New York:
        Macmillan.

1907   On the origin of the classificatory system
        of relationships. Pp. 309-323 in Anthropo-
        logical essays presented to Edward Burnett
        Tylor, edited by H. Balfour et al. Oxford:
        Clarendon.

1910   The genealogical method of anthropological
        inquiry. Sociological Review 3.1:1-12.
        Keele. (Reprinted, see Rivers 1968.)

1912   A general account of method [and other
        topics]. In sections of Part III, Sociology,
        pp. 108-180, in Notes and queries on anthro-
        pology, 4th edition, edited by B. Freire-
        Marreco and J. L. Myres. London.

1914   Kinship and social organization. vii, 96 pp.
        London: Constable. (Reprinted, see Rivers
        1968.)

1921   Kinship and marriage in India. Man in India
        1.1:6-10. Ranchi.

1968   Kinship and social organization. With
        'Genealogical method of anthropological
        inquiry.' Reprinting of 1910 and 1914
        publications, with commentaries by Raymond
        Firth and David Schneider. (London School
        of Economics Monographs of Social Anthro-
        pology, No. 34.) vi, 116 pp. London:
        Athlone.

Roark, Richard
1961   The mathematics of American cousinship.
        Papers of the Kroeber Anthropological
        Society 24:17-18. Berkeley.

Romney, A. Kimball
1965   Kalmuk Mongol and the classification of
        lineal kinship terminologies. Pp. 127-
        141 in Formal semantic analysis, (American
        Anthropologist 67.5[Part 2], Special Publi-
        cation), edited by E. A. Hammel. Menasha.

1967a   Internal reconstruction of Yuman kinship
        terminology. Pp. 379-386 in Studies in
        southwestern ethnolinguistics, edited by
        D. H. Hymes and W. E. Bittle. The Hague:
        Mouton.

1967b   Kinship and family. Pp. 207-237 in Vol. 6
        of Handbook of Middle American Indians,

[1:38]

edited by R. Wauchope and M. Nash. Austin: University of Texas Press.

Romney, A. Kimball and Roy G. D'Andrade
1964 Cognitive aspects of English kin terms. Pp. 79-98 in Transcultural studies in cognition, (American Anthropologist 66.3[Part 2], Special Publication), edited by A. K. Romney and R. G. D'Andrade. Menasha.

Romney, A. Kimball and Philip J. Epling
1958 A simplified model of Kariera kinship. American Anthropologist 60.1:59-74. Menasha.

Roumeguère-Eberhardt, Jacqueline
1961 Les Dynamismes internes des systèmes de parenté. Cahiers Internationaux de Sociologie 8:95-112. Paris.

Ruel, Malcolm J.
1962 Genealogical concepts or 'category words'? A study of Banyang kinship terminology. Journal of the Royal Anthropological Institute of Great Britain and Ireland 92(Part 2):157-176. London.

Ruhemann, Barbara
1945 A method for analysing classificatory systems. Southwestern Journal of Anthropology 1.4:531-576. Albuquerque.

1967 Purpose and mathematics--a problem in the analysis of classificatory kinship systems. Bijdragen tot de Taal-, Land- en Volkenkunde 123.1:83-124. 's-Gravenhage.

Rygaloff, Alexis
1962 Deux points de nomenclature dans les systèmes chinois de parenté. L'Homme 2.3:53-74. Paris.

Saladin d'Anglure, Bernard
1970 Nom et parenté chez les Esquimaux Tarramiut du Nouveau Québec (Canada). Pp. 1013-1039 in Échanges et communications; mélanges offerts à Claude Lévi-Strauss à l'occasion de son 60ème anniversaire, edited by J. Pouillon and P. Maranda. The Hague and Paris: Mouton.

Saltarelli, M. and M. Durbin
1967 A semantic interpretation of kinship systems. Linguistics 33:87-94. The Hague.

Sanday, Peggy R.
1966   The problem of kinship terms and "psycho-
        logical reality": an information process-
        ing approach. Doctoral dissertation in the
        University of Pittsburgh. Pittsburgh.

1968   The "psychological reality" of American-
        English kinship terms: an information-
        processing approach. American Anthropolo-
        gist 70.3:508-523. Menasha.

Sapir, Edward
1913   A note on reciprocal terms of relationships
        in America. American Anthropologist 15.1:
        132-138. Menasha.

1916   Terms of relationship and the Levirate.
        American Anthropologist 18.3:327-337.
        Menasha.

Scheffler, Harold W.
1967   On scaling kinship terminologies. South-
        western Journal of Anthropology 23.2:159-
        175. Albuquerque.

1969   Kinship and adoption in the northern New
        Hebrides. Pp. 69-89 in Adoption in eastern
        Oceania, edited by V. Carroll. Honolulu:
        University of Hawaii Press.

1970a   The elementary structures of kinship by
        Claude Lévi-Strauss: a review article.
        American Anthropologist 72.2:251-268.
        Menasha.

1970b   Ambrym revisited: a preliminary report.
        Southwestern Journal of Anthropology 26.1:
        52-66. Albuquerque.

1971a   Studies in kinship semantics: a bibliogra-
        phy. 33 pp. New Haven: Department of
        Anthropology, Yale University.

1971b   Some aspects of Australian systems of kin
        classification: a correction. Mankind
        8.1:25-30. Sydney.

1971c   Dravidian-Iroquois: the Melanesian evidence.
        Pp. 231-254 in Anthropology in Oceania,
        essays presented to Ian Hogbin, edited by
        L. R. Hiatt and C. Jayawardena. Sydney:
        Angus and Robertson.

[1:40]

Scheffler, Harold W. and Floyd G. Lounsbury
1971   A study in structural semantics, the Siriono
         kinship system. 260 pp. Englewood Cliffs,
         N. J.: Prentice-Hall.

Schmitz, Carl August
1964   Grundformen der Verwandschaft. 134 pp.
         Basel: Paros.

Schneider, David M.
1965a   American kin terms and terms for kinsmen:
         a critique of Goodenough's componential
         analysis of Yankee kinship terminology.
         Pp. 288-308 in Formal semantic analysis,
         (American Anthropologist 67.5[Part 2],
         Special Publication), edited by E. A.
         Hammel. Menasha.

1965b   Some muddles in the models; or, how the
         system really works. Pp. 25-86 in The
         relevance of models for social anthropology,
         (Association of Social Anthropologists
         Monographs, 1). London: Tavistock.

1967   Descent and filiation as cultural constructs.
         Southwestern Journal of Anthropology 23.1:
         65-73. Albuquerque.

1968a   American kinship: a cultural account. x,
         117 pp. Englewood Cliffs, N. J.: Prentice-
         Hall.

1968b   Rivers and Kroeber in the study of kinship.
         Pp. 7-36 (Commentary) in Kinship and social
         organization, (London School of Economics
         Monograph in Social Anthropology, No. 34),
         by W. H. R. Rivers. London: Athlone.

1969   Kinship, nationality and religion in Ameri-
         can culture: toward a definition of kinship.
         Pp. 116-125 in Forms of symbolic action,
         (Proceedings of the 1969 Annual Spring
         Meeting of the American Ethnological Society),
         edited by R. F. Spencer. Seattle: Univer-
         sity of Washington Press.

1970a   American kin categories. Pp. 370-381 in
         Échanges et communications; mélanges offerts
         à Claude Lévi-Strauss à l'occasion de son
         60ème anniversaire, edited by J. Pouillon
         and P. Maranda. The Hague and Paris:
         Mouton.

188

1970b   What should be included in a vocabulary of
         kinship terms? Proceedings of the VIII
         Congress of Anthropological and Ethnological
         Sciences, Tokyo, 1968, Vol. 2 (Ethnology):
         88-90. Tokyo.

Schneider, David M. and George C. Homans
   1955   Kinship terminology and the American kinship
            system. American Anthropologist 57.6:1194-
            1208. Menasha.

Schneider, David M. and John M. Roberts
   1956   Zuni kin terms. (Laboratory of Anthropology
            Notebook No. 3, Monograph II.)   23 pp.
            Lincoln: University of Nebraska.

Seligman, Brenda Z.
   1923-   Studies in Semitic kinship. Bulletin of
   1924   the School of Oriental and African Studies
            3:51-68; 3:263-279. London.

   1927   Bilateral descent and the formation of
            marriage classes. Journal of the Royal
            Anthropological Institute of Great Britain
            and Ireland 57.2:349-375. London.

   1928   Asymmetry in descent with special reference
            to Pentecost. Journal of the Royal Anthro-
            pological Institute of Great Britain and
            Ireland 58.2:533-558. London.

Service, Elman R.
   1960a   Sociocentric relationship terms and the
            Australian class system. Pp. 416-436 in
            Essays in the science of culture, edited
            by G. E. Dole and R. L. Carneiro. New
            York: Crowell.

   1960b   Kinship terminology and evolution. American
            Anthropologist 62.5:747-763. Menasha.
            (Reprinted 1968, pp. 331-349 in Vol. 2 of
            Readings in anthropology, 2d edition,
            edited by M. H. Fried, New York: Crowell.)

Shapiro, Warren
   1966a   Secondary unions and kinship terminology:
            the case of avuncular marriage. Bijdragen
            tot de Taal-, Land- en Volkenkunde 124.1:
            40-55. 's-Gravenhage.

   1966b   On the classification of bifurcate merging
            systems. Anthropologica 8.1:145-150.
            Ottawa.

189

Shapiro, Warren (cont.)
1967   Relational affiliation in 'unilineal'
        descent systems. Man 2.3:461-463. London.

1968   Kinship and marriage in Siriono society:
        a reexamination. Bijdragen tot de Taal-,
        Land- en Volkenkunde 124.1(Anthropologica
        X):40-55. 's-Gravenhage.

1970   The ethnography of two-section systems.
        Ethnology 9.4:380-389. Pittsburgh.

1971   Patri-groups, patri-categories, and sections
        in Australian aboriginal social classifica-
        tion. Man (n.s.)6.4:590-600. London.

Sider, Karen Blu
1967   Kinship and culture: affinity and the role
        of a father in the Trobriands. Southwestern
        Journal of Anthropology 23.1:90-109.
        Albuquerque.

Silverman, Martin G.
1971   Disconcerting issue: meaning and struggle
        in a Pacific island community. 362 pp.
        Chicago: University of Chicago Press.

Sousberghe, Léon de
1955   Structures de parenté et d'alliance
        d'après les formules Pende; (ba-Pende,
        Congo Belge). (Académie Royale des
        Sciences Coloniales, Classe des Sciences
        Morales et Politiques, Mémoirs 8°[n.s.]5.1
        [Ethnographie].) 93 pp. Brussels.

1963   Nomenclature et structure de parenté des
        Maya du Yucatan d'après les sources
        anciennes (Motul, Beltran). L'Homme 3.2:
        77-112. Paris.

1965   Cousins croisés et descendants: les sys-
        tèmes du Rwanda comparés à ceux du Bas-
        Congo. Africa 35.4:396-420. London.

1966   L'Immutabilité des relations de parenté par
        alliance dans les sociétés matrilinéaires
        du Congo (ex-Belge). L'Homme 6.1:82-94.
        Paris.

1968   Les Unions entre cousins croisés; une
        comparaison des systèmes du Rwanda-Burundi
        avec ceux du Bas-Congo. (Museum Lessianum,

Section Missiologique 50.) 120 pp. Paris: Desclée, de Brouwer.

Southall, Aidan, editor
1971   Kinship, descent, and residence in Madagascar. American Anthropologist 73.1:144-208. Menasha.

Southwold, Martin
1971   Meanings of kinship. Pp. 35-56 in Rethinking kinship and marriage, (Association of Social Anthropologists Monographs, 11), edited by R. Needham. London: Tavistock.

Spier, Leslie
1925   The distribution of kinship systems in North America. University of Washington Publications in Anthropology 1.2:69-88. Seattle.

Spoehr, Alexander
1942   Kinship systems of the Seminole. Field Museum of Natural History Anthropological Series 33.2:31-113. Chicago.

1947   Changing kinship systems. Field Museum of Natural History Anthropological Series 33.4: 155-235. Chicago.

1950   Observations on the study of kinship. American Anthropologist 52.1:1-15. Menasha.

Stevens, Hrolf Vaughan
1902   Namengebung und Heirat bei den Orang Těmiā auf der Halbinsel Malāka. Globus 82.16: 253-257. Braunschweig.

Sturtevant, William C.
1964   Studies in ethnoscience. Pp. 99-131 in Transcultural studies in cognition, (American Anthropologist 66.3[Part 2], Special Publication), edited by A. K. Romney and R. G. D'Andrade. Menasha.

Swanton, John Reed
1916   The terms of relationship of Pentecost Island. American Anthropologist 18.4: 455-465. Menasha.

Swartz, Marc Jerome
1960   Situational determinants of kinship terminology. Southwestern Journal of Anthropology 16.4:393-397. Albuquerque.

[1:44]

Tax, Sol
1955a   The social organization of the Fox Indians.
         Pp. 243-284 in Social anthropology of the
         North American tribes, (enlarged edition),
         edited by F. Eggan. Chicago: University
         of Chicago Press.

1955b   From Lafitau to Radcliffe-Brown: a short
         history of the study of social organization.
         Pp. 445-481 in Social anthropology of North
         American tribes, (enlarged edition), edited
         by F. Eggan. Chicago: University of
         Chicago Press.

Thomas, Northcote Whitridge
1906   Kinship organization and group marriages in
         Australia. xiii, 163 pp. Cambridge:
         Cambridge University Press.

Thomson, Donald F.
1946   Names and naming in the Wik Monkan tribe.
         Journal of the Royal Anthropological Insti-
         tute of Great Britain and Ireland 76(Part
         2):157-167. London.

Titiev, Mischa
1943   The influence of common residence on the
         unilateral classification of kindred.
         American Anthropologist 45.4(Part 1):511-
         530. Menasha.

1956   The importance of space in primitive kinship.
         American Anthropologist 58:854-865. Menasha.

1967   The Hopi use of kinship terms for expressing
         socio-cultural values. Anthropological
         Linguistics 9.5:44-49. Bloomington, Ind.

Tornay, Serge
1969   Essai sur le vocabulaire de parenté des
         Keyo du Kenya. L'Homme 9.2:113-135. Paris.

Tornay, S. and H. Raynaud
1969   Test des triades et parenté: essai methodolo-
         gique sur un example Kalenjin et Kikuyu.
         Mathématiques et Sciences Humaines 7.1:17-34.
         Paris.

Trubachev, O. N.
1959   Istorija slavjanskikh terminov rodstva i
         nekotorykh drevnejshikh terminov
         obshchestvenogo stroja. 212 pp. Moscow:
         USSR Academy of Sciences.

Turner, Paul R. and David L. Olmsted
1966   Tequistlatecan kinship and limitations on
        the choice of spouse. Ethnology 5.3:245-
        250. Pittsburgh.

Tyler, Stephen A.
1965   Koya language morphology and patterns of
        kinship behavior. American Anthropologist
        67.6(Part 1):1428-1440. Menasha.

1966a   Parallel-cross: an evaluation of definitions.
        Southwestern Journal of Anthropology 22.4:
        416-432. Albuquerque.

1966b   Whose kinship reckoning? Comments on Buchler.
        American Anthropologist 68.2(Part 1):513-
        516. Menasha.

1966c   Context and variation in Koya kinship termi-
        nology. American Anthropologist 68.3:693-707.
        Menasha.

1969a   Introduction. Pp. 1-23 in Cognitive anthro-
        pology, edited by S. A. Tyler. New York:
        Holt, Rinehart and Winston.

1969b   The myth of P: epistemology and formal
        analysis. American Anthropologist 71.1:
        71-78. Menasha.

Unwin, Joseph D.
1929   The classification system of relationship.
        Man 29:164(Art. 124). London.

1930   Kinship. Man 30:76(Art. 61). London.

Vincke, Jacques L.
1961   Systemes des termes de parenté. Cahiers
        d'Etudes Africaines 2:271-279. Paris.

Voegelin, Charles F. and Florence M. Voegelin
1970   Cross-cultural typologies and folk taxonomies.
        Pp. 1132-1147 in Échanges et communications;
        mélanges offerts à Claude Lévi-Strauss à
        l'occasion de son 60ème anniversaire, edited
        by J. Pouillon and P. Maranda. The Hague
        and Paris: Mouton.

Wake, Charles Staniland
1879   The origin of the classificatory system of
        relationships used among primitive peoples.
        Journal of the Anthropological Institute of

[1:46]

        Great Britain and Ireland 8:144-179.
        London.

Wake, Charles Staniland (cont.)
   1889   The development of marriage and kinship.
        London: George Redway. (Reprinted 1967,
        edited, with an introduction by Rodney
        Needham, lvi, 510 pp. Chicago: University
        of Chicago Press.)

Wallace, Anthony F. C.
   1962   Culture and cognition.   Science 135.3501:
        351-357. Washington.

   1965   The problem of psychological validity of
        componential analyses. Pp. 229-248 in
        Formal semantic analysis, (American Anthro-
        pologist 67.5[Part 2], Special Publication),
        edited by E. A. Hammel. Menasha.

   1969   Review of American kinship, by David M.
        Schneider. American Anthropologist 71.1:
        100-106. Menasha.

   1970   A relational analysis of American kinship
        terminology. American Anthropologist 72.4:
        841-845. Menasha.

Wallace, Anthony F. C. and John Atkins
   1960   The meaning of kinship terms. American
        Anthropologist 62.1:58-80. Menasha.

Weil, André
   1949   Sur l'étude algébrique de certains types de
        lois de mariage (système Murngin). Pp. 257-
        265 in Les Structures elémentaire de la
        parenté, by C. Lévi-Strauss. Paris: Presses
        Universitaire de France. (Translated 1963
        as "On the algebraic study of certain types
        of marriage laws [Murngin system]" and
        appended to An anatomy of kinship, by H. C.
        White, Englewood Cliffs, N. J.: Prentice-
        Hall. Reprinted 1958; translated 1969, see
        Lévi-Strauss 1949.)

White, Harrison C.
   1963   An anatomy of kinship: mathematical models
        for structures of cumulated roles. 180 pp.
        Englewood Cliffs, N. J.: Prentice-Hall.

White, Leslie A.
   1939   A problem in kinship terminology. American

Anthropologist 41.4:566-573. Menasha.

1958   What is a classificatory kinship term?
        Southwestern Journal of Anthropology 14.4:
        378-385. Albuquerque.

Wicke, Charles R. and Miguel Chase-Sardi
1969   Componential analysis of Chulupi (Ashluslay)
        kinship terminology. Ethnology 8.4:484-493.
        Pittsburgh.

Wilson, Peter J.
1967   Tsimehety kinship and descent. Africa 37.2:
        133-154. London.

Witherspoon, Gary J.
1970   A new look at Navajo social organization.
        American Anthropologist 72.1:55-65. Menasha.

1971   Navajo categories of objects at rest.
        American Anthropologist 73.1:110-127.
        Menasha.

Wouden, F. van
1968   Types of social structure in eastern Indo-
        nesia. Translated by R. Needham from 1935
        edition. Koninklijk Instituut voor Taal-,
        Land- en Volkenkunde, Translation Series,
        No. 11. The Hague: Martinus Nijhoff.

Yalman, Nur
1962   The structure of the Sinhalese kindred: a
        re-examination of the Dravidian terminology.
        American Anthropologist 64.3(Part 1):548-
        575. Menasha.

1967   Under the Bo tree: studies in caste, kin-
        ship, and marriage in the interior of
        Ceylon. xii, 406 pp. Berkeley and Los
        Angeles: University of California Press.

1969   The semantics of kinship in South India and
        Ceylon. Pp. 607-626 in Vol. 5 of Current
        trends in linguistics, edited by T. A.
        Sebeok. The Hague: Mouton.

Young, Philip D.
1970   A structural model of Ngawe marriage.
        Ethnology 9.1:85-95. Pittsburgh.

2. Archeological Classification

[Including references to pertinent archeological works on artifactual and contextual classification problems analogous to and overlapping with those encountered in folk system analysis; cf. 3.]

Arnold, Dean E.
1971   Ethnomineralogy of Ticul, Yucatan potters:
        etics and emics. American Antiquity 36.1:
        20-40. Washington.

Beck, Horace C.
1928   Classification and nomenclature of beads and
        pendants. Archaeologia 77:1-76. Oxford.

Beirne, Daniel Randall
1971   Cultural patterning as revealed by a study
        of pre-Columbian ax and adz hafting in the
        Old and New Worlds. Pp. 139-177 in Man
        across the sea: problems of pre-Columbian
        contacts, edited by C. L. Riley et al.
        Austin and London: University of Texas Press.

Benfer, Robert A.
1967   A design for the study of archaeological
        characteristics. American Anthropologist
        69.6:719-730. Menasha.

Binford, Lewis R.
1963   A proposed attribute list for the description
        and classification of projectile points.
        Pp. 193-221 in Miscellaneous studies in
        typology and classification, (Anthropological
        Papers of the Museum of Anthropology, No. 19.)
        Ann Arbor: University of Michigan.

1965   Archaeological systematics and the study of
        cultural process. American Antiquity 31.2:
        203-210. Salt Lake City.

Binford, Lewis R. and Sally R. Binford
1966   A preliminary analysis of functional varia-
        bility in the Mousterian of Levallois facies.
        American Anthropologist 82.2(Part 2):238-295.
        Menasha.

Binford, Sally R. and Lewis R. Binford, editors
1968   New perspectives in archaeology. 373 pp.
        Chicago: Aldine.

Black, Glenn Albert and Paul Weer
1936   A proposed terminology for shape classifica-
        tion of artifacts. American Antiquity 1.4:
        280-294. Salt Lake City.

Blackwood, Beatrice Mary
1970   The classification of artifacts in the Pitt
        Rivers Museum, Oxford. (Pitt Rivers Museum
        Occasional Papers on Technology No. 11.)
        94 pp. Oxford: Oxford University Press.

Bordaz, Jacques and Victoria Bordaz
1966   A critical examination of data processing in
        archaeology, with an evaluation of a new
        inverted data system. American Antiquity
        31.4:494-501. Salt Lake City.

Bordaz, Victoria von Hagen and Jacques Bordaz
1970   A computer pattern recognition method of
        classification and seriation applied to
        archaeological material. Pp. 229-244 in
        Archéologie et calculateurs, by J.-C.
        Gardin et al. Paris: Éditions du Centre
        National de la Recherche Scientifique.

Bordes, François
1953   Essai de classification des industries
        "moustériennes." Bulletin de la Société
        Préhistorique Française 50:457-466. Paris.

Boser, Renée and Irmgard Müller
1969   Stickerei, Systematik der Stichformen.
        88 pp. Basel: Museum für Völkerkunde.

Braidwood, Robert John
1946a   Artifacts. Pp. 113-120(Art. 12) in Human
        origins: selected readings, Series II,
        2d edition. Chicago: University of
        Chicago Bookstore.

1946b   Terminology in prehistory. Pp. 127-144
        (Art. 14) in Human origins: selected read-
        ings, Series II, 2d edition. Chicago:
        University of Chicago Bookstore.

Brainerd, George W.
1951   The plan of chronological ordering in
        archaeological analysis. American Antiquity
        16.4:301-313. Salt Lake City.

Brew, J. O.
1946   The use and abuse of taxonomy. Pp. 44-66 in
        Archaeology of Alkali Ridge, southeastern

Utah, (Papers of the Peabody Museum of
American Archaeology and Ethnology, Harvard
University No. 21), by J. O. Brew. Cambridge.

Brothwell, Don and A. T. Sandison, editors
1967   Diseases in antiquity: a survey of the
         diseases, injuries and surgery of early
         populations. lxx, 766 pp. Springfield,
         Ill.: C. C. Thomas.

Bruckner, Geraldine
1968   A terminology for describing objects in a
         museum of anthropology. Chapter 11 in
         Museum registration methods, 2d edition,
         revised and edited by D. H. Dudley et al.
         Washington: American Association of
         Museums and Smithsonian Institution.

Buck, P. H., K. P. Emory, H. D. Skinner, and J. F. G.
         Stokes
1930   Terminology for ground stone cutting-implements
         in Polynesia. Journal of the Polynesian
         Society 39.2:174-180. Wellington.

Chang, Kwang-chih
1962   A typology of settlement and community
         patterns in some circumpolar societies.
         Arctic Anthropology 1.1:28-41. Madison,
         Wisc.

1967a   Rethinking archaeology. xiv, 172 pp. New
         York: Random House.

1967b   Major aspects of the interrelationship of
         archaeology and ethnology. Current Anthro-
         pology 8.3:227-248. Utrecht.

Chang, Kwang-chih, editor
1968   Settlement archaeology. ix, 229 pp. Palo
         Alto: National Press.

Chengall, Robert G.
1967   The description of archaeological data in
         computer language. American Antiquity
         32.2:161-167. Salt Lake City.

Clarke, David Leonard
1966   Archaeological classification: symposium on
         the classification of changing phenomena.
         London: The Linnean and Classification
         Societies.

[2:4]

Clarke, David Leonard (cont.)
1968   Analytical archaeology. xx, 684 pp.
          London: Methuen.

1970   Reply to the comments on Analytical
          Archaeology. Norwegian Archaeological
          Review 3:25-32. Oslo.

Coe, Michael D.
1961   Social typology and the tropical forest
          civilizations. Comparative Studies of
          Society and History 4:65-85. The Hague.

Colton, Harold Sellers
1939   Prehistoric cultural units and their rela-
          tionships in northern Arizona. (Museum of
          Northern Arizona, Bulletin 17.) 76 pp.
          Flagstaff.

Colton, Harold Sellers and Lyndon Lane Hargrove
1937   Handbook of northern Arizona pottery wares.
          (Museum of Northern Arizona, Bulletin 11.)
          xiii, 267 pp. Flagstaff.

Deetz, James F.
1965   The dynamics of stylistic change in Arikara
          ceramics. (Illinois Studies in Anthropology
          No. 4.) 111 pp. Urbana: University of
          Illinois Press.

1967   Invitation to archaeology. x, 150 pp.
          Garden City, N. Y.: Natural History Press.

Dembeck, Adeline
1969   Guidebook to man-made textile fibers and
          textured yarns of the world: film-to-yarn
          non-wovens. 3d edition. 345 pp. New York:
          United Piece Dye Works.

Deshayes, Jean
1970   Points de vue subjectifs sur la construction
          d'une typologie. Pp. 2-24 in Archéologie et
          calculateurs, by J.-C. Gardin et al. Paris:
          Éditions du Centre National de la Recherche
          Scientifique.

Dethlefsen, Edwin and James Deetz
1966   Death's heads, cherubs, and willow trees:
          experimental archaeology in colonial
          cemeteries. American Antiquity 31.4:502-
          510. Salt Lake City.

200

Doran, J. E. and F. R. Hodson
1966   A digital computer analysis of palaeolithic
        flint assemblages. Nature 210:688-689.
        London.

Drier, Roy Ward
1939   A new method of sherd classification.
        American Antiquity 5.1:31-35. Menasha.

Driver, Harold E.
1965   Survey of numerical classification in anthro-
        pology. Pp. 301-344 in The use of computers
        in anthropology, edited by D. H. Hymes.
        The Hague: Mouton.

Dunnell, Robert C.
1971a   Systematics in prehistory, x, 214 pp. Lon-
        don: Collier-Macmillan; New York: Free Press.

1971b   Sabloff and Smith's "The importance of both
        analytic and taxonomic classification in the
        type-variety system." American Antiquity
        36.1:115-118. Washington.

Emery, Irene
1966   The primary structures of fabrics, an illus-
        trated classification. xxvi, 339 pp.
        Washington: Textile Museum.

Ford, James A.
1954a   On the concept of types: the type concept
        revisited. American Anthropologist 56.1:
        42-54. Menasha. (See also Ford and Steward.)

1954b   Comment on Statistical techniques for the
        discovery of artifact types, by A. C. Spauld-
        ing. American Antiquity 19.4:390-391.
        Salt Lake City.

1961   In favor of simple typology. American
        Antiquity 27.1:113-114. Salt Lake City.

1962   A quantitative method for deriving cultural
        chronology. Washington: Pan American Union.

Ford, James A. and James B. Griffin
1960   (A proposal for) A conference on pottery
        nomenclature for the Southeastern United
        States. Southeastern Archaeological
        Conference Newsletter 7.1:5-9.

Ford, James A. and Julian H. Steward
1954   On the concept of types. American

[2:6]

Anthropologist 56.1:42-57. Menasha.

Friedrich, Margaret Hardin
1970   Design structure and social interaction:
        archaeological implications of an ethnographic
        analysis. American Antiquity 35.3:332-343.
        Washington.

Fritz, John M. and Fred T. Plog
1970   The nature of archaeological explanation.
        American Antiquity 35.4:405-412. Washington.

Gardin, Jean-Claude
1956   Le Fichier mécanographique de l'outillage.
        Outils en métal de l'âge du bronze, des
        Balkans à l'Indus. 20 pp. Beyrouth:
        Institut Français d'Archéologie de Beyrouth.

1958a   Four codes for the description of artifacts:
        an essay in archeological technique and
        theory. American Anthropologist 60.2:335-
        357. Menasha.

1958b   On the coding of geometrical shapes and other
        representations, with reference to archaeo-
        logical documents. Pp. 889-901 in Vol. 2 of
        Proceedings of the International Conference
        on Scientific Information. Washington:
        National Academy of Sciences, National Re-
        search Council.

1965   On a possible interpretation of componential
        analysis in archeology. Pp. 1-8 in Formal
        semantic analysis, (American Anthropologist
        67.5[Part 2], Special Publication), edited
        by E. A. Hammel. Menasha.

1967   Methods for the descriptive analysis of
        archaeological material. American Antiquity
        32.1:13-30. Salt Lake City.

Gardin, Jean-Claude et al.
1970   Archéologie et calculateurs: problèmes
        sémiologiques et mathématiques: Marseille
        7-12 avril 1969. 371 pp. Paris: Éditions
        du Centre National de la Recherche Scienti-
        fique.

Gifford, James C.
1960   The type-variety method of ceramic classifi-
        cation as an indicator of cultural phenomena.
        American Antiquity 25.3:341-347. Salt Lake
        City.

202

Gilborn, Craig
1968   Pop pedagogy: description, classification,
        interpretation; an analysis of the object.
        Museum News 47.4:12-18. Washington.

Gladwin, Winifred and Harold S.
1930   A method for designation of southwestern
        pottery types. (Gila Pueblo-Medallion
        Papers No. 7.) 3 unnumbered pp. Globe, Ariz.

1934   A method for the designation of cultures and
        their variations. (Medallion Papers No. 15.)
        30 pp. Globe, Ariz.

Gorodzov, V. A.
1933   The typological method in archaeology.
        American Anthropologist 35.1:95-103. Menasha.

Griffin, James B.
1943   Comments on the classification. Pp. 327-341
        in The Fort Ancient aspect, its cultural and
        chronological position in Mississippi Valley
        archaeology, by J. B. Griffin. Ann Arbor:
        University of Michigan Press.

Grillin, J.
1938   A method notation for the description and
        comparison of southwestern pottery sherds
        by formula. American Antiquity 4.1:22-29.
        Menasha.

Guthe, Alfred K.
1954   Some thoughts on pottery types [abstract].
        Eastern States Archaeological Federation
        Bulletin No. 13:9. Harrisburg, Pa.

Hawkes, Christopher
1954   Archaeological theory and method: some
        suggestions from the Old World. American
        Anthropologist 56.2:155-168. Menasha.

Heizer, Robert F.
1958   Classification systems for archaeological
        cultures. Pp. 97-101 in A guide to archaeo-
        logical field methods, edited by R. F.
        Heizer. Palo Alto: National Press.

Heizer, Robert F., editor
1958   A guide to archaeological field methods.
        162 pp. Palo Alto: National Press.

Hodson, F. R., D. G. Kendall, and P. Tăutu, editors
1971   Mathematics in the archaeological and histor-

ical sciences. Proceedings of a conference, Mamaia, Romania, 1970. x, 566 pp. Edinburgh: Edinburgh University Press.

Hodson, F. R., P. H. A. Sneath, and J. E. Doran
1966   Some experiments in the numerical analysis of archaeological data. Biometrika 53.3-4: 311-324. London.

Hole, Frank and Robert F. Heizer
1965   An introduction to prehistoric archeology. x, 306 pp. New York: Holt, Rinehart and Winston.

Hymes, Dell H.
1970a   Comments on Analytical archaeology. Norwegian Archaeological Review 3:16-21. Oslo.

1970b   Linguistic models in archaeology. Pp. 91-118 in Archéologie et calculateurs, by J.-C. Gardin et al. Paris: Édition du Centre National de la Recherche Scientifique.

Ihm, P.
1970   Distance et similitude en taxométrie. Pp. 309-316 in Archéologie et calculateurs, by J.-C. Gardin et al. Paris: Éditions du Centre National de la Recherche Scientifique.

Ives, John Chester
1960   The type concept: a methodological inquiry into archaeological classification. Ph.D. dissertation in Harvard University, Cambridge.

Jaulin, M. B.
1970   Mesure de la ressemblance en archéologie. Pp. 343-355 in Archéologie et calculateurs, by J.-C. Gardin et al. Paris: Éditions du Centre National de la Recherche Scientifique.

Karlgren, Berhard
1936   Yin and Chou in Chinese bronzes. Bulletin of the Museum of Far Eastern Antiquities No. 8: 9-154. Stockholm.

Kidder, Alfred V. and Anna O. Shepard
1936   The pottery of Pecos. Vol. 2. (Papers of the Phillips Academy Southwestern Expedition, No. 7.) Illustration, plates, diagrams. New Haven: Yale University Press.

Kluckhohn, Clyde
1960   The use of typology in anthropological

theory. Pp. 134-140 in Men and cultures, (Selected papers of the Fifth International Congress of Anthropological and Ethnological Sciences, Philadelphia, 1956), edited by A. F. C. Wallace. Philadelphia: University of Pennsylvania Press.

1962   The position of Bc 51. Pp. 74-87 in Culture and behavior: the collected essays of Clyde Kluckhohn, edited by Richard Kluckhohn. New York: Free Press.

Korobkov, I. I.
1964   On the methodology of classifying cores. Soviet Anthropology and Archaeology 2.4: 32-40. New York.

Kovalevskaja, V. B.
1970   Recherches sur les systèmes sémiologiques en archéologie par les méthodes de la théorie de l'information. Pp. 187-190 in Archéologie et calculateurs, by J.-C. Gardin et al. Paris: Éditions du Centre National de la Recherche Scientifique.

Krieger, Alex D.
1944   The typological concept. American Antiquity 9.3:271-288. Salt Lake City.

1960   Archeological typology in theory and practice. Pp. 141-151 in Men and cultures, (Selected papers of the Fifth International Congress of Anthropological and Ethnological Sciences, Philadelphia, 1956), edited by A. F. C. Wallace. Philadelphia: University of Pennsylvania Press.

Kroeber, A. L.
1940   Statistical classification. American Antiquity 6.1:29-44. Salt Lake City.

Leach, Edmund R.
1966   Classification in social and cultural anthropology, and prehistoric archaeology, a select bibliography. Classification Society Bulletin 1.2:19-26. Leicester, England.

Lehmer, Donald Jayne
1951   Robinson's coefficient of agreement--a critique. American Antiquity 16.4:293-301. Salt Lake City.

Lerman, I. C.
 1970   H-classificabilité. Pp. 319-236 in Arché-
         ologie et calculateurs, by J.-C. Gardin et
         al. Paris: Éditions du Centre National de
         la Recherche Scientifique.

Leroi-Gourhan, André
 1970   Observations technologiques sur le rythme
         statuaire. Pp. 658-676 in Échanges et
         communications, edited by J. Pouillon and
         P. Maranda. The Hague and Paris: Mouton.

Loud, Llewellyn L.
 1918   Ethnogeography and archaeology of the Wiyot
         territory. University of California Publica-
         tions in American Archaeology and Ethnology
         14.3:221-436. Berkeley.

McKern, William Carlton
 1939   The midwestern taxonomic method as an aid
         to archaeological culture study. American
         Antiquity 4.4:301-313. Menasha.

 1942   Taxonomy and the direct historical approach.
         American Antiquity 8.2:170-172. Menasha.

MacNeish, Richard S.
 1952   Iroquois pottery types: technique for the
         study of Iroquois prehistory. (National
         Museum of Canada Bulletin No. 124.) 166 pp.
         Ottawa.

Malmer, Mats P.
 1963   Metodproblem inom järnålderns Konsthistoria.
         Acta Archaeologica Lundensia 8.3. Lund.

March, Benjamin
 1934   Standards of pottery description. (Occasion-
         al Contributions from the Museum of Anthro-
         pology of the University of Michigan, No. 3.)
         55 pp. Ann Arbor.

Mason, Otis Tufton
 1904   Aboriginal American basketry: studies in a
         textile art without machinery. Pp. 171-548
         in United States National Museum Report for
         1902. Washington.

Matthews, J.
 1963   Application of matrix analysis to archaeo-
         logical problems. Nature 198.4884:930-934.
         London.

Mayer-Oakes, William J.
1970   Comments on Analytical archaeology. Norwegian
        Archaeological Review 3:12-16. Oslo.

Millier, C. and R. E. Tomassone
1970   Méthodes d'ordination et de classification:
        leur efficacité et leurs limites. Pp. 207-
        226 in Archéologie et calculateurs, by J.-C.
        Gardin et al. Paris: Éditions du Centre
        National de la Recherche Scientifique.

Moberg, Carl-Axel
1970   Comments on Analytical archaeology. Norwegian
        Archaeological Review 3:21-24. Oslo.

Morris, Earl H. and Robert F. Burgh
1941   Anasazi basketry, Basket Maker II through
        Pueblo III, a study based on specimens from
        the San Juan River country. (Carnegie
        Institution of Washington, Publication 533.)
        viii, 66 pp. Washington.

Muller, Jon
1971   Style and culture contact. Pp. 66-78 in
        Man across the sea: problems of pre-Columbian
        contacts, edited by C. L. Riley et al. Austin
        and London: University of Texas Press.

Needham, R. M.
1965   Computer methods for classification and
        grouping. Pp. 345-356 in The use of computers
        in anthropology, edited by D. Hymes. The
        Hague: Mouton.

Phillips, Philip
1959   Application of the Wheat-Gifford-Wasley
        taxonomy to eastern ceramics. American
        Antiquity 24.2:117-125. Salt Lake City.

Phillips, Philip, James A. Ford, and James B. Griffin
1951   Archaeological survey of the lower Mississippi
        alluvial valley 1940-1947. (Papers of the
        Peabody Museum of American Archaeology and
        Ethnology, Harvard University, No. 25.)
        Cambridge.

Phillips, Philip and Gordon Willey
1953   Method and theory in American archaeology.
        American Anthropologist 55.5:615-633. Menasha.

Proulx, Donald A.
1968   Local differences and time differences in
        Nasca pottery. (University of California

Publications in Anthropology 5.) 188 pp.
Berkeley and Los Angeles.

Rands, Robert L.
1961   Elaboration and invention in ceramic traditions. American Antiquity 26.3:331-340.
Salt Lake City.

Régnier, Simon
1970   Non-fécondité du modèle statistique général
de la classification automatique. Pp. 301-
307 in Archéologie et calculateurs, by
J.-C. Gardin et al. Paris: Édition du
Centre National de la Recherche Scientifique.

Renaud, Étienne Bernardeau
1941   Classification and description of Indian
stone artifacts. Gunnison: Colorado
Archaeological Society.

Riley, Carroll L., J. Charles Kelley, Campbell W.
Pennington, and Robert L. Rands, editors
1971   Man across the sea: problems of pre-Columbian
contacts. Austin and London: University of
Texas Press.

Ritchie, William A. and Richard S. MacNeish
1949   The pre-Iroquoian pottery of New York State.
American Antiquity 15.2:97-124. Menasha.

Rouse, Irving
1937   New evidence pertaining to Puerto Rican
prehistory. Proceedings of the National
Academy of Sciences 23.3:182-187.
Washington.

1939   Prehistory in Haiti: a study in method.
(Yale University Publications in Anthropology No. 21.) 202 pp. New Haven.

1944   On the typological method. American Antiquity
10.2:202-204. Menasha.

1952   Porto Rican prehistory: introduction:
excavations the west and north. Scientific
Survey of Porto Rico and the Virgin Islands
18(Part 3):307-460. New York: New York
Academy of Sciences.

1960   The classification of artifacts in archaeology. American Antiquity 25.3:313-323. Salt
Lake City.

1965a   Caribbean ceramics: a study in method and
        theory. Pp. 88-103 in Ceramics and man,
        (Viking Fund Publications in Anthropology,
        No. 41), edited by F. R. Matson. New York:
        Wenner-Gren Foundation for Anthropological
        Research.

1965b   The place of 'peoples' in prehistoric research.
        Journal of the Royal Anthropological Institute
        95(Part 1):1-15. London.

1967   Seriation in archaeology. Pp. 153-195 in
        American historical anthropology: essays in
        honor of Leslie Spier, edited by C. L. Riley
        and W. W. Taylor. Carbondale: Southern
        Illinois University Press.

1970   Comments on Analytical archaeology: classi-
        fication for what? Norwegian Archaeological
        Review 3:4-12. Oslo.

Sabloff, Jeremy A. and Robert E. Smith
1969   The importance of both analytic and taxonomic
        classification in the type-variety system.
        American Antiquity 34.3:278-285. Salt Lake
        City.

Sackett, James R.
1966   Quantitative analysis of Upper Paleolithic
        stone tools. Pp. 356-394 in Recent studies
        in paleoanthropology, (American Anthropolo-
        gist 68.2[Part 2], Special Publication),
        edited by J. D. Clark and F. C. Howell.
        Menasha.

1969   Factor analysis and artifact typology.
        American Anthropologist 71.6:1125-1130.
        Menasha.

Scheans, Daniel J.
1966   A new view of Philippines pottery manufacture.
        Southwestern Journal of Anthropology 22.2:
        206-219. Albuquerque.

Schwartz, Douglas W.
1962   A key to prehistoric Kentucky pottery.
        Transactions of the Kentucky Academy of
        Science 22.3-4:82-85. Lexington.

Sears, William H.
1960   Ceramic systems and eastern archaeology.
        American Antiquity 25.3:324-329. Salt
        Lake City.

[2:14]

Shepard, Anna O.
1956   Ceramics for the archaeologist. (Carnegie
        Institution of Washington Publication 609.)
        xii, 414 pp. Washington.

Sher, J. A.
1970   Un algorithme de classification typologique.
        Pp. 193-203 in Archéologie et calculateurs,
        by J.-C. Gardin et al. Paris: Édition du
        Centre National de la Recherche Scientifique.

Smith, M. W.
1954   Attributes and the discovery of projectile
        point types: with data from the Columbia-
        Fraser region. American Antiquity 20.1:15-
        26. Salt Lake City.

Smith, Robert E., Gordon R. Willey, and James C. Gifford
1960   The type-variety concept as a basis for the
        analysis of Maya pottery. American Antiquity
        25.3:330-340. Salt Lake City.

Smith, Watson
1962   Schools, pots, and potters. American
        Anthropologist 64.6:1165-1177. Menasha.

Sneath, P. H. A.
1968   Goodness of intuitive arrangements into time
        trends based on complex pattern. Systematic
        Zoology 17.3:256-260. Lawrence, Kans.

[Sneath, P. H. A., editor]
1969   Report of a meeting on classification in
        linguistics and archaeology. Classification
        Society Bulletin 2.1:22-28. Leicester,
        England.

Sokal, Robert R.
1966   Numerical taxonomy. Scientific American
        215.6:106-116. New York.

Sonneville-Bordes, Denise de and J. Perrot
1954-   Lexique typologique de paléolithique
1956   supérieur. Bulletin de la Société Préhistor-
        ique Française, (in 4 installments). Paris.

Sparck-Jones, Karen
1970   The evaluation of archaeological classifica-
        tion. Pp. 245-272 in Archéologie et calcula-
        teurs, by J.-C. Gardin et al. Paris:
        Éditions du Centre National de la Recherche
        Scientifique.

Spaulding, Albert C.
1953   Statistical techniques for the discovery of
        artifact types. American Antiquity 18.4:
        305-313. Salt Lake City.

1954   Reply to Ford. American Antiquity 19.4:391-
        393. Salt Lake City.

1960a   The dimensions of archaeology. Pp. 435-456
        in Essays in the science of culture, edited
        by G. E. Dole and R. L. Carneiro. New York:
        Crowell.

1960b   Statistical description and comparison of
        artifact assemblages. Pp. 60-83 in The
        application of quantitative methods in
        archaeology, (Viking Fund Publications in
        Anthropology, 28), edited by R. F. Heizer
        and S. F. Cook. New York: Wenner-Gren
        Foundation for Anthropological Research.

1968   Review of Rethinking archaeology, by Kwang-
        Chih Chang. American Anthropologist 70.3:
        626-628. Menasha.

Sprague, Roderick
1968   A suggested terminology and classification
        for burial description. American Antiquity
        33.4:479-485. Salt Lake City.

Steensberg, Axel
1966   A classification of ploughing implements before
        c. 1000 A.D. A functional outline. 19 pp.
        Lyngby, Denmark: International Secretariat
        for Research on the History of Agricultural
        Implements.

Steward, Julian H.
1954   On the concept of types: types of types.
        American Anthropologist 56.1:54-57. Menasha.
        (See also Ford and Steward.)

Streuver, Stuart
1971   Comments on archaeological data, require-
        ments and research strategy. American
        Antiquity 36.1:9-19. Washington.

Taylor, Walter W.
1948   A study of archaeology. (American Anthropo-
        logical Association Memoir 69.) 256 pp. Menasha.

Taylor, Walter W., editor
1957   The identification of non-artifactual

archaeological materials. (National Academy of Sciences, National Research Council, Publication No. 565.) Washington.

Thompson, Raymond H.
1957   Modern Yucatan Maya pottery. (Memoirs of the Society for American Archaeology, No. 15.) 157 pp. Menasha.

Trigger, Bruce G.
1967   Settlement archaeology, its goals and promise. American Antiquity 32.2:149-160. Salt Lake City.

Tugby, Donald J.
1958   A typological analysis of axes and choppers from southeast Australia. American Antiquity 24.1:24-34. Salt Lake City.

1965   Archaeological objectives and statistical methods: a frontier in archaeology. American Antiquity 31.1:1-16. Salt Lake City.

Vanstone, James W.
1971   Historic settlement patterns: the Nashagak River region, Alaska. (Fieldiana: Anthropology, Vol. 61.) 149 pp. Chicago: Field Museum of Natural History.

Vega, W. F. de la
1970   Quelques propriétés des hiérarchies de classification. Pp. 329-342 in Archéologie et calculateurs, by J.-C. Gardin et al. Paris: Éditions du Centre National de la Recherche Scientifique.

Wheat, Joe Ben et al.
1958   Ceramic variety, type cluster, and ceramic system in southwestern pottery analysis. American Antiquity 24.1:34-47. Salt Lake City.

White, Anta M., Lewis R. Binford, and Mark L. Papworth
1963   Miscellaneous studies in typology and classification. (Anthropological Papers of the Museum of Anthropology, No. 19.) 221 pp. Ann Arbor: University of Michigan.

Whiteford, Andrew Hunter
1947   Description for artifact analysis. American Antiquity 12.4:226-238. Menasha.

Willey, Gordon R.
1956   An archaeological classification of culture
        contact situations. (Society for American
        Archaeology, Memoir No. 11.) 30 pp. Beloit.

Willey, Gordon R. and Philip Phillips
1958   Method and theory in American archaeology.
        xi, 270 pp. Chicago: University of Chicago
        Press.

Williams, Stephen
1962   Ceramic classification (Session II).
        Proceedings of the Southeastern Archaeo-
        logical Conference 8:24-62. Athens, Georgia.

3. Anthropological Classification

[Including references to interactional, technological, and comparative aspects of classification in social and cultural anthropology.
Cf. 0., 1., and 2.]

Aarne, Antti
 1971   The types of the folk-tale: a classification
 (1928) and bibliography. Translated and enlarged
         by Stith Thompson. 279 pp. New York: Burt
         Franklin. (Originally published 1928.)

Albisetti, César and Ângelo Jayme Venturelli
 1962,   Enciclopédia Bororo. Vols. 1, 2. (Museu
 1969   Dom Bosço Publication Nos. 1, 2.) Vol. 1,
         Vocabulários e etnografia, 1047 pp.; vol. 2,
         Lendase antropónimos, 1269 pp. Campo Grande,
         Mato Grosso, Brazil.

Altmann, G. and A. Riška
 1966   Towards a typology of courtesy in language.
         Anthropological Linguistics 8.1:1-10.
         Bloomington, Ind.

Anderson, Johannes
 1942   Maori place-names, also personal names and
         names of colour, weapons, and natural
         objects. (Polynesian Society, Memoir No.
         20.) xi, 494 pp. Wellington.

Antoun, Richard Taft
 1968   On the significance of names in an Arab
         village. Ethnology 7.2:158-170. Pittsburgh.

Appell, George N. and Robert Harrison
 1969   Ethnographic classification of the Dusun-
         speaking peoples of northern Borneo.
         Ethnology 8.2:212-227. Pittsburgh.

Ardener, Edwin
 1971   Introductory essay: social anthropology and
         language. Pp. ix-ci in Social anthropology
         and language, edited by E. Ardener. London:
         Tavistock.

Ardener, Edwin, editor
 1971   Social anthropology and language. (Associa-
         tion of Social Anthropologists Monographs,
         10.) ci, 318 pp. London: Tavistock.

Ashley, Clifford W.
1944   The Ashley book of knots. x, 620 pp.
        Garden City, N. Y.: Doubleday.

Ashley, Leonard R. N.
1968   Scoff lore: an introduction to British
        words for food and drink. Names 16.3:238-
        272. Potsdam, N. Y.

Balfet, Hélène
1952   La Vannerie: essai de classification.
        L'Anthropologie 56.3-4:259-280. Paris.

1957   Basketry: a proposed classification.
        Translated by M. A. Baumhoff. Pp. 1-21 in
        Reports of the University of California
        Archaeological Survey, No. 37; Papers on
        California Archaeology, No. 47. Berkeley.

Barker, Roger G. and Herbert F. Wright
1954   Midwest and its children: the psychological
        ecology of an American town. viii, 532 pp.
        Evanston, Ill.: Row, Peterson.

Barrett, Samuel Alfred
1908   Pomo Indian basketry. University of
        California Publications in American
        Archaeology and Ethnology 5.3:133-308.
        Berkeley.

1910   The material culture of the Klamath Lake and
        Modoc Indians of northeastern California and
        southern Oregon. University of California
        Publications in American Archaeology and
        Ethnology 7.4:239-292. Berkeley.

1952   Material aspects of Pomo culture. (Bulletins
        of the Public Museum of the City of Milwaukee,
        No. 22.) 508 pp. Milwaukee.

Barrett, Samuel Alfred and Edward Winslow Gifford
1933   Miwok material culture. Bulletins of the
        Public Museum of the City of Milwaukee
        2.4:117-376. Milwaukee.

Barth, Fredrik
1964   Ethnic processes on the Pathan-Baluch
        boundary. In Indo-Iranica: mélanges
        présentes à Georg Morgenstierne à l'occasion
        de son soixantedixième anniversaire.
        Wiesbaden: Harrassowitz.

1966   Anthropological models and social reality. (The Second Royal Society Nuffield Lecture.) Proceedings of the Royal Society, B, 165: 20-34. London.

Barth, Fredrik, editor
1969   Ethnic groups and boundaries: the social organization of culture difference. 153 pp. Bergen-Oslo: Universitets Forlaget; London: Allen and Unwin.

Barthes, Roland
1967   Système de la mode. 327 pp. Paris: Éditions du Seuil.

Bascom, William Russell
1966   Two studies of Ifa divination. I. Odu Ifa: the names of the signs. Africa 36.4:408-421. London.

Basso, Keith H.
1967   Semantic aspects of linguistic acculturation. American Anthropologist 69.5:471-477. Menasha.

1970   To give up on words: silence in western Apache culture. Southwestern Journal of Anthropology 26.3:213-230. Albuquerque.

Beattie, John
1968   Aspects of Nyoro symbolism. Africa 38.4: 413-442. London.

Beck, Horace C.
1928   Classification and nomenclature of beads and pendants. Archaeologia 77:1-76. Oxford.

Beidelman, Thomas O.
1964   Pig (Guluwe): an essay on Ngulu sexual symbolism and ceremony. Southwestern Journal of Anthropology 20.4:359-392. Albuquerque.

1966   The ox and Nuer sacrifice: some Freudian hypotheses about Nuer symbolism. Man 1.4: 453-467. London.

1968   Some Nuer notions of nakedness, nudity, and sexuality. Africa 38.2:113-132. London.

Benjamin, Geoffrey
1968   Temiar personal names. Bijdragen tot de Taal-, Land- en Volkenkunde 124.1:99-134. 's-Gravenhage.

[3:4]

Benveniste, Émile
1969   Le Vocabulaire des institutions indo-
        européennes. 2 vols. Vol. 1., Économie,
        parenté, société, 376 pp.; Vol. 2., Pouvoir,
        droit, religion, 340 pp. Paris: Les
        Éditions de Minuit.

Berg, Gösta
1966   Die Merkbücher auf Gotland. Folk-Liv
        30:48-62. Stockholm.

Berliner, Joseph S.
1962   The feet of the natives are large: an essay
        on anthropology by an economist. Current
        Anthropology 3.1:47-77. Chicago.

Berreman, Gerald D.
1966   Anemic and emetic analyses in social anthro-
        pology. American Anthropologist 68.2:346-
        354. Menasha.

Béteille, André
1967   Race and descent as social categories in
        India. Daedalus 96.2:444-463. Cambridge,
        Mass.

Bialor, Perry A.
1967   What's in a name? Aspects of the social
        organization of a Greek farming community
        related to naming customs. Kroeber
        Anthropological Society Special Publications
        1:95-108. Berkeley.

Birdwhistell, Ray L.
1952   Introduction to kinesics: an annotation
        system for analysis of body motion and
        gesture. 75 pp. Louisville: University
        of Kentucky.

Birnbaum, Eleazar
1968   Ottoman Turkish names: the choice of entry
        words for alphabetical listing. Journal of
        the American Oriental Society 88.2:228-238.
        New Haven.

Black, Mary B.
1963   On formal ethnographic procedures. American
        Anthropologist 65.6:1347-1351. Menasha.

Black, Mary and Duane Metzger
1965   Ethnographic description and the study of
        law. Pp. 141-165 in The ethnography of law,

(American Anthropologist 67.6[Part 2],
Special Publication), edited by L. Nader.
Menasha.

Blackwood, Beatrice Mary
1970   The classification of artifacts in the Pitt
        Rivers Museum, Oxford. (Pitt Rivers Museum
        Occasional Papers on Technology, No. 11.)
        94 pp. Oxford: Oxford University Press.

Blaut, James M.
1970   Geographic models of imperialism. Antipode:
        A Radical Journal of Geography 2.1:65-85.
        Worcester, Mass.

Boas, Franz
1887   Museums of ethnology and their classifica-
        tion. Science 3:587-589. Washington.

1902   The ethnological significance of esoteric
        doctrines. Science 16:872. Washington.

Bock, Philip K.
1964   Social structure and language structure.
        Southwestern Journal of Anthropology 20.4:
        393-403. Albuquerque.

Boddewyn, J.
1967   The names of U. S. industrial corporations:
        a study in change. Names 15.1:39-52.
        Potsdam, N. Y.

Bohannan, Paul J.
1969   Ethnography and comparison in legal anthro-
        pology. Pp. 401-418 in Law in culture and
        society, edited by L. Nader. Chicago:
        Aldine.

Boser, Renée and Irmgard Müller
1969   Stickerei, Systematik der Stichformen.
        88 pp. Basel: Museum für Völkerkunde.

Bouissac, Paul A. R.
1970   The circus as a multimedia language.
        Language Sciences 11:1-7. Bloomington, Ind.

[Brand, Stewart, editor]
1971   The last whole earth catalog: access to
        tools. 448 pp. Menlo Park, Calif.:
        Portola Institute.

[3:6]

Brandenstein, Carl Georg von
  1970   The meaning of section and section names.
        Oceania 41.1:39-49. Sydney.

Bright, William
  1963   Language and music: areas for cooperation.
        Ethnomusicology 7.1:26-32. Middletown, Conn.

  1968   Toward a cultural grammar. Pp. 20-29 in
        Indian linguistics, Vol. 29, (Katre Felici-
        tation Volume, Part 1), edited by A. M.
        Ghatage, et al. Poona: Deccan College,
        Linguistic Society of India.

Bright, William, editor
  1966   Sociolinguistics. Proceedings of the UCLA
        Sociolinguistics Conference, 1964. (Janua
        Linguarum, Series Maior 20.) 324 pp. Paris
        and The Hague: Mouton.

Bruckner, Geraldine
  1968   A terminology for describing objects in a
        museum of anthropology. Chapter 11 in
        Museum registration methods, 2d edition,
        revised, edited by D. H. Dudley et al.
        Washington: American Association of Museums
        and Smithsonian Institution.

Brunvand, Jan Harold
  1962   A note on names for cars. Names 10.4:279-
        284. Youngstown, Ohio.

Buchler, Ira R.
  1966   Sémantique descriptive des catégories
        religieuses nuer. L'Homme 6.4:35-58. Paris.

Buck, Peter H. (Te Rangi Hiroa)
  1930   Samoan material culture. (Bernice P. Bishop
        Museum Bulletin, No. 75.) Honolulu.

  1944   Arts and crafts of the Cook Islands.
        (Bernice P. Bishop Museum Bulletin, No. 179.)
        533 pp. Honolulu.

Budge, Sir Ernest Alfred Thompson Wallis
  1930   Amulets and superstitions. xxxix, 543 pp.
        London: Oxford University Press.

Bukofzer, Manfred
  1942   Speculative thinking in medieval music.
        Speculum 17.2:165-180. Cambridge, Mass.

Bunzel, Ruth L.
1929   The Pueblo potter: a study of creative
        imagination in primitive art. (Columbia
        University Contributions to Anthropology,
        No. 8.) xii, 134 pp. New York.

Burling, Robbins
1965   How to choose a Burmese numeral classifier.
        Pp. 243-264 in Context and meaning in cul-
        tural anthropology, edited by M. E. Spiro.
        New York: Free Press; London: Collier-
        Macmillan.

1970   Man's many voices: language in its cultural
        context. xi, 222 pp. New York: Holt,
        Rinehart and Winston.

Cafagna, Albert Carl
1960   A formal analysis of definitions of 'culture.'
        Pp. 111-132 in Essays in the science of
        culture, edited by G. E. Dole and R. L.
        Carneiro. New York: Crowell.

Calame-Griaule, Geneviève
1965   Ethnologie et langage: la parole chez les
        Dogon. 589 pp. Paris: Gallimard.

Cancian, Frank
1963   Informant error and native prestige ranking
        in Zinacantan. American Anthropologist
        65.3:1068-1075. Menasha.

Carvalho Neto, Paulo
1956   Teoria do tabú simbólico. Un ensaio de
        folklore psicoanalitico. Pp. 311-316 in
        Estudios Antropológicos Publicados en
        Homenaje al Doctor Manuel Gamio. Mexico
        City: Universidad Nacional Autónoma de
        México y Sociedad Mexicana de Antropología.

Cassidy, Frederic G. and David DeCamp
1966   Names for an albino among Jamaican Negroes.
        Names 14.3:129-133. Potsdam, N. Y.

Casson, Lionel
1956   Fore-and-aft sails in the ancient world.
        Mariners' Mirror 42.1:3-5. London.

Castañeda, Carlos
1968   The teachings of Don Juan: a Yaqui way of
        knowledge. viii, 196 pp. Berkeley:
        University of California Press.

[3:8]

Chang, Kwang-chih
 1962 A typology of settlement and community
   patterns in some circumpolar societies.
   Arctic Anthropology 1.1:28-41. Madison,
   Wisc.

Chisholm, M.
 1964 Problems in the classification and use of
   the farming type region. Transactions of
   the Institute of British Geographers
   35:91-103. London.

Circourel, Aaron V.
 1964 Method and measurement in sociology. viii,
   247 pp. Glencoe, Ill.: Free Press.

Coe, Michael D.
 1961 Social typology and the tropical forest
   civilizations. Comparative Studies of
   Society and History 4:65-85. The Hague.

Cohen, Rosalie, Gerd Fraenkel, and John Brewer
 1968 Implications for 'culture conflict' from a
   semantic feature analysis of the lexicon of
   the hard core poor. Linguistics 44:11-21.
   The Hague.

Cohen, Yehudi A.
 1969 Social boundary systems. Current Anthropology 10.1:103-126. Glasgow.

Colby, Benjamin N.
 1966a The analysis of culture content and the
   patterning of narrative concern in texts.
   American Anthropologist 68.2:374-388.
   Menasha.

 1966b Cultural patterns in narrative. Science
   151.3712:793-798. Washington.

Cole, Michael, John Gay, Joseph A. Glick, Donald W.
   Sharp, et al.
 1971 The cultural context of learning and thinking,
   an exploration in experimental anthropology.
   304 pp. New York: Basic Books.

Collier, George A. and Victoria R. Bricker
 1970 Nicknames and social structures in Zinacantan.
   American Anthropologist 72.2:289-302. Menasha.

Conant, Francis P.
 1965 Korok: a variable unit of physical and
   social space among the Pokot of east Africa.

American Anthropologist 67.2:429-434. Menasha.

Condominas, Georges
1957   Nous avons mangé la forêt de la Pierre-Génie Gôo. 495 pp. Paris: Mercure de France.

Conklin, Harold C.
1953a   Buhíd pottery. University of Manila Journal of East Asiatic Studies 3.1:1-12. Manila.

1953b   Hanunóo-English vocabulary. (University of California Publications in Linguistics, Vol. 9.) 290 pp. Berkeley and Los Angeles.

1956   Tagalog speech disguise. Language 32.1: 136-139. Baltimore.

1957   Hanunóo agriculture, a report on an integral system of shifting cultivation in the Philippines. (FAO Forestry Development Paper, No. 12.) xii, 209 pp. Rome: Food and Agriculture Organization of the United Nations.

1959   Linguistic play in its cultural context. Language 35.4:631-636. Baltimore.

1961   The study of shifting cultivation. Current Anthropology 2.1:27-61, outline, bibliog. Chicago.

1967   Some aspects of ethnographic research in Ifugao. Transactions of the New York Academy of Sciences, Series 2, 30.1:99-121. New York.

1968   Ethnography. International Encyclopedia of the Social Sciences 5:172-179. New York: Macmillan and Free Press.

Conklin, Harold C. and William C. Sturtevant
1953   Seneca singing tools at Coldspring Longhouse: musical instruments of the modern Iroquois. Proceedings of the American Philosophical Society 97.3:262-290. Philadelphia.

Coppet, Daniel de
1970   Cycles de meurtres et cycles funéraires. Esquisse de deux structures d'échange. Pp. 759-781 in Échanges et communications, edited by J. Pouillon and P. Maranda. The Hague and Paris: Mouton.

[3:10]

Coulborn, Rushton
  1969   A paradigm for comparative history? Current
          Anthropology 10.2-3:175-178. Glasgow.

Cowan, George M.
  1946   Mazateco house building. Southwestern
          Journal of Anthropology 2.4:375-390.
          Albuquerque.

Crumrine, Lynne S. and N. Ross Crumrine
  1970   Ritual service and blood sacrifice as
          mediating binary oppositions: a structural
          analysis of several Mayo myths and rituals.
          Journal of American Folklore 83.327:69-76.
          Austin.

Cunningham, Clark E.
  1964   Order in the Atoni house. Bijdragen tot de
          Taal-, Land- en Volkenkunde 120.1:34-68.
          's-Gravenhage.

  1965   Order and change in an Atoni diarchy.
          Southwestern Journal of Anthropology
          21.4:359-382. Albuquerque.

Danzel, Theodor Wilhelm
  1967   Ethnologische Kulturkunde. Versuch einer
          universalen Systematik der Kulturwissen-
          schaften. 1119 pp. Hamburg: Christans.

Davidson, Daniel S.
  1941   Aboriginal Australian string figures.
          Proceedings of the American Philosophical
          Society 84.6:793-901. Philadelphia.

  1953   Snowshoes. (American Philosophical Society,
          Memoir No. 6.) x, 207 pp. Philadelphia.

Dawson, Lawrence and James Deetz
  1964   Chumash Indian art. 16 pp., + 14 plates.
          Santa Barbara: The Art Gallery, University
          of California, Santa Barbara.

  1965   A corpus of Chumash basketry. Archaeologi-
          cal Survey Annual Report 7:197-212, + 31
          plates. Los Angeles.

Dembeck, Adeline
  1969   Guidebook to man-made textile fibers and
          textured yarns of the world: film-to-yarn
          non-wovens. 3d edition. 345 pp. New York:
          United Piece Dye Works.

Dentan, Robert K.
1970   Labels and rituals in Semai classification.
        Ethnology 9.1:16-25. Pittsburgh.

Deutsch, Karl
1966   On theories, taxonomies, and models as
        communication codes for organizing informa-
        tion. Behavioral Science 11.1:1-17. Ann
        Arbor.

Diamond, Sydney G. and Muriel Dimen Schein
1966   The waste collectors. iv, 46 pp. New York:
        Columbia University Department of Anthropology.

Dieterlen, Germaine
1970   La Serrure et sa clef (Dogon, Mali). Pp. 7-
        28 in Échanges et communications, edited by
        J. Pouillon and P. Maranda. The Hague and
        Paris: Mouton.

Dorian, Nancy C.
1970   A substitute name system in the Scottish
        highlands. American Anthropologist 72.2:
        303-319. Menasha.

Douglas, Mary Tew
1966   Purity and danger. An analysis of the
        concepts of pollution and taboo. 179 pp.
        London: Routledge and Kegan Paul.

1968a   Dogon culture--profane and arcane. Africa
        38.1:16-25. London.

1968b   The social control of cognition: some
        factors in joke perception. Man (n.s.)3.3:
        361-376. London.

Driver, Harold E.
1941   Culture element distribution: XVI. Girls
        puberty rites in western North America.
        University of California Anthropological
        Records 6.2:21-90. Berkeley.

1965   Survey of numerical classification in
        anthropology. Pp. 301-344 in The use of
        computers in anthropology, edited by D.
        Hymes. The Hague: Mouton.

Driver, Harold E. and A. L. Kroeber
1932   Quantitative expression of cultural rela-
        tionship. University of California Publica-
        tions in American Archaeology and Ethnology
        31:211-256. Berkeley.

Driver, Harold E. and Karl F. Schussler
1957   Factor analysis of ethnographic data.
        American Anthropologist 59.4:655-663.
        Menasha.

Dubb, Allie A.
1966   Red and school: a quantitative approach.
        Africa 36.3:292-302. London.

Dunăre, Nicolas
1964-   Les Motifs ornementaux dans l'art populaire
1965   roumain. L'Ethnographie 58-59:12-25. Paris.

Duncan, Hugh Dalziel
1962   Communication and social order. 475 pp.
        New York: Bedminster Press.

1969   Symbols and social theory. 334 pp. Oxford:
        Oxford University Press.

Dundes, Alan
1962   From etic to emic units in the structural
        study of folktales. Journal of American
        Folklore 75.296:95-105. Richmond, Va.

1969   Thinking ahead: a folkloristic reflection
        of the future orientation in American world
        view. Anthropological Quarterly 42.2:53-72.
        Washington.

Durkheim, Emile and Marcel Mauss
1903   De quelques formes primitives de classifica-
        tion; contribution à l'étude des représenta-
        tions collectives. L'Année Sociologique
        6:1-72. Paris.

1963   Primitive classification. Translated and
        edited, with an introduction by Rodney
        Needham. xlvii, 96 pp. Chicago: Universi-
        ty of Chicago Press.

Dyen, Isidore
1960   Comment on Leach's The frontiers of "Burma."
        Comparative Studies in Society and History
        3.1:69-73. The Hague.

Eberhard, Wolfram
1968   On some Chinese terms of abuse. Asian
        Folklore Studies 27.1:25-40. Tokyo.

Ehrmann, Jacques, editor
1970   Structuralism. 264 pp. Garden City, N. Y.:

Anchor Books. (Originally printed 1966, Yale French Studies 36-37, New Haven.)

Ekvall, Robert B.
1959   Significance of thirteen as a symbolic num-
        ber in Tibetan and Mongolian cultures.
        Journal of the American Oriental Society
        79.3:188-192. New Haven.

Elkin, Adolphus Peter
1969   Elements of Australian aboriginal philosophy.
        Oceania 40.2:85-98. Sydney.

Ellis, Catherine J.
1969   Structure and significance in aboriginal
        song. Mankind 7.1:3-14. Sydney.

Ember, Melvin
1970   Taxonomy in comparative studies. Pp. 697-
        706 in A handbook of method in cultural
        anthropology, edited by R. Naroll and
        R. Cohen. Garden City, N. Y.: Natural
        History Press.

Emery, Irene
1966   The primary structures of fabrics: an
        illustrated classification. xxvi, 339 pp.
        Washington: Textile Museum.

Evans-Pritchard, E. E.
1948   Nuer modes of address. Ugundu Journal
        12:166-171. Kampala. (Reprinted 1964,
        pp. 221-227 in Language in culture and
        society, edited by D. Hymes. New York:
        Harper and Row.)

1966   Twins, birds and vegetables. Man (n.s.)
        1.1:398. London.

1970   Comment on Twins, birds, etc., by James
        Littlejohn. Bijdragen tot de Taal-, Land-
        en Volkenkunde 126.1:109-113. 's-Gravenhage.

Eyde, David B.
1969   On Tikopia social space. Bijdragen tot de
        Taal-, Land- en Volkenkunde 125.1:40-70.
        's-Gravenhage.

Farfán, Joseph Mario B.
1957   Onomastica de vehículos. Folklore
        Americano 5:140-154. Lima.

[3:14]

Faris, James C.
1968   Validation in ethnographical description:
the lexicon of 'occasions' in Cat Harbour.
Man (n.s.)3.1:111-124. London.

Felton, Gary S.
1968   Stimulus implications of television soap
opera names. Names 16.2:130-133. Potsdam,
N. Y.

Fenton, William N.
1941   Masked medicine societies of the Iroquois.
Pp. 397-430 in Smithsonian Institution
Annual Report for 1940. Washington.

1956   Some questions of classification, typology,
and style raised by Iroquois masks. Transactions of the New York Academy of Sciences,
Series 2, 18.4:347-357. New York.

Firth, Raymond
1966a   The meaning of pali in Tikopia. Pp. 96-115
in In memory of J. R. Firth, edited by C. E.
Bazell et al. London: Longmans.

1966b   Twins, birds and vegetables: problems of
identification in primitive religious thought.
Man (n.s.)1.1:1-17. London.

1967   Twins, birds and vegetables. Man (n.s.)2.1:
129-130. London.

1969   Tikopia social space--a commentary.
Bijdragen tot de Taal-, Land- en Volkenkunde
125.1:64-70. 's-Gravenhage.

1970   Postures and gestures of respect. Pp. 188-
209 in Échanges et communications, edited by
J. Pouillon and P. Maranda. The Hague and
Paris: Mouton.

Fischer, John L.
1958a   The classification of residence in censuses.
American Anthropologist 60.3:508-517. Menasha.

1958b   Social influences on the choice of a linguistic variant. Word 14.1:47-56. New York.

1960   Sequence and structure in folktales. Pp. 442-
446 in Men and cultures, (Selected papers of
the Fifth International Congress of Anthropological and Ethnological Sciences, Philadelphia

228

1956), edited by A. F. C. Wallace. Philadelphia: University of Pennsylvania Press.

1961 Art styles as cultural cognitive maps. American Anthropologist 63.1:79-93. Menasha.

1963a Linguistic class-indicators. Current Anthropology 4.1:116. Chicago.

1963b Sociopsychological analysis of folklore. Current Anthropology 4.3:235-295. Chicago.

Fishman, Joshua A.
1965 Who speaks what language to whom and when. La Linguistique 1.1:67-88. Paris.

Ford, Clellan S.
1937 A sample comparative analysis of material culture. Pp. 225-246 in Studies in the science of society presented to Albert Galloway Keller, edited by G. P. Murdock. New Haven: Yale University Press.

1970 Human Relations Area Files: 1949-1969; a twenty-year report. Behavior Science Notes 5.1:1-61. New Haven.

1971 The development of the Outline of cultural materials. Behavior Science Notes 6.3: 173-185. New Haven.

Ford, James A.
1954 On the concept of types: the type concept revisited. American Anthropologist 56.1: 42-54. Menasha. (See also Ford and Steward.)

Ford, James A. and Julian H. Steward
1954 On the concept of types. American Anthropologist 56.1:42-57. Menasha. (See also under individual authors.)

Forde, C. Daryll, editor
1954 African worlds: studies in the cosmological ideas and social values of African peoples. xvii, 243 pp. London: Oxford University Press.

Fortes, Meyer
1966 Totem and taboo. (Presidential address 1966.) Pp. 5-22 in Proceedings of the Royal Anthropological Institute of Great Britain and Ireland. London.

Fortes, M. and E. E. Evans-Pritchard
1940 Introduction. Pp. 5-23 in African political systems, edited by M. Fortes and E. E. Evans-Pritchard. London: Oxford University Press.

Foskett, Douglas John
1963 Classification and indexing in the social sciences. x, 190 pp. Washington and London: Butterworths.

1970 Classification and indexing in the social sciences. Aslib Proceedings 22.3:90-101. London.

Fowler, Catherine Sweeney and Joy Leland
1967 Some northern Paiute native categories. Ethnology 6.4:381-404. Pittsburgh.

Fox, James J.
1971 Semantic parallelism in Rotinese ritual language. Bijdragen tot de Taal-, Land- en Volkenkunde 127.2:215-255. 's-Gravenhage.

Frake, Charles O.
1960a The Eastern Subanun of Mindanao. Pp. 51-64 in Social structure in Southeast Asia, (Viking Fund Publications in Anthropology, No. 29) edited by G. P. Murdock. New York: Wenner-Gren Foundation for Anthropological Research.

1960b Review of The use of names by Micronesians, edited by John de Young. Journal of American Folklore 73.288:177-178. Montpelier, Vt.

1964 A structural description of Subanun religious behavior. Pp. 111-129 in Explorations in cultural anthropology: essays in honor of George Peter Murdock, edited by W. H. Goodenough. New York: McGraw-Hill.

1969 Struck by speech: the Yakan concept of litigation. Pp. 147-167 in Law in culture and society, edited by L. Nader. Chicago: Aldine.

1971 Lexical origins and semantic structure in Philippine creole Spanish. Pp. 223-242 in Pidginization and creolization of languages, edited by D. Hymes. London: Cambridge University Press.

Franciscan Fathers
1910 An ethnologic dictionary of the Navaho

language. 536 pp. Saint Michaels, Ariz.

Franklin, Karl J.
1967   Names and aliases in Kewa. Journal of the
Polynesian Society 76.1:76-81. Wellington.

Friedrich, Margaret Hardin
1970   Design structure and social interaction:
archaeological implications of an ethnographic analysis. American Antiquity 35.3:
332-343. Washington.

Furst, Peter
1967   Huichol conceptions of the soul. Folklore
Americas   27.2:39-106. Coral Gables, Fla.

Garfinkel, Harold
1964   Studies of the routine grounds of everyday
activities. Social Problems 11.3:225-250.
Spencer, Ind.

1967   Studies in ethnomethodology. xvi, 288 pp.
Englewood Cliffs, N. J.: Prentice-Hall.

Geertz, Clifford
1960   The religion of Java. xv, 392 pp. Glencoe,
Ill.: Free Press.

1966   Person, time, and conduct in Bali: an essay
in cultural analysis. (Southeast Asia Studies
Cultural Report Series, No. 14.) 85 pp.
New Haven: Yale University.

Gifford, Edward Winslow and Stanislaw Klimek
1936   Culture element distributions: II. Yana.
University of California Publications in
American Archaeology and Ethnology 37.2:
71-100. Berkeley.

Gifford, Edward Winslow and Alfred L. Kroeber
1937   Culture element distributions: IV. Pomo.
University of California Publications in
American Archaeology and Ethnology 37.4:
117-254. Berkeley.

Gilborn, Craig
1968   Pop pedagogy: description, classification,
interpretation; an analysis of the object.
Museum News 47.4:12-18. Washington.

Gilman, Albert and Roger Brown
1958   Who says "tu" to whom. Etc. 15:169-174.
Bloomington, Ill.

Gluckman, Max
 1959   The technical vocabulary of Barotse juris-
       prudence. American Anthropologist 61.5(Part
       1):743-754. Menasha.

 1969   Concepts in the comparative study of tribal
       law. Pp. 349-373 in Law in culture and
       society, edited by L. Nader. Chicago:
       Aldine.

Goffman, Erving
 1956   The nature of deference and demeanor.
       American Anthropologist 58.3:473-502.
       Menasha.

 1959   Presentation of self in everyday life. xii,
       259 pp. Garden City, N. Y.: Doubleday.

 1963   Behavior in public places, notes on the
       social organization of gatherings. vii, 248
       pp. New York: Free Press of Glencoe.

Goitein, S. D.
 1970   Nicknames as family names. Journal of the
       American Oriental Society 90.4:517-524.
       New Haven.

Gonda, J.
 1948   The Javanese vocabulary of courtesy. Lingua
       1.3:333-376. Haarlem.

Goodenough, Ward H.
 1951   Property, kin, and community on Truk. (Yale
       University Publications in Anthropology, No.
       46.) 192 pp. New Haven.

 1956   Residence rules. Southwestern Journal of
       Anthropology 12.1:22-37. Albuquerque.

 1965a   Rethinking 'status' and 'role' toward a
       general model of the cultural organization
       of social relationships. Pp. 1-22 in The
       relevance of models for social anthropology,
       (Association of Social Anthropologists
       Monographs, 1). London: Tavistock.

 1965b   Personal names and modes of address in two
       oceanic societies. Pp. 265-276 in Context
       and meaning in cultural anthropology,
       edited by M. E. Spiro. New York: Free
       Press; London: Collier-Macmillan.

1970   Description and comparison in cultural
        anthropology. xi, 173 pp. Chicago: Aldine.

Goodenough, Ward H., editor
1964   Explorations in cultural anthropology:
        essays in honor of George Peter Murdock.
        xiii, 635 pp. New York: McGraw-Hill.

Goss, James A.
1967   Ute language, kin, myth, and nature: a
        demonstration of a multi-dimensional folk-
        taxonomy. Anthropological Linguistics 9.9:
        1-11. Bloomington, Ind.

Grayson, T. J.
1967   Some aspects of industrial classification in
        the Soviet Union. Aslib Proceedings 19.5:
        129-145. London.

Greenberg, Joseph H.
1948   Linguistics and ethnology. Southwestern
        Journal of Anthropology 4.2:140-147.
        Albuquerque.

Gutmans, Théodore
1970   Une terminologie occidentale unifée dès le
        Moyen Age: les quatre points cardinaux.
        La Linguistique 6.1:147-151. Paris.

Gwaltney, John L.
1970   The thrice shy: cultural accommodation to
        blindness and other disasters in a Mexican
        community. xii, 219 pp. New York: Columbia
        University Press.

Haas, Mary R.
1968   The Menomini terms for playing cards.
        International Journal of American Linguistics
        34.3:217. Baltimore.

Haddon, A. C. and James Hornell
1936-   Canoes of Oceania. 3 vols. (Bernice P.
1938   Bishop Museum Special Publications, Nos.
        27-29.) Vol. 1, The canoes of Polynesia,
        Fiji, and Micronesia, by James Hornell,
        454 pp.; Vol. 2, The canoes of Melanesia,
        Queensland, and New Guinea, by A. C. Haddon,
        342 pp.; Vol. 3, Definition of terms, general
        survey and conclusions, by A. C. Haddon and
        James Hornell, 88 pp. Honolulu.

[3:20]

Haeberlin, Herman K.
1916   The idea of fertilization in the culture of
        the Pueblo Indians. (American Anthropolo-
        gist, Memoir No. 3.) 55 pp. Menasha.

Hall, Edward T.
1959   The silent language. 240 pp. Garden City:
        Doubleday.

Hallowell, A. Irving
1960   Ojibwa ontology, behavior, and world view.
        Pp. 49-82 in Culture in history, edited by
        S. Diamond. New York: Columbia University
        Press.

Hammel, Eugene A.
1967   Sexual symbolism in flatware. Kroeber
        Anthropological Society Papers 37:23-30.
        Berkeley.

Hammer, Muriel
1966   Some comments on formal analysis of grammati-
        cal and semantic systems. American Anthro-
        pologist 68.2(Part 1):362-373. Menasha.

Hammond, Dorothy
1970   Magic: a problem in semantics. American
        Anthropologist 72.6:1349-1356. Menasha.

Hamnett, Ian
1967   Ambiguity, classification and change: the
        function of riddles. Man (n.s.)2.3:379-392.
        London.

Harris, Marvin
1964   The nature of cultural things. xv, 209 pp.
        New York: Random House.

1970   Referential ambiguity in the calculus of
        Brazilian racial identity. Southwestern
        Journal of Anthropology 26.1:1-14.
        Albuquerque.

Harrison, H. Spencer
1924   A handbook to the cases illustrating stages
        in the evolution of the domestic arts. 2d
        edition. (Horniman Museum and Library,
        Publication Nos. 9-10.) London.

Harwood, Alan
1970   Witchcraft, sorcery, and social categories
        among the Safwa. xvii, 160 pp. London:
        Oxford University Press.

Hatt, Gudmund
  1918   Moccasins. American Anthropologist 20.1:112-
          115. Menasha.

Hayley, Audrey
  1968   Symbolic equations: the ox and the cucumber.
          Man (n.s.)3.2:262-271. London.

Heider, Karl Gustav
  1969   Attributes and categories in the study of
          material culture: New Guinea Dani attire.
          Man (n.s.)4.3:379-391. London.

Helm, June, editor
  1968   Essays on the problem of tribe. (Proceedings
          of the 1967 Annual Spring Meeting of the
          American Ethnological Society.) 227 pp.
          Seattle: University of Washington Press.

Herold, Elaine Bluhm
  1968   Review of The primary structures of fabrics,
          an illustrated classification, by Irene
          Emery. American Antiquity 33.1:109-110.
          Salt Lake City.

Hiatt, Betty
  1967,   The food quest and the economy of the Tasman-
  1968   ian aborigines, I and II. Oceania 38.2:99-
          133; 38.3:190-219. Sydney.

Hiatt, Lester Richard
  1969   Totemism tomorrow: the future of an illusion.
          Mankind 7.2:83-93. Sydney.

Hirschberg, Walter, Alfred Janata, Wilhelm P. Bauer,
          and Christian F. Fiest
  1966   Technologie und Ergologie in der Völkerkunde.
          321 pp., bibliog. Mannheim: Bibliographisches
          Institut.

Hockett, Charles F.
  1964   Scheduling. Pp. 125-144 in Cross-cultural
          understanding: epistemology in anthropology,
          edited by F. S. C. Northrop and H. H.
          Livingston. New York: Harper and Row.

Hoffman, John
  1930-   Encyclopaedia Mundarica. 13 vols. Bihar
  1938   and Orissa, Patna (India): Government
          Printing Office.

[3:22]

Hornell, James
1943   Outrigger devices: distribution and origin.
        Journal of the Polynesian Society 52.3:91-
        100. Wellington.

1946   Water transport; origins and early evolution.
        308 pp. London: Cambridge University Press.

Horton, Robin
1962   The Kalabiri world view: an outline and
        interpretation. Africa 32:197-220. London.

1967a   African traditional thought and western
        science, Part I. Africa 37.1:50-71. London.

1967b   African traditional thought and western
        science, Part II, The 'closed' and 'open'
        predicaments. Africa 37.2:155-187. London.

Howard, Alan
1963   Land, activity systems, and decision making
        models in Rotuma. Ethnology 2.4:407-440.
        Pittsburgh.

Hudson, Charles
1966   Folk history and ethnohistory. Ethnohistory
        13.1-2:52-70. Buffalo.

Hymes, Dell H.
1961   On typology of cognitive styles in language
        (with examples from Chinookan). Anthropo-
        logical Linguistics 3.1:22-54. Bloomington,
        Ind.

1966   Two types of linguistic relativity (with
        examples from Amerindian ethnography).
        Pp. 114-167 in Sociolinguistics, (Janua
        Linguarum, Series Maior 20), edited by
        W. Bright. Paris and The Hague: Mouton.

1967   Models of the interaction of language and
        social setting. Journal of Social Issues
        13.2:8-29. Ann Arbor.

1970   Linguistic method of ethnography: its
        development in the United States. Pp. 249-
        325 in Method and theory in linguistics,
        (Janua Linguarum, Series Maior 40), edited
        by P. L. Garvin. Paris and The Hague:
        Mouton.

Hymes, Dell H., editor
1964   Language in culture and society: a reader

236

in linguistics and anthropology. 764 pp.
New York: Harper and Row.

1965   The use of computers in anthropology. 558 pp.
        The Hague: Mouton.

Ihm, Peter
1965   Automatic classification in anthropology.
        Pp. 357-376 in The use of computers in
        anthropology, edited by D. Hymes. The
        Hague: Mouton.

Ikegami, Yoshiko
1965   Semantic change in poetic words. Linguistics
        19:64-79. The Hague.

Inverarity, Robert Bruce
1960   Visual files coding index. (Publication 15,
        Indiana University Research Center in Anthro-
        pology, Folklore and Linguistics.) 185 pp.
        Bloomington, Ind.

Izutsu, Toshihiko
1966   Ethico-religious concepts in the Qur'ān. Re-
(1959) vised edition. (McGill Islamic Studies, I.)
        284 pp. Montreal: McGill University Press.
        (First published 1959 as The structure of the
        ethical terms in the Koran: a study in
        semantics. [Keio University Studies in the
        Humanities and Social Relations, Vol. 2.]
        275 pp. Tokyo.)

Jakobson, Roman and Claude Lévi-Strauss
1962   "Les Chats" de Charles Baudelaire. L'Homme
        2.1:5-21. Paris.

James, George Wharton
1902   Indian basketry. 2d edition, revised and
        enlarged. 274 pp., 360 illus., bibliog. of
        Indian basketry. New York: H. Malkan.

Jenkins, C. David and Stephen J. Zyzanski
1968   Dimensions of belief and feeling concerning
        three diseases, poliomyelitis, cancer, and
        mental illness: a factor analytic study.
        Behavioral Science 13.5:372-381. Ann Arbor.

Katz, Aaron
1964   Toward high information-level culture.
        Cybernetica 7.3:203-245. Namur, Belgium.

Kay, Paul
1971   Explorations in mathematical anthropology.

xviii, 286 pp. Cambridge, Mass. and London: MIT Press.

Keesing, Roger M.
1966   Descriptive categories in the analysis of social organization: a rejoinder to Nelson. American Anthropologist 68.2(Part 1):474-477. Menasha.

Keesing, Roger M. and Jonathan Fifi?i
1969   Kwaio word tabooing in its cultural context. Journal of the Polynesian Society 78.2:154-177. Wellington.

Kennedy, Kenneth A. R.
1960   The phylogenetic tree: an analysis of its development in studies of human evolution. Kroeber Anthropological Society Papers 23: 7-53. Berkeley.

Kilson, Marion
1968-   The Ga naming rite. Anthropos 63/64:904-
1969   920. Fribourg.

Kluckhohn, Clyde
1960   The use of typology in anthropological theory. Pp. 134-140 in Men and cultures, (Selected papers of the Fifth International Congress of Anthropological and Ethnological Sciences, Philadelphia, 1956), edited by A. F. C. Wallace. Philadelphia: University of Pennsylvania Press.

Kobychev, V. P. and A. I. Robakidze
1969   Basic typology and mapping of dwellings of the Caucasian peoples. Soviet Anthropology and Archeology 7.4:13-28. New York.

Kochman, Thomas
1970   Toward an ethnography of black American speech behavior. Pp. 145-162 in Afro-American anthropology, edited by N. E. Whitten, Jr. and J. F. Szwed. New York: Free Press.

Koh, Hesung Chun
1966   A social science bibliographic system: orientation and framework. Behavior Science Notes 1.3:145-163. New Haven.

Kongas, Elli-Kaija and Pierre Maranda
1962   Structural models in folklore. Midwest Folklore 12.3:133-192. Bloomington, Ind.

Kopytoff, Igor
1964   Classifications of religious movements:
          analytical and synthetic. Pp. 77-90 in
          Symposium on New Approaches to the Study
          of Religion (Proceedings of the 1964 Annual
          Spring Meeting of the American Ethnological
          Society), edited by J. Helm. Seattle:
          University of Washington Press.

Kosambi, D. D.
1966   Scientific numismatics. Scientific American
          214.2:102-111. New York.

Kranz, Peter
1970   What do people do all day? Behavioral
          Science 15.3:286-291. Ann Arbor.

Kroeber, A. L.
1940   Statistical classification. American
          Antiquity 6.1:29-44. Menasha.

1955   Nature of the landholding group. Ethnohis-
          tory 2.4:303-314. Bloomington, Ind.

1962   A roster of civilizations and culture.
          (Viking Fund Publications in Anthropology,
          No. 33.) 96 pp. New York: Wenner-Gren
          Foundation for Anthropological Research.

Kuusi, M.
1966   Ein Vorschlag für die Terminologie der
          parömiologischen Strukturnanalyse.
          Proverbium 5:108-1091. Helsinki.

Lagercrantz, Sture
1968-   African tally-strings. Anthropos 63-64.1-2:
1969   115-128. Fribourg.

La Barre, Weston
1947   Kiowa folk sciences. Journal of American
          Folklore 60.236:105-114. Philadelphia.

Laplace, Georges
1966   Pourquoi une typologie analytique?
          L'Anthropologie 70.1-2:193-201. Paris.

Lauria, Anthony, Jr.
1964   "Respeto," "relajo" and inter-personal
          relations in Puerto Rico. Anthropological
          Quarterly 37.2:53-67. Washington.

Leach, Edmund R.
1960   The "frontiers" of Burma. Comparative

[3:26]

Studies in Society and History 3.1:49-68.
The Hague.

Leach, Edmund R. (cont.)
1961   Rethinking anthropology. (London School of
Economics Monographs on Social Anthropology,
No. 22.) 143 pp. London: Anthlone.

1962   Classification in social anthropology. Aslib
Proceedings 14.8:239-242. London.

1964   Anthropological aspects of language: animal
categories and verbal abuse. Pp. 23-63 in
New directions in the study of language,
edited by E. H. Lenneberg. Cambridge:
MIT Press.

1965   Lévi-Strauss in the garden of Eden: an
(1958)   examination of some recent developments in
the analysis of myth. Pp. 574-581 in
Reader in comparative religion, edited by
W. A. Lessa and E. Z. Vogt. New York:
Harper and Row.

1966a   Classification in social and cultural anthropology, and prehistoric archaeology: a
select bibliography. Classification Society
Bulletin 1.2:19-26. Leicester, England.

1966b   The legitimacy of Solomon: some structural
aspects of Old Testament history. Archives
Europeennes de Sociologie, European Journal
of Sociology 7:58-101. Paris.

1966c   Twins, birds and vegetables. Man (n.s.)1.4:
557-558. London.

1967a   Caste, class and slavery: the taxonomic
problem. Pp. 5-16 in Ciba Foundation Symposium on Caste and Race: Comparative
approaches, 1967, edited by A. V. S. de
Rueck and J. Knight. London: J. and A.
Churchill.

1967b   Introduction. Pp. vii-xix in The structural
study of myth and totemism, (Association of
Social Anthropologists Monographs, 5), edited
by E. R. Leach. London: Tavistock.

1969   Genesis as myth: and other essays. (Cape
Editions 39.) 123 pp. London: Jonathan Cape.

1970   Lévi-Strauss. 127 pp. (Fontana Modern
            Masters Series.) London: Wm. Collins.

LeBar, Frank M.
1970   Coding ethnographic materials. Pp. 707-720
            in A handbook of method in cultural anthro-
            pology, edited by R. Naroll and R. Cohen.
            Garden City, N. Y.: Natural History Press.

Le Coeur, Charles
1950   Dictionnaire ethnographique téda. Précédé
            d'un lexique français-téda. (Mémoires de
            l'Institut Français d'Afrique Noire 9.)
            211 pp. Paris: Larose.

Lehman, Frederic K.
1967   Ethnic categories in Burma and the theory of
            social systems. Pp. 93-124 in Vol. 1 of
            Southeast Asian tribes, minorities, and
            nations, edited by P. Kunstadter. Princeton:
            Princeton University Press.

Lehmann, Siegfried
1968   Bäuerliche Symbolik: versuch einer Genese
            und Systematik. Symbolon 6:72-106. Basel.

Lehrer, Adrienne
1969   Semantic cuisine. Journal of Linguistics
            5.1:39-55. London.

Leroi-Gourhan, André
1943,   Evolution et technique. 2 vols. Vol. 1,
1945   L'Homme et la matière; Vol. II, Milieu et
            techniques. Paris: Albin Michel.

1970   Observations technologiques sur le rythme
            staturaie. Pp. 658-676 in Échanges et
            communications, edited by J. Pouillon and
            P. Maranda. The Hague and Paris: Mouton.

Lessa, William Armand
1959   Divining by knots in the Carolines. Journal
            of the Polynesian Society 68:188-210.
            Wellington.

1968   Chinese body divination: its forms, affin-
            ities, and functions. xiii, 220 pp. Los
            Angeles: United World Academy and Fellowship.

Lévi-Strauss, Claude
1948   La Vie familiale et sociale des Indiens
            Nambikwara. Journal de la Société des
            Americanistes 37:1-131. Paris.

241

[3:28]

Lévi-Strauss, Claude (cont.)
  1958   Anthropologie structurale. 454 pp. Paris:
          Plon. (Translated 1963 by Claire Jacobson
          and Brooke Grundfest Schoepf as Structural
          anthropology. xvi, 410 pp. New York:
          Basic Books.)

  1962   La Pensée sauvage. 395 pp. Paris: Plon.
  (1966) (Translated 1966 as The savage mind. xii,
          290 pp. London: Wiedenfeld and Nicolson.)

  1964   Mythologiques 1: le cru et le cuit. 402 pp.
          Paris: Plon. (Translated 1969 by John and
          Doreen Weightman as The raw and the cooked:
          introduction to a science of mythology, I.
          xiii, 387 pp. New York and Evanston:
          Harper and Row.)

  1966   Mythologiques 2: du miel aux cendres.
          446 pp. Paris: Plon.

  1968   Mythologiques 3: l'origine des manières de
          table. 478 pp. Paris: Plon.

  1971   Mythologiques 4: l'homme nu. 688 pp. Paris:
          Plon.

Lewis, G. Griffen
  1945   The practical book of oriental rugs. xvii,
          317 pp. Philadelphia and New York:
          Lippincott.

Lieberson, Stanley
  1966   Language questions in censuses. Sociological
          Inquiry 36:262-279. Mancester, England.

Lienhardt, R. Godfrey
  1954   Modes of thought. Pp. 95-107 in The institu-
          tions of primitive society, by E. E. Evans-
          Pritchard et al. Oxford: Basel Blackwell.

List, George
  1963   The boundaries of speech and song. Ethno-
          musicology 7.1:1-16. Middletown, Conn.

Littlejohn, James
  1968a   Twins, birds,etc. Bijdragen tot de Taal-,
          Land- en Volkenkunde 126.1:91-109.
          's-Gravenhage.

  1968b   Reply to E. E. Evans-Pritchard. Bijdragen
          tot de Taal-, Land- en Volkenkunde 126.1:
          113-114. 's-Gravenhage.

Lord, Albert B.
1960   The singer of tales. xv, 309 pp.   Cambridge:
         Harvard University Press.

Lowenthal, David
1967   Race and color in the West Indies.   Daedalus
         96.2:580-626.   Cambridge, Mass.

McClelland, E. M.
1966   Two studies of Ifa divination.   II. The
         significance of number in the Odu of Ifa.
         Africa 36.4:421-431.   London.

Macgaffey, Wyatt
1968   Kongo and the king of the Americans.   Journal
         of Modern African Studies 6:171-181.   London.

McKern, Will Carleton
1923   Patwin houses.   University of California
         Publications in American Archaeology and
         Ethnology 20.10:159-171.   Berkeley.

McQuown, Norman A.
1954   Analysis of the cultural content of language
         materials.   Pp. 20-31 in Language in culture,
         (American Anthropologist 56.6[Part 2];
         Memoir No. 79; Comparative Studies of Cultures
         and Civilizations No. 3), edited by H. Hoijer.
         Menasha.

Malinowski, Bronislaw
1935   The language of magic and gardening.   (Coral
         gardens and their magic, Vol. 2.)   xxxiii,
         350 pp.   London: Allen and Unwin; New York:
         American Book.   (Reprinted 1965, 384 pp.
         Bloomington: Indiana University Press.)

Mandelbaum, David G., editor
1949   Selected writing of Edward Sapir in language,
         culture, and personality.   617 pp.   Berkeley
         and Los Angeles: University of California
         Press.

Maranda, Pierre and E.-K. Köngäs
1962   Structural models in folklore.   Midwest
         Folklore 12.3:132-193.   Bloomington, Ind.

Maranda, Pierre and E. Köngäs Maranda, editors
1971   Structural analysis of oral tradition.   xxxiv,
         324 pp.   Philadelphia: University of Penn-
         sylvania Press.

Martin, Richard T.
1970   The role of coca in the history, religion,
         and medicine of South American Indians.
         Economic Botany 24.4:422-438. Lawrence, Kans.

Martin, Samuel E.
1964   Speech levels in Japan and Korea. Pp. 407-
         415 in Language in culture and society, edited
         by D. Hymes. New York: Harper and Row.

Mason, Otis T.
1904   Aboriginal American basketry: studies in a
         textile art without machinery. Pp. 171-548
         in United States National Museum Report for
         1902. Washington.

1908   Vocabulary of Malaysian basketwork: a study
         in the W. L. Abbott collections. Proceedings
         of the United States National Museum 35.1631:
         1-51. Washington.

Matta, Roberto da
1967   La panema: un essai d'analyse structurale.
         L'Homme 7.3:5-24. Paris.

Maxwell, Allen R.
1966   Bibliography: anthropology. Pp. 256-262 in
         Structuralism, (Yale French Studies 36-37),
         edited by J. Ehrmann. New Haven. (Reprinted
         1970, Garden City, N. Y.: Anchor Books.)

Mbaga, K. and W. H. Whiteley
1961   Formality and informality in Yao speech.
         Africa 31.2:137-146. London.

Meggitt, Mervyn J.
1964   Male-female relationships in the highlands
         of Australian New Guinea. American Anthro-
         pologist 66.4(Part 2):204-224. Menasha.

Messing, Simon D.
1960   The nonverbial language of the Ethiopian
         toga. Anthropos 55.3-4:558-560. Fribourg.

Metzger, Duane G. and Gerald E. Williams
1966   Some procedures and results in the study of
         native categories: Tzeltal "firewood."
         American Anthropologist 68.2:389-407.
         Menasha.

Middleton, John and David A. Tait
1958   Tribes without rulers. xi, 234 pp. London:
         Routledge and Kegan Paul.

Milke, Wilhelm
1949   The quantitative distribution of cultural
        similarities and their cartographic repre-
        sentation. American Anthropologist 51.2:
        237-252. Menasha.

Miller, R. B.
1967   Task taxonomy: science or technology? In
        The human operator in complex systems,
        edited by W. T. Singleton et al. London:
        Taylor and Francis.

Milner, George B.
1969a   Siamese twins, birds and the double helix.
        Man (n.s.)4.1:5-23. London.

1969b   De l'armature des locutions proverbiales.
        Essai de taxonomie sémantique. L'Homme
        9.3:49-70. Paris.

Mintz, Sidney W.
1961   Standards of value and units of measure in
        the Fond des Nègres market place, Haiti.
        Journal of the Royal Anthropological Insti-
        tute 91:22-38. London.

Moerman, Michael
1965   Ethnic identification in a complex civiliza-
        tion: who are the Lue? American Anthropolo-
        gist 67.5(Part 1):1215-1230. Menasha.

Montagu, Jeremy and John Burton
1971   A proposed new classification system for
        musical instruments. Ethnomusicology 15.1:
        49-70. Middletown, Conn.

Montandon, George
1934   Ergologie systématique. Pp. 213-732 in
        L'Ologénèse culturelle: traité d'ethnologie
        cyclo-culturelle et d'ergologie systématique.
        Paris: Payot.

Montgomery Ward and Co.
1969   Montgomery Ward and Co. catalogue and buyers'
(1895) guide No. 57, spring and summer 1895. An
        unabridged facsimile reprint of the original
        edition with a new introduction by Boris
        Emmet. xviii, 624 pp. New York: Dover.

Moore, Frank W.
1971   The outline of cultural materials: contem-
        porary problems. Behavior Science Notes
        6.3:187-189. New Haven.

[3:32]

Morazé, Charles
1970   Pensée sauvage et logique géométrique. Pp.
        964-980 in Échanges et communications,
        edited by J. Pouillon and P. Maranda. The
        Hague and Paris: Mouton.

Morton-Williams, Peter
1966   Two studies of Ifa divination. Introduction:
        the mode of divination. Africa 36.4:406-408.
        London.

Mounin, Georges
1970   Sémiologie et linguistique: l'exemple du
        blason. La Linguistique 6.2:5-16. Paris.

Munn, Nancy D.
1966   Visual categories: an approach to the study
        of representational systems. American Anthro-
        pologist 68.4:936-950. Menasha.

Murdock, George Peter
1949   Social structure. xvii, 387 pp. New York:
        Macmillan.

1960   Typology in the area of social organization.
        Pp. 183-188 in Men and cultures, (Selected
        Papers of the Fifth International Congress
        of Anthropological and Ethnological Sciences,
        Philadelphia, 1956), edited by A. F. C.
        Wallace. Philadelphia: University of Penn-
        sylvania Press.

Murdock, George Peter et al., editors
1971   Outline of cultural materials. 4th revised
(1938) edition. (Behavior Science Outlines, Vol. 1.)
        xxv, 164 pp. New Haven: Human Relations
        Area Files. (Earlier editions: 1st, 1938
        [1937], by the Cross-cultural Survey; 2d, 1945
        [1942], by the Yale University Press; 3d
        [revised], 1950, by the Human Relations Area
        Files, New Haven.)

Murphy, Robert F.
1964   Social distance and the veil. American
        Anthropologist 66.6:1257-1274. Menasha.

Nader, Laura, editor
1965   The ethnography of law. (American Anthro-
        pologist 67.6[Part 2], Special Publication.)
        v, 212 pp. Menasha.

Naroll, Raoul
1964   On ethnic unit classification. Current

Anthropology 5.4:283-312. Chicago.

1970   The culture-bearing unit in cross-cultural
survey. Pp. 721-765 in A handbook of method
in cultural anthropology, edited by R. Naroll
and R. Cohen. Garden City, N. Y.: Natural
History Press.

Needham, Joseph
1954-   Science and civilisation in China, vols. 1-4.
1965   Cambridge: Cambridge University Press.

Needham, Rodney
1959   Mourning-terms. Bijdragen tot de Taal-,
Land- en Volkenkunde 115.1:58-89.
's-Gravenhage.

1960   Alliance and classification among the Lamer.
Sociologus 10.2:97-119. Berlin.

1963   Introduction. Pp. vii-xlvii in Primitive
classification, by E. Durkheim and M. Mauss.
Chicago: University of Chicago Press.

1964   Temer names. Journal of the Royal Asiatic
Society, Malaysian Branch, 37.1:121-125.
Singapore.

1965   Death-names and solidarity in Penan society.
Bijdragen tot de Taal-, Land- en Volkenkunde
121.1:58-76. 's-Gravenhage.

1966   Twins, birds and vegetables. Man (n.s.)1.3:
398. London.

1967   Right and left in Nyoro symbolic classification. Africa 37.4:425-452. London.

1969   Gurage social classification: formal notes
on an unusual system. Africa 39.2:153-166.
London.

Newell, Leonard E.
1968   A Batad Ifugao vocabulary. (HRAFlex book.)
vii, 230. New Haven: Human Relations Area
Files.

Nketia, J. H. Kwabena
1962   The problem of meaning in African music.
Ethnomusicology 6.1:1-7. Middletown, Conn.

Nordenskiöld, Erland
1929   The American Indian as an inventor. Journal

of the Royal Anthropological Institute 59:273-309. London. (Also 1931, pp. 489-505 in Source book in anthropology, edited by A. L. Kroeber and T. T. Waterman. New York.)

Oberg, Kalervo
1955   Types of social structure among the lowland tribes of South and Central America. American Anthropologist 57.3(Part 1):472-487. Menasha.

O'Neale, Lila M.
1932   Yurok-Karok basket-weavers. (University of California Publications in American Archaeology and Ethnology 32.1.) 184 pp., + 58 plates. Berkeley.

Opitz, Herwart
1970   A classification system to describe workpieces. 1st English edition. Compiled by H. Opitz. Translation by R. A. Acton Taylor of Werkstückbeschreibendes Klassifizierungssystem. Edited by W. R. MacConnell. Oxford and New York: Pergamon.

Ortiz, Alfonso
1969   The Tewa world; space, time, being, and becoming in a Pueblo society. xviii, 197 pp. Chicago: University of Chicago Press.

Osgood, Cornelius
1940   Ingalik material culture. (Yale University Publications in Anthropology, No. 22.) 500 pp. New Haven.

Osman, Moh Taib
1964   A text on the rules of the Kelantan bull fight. Journal of the Royal Asiatic Society, Malaysian Branch 37.2:1-10. Singapore.

Panoff, Michel
1968   The notion of double self among the Maenge. Journal of the Polynesian Society 77.3:275-295. Wellington.

Panoff, Michel and Françoise
1968   L'Ethnologue et son ombre. 193 pp. Paris: Payot.

Pearce, T. M.
1962   The names of objects in aerospace. Names 10.1:1-10. Youngstown, Ohio.

Perchonock, Norma and Oswald Werner
1969   Navaho systems of classification: some
        implications for ethnoscience. Ethnology
        8.3:229-242. Pittsburgh.

Pike, Kenneth L.
1967   Language in relation to a unified theory of
        the structure of human behavior. 762 pp.
        New York: Humanities Press; The Hague:
        Mouton.

Pilcher, William W.
1967   Some comments on the folk taxonomy of the
        Papago. American Anthropologist 69.2:204-
        208. Menasha.

Pilling, Arnold R.
1968   Statistics, sorcery, and justice. American
        Anthropologist 64.5(Part 1):1057-1059.
        Menasha.

Pitt-Rivers, Julian A.
1967   Contextual analysis and the locus of the
        model. Archives Europeennes de Sociologie,
        European Journal of Sociology 8:15-34.
        Paris.

Plank, Robert
1964   Names of twins. Names 12.1:1-5. Youngstown,
        Ohio.

Platt, J. T.
1967   The Kukata-Kukatja distinction. Oceania 38.1:
        61-64. Sydney.

Pospisil, Leopold
1965a   A formal analysis of substantive law: Kapauku
        Papuan laws of land tenure. Pp. 186-214 in
        Formal semantic analysis, (American Anthro-
        pologist 67.5[Part 2], Special Publication),
        edited by E. A. Hammel. Menasha.

1965b   A formal analysis of substantive law: Kapauku
        Papuan laws of inheritance. Pp. 166-185 in
        The ethnography of law, (American Anthropolo-
        gist 67.6[Part 2], Special Publication),
        edited by L. Nader. Menasha.

1971   Anthropology of law: a comparative theory.
        xiii, 385 pp. New York: Harper and Row.

Pouillon, Jean and Pierre Maránda, editors
1970   Échanges et communications: mélanges offerts

[3:36]

à Claude Lévi-Strauss à l'occasion de son
60ème anniversaire. 2 vols. 1452 pp. The
Hague and Paris: Mouton.

Price, Richard and Sally Price
1966   A note on canoe names in Martinique. Names
14.3:157-160. Potsdam, N. Y.

Propp, Vladimir
1958   Morphology of the folktale. (Indiana University Research Center in Anthropology, Folklore and Linguistics, Publication 10;
Publications of the American Folklore
Society, Bibliographical and Special Series,
Vol. 9.) xxvi, 158 pp. Bloomington, Ind.

Psathas, George and James M. Henslin
1967   Dispatched orders and the cab driver: a
study of locating activities. Social
Problems 14.4:424-443. Brooklyn.

Pukui, Mary K. and Samuel H. Elbert
1957   Hawaiian-English dictionary. xxx, 362 pp.
Honolulu: University of Hawaii Press.

Radcliffe-Brown, A. R.
1952   Structure and function in primitive society.
219 pp. Glencoe, Ill.: Free Press.

Rankin, Bunyan Kirk, III
1965   A linguistic study of the formation of
Chinese characters. xviii, 219 pp.
(Published by University Microfilms, Ann
Arbor, Mich., [No. 66-293].)

Reichard, Gladys A.
1950   Navaho religion, a study of symbolism.
2 vols. xxxvi, 800 pp. New York: Pantheon.

Reichel-Dolmatoff, Gerardo
1968   Desana: simbolismo de los Indios Tukano del
(1971) Vaupés. xiii, 270 pp. Bogotá: Universidad
de los Andes. (Translated 1971 by the author
as Amazonian cosmos, the sexual and religious
symbolism of the Tukano Indians. xxiii, 290
pp. Chicago: University of Chicago Press.)

Rennick, Robert M.
1968   Obscene names and naming in folk tradition.
Names 16.3:207-229. Potsdam, N. Y.

Richards, Audrey I.
1967   African systems of thought: an Anglo-French

dialogue. Man 2.2:286-298. London.

Riesman, Paul
1966   Mariage et vol du feu; quelques catégories
        de la pensée symbolique des Haoussa.
        L'Homme 6.4:82-103. Paris.

Rigby, Peter
1966   Dual symbolic classification among the Gogo
        of central Tanzania. Africa 36.1:1-17.
        London.

1968   Joking relationships, kin categories, and
        clanship among the Gogo. Africa 38.2:133-
        155. London.

Rivers, W. H. R. and A. C. Haddon
1902   A method of recording string figures and
        tricks. Man 2:146-153(Art. 109). London.

Roberts, John M., Hans Hoffman, and Brian Sutton-Smith
1965   Pattern and competence: a consideration of
        tick tack toe. El Palacio 72.3:17-30.
        Santa Fe.

Rohdie, Sylvia
1968   Symbolic equations. Man (n.s.)3:659. London.

Romney, A. Kimball and Roy G. d'Andrade, editors
1964   Transcultural studies in cognition. (Amer-
        ican Anthropologist 66.3[Part 2], Special
        Publication.) Menasha.

Roseberg, Bruce
1970   The formulaic quality of spontaneous sermons.
        Journal of American Folklore 83.327:3-20.
        Austin.

Ross, Alan S. C.
1962   U and non-U: an essay in sociological
        linguistics. Pp. 91-106 in The importance
        of language, edited by M. Black. Englewood
        Cliffs, N. J.: Prentice-Hall.

Ruesch, Jurgen and Weldon Kees
1956   Nonverbial communication: notes on the
        visual perception of human relations. 205
        pp. Berkeley and Los Angeles: University
        of California Press.

Ruffner, Frederick G., compiler
1960   Acronyms dictionary. 211 pp. Detroit:
        Gale Research Co.

[3:38]

Samarin, William J.
1969   The art of Gbeya insults. International
        Journal of American Linguistics 35.4:323-
        329. Baltimore.

Sapir, Edward   (See David G. Mandelbaum.)

Santerre, Renaud
1966   La Méthode d'analyse de l'homme. Anthro-
        pologica (n.s.)8.1:111-114. Ottawa.

Saraf, Samarendra
1970   The trichotomous theme: a ritual category
        in Hindu culture. Anthropos 65.5-6:948-972.
        Fribourg.

Sarnoff, Paul
1963   The Wall Street thesaurus. xx, 250 pp.
        New York: Ivan Obolensky.

Schapera, Isaac
1966   Tswana, legal maxims. Africa 36.2:121-134.
        London.

Schapiro, Meyer
1970   On some problems in the semiotics of visual
        art: field and vehicle in image-signs.
        Pp. 487-502 in Sign·language·culture, (Janua
        Linguarum, Series Maior 1), edited by A. J.
        Greimas et al. The Hague and Paris: Mouton.

Scheans, Daniel J.
1966   A new view of Philippine pottery manufacture.
        Southwestern Journal of Anthropology 22.2:
        206-219. Albuquerque.

Scheffler, Harold W.
1966   Structuralism in anthropology. Pp. 68-88 in
        Structuralism, (Yale French Studies 36-37),
        edited by Jacques Ehrmann. New Haven.
        (Reprinted 1970, Garden City: Anchor Books.

Schegloff, Emanuel A.
1968   Sequencing in conversational openings.
        American Anthropologist 70.6:1075-1095.
        Menasha.

Schlesier, Erhard
1966   Sippen-diagramme und lokale Ethnohistorie.
        Mitteilungen zur Kulturkunde 1:41-52.
        Wiesbaden.

Schneider, Marius
1966   Das Morgenrot in der vedischen Kosmogonie.
        Symbolon 5:61-75. Basel.

Schroeder, Joseph J., Jr., editor
1969   Sears, Roebuck and Co., 1908 Catalogue
(1908) No. 117, The great price maker. XI, 3,
        1184 pp. Chicago: Gun Digest Co.

Scott, William Henry
1960   The Apo-Dios concept in northern Luzon.
        Philippine Studies 8.4:772-788. Manila.

1962   Cordillera architecture of northern Luzon.
        Folklore Studies 21:186-220. Tokyo.

Sears Roebuck
1969   The 1902 edition of the Sears Roebuck
(1902) Catalogue. An unabridged facsimile reprint
        of the original edition, with an introduction
        by Cleveland Amory. 1162 pp. New York:
        Crown. (See also Schroeder 1969.)

Seaton, S. Lee and Karen Ann Watson
1970   A proto-ethnosemantic differential for
        American cultural insignia: team totems in
        major league sports. Anthropological Lin-
        guistics 12.8:304-318. Bloomington, Ind.

Seeger, Charles
1961   Semantic, logical and political considera-
        tions bearing upon research in ethnomusicolo-
        gy. Ethnomusicology 5.2:77-80. Middletown,
        Conn.

1962   Music as a tradition of communication,
        discipline, and play, I. Ethnomusicology
        6.3:156-163. Middletown, Conn.

Seki, Keigo
1966   Types of Japanese folktales. Asian Folklore
        Studies 25:1-220. Tokyo.

Serruys, Henry
1958   A note on arrows and oaths among the Mongols.
        Journal of the American Oriental Society
        78:279-294. New Haven.

Shepard, Anna O.
1948   The symmetry of abstract design, with special
        reference to ceramic decoration. Pp. 211-
        293 in Carnegie Institution of Washington,

[3:40]

Contributions to American Anthropology and History, No. 47. Washington.

Silverman, Sydel F.
1966   An ethnographic approach to social stratification: prestige in a central Italian community. American Anthropologist 68.4: 899-921. Menasha.

Simmons, William Scranton
1967   The supernatural world of the Badyaranķe of Tonghia (Senegal). Journal de la Société des Africanistes 37.1:41-72. Paris.

Simoons, Frederick J.
1961   Eat not this flesh: food avoidances in the world. 241 pp. Madison: University of Wisconsin Press.

Skinner, Alanson
1921   Material culture of the Menomini. (Museum of the American Indian, Heye Foundation, Indian Notes and Monographs, Monograph No. 20.) 478 pp. New York.

Slobin, Dan I., editor
1967   A field manual for cross-cultural study of the acquisition of communicative competence. 2d version. xv, 248 pp. Berkeley: University of California.

Spilerman, Seymour
1966   Structural analysis and the generation of sociograms. Behavioral Science 11.4:312-318. Ann Arbor.

Spiro, Melford E.
1965   A typology of social structure and the patterning of social institutions: a cross-cultural study. American Anthropologist 67.5(Part 1):1097-1119. Menasha.

Spiro, Melford E., editor
1965   Context and meaning in cultural anthropology. xxii, 442 pp. New York: Free Press; London: Collier-Macmillan.

Spradley, James P.
1970a   Adaptive strategies of urban nomads: the ethnoscience of tramp culture. In Urban anthropology, (Human Organization Monograph 2.11), edited by T. Weaver and D. White. St. Paul, Minn.: Macalester College.

1970b   You owe yourself a drunk, an ethnography
         of urban nomads. xii, 301 pp. Boston:
         Little, Brown.

Stevens, Alan M.
1965   Language levels in Madurese. Language 41.2:
         294-302. Baltimore.

Stevens, Hrolf Vaughan
1902   Namengebung und Heirat bei den Orang Tĕmiā
         auf der Halbinsel Malāka. Globus 82.16:
         253-257. Braunschweig.

Steward, Julian H.
1954   On the concept of types: types of types.
         American Anthropologist 56.1:54-57. Menasha.
         (See also Ford and Steward.)

Strathern, Andrew
1970   Wiru penthonyms. Bijdragen tot de Taal-,
         Land- en Volkenkunde 126.1:59-74.
         's-Gravenhage.

Strickon, Arnold
1967   Folk models of stratification,political
         ideology, and socio-cultural systems. Pp. 93-
         118 in Latin American sociological studies,
         (Sociological Review Monograph No. 11),
         edited by P. Halmos. Keele, England.

Sturtevant, William C.
1955   A selected bibliography of material culture.
         vi, 69 pp. New Haven: Peabody Museum,
         Yale University.

1966   Anthropology, history, and ethnohistory.
         Ethnohistory 13.1-2:1-51. Buffalo.
         (Reprinted 1968, pp. 450-475 [Chapter 17]
         in Introduction to cultural anthropology,
         edited by J. A. Clifton. Boston: Houghton
         and Mifflin.)

1967   Seminole men's clothing. Pp. 160-174 in
         Essays on the verbal and visual arts,
         (Proceedings of the 1966 Annual Spring
         Meeting of the American Ethnological Society),
         edited by J. Helm. Seattle: University of
         Washington Press.

Swartz, B. K., Jr.
1958   A study of the material aspects of north-
         eastern Maidu basketry. Papers of the

Kroeber Anthropological Society 19:67-84.
Berkeley.

Tajfel, Henri
1968   Social and cultural factors in perception.
Pp. 315-393 in Vol. 3 of The handbook of
social psychology, 2d edition, edited by G.
Lindzey and E. Aronson. Reading, Mass.:
Addison-Wesley.

Takaki, Michiko
1969   Review of Mountain arbiters: the changing
life of a Philippine hill people, by Edward
P. Dozier. American Anthropologist 71.3:
515-518. Menasha.

Tamony, Peter
1969   Coca-Cola: the most-lawed name. Names
17.4:278- 283. Potsdam, N. Y.

Taylor, Charles W.
1966   Ethno-/xeno views of other-/own cultures:
comments on Haas and White [letter]; and
Reply to Taylor, by M. R. Haas. American
Anthropologist 68.4:1017-1020. Menasha.

Te Rangi Hiroa (See Peter H. Buck)

Ten Raa, Eric
1969   The moon as a symbol of life and fertility
in Sandawe thought. Africa 39.1:24-53.
London.

Textile Information Center
1966   Textile technology terms: an information
retrieval thesaurus. 1st edition. ix,
329 pp. Charlottesville, Va.: Institute
of Textile Technology.

Thierry, Solange
1966-   Quelques aspects du rôle culturel des fleurs
1967   en asie méridionale. L'Ethnographie 60-61:
123-150. Paris.

Thomas Publishing Company
1970   Thomas register of American manufacturers.
(1905) 60th edition. 10 vols. Vols. 1-6, product
classifications, pp. 1-9494; vol. 7, manufacturers' indices, vols. 9-10, manufacturers' catalogs, variously paginated. New
York: Thomas. (1st edition 1905-1906.)

Thompson, Raymond H.
1957   Modern Yucatan Maya pottery. (Memoirs of
        the Society for American Archaeology, No.
        15.) 157 pp. Menasha.

Thompson, Stith
1953   Advances in folklore studies. Pp. 587-596
        in Anthropology today, edited by A. L. Kroeber.
        Chicago: University of Chicago.

Thomson, Donald F.
1946   Names and naming in the Wik Minkan tribe.
        Journal of the Royal Anthropological Insti-
        tute 76.2:157-168. London.

Tokarev, Sergei A.
1966   Principles of the morphological classification
        of religions, Parts I and II. Soviet Anthro-
        pology and Archeology 4.4:3-10; 5.1:11-25.
        New York.

Trager, George L. and Edward T. Hall, Jr.
1953   Culture and communication: a model and an
        analysis. Explorations 3:137-149. Toronto.

Tsiviane, Tatjana V.
1970   Contribution à l'étude de certains systèmes
        sémiotiques simples. Pp. 390-400 in Sign·
        language·culture, (Janua Linguarum, Series
        Maior 1), edited by A. J. Greimas et al.
        The Hague and Paris: Mouton.

Tudorovskaia, E. A.
1967   On the classification of fairy tales.
        Soviet Anthropology and Archeology 6.1:23-31.
        New York.

Turner, Terence S.
1969   Tchikrin: a central Brazilian tribe and its
        symbolic language of bodily adornment.
        Natural History 78.8:50-59, 70. New York.

Turner, Victor W.
1967   The forest of symbols, aspects of Ndembu
        ritual. 405 pp. Ithaca: Cornell Universi-
        ty Press.

1969   The ritual process, structure and anti-
        structure. (The Lewis Henry Morgan Lectures
        1966.) 213 pp. Chicago: Aldine.

Uhlenbeck, E. M.
1969   Systematic features of Javanese personal

[3:44]

names. Word 25.1-3:321-335. London.

Umali, Agustin F.
1950   Guide to the classification of fishing gear
        in the Philippines. (Research Report 17,
        Fish and Wildlife Service, U.S. Department
        of the Interior.) iv, 165 pp. Washington.

United States Department of the Army
1960   Use and care of handtools and measuring
        tools. (Department of the Army Technical
        Manual 9-243.) 223 pp. Washington.

Verguin, Joseph
1957   Deux systèmes de vocabulaire parallèle à
        Madagascar. Word 13:153-156. New York.

Verplanck, William S.
1962   Unaware of where's awareness: some verbal
        operants--notates, monents, and notants.
        In Behaviour and awareness, edited by C. W.
        Eriksen. Durham, N. C.: Duke University
        Press.

Vickery, B. C.
1960   Faceted classification: a guide to construc-
        tion and use of special schemes. iii, 70 pp.
        London: Aslib.

Voegelin, Charles F. and Florence M. Voegelin
1957   Hopi domains: a lexical approach to the
        problem of selection. (International Journal
        of American Linguistics, Memoir 14.) 82 pp.
        Baltimore.

1970   Cross-cultural typologies and folk taxonomies.
        Pp. 1132-1147 in Échanges et communications,
        edited by J. Pouillon and P. Maranda. The
        Hague and Paris: Mouton.

Vogt, Evon Z.
1965   Structural and conceptual replication in
        Zinacantan culture. American Anthropologist
        67.2:342-353. Menasha.

1969   Zinacantan, a Maya community in the highlands
        of Chiapas. xxx, 733 pp. Cambridge: Belknap
        Press of Harvard University Press.

Vreeland, Herbert H.
1958   The concept of ethnic groups as related to
        whole societies. Georgetown University

Monograph Series on Language and Linguistics,
No. 11:81-88. Washington.

Wallace, Anthony F. C.
1965   Driving to work. Pp. 277-292 in Context
        and meaning in cultural anthropology, edited
        by M. E. Spiro. New York: Free Press;
        London: Collier-Macmillan.

Waller, G. F.
1971   Transition in Renaissance ideas of time and
        the place of Giordano Bruno. Neophilologus
        55.1:3-15. Groningen.

Watt, William C.
1966   Morphology of the Nevada cattlebrands and
        their blazons, Part I. 123 pp. Washington:
        U. S. Department of Commerce, National
        Bureau of Standards.

1967a   Morphology of the Nevada cattle brands and
        their blazons, Part II. iii, 57 pp.
        Pittsburgh: Department of Computer Science,
        Carnegie-Mellon University.

1967b   Structural properties of the Nevada cattle-
        brands. Computer Science Research Review,
        No. 2:20-27. Pittsburgh.

Whiteley, Wilfred Howell
1966   Social anthropology, meaning and linguistics.
        Man (n.s.)1.2:139-147. London.

Whorf, Benjamin Lee
1953   Linguistic factors in the terminology of
        Hopi architecture. International Journal
        of American Linguistics 19.2:141-145.
        Baltimore.

Wijeyewardene, Gehan
1968   Address, abuse and animal categories in
        northern Thailand. Man (n.s.)3.1:76-93.
        London.

Willis, Roy G.
1967   The head and the loins: Lévi-Strauss and
        beyond. Man 2.4:519-534. London.

1968   Changes in mystical concepts and practices
        among the Fipa. Ethnology 7.2:139-157.
        Pittsburgh.

[3:46]

Winslow, David J.
    1969   Children's derogatory epithets. Journal of
    American Folklore 82.325:255-263. Austin.

Wyman, Leland C. and Clyde Kluckhohn
    1938   Navaho classification of their song ceremoni-
    als. American Anthropological Association,
    Memoir No. 50.) 38 pp. Menasha.

Yalman, Nur
    1965   Dual organization in central Ceylon? Or the
    goddess on the tree-top. Journal of Asian
    Studies 24.3:441-457. Ann Arbor.

    1967   Under the Bo tree: studies in caste, kin-
    ship, and marriage in the interior of Ceylon.
    xii, 406 pp. Berkeley and Los Angeles:
    University of California Press.

Zuidema, R. T.
    1964   The ceque system of Cuzco: the social
    organization of the capital of the Inca.
    Translated by Eva M. Hooykass. (Internation-
    al Archives of Ethnography, Supplement to
    Vol. 50.) 265 pp. Leiden.

4. **Ethnobotany** (and systematic botany)

[Including references to various types of
ethnobotanical reports and pertinent background works on botanical classification,
as well as analyses of specific folk systems
of plant categorization; cf. 1., 5., and 6.]

Abrahams, Harold J.
1970   The Compendium Pharmaceuticum of Jean
          François Coste. Economic Botany 24.4:374-
          398. Lawrence, Kans.

Adanson, Michel
1763   Familles des plantes. Vol. 1. cccxxv,
          189 pp. Paris: Vincent.

Alefeld, A.
1866   Landwirthschaftliche Flora oder die nutz-
          barenkultivirten Garten und Feldgewächse.
          Mitteleuropas in allen ihren wilden und
          Kulturvarietaten für Landwirthe, Gärtner,
          Gartenfreunde und Botaniker für landwirth-
          schaftliche Lehranstalten. 364 pp. Berlin:
          Wiegandt und Hempel.

Alkire, William H.
1968   Porpoises and taro. Ethnology 7.3:280-289.
          Pittsburgh.

Almstedt, Ruth F.
1968   Diegueño tree: an ecological approach to a
          linguistic problem. International Journal
          of American Linguistics 34.1:9-15. Baltimore.

Alston, R. E. and B. L. Turner
1963   Biochemical systematics. 404 pp. Englewood
          Cliffs, N. J.: Prentice-Hall.

Altschul, Siri von Reis
1970   Ethnogynecological notes in the Harvard
          University Herbaria. Botanical Museum
          Leaflets, Harvard University, 22.10:333-
          343. Cambridge.

Ames, Oakes
1939   Economic annuals and human cultures. vii,
          153 pp. Cambridge: Botanical Museum of
          Harvard University. (Reprinted in 1953.)

Anderson, Edgar
1940   The concept of genus: II. A survey of

modern opinion. Bulletin of the Torrey
Botanical Club 67.5:363-369. New York.
(See also Bartlett et al. 1940.)

Anderson, Edgar (cont.)
1949   Introgressive hybridization. 109 pp. New
York: John Wiley.

1952   Plants, man and life. 245 pp. Boston:
Little, Brown. (Reprinted 1967, ix, 251 pp.,
Berkeley and Los Angeles: University of
California Press.)

1954   Efficient and inefficient methods of measuring species differences. Pp. 93-106 in
Statistics and mathematics in biology,
edited by O. Kempthorne et al. Ames: Iowa
State College Press.

1960   The evolution of domestication. Pp. 67-84
in Vol. 2 of The evolution of man, edited
by S. Tax. Chicago: University of Chicago
Press.

1969   Experimental studies of the species concept.
Annals of the Missouri Botanical Garden
55.3:179-192. St. Louis.

Anderson, Edgar and Hugh Cutler
1942   Races of Zea mays: I. Their recognition
and classification. Annals of the Missouri
Botanical Garden 29.1:69-86. St. Louis.

Anderson, Myrdene
1971   L'Ethnobiologie. La Recherche, No. 18:1029-
1038. Paris.

André, Jacques
1956   Lexique les termes de botanique en latin.
(Études et commentaires, Vol. 23; Ouvrage
publié avec le concours du Centre National
de la Recherche Scientifique.) 343 pp.
Paris: Klincksieck.

1958   Notes de lexicographie botanique grecque.
(Bibliothèque de l'Ecole des Hautes Études,
Sciences historiques et philologiques,
fasc. 311.) 76 pp. Paris.

1963   Noms de plantes et noms d'animaux en latin.
Latomus 22.4:649-663. Brussels.

Anonymous
1954   The nature of plant species. Nature 174.
          4423:245-247. London.

1961   Visiting anthropologist shows drawings clue
          to form of culture. Rockefeller Institute
          Quarterly 5.4:(1 p.) New York.

1970   Atlas de biologie (Atlas zur Biologie).
          Preface by Jean Bernard. Translated by
          Anne Sebisch et al. ii, 569 pp., color
          plates. Paris: Librairie Stock and Librair-
          ie Générale Française.

António Soares, F.
1963   Nomes vernáculos chineses de algunas plantas
          de Macau. Garcia de Orta 11.3:573-591.
          Lisbon.

Arber, Agnes
1940   The colouring of 16th century herbals.
          Nature 154:803-804. London.

Austerlitz, Robert
1962   A linguistic approach to the ethnobotany
          of South-Sahalin. Proceedings of the Ninth
          Pacific Science Congress of the Pacific
          Science Association, 1957, 4:302-303.
          Bangkok.

Bailey, Liberty Hyde
1935   The standard cyclopedia of horticulture.
(1900)   3 vols. New York: Macmillan. (Numerous
          earlier and later editions; first published
          1900-1902.)

1963   How plants get their names. 181 pp. New
(1933)   York: Dover. (First published in 1933 by
          Macmillan.)

1966   Manual of cultivated plants most commonly
(1949)   grown in the continental United States and
          Canada. Revised edition, completely
          restudied. 1116 pp. New York: Macmillan.

Baker, Herbert G. and G. Ledyard Stebbins, editors
1965   The genetics of colonizing species: Pro-
          ceedings of the First International Union
          of Biological Sciences Symposia on General
          Biology, 1964. xv, 588 pp. New York and
          London: Academic Press.

Bal, S. N.
   1942   Useful plants of Mayurbhanj State in Orissa.
           Records of the Botanical Survey of India
           6.10:1-119. Calcutta.

Balls, Edward K.
   1962   Early uses of California plants. 103 pp.
           Berkeley and Los Angeles: University of
           California Press.

Bank, Theodore P., II
   1952   Botanical and ethnobotanical studies in the
           Aleutian Islands. Papers of the Michigan
           Academy of Science, Arts, and Letters,
           36(1950):13-30. Ann Arbor and London.

Baranov, A. I.
   1967   Wild vegetables of the Chinese in Manchuria.
           Economic Botany 21.2:140-155. Baltimore.

Barrau, Jacques
   1950   Liste préliminaire de plantes économiques
           de la Nouvelle-Cáledonie. (Commission du
           Pacifique Sud, Le Document Technique No. 6.)
           32 pp. Noumea.

   1956a   L'Agriculture vivrière autochtone de la
           Nouvelle-Caledonie. Commission du Pacifique
           Sud, Le Document Technique No. 87:45-153.
           Noumea.

   1956b   Para--a former staple food plant of the
           Polynesians. South Pacific Commission
           Quarterly Bulletin 6.1:29. Noumea.

   1958   Subsistence agriculture in Melanesia.
           (Bernice P. Bishop Museum Bulletin No. 219.)
           111 pp. Honolulu.

   1961   Subsistence agriculture in Polynesia and
           Micronesia. (Bernice P. Bishop Museum
           Bulletin No. 223.) 94 pp. Honolulu.

   1962a   Les Plantes alimentaires de l'Océanie,
           origines, distribution et usages. (Annales
           du Musée Colonial de Marseille, 7ᵉ, série
           3ᵉ à 9ᵉ Volume (1955-1961) Fascicule unique.)
           275 pp. Marseille: Faculté des Sciences
           de l'Université d'Aix-Marseille.

   1962b   Notes on the significance of some vernacular
           names of food plants in the South Pacific

islands. Proceedings of the Ninth Pacific
Science Congress (1957), 4:296-298. Bangkok.

1965   L'Humide et le sec, an essay on ethnobio-
logical adaptation to contrastive environ-
ments in the Indo-Pacific area. Journal of
the Polynesian Society 74.3:329-346.
Wellington.

[1967]   An ethnobotanical guide for anthropological
research in Malayo-Oceania. Preliminary
version. 149 pp. [Singapore]: UNESCO
Science Cooperation Office for Southeast
Asia.

1970a   Note sur le langage des plantes en Nouvelle
Calédonie Mélanésienne. Journal d'Agriculture Tropicale et de Botanique Appliquée
17.10-11:461-463. Paris.

1970b   L'Homme et son environnement végétal en
région tropicale humide: l'exemple Malayo-
Océanien. Article B (52 pp.) in Cours de
ethno-botanique et ethno-zoologie (1969-
1970), Vol. 2, edited by J.-F. Leroy.
Paris: Muséum National d'Histoire Naturelle;
Laboratoire d'Ethno-Botanique et d'Ethno-
Zoologie.

Barrau, Jacques, editor
1963   Plants and the migrations of Pacific peoples,
a symposium, (10th Pacific Science Congress,
Honolulu, 1961). 136 pp. Honolulu: Bishop
Museum Press.

Barrau, Jacques and E. Massal
1954-   Cultures vivrières du Pacifique Sud.
1956   Bulletin du Pacifique Sud. Noumea.
    (1) L'Arbre à pain. 4.4:63-69. 1954.
    (2) La Sagoutier. 5.1:39-47. 1955.
    (3) Les Taros. 5.2:42-53. 1955.
    (4) La Patate douce. 5.3:20-29. 1955.
    (5) Le Manioc. 5.4:23-32. 1955.
    (6) Les Bananiers. 5.1:13-21. 1956.
    (7) Le Cocotier. 6.2:12-19. 1956.

1956a   Quelques plantes alimentaires moins connues
des îles du Pacifique Sud. Bulletin du
Pacifique Sud 7.2:81-85. Noumea.

1956b   L'Agriculture vivrière et l'alimentation dans
les îles du Pacifique Sud. Bulletin du
Pacifique Sud 7.2:81-85. Noumea.

Barrows, David P.
1900   The ethnobotany of the Coahuilla Indians of
        southern California. 82 pp. Chicago:
        University of Chicago Press.

Bartlett, Harley Harris
1915   The experimental study of genetic relation-
        ships. American Journal of Botany 2.3:132-
        155. Lancaster, Pa.

1927   Sumatran plants collected in Asahan and
        Karoland, with notes on their vernacular
        names. Papers of the Michigan Academy of
        Science, Arts and Letters 6(1926):1-66.
        New York and London.

1936   A method of procedure for field work in
        tropical American phytogeography based upon
        a botanical reconnaissance in parts of
        British Honduras and the Peten forest of
        Guatemala. Pp. 1-25 (Miscellaneous Paper 1)
        in Botany of the Maya area, (Carnegie Insti-
        tution of Washington, Publication No. 461).
        Washington.

1940   The concept of genus: I. History of the
        generic concept in botany. Bulletin of
        the Torrey Botanical Club 67.5:349-362.
        New York. (See also Bartlett et al. 1940.)

1953   English names of some East-Indian plants and
        plant products. Asa Gray Bulletin 2.2:149-
        176. Ann Arbor.

1955   Fire in relation to primitive agriculture
        and grazing in the tropics: annotated
        bibliography. 568 pp., mimeographed. Ann
        Arbor: University of Michigan Botanical
        Gardens.

Bartlett, Harley Harris, Edgar Anderson, J. M. Greenman,
        E. E. Sherff, and W. A. Camp
1940   The concept of genus: I-V. Bulletin of the
        Torrey Botanical Club 67.5:349-389. New
        York. (See also under individual authors.)

Bather, Francis Arthur
1927   Biological classification, past and future.
        Quarterly Journal of the Geological Society
        of London 83(Part 2):lxii-civ. London.

Baum, B. R.
1969   On the application of nomenclature to the

taxonomy of hybrids. Taxon 18.6:670-671.
Utrecht.

Bean, Lowell John and Katherine Siva Saubel
1961   Cahuilla ethnobotanical notes: the aborigi-
        nal use of the oak. UCLA Archaeological
        Survey, Annual Report 1960-1961:237-245.
        Los Angeles.

1963   Cahuilla ethnobotanical notes: the aborigi-
        nal uses of the mesquite and screwbean.
        UCLA Archaeological Survey, Annual Report
        1962-1963:51-75. Los Angeles.

Beauchamp, William M.
1902   Onondaga plant names. Journal of American
        Folklore 15.57:91-103. Boston and New York.

Beckner, Morton
1959   The biological way of thought. vii, 200 pp.
        New York: Columbia University Press.

Beckwith, Martha Warren
1927   Notes on Jamaican ethnobotany. (Publications
        of the Folk-lore Foundation, No. 8.) 47 pp.
        Poughkeepsie: Vassar College.

Beidelman, Thomas O.
1964   Some Kaguru plants: terms, names and uses.
        Man 64:79-82(Art. 93). London.

Bell, C. Ritchie
[1964] Plant variation and classification. vi,
        135 pp. London: Macmillan.

Bell, Willis H. and Edward F. Castetter
1937   The utilization of mesquite and screwbean by
        the aborigines of the American Southwest.
        (Ethnobiological Studies in the American
        Southwest, V; University of New Mexico
        Bulletin No. 314, Biological Series 5.2.)
        55 pp. Albuquerque.

1941   The utilization of yucca, sotal, and bear-
        grass by the aborigines of the American
        Southwest. (Ethnobiological Studies in
        the American Southwest, VII; University of
        New Mexico Bulletin No. 372, Biological
        Series 5.5.) 74 pp. Albuquerque.

Benson, Lyman
1957   Plant classification. 688 pp. Boston:
        Heath.

[4:8]

Benson, Lyman (cont.)
1962   Plant taxonomy; methods and principles. ix,
        494 pp. New York: Ronald Press.

Benson, Lyman and Robert A. Darrow
1945   A manual of southwestern desert trees and
        shrubs. (University of Arizona Biological
        Science Bulletin No. 6.) 411 pp. Tucson.

Bergen, Fanny D.
1894,   Popular American plant names. Journal of
1896   American Folklore 7.25:89-104; 9.34:179-193.
        Boston and New York.

Berlin, Brent
1971   Speculations on the growth of ethnobotanical
        nomenclature. (Working Paper No. 39.) 51
        pp. Berkeley: Language-Behavior Research
        Laboratory, University of California.

Berlin, Brent, Dennis E. Breedlove and Peter H. Raven
1966   Folk taxonomies and biological classifica-
        tion. Science 154.3746:273-275. Washington.

1968   Covert semantic categories and folk taxono-
        mies. American Anthropologist 70.2:290-299.
        Menasha.

Blackwelder, R. E.
1967   A critique of numerical taxonomy. Systemat-
        ic Zoology 16.1:64-72. Lawrence, Kans.

Blackwood, B.
1940   Use of plants among the Kukukuku of south-
        east central New Guinea. Proceedings of
        the Sixth Pacific Science Congress 6:111-
        126. Berkeley.

Bois, Désiré Georges Jean Marie
1927-   Les Plantes alimentaires chez tous les
1937   peuples et à travers les âges. Histoire,
        utilisation, culture. 4 vols. (Encyclo-
        pédie biologique I, III, VII, XVII.)
        Paris: Paul Lechevalier.

Brand, Donald D.
1966   Cochineal: aboriginal dyestuff from Nueva
        España. 36th Congreso Internacional de
        Americanistas, España, 1964, Actas y memori-
        as 2:77-91. Seville: Editorial Católica
        Española, S. A.

Bristol, Melvin L.
1964   Philoglossa--a cultivar of the Sibundoy of
        Colombia. Botanical Museum Leaflets, Harvard
        University, 20.10:325-333. Cambridge.

1965   Sibundoy ethnobotany. 361 pp. Ph.D. disser-
        tation in botany, Harvard University,
        Cambridge.

Brookfield, Harold C.
1962   Geography and anthropology. Pacific View-
        point 3.2:11-16. Wellington.

Brown, Robert
1868   On the vegetable products used by the
        North-west American Indians, as food and
        medicine, in the arts, and in superstitious
        rites. Transactions of the Botanical
        Society of Edinburgh 9(May):378-396.
        Edinburgh.

Brown, William Henry
1920   Wild food plants of the Philippines.
        (Department of Agriculture and Natural Re-
        sources, Bureau of Forestry, Bulletin No.
        21.) 165 pp. Manila: Bureau of Printing.

1951-   Useful plants of the Philippines. (Philip-
1957   pine Department of Agriculture and Natural
(1941- Resources, Technical Bulletin No. 10.)
1943)   3 vols. Manila.

Browne, C. A.
1935   The chemical industries of the American
        aborigines. Isis 23.2:406-424. Bruges.

Brummitt, R. K. and A. O. Chater
1968   Proposals mainly concerning names of taxa
        which include the type of the name of the
        next higher taxon. Taxon 17.6:652-658.
        Utrecht.

Buchanan, Robert Earle et al., editors
1958   International code of nomenclature of
        bacteria and viruses: bacteriological code,
        publication data. Edited by the Editorial
        Board of the International Committee on
        Bacteriological Nomenclature of Internation-
        al Association of Microbiological Societies.
        xxii, 186 pp. Ames: Iowa State College
        Press.

[4:10]

Buck, Peter H. (Te Rangi Hiroa)
1927   The material culture of the Cook Islands
        (Aitutaki). (Memoirs of the Board of Maori
        Ethnological Research, Vol. 1.) xxv, 384 pp.
        New Plymouth, N. Z.: T. Avery.

Buck, Roger C. and David L. Hull
1966   The logical structure of the Linnean hier-
        archy. Systematic Zoology 15.2:97-111.
        Lawrence, Kans.

Buisson, Emile
1941   Enquête sur les végétaux dans le folklore
        et l'ethnographie. L'Ethnographie (n.s.)
        39:93-118. Paris.

Bullock, A. A.
1958   Indicis Nominum Familiarum Angiospermarum
        Prodromus. Taxon 7.1:1-35. Utrecht.

1968   What is a new taxon? Taxon 17.5:504-506.
        Utrecht.

Bulmer, Ralph N. H.
1965   Beliefs concerning the propagation of new
        varieties of sweet potato in two New Guinea
        Highlands societies. Journal of the Poly-
        nesian Society 74.2:237-239. Wellington.

Burkill, I. H.
1935   A dictionary of the economic products of
        the Malay Peninsula. With contributions by
        William Birtwhistle and others. 2 vols.
        i-xi, 1-1220; 1221-2402. London: The
        Crown Agents for the Colonies.

——— 1953   Habits of man and the origins of the
        cultivated plants of the Old World.
        (The Hooker Lecture.) Proceedings of the
        Linnean Society 164(Part 1):12-42. London.

Burma, Benjamin H.
1949a   The species concept: a semantic review.
        Evolution 3.4:369-370. Lancaster, Pa.

1949b   Postscriptum [see Burma 1949a, Mayr 1949].
        Evolution 3.4:372-373. Lancaster, Pa.

1954   Reality, existence, and classification: a
        discussion of the species problem.
        Madroño 12.7:193-209. Berkeley.

Burtt, B. L.
1970   Infraspecific categories in flowering plants.
        Biological Journal of the Linnean Society
        2.3:233-238. London. (See also Valentine
        et al. 1970.)

Cain, Arthur James
1958   Logic and memory in Linnaeus's system of
        taxonomy. Proceedings of the Linnean
        Society 169(Parts 1 and 2):144-163. London.

1959a   Taxonomic concepts. Ibis 101.3-4:302-318.
        London.

1959b   Deductive and inductive methods in post-
        Linnean taxonomy. Proceedings of the
        Linnean Society 170(Part 2):185-217. London.

1959c   The post-Linnean development of taxonomy.
        Proceedings of the Linnean Society 170(Part
        3):234-244. London.

1962   The evolution of taxonomic principles.
        Pp. 1-13 in Microbial classification, (12th
        Symposium of the Society for General Micro-
        biology, 1962), edited by G. C. Ainsworth
        and P. H. A. Sneath. Cambridge: Cambridge
        University Press.

Cain, A. J. and G. A. Harrison
1958   An analysis of the taxonomist's judgement
        of affinity. Proceedings of the Zoological
        Society of London 131(Part 1):85-98.
        London.

Camin, Joseph H. and Robert R. Sokal
1965   A method for deducing branching sequences
        in phylogeny. Evolution 19.3:311-326.
        Lawrence, Kans.

Camp, W. H.
1940   The concept of genus: V. Our changing
        generic concepts. Bulletin of the Torrey
        Botanical Club 67.5:381-389. New York.
        (See also Bartlett et al. 1940.)

1951   Biosystematy. Brittonia 7.3:113-127.
        New York.

Camp, W. H., H. W. Rickett, and C. A. Weatherby,
        editors
1947   International rules of botanical nomencla-
        ture. Unofficial special edition;

271

formulated by the International Botanical
Congresses of Vienna, 1905, Brussels, 1910,
and Cambridge, 1930; adopted and revised by
the International Botanical Congress of
Amsterdam, 1935. Brittonia 6.1:1-120.
New York.

Candolle, Alphonse Louis Pierre Pyramous de
1855 Géographie botanique raisonée; ou, Exposition des faits principaux et des lois
concernant la distribution géographique
des plantes de l'époque actuelle. 2 vols.
2 folding maps. Paris: V. Masson.

1883 Origine des plantes cultivées. (Bibliothèque
Scientifique Internationale, 43.) viii,
377 pp. Paris: Germer Baillière. (Later
versions.)

1885 Origin of cultivated plants. First American edition. (International Scientific
Series, Vol. 48.) viii, 468 pp. New York:
D. Appleton. (Reprint of the 1886 2d edition in 1959 and 1964. New York: Hafner.)

Candolle, Augustin Pyramus de
1813 Théorie élémentaire de la botanique, ou
exposition des principes de la classification naturelle et de l'art de décrire et
d'étudier les végétaux. viii, 528 pp.
Paris: Peterville.

Cárdenas, Martín
1969 Manual de plantas económicas de Bolivia.
421 pp. Cochabamba: Imprenta Icthus.

Carlson, Gustav G. and Volney H. Jones
1939 Some notes on uses of plants by the
Comanche Indians. Papers of the Michigan
Academy of Science, Arts and Letters 25.4:
517-542. Ann Arbor.

Carter, George Francis
1938 Aboriginal use of medicinal plants in
southern California. California Garden
29.9:4, 8; 29.11:4-5. San Diego.

1945 Plant geography and culture history in the
American Southwest. (Viking Fund Publica-
tions in Anthropology, No. 5.) 140 pp.
New York: Viking Foundation.

1947   A California account of uses of medicinal
        herbs. Western Folklore 6.3:199-203.
        Berkeley.

1950   Ecology--geography--ethnobotany. Scientific
        Monthly 70.2:73-80. Washington.

Castetter, Edward F.
1935   Uncultivated native plants used as sources
        of food. (Ethnobiological Studies in the
        American Southwest, I; University of New
        Mexico Bulletin No. 266, Biological Series
        4.1.) 62 pp. Albuquerque.

1944   The domain of ethnobiology. American
        Naturalist 78.775:158-170. Lancaster, Pa.

Castetter, Edward F. and Willis H. Bell
1951   Yuman Indian agriculture: primitive subsis-
        tence on the lower Colorado and Gila Rivers.
        274 pp. Albuquerque: University of New
        Mexico Press.

Castetter, Edward F., Willis H. Bell and Alvin R. Grove
1938   The early utilization and the distribution
        of agave in the American Southwest. (Ethno-
        biological Studies in the American Southwest,
        VI; University of New Mexico Bulletin No.
        335, Biological Series 5.4.) 92 pp.
        Albuquerque.

Castetter, Edward F. and Morris E. Opler
1936   The ethnobiology of the Chiricahua and
        Mescalero Apache; A. The use of plants for
        foods, beverages, and narcotics. (Ethno-
        biological Studies in the American Southwest,
        III; University of New Mexico Bulletin No.
        297, Biological Series 4.5.) 63 pp.
        Albuquerque.

1937   The aboriginal utilization of the tall
        cacti in the American Southwest. (Ethno-
        biological Studies in the American South-
        west, IV; University of New Mexico Bulletin
        No. 307, Biological Series 5.1.) 48 pp.
        Albuquerque.

Castetter, Edward F. and Ruth M. Underhill
1935   The ethnobiology of the Papago Indians.
        (Ethnobiological Studies in the American
        Southwest, II; University of New Mexico
        Bulletin No. 275, Biological Series 4.3.)
        84 pp. Albuquerque.

[4:14]

Chamberlain, Alex. J.
  1895   Beitrag zur Pflanzenkunde der Naturvölker
          America's. Pp. 551-556 in Verhandlungen
          der Berliner Gesellschaft für Anthropologie,
          Ethnologie, und Urgeschichte, Jahrgang 1895.
          Berlin.

Chamberlain, Lucia Sarah
  1901   Plants used by the Indians of eastern North
          America. American Naturalist 35.409:1-10.
          Boston.

Chamberlain, Ralph V.
  1909   Some plant names of the Ute Indians.
          American Anthropologist 11.1:27-40. Menasha.

Chao, Yuen Ren
  1953   Popular Chinese plant words: a descriptive
          lexico-grammatical study. Language 29.3:
          379-414. Baltimore.

Chevalier, Auguste
  1923   L'Oeuvre d'Alexis Jordan et la notion
          actuelle d'espèce en systématique. Revue
          de Botanique Appliquée et d'Agriculture
          Coloniale 3:441-459. Paris.

Chock, Alvin K.
  1968   Hawaiian ethnobotanical studies I. Native
          food and beverage plants. Economic Botany
          22.3:221-238. Baltimore.

Christensen, Carl Frederik Albert
  1906   Index filicum; sive, enumeratio omnium
          generum specie-rumque Filicum et Hydropteri-
          dum ab anno 1753 ad finen anni 1905 descrip-
          torum, adjectis synonymis principalibus,
          area geographica etc. lix, 744 pp.
          Hafniae: H. Hagerup.

  1913   Index filicum Supplementum, 1906-1912.
          131 pp. Hafniae: H. Hagerup.

  1917   Index filicum Supplément préliminaire pour
          les années 1913, 1914, 1915, 1916. 60 pp.
          (Publié aux frais de S.A.I. le prince
          Bonaparte.) Hafniae: Types Triers
          bodtrykkeri.

  1934   Index filicum Supplementum tertium, pro
          annis 1917-1933. 219 pp. Hafniae:
          H. Hagerup.

1965   Index filicum Supplementum quartum, pro
        annis 1934-1960. Prepared by Rodolfo E. G.
        Pichi-Sermolli, with the collaboration of
        F. Ballard [and others], being the Committee
        for the Index Filicum of the International
        Association for Plant Taxonomy. (Regnum
        Vegetabile Vol. 37.) xiv, 370 pp. Utrecht:
        International Bureau for Plant Taxonomy and
        Nomenclature.

Clausen, Jens Christian
1951   Stages in the evolution of plant species.
        (Cornell University, Messenger Lectures on
        the Evolution of Civilization, 1950.) viii,
        206 pp. Ithaca: Cornell University Press.

Cleland, J. B.
1957   Our natives and the vegetation of southern
        Australia. Mankind 5.4:149-162. Sydney.

Clercq, Frederik Sigismund Alexander, A. Pulle, and
        A. H. J. G. Walbeehm
1927   Nieuw plantkundig woordenboek voor Neder-
(1909) landsch Indië. Met korte aanwijzingen van
        het nuttig gebruik der planten en hare
        beteekenis in het volksleven, en met regis-
        ters der inlandsche en wetenschappelijke
        benamingen. 2d edition. xxiv, 443 pp.
        Amsterdam: J. H. deBussy. (1st edition
        1909, xx, 395 pp.)

Cobb, Boughton
1956   A field guide to the ferns and their
        related families (northeastern and central
        North America). (Peterson Field Guide 10.)
        xviii, 281 pp. Boston: Houghton Mifflin.

Colless, Donald H.
1967   An examination of certain concepts in
        phenetic taxonomy. Systematic Zoology
        16.1:6-27. Lawrence, Kans.

Condominas, Georges and André Haudricourt
1952   Première contribution à l'ethnobotanique
        indochinoise. Essai d'ethnobotanique Mnong
        Gar (Protoindochinois du Vietnam). Revue
        Internationale de Botanique Appliquée et
        d'Agriculture Tropicale, No. 351-352:19-27,
        169-180. Paris.

Conklin, Harold C.
1954   The relation of Hanunóo culture to the
        plant world. 471 pp. Ph.D. dissertation

[4:16]

in anthropology, Yale University, New Haven.
(Published by University Microfilms, Ann
Arbor, Mich., 1967, [No. 67-4119].)

Conklin, Harold C. (cont.)
1957   Hanunóo agriculture, a report on an integral
        system of shifting cultivation in the Philip-
        pines. (FAO Forestry Development Paper, No.
        12.) xii, 209 pp. Rome: Food and Agricul-
        ture Organization of the United Nations.

1958   Betel chewing among the Hanunóo. 41 pp.
        Quezon City: National Research Council of
        the Philippines.

1959   Ecological interpretations and plant domesti-
        cation. American Antiquity 25.2:260-262.
        Salt Lake City.

1960   Cultural significance of land resources.
        Bulletin of the Philadelphia Anthropological
        Society 13.2:38-42. Philadelphia.

1962a   Ethnobotanical problems in the comparative
        study of folk taxonomy. Proceedings of the
        Ninth Pacific Science Congress of the Pacific
        Science Association, 1957, 4(Botany):299-301.
        Bangkok.

1962b   Lexicographical treatment of folk taxonomies.
        Pp. 119-141 in Problems in lexicography:
        report of the Conference on Lexicography
        held at Indiana University, November 11-12,
        1960, (International Journal of American
        Linguistics 28.2[Part 4]; Publication 21,
        Indiana University Research Center in Anthro-
        pology, Folklore, and Linguistics), edited
        by F. W. Householder and S. Saporta.
        Bloomington. (Volume reprinted with addi-
        tions and corrections 1967.)

1963   The Oceanian-African hypotheses and the
        sweet potato. Pp. 129-136 in Plants and the
        migrations of Pacific peoples, edited by
        J. Barrau. Honolulu: Bishop Museum Press.

1967   Ifugao ethnobotany 1905-1965; the 1911 Beyer-
        Merrill report in perspective. Pp. 204-262
        in Studies in Philippine anthropology, in
        honor of H. Otley Beyer, edited by M. D.
        Zamora. Manila: Alemar-Phoenix. (Reprinted
        with minor changes in Economic Botany 21.3:
        243-273. Baltimore.)

Core, Earl L.
1967   Ethnobotany of the southern Appalachian
        aborigines. Economic Botany 21.3:199-214.
        Baltimore.

Coville, Frederick Vernon
1897   Notes on the plants used by the Klamath
        Indians of Oregon. Contributions from the
        United States National Herbarium 5.(Part 2):
        87-108. Washington.

1904a   Plants used in basketry. Pp. 199-214 in
        Aboriginal American Basketry: studies in
        a textile art without machinery, (United
        States National Museum Report for 1902),
        edited by O. T. Mason. Washington.

1904b   Wokas, a primitive food of the Klamath
        Indians. Pp. 725-739 in United States
        National Museum Report for 1902. Washington.

Cowan, Samuel T.
1968   A dictionary of microbial taxonomic usage.
        (University Reviews in Botany, Vol. 1.)
        x, 118 pp. Edinburgh: Oliver and Boyd.

Cronquist, Arthur
1957   Outline of a new system of families and
        orders of dicotyledons. Bulletin de Jardin
        Botanique de l'État, Jubilee Vol. 27.1:3-40.
        Brussels.

1969   On the relationship between taxonomy and
        evolution. Taxon 18.2:177-187. Utrecht.

Crowson, Roy A.
1970   Classification and biology. ix, 350 pp.
        New York: Atherton.

Crundwell, A. C.
1970   Infraspecific categories in Bryophyta.
        Biological Journal of the Linnean Society
        2.3:221-224. London. (See also Valentine
        et al. 1970.)

Cutler, Hugh C.
1953   Review of Agricultural origins and disper-
        sals, by Carl O. Sauer. American Anthro-
        pologist 55.3:434-436. Menasha.

1962   Review of The ethnobotany of pre-Columbian
        Peru, by Margaret A. Towle. American
        Antiquity 28.2:256-257. Salt Lake City.

[4:18]

Cutler, Hugh and Lawrence Kaplan
    1956   Some plant remains from Montezuma Castle and
            nearby caves (NA 4007 B and C on Dry Beaver
            Creek). Plateau 28.4:98-100. Flagstaff.

Dagognet, François
    1970   Le Catalogue de la vie: étude méthodolo-
            gique sur la taxinomie. 1st edition. 187
            pp. Paris: Presses Universitaires de France.

Dalziel, John M.
    1916   A Hausa botanical vocabulary. 119 pp.
            London: T. Fisher Unwin.

Darlington, Cyril Dean and Ann Philippa Wylie
    1955   Chromosome atlas of flowering plants.
            2d edition. xix, 519 pp. London: Allen
            and Unwin.

Davidson, J. F.
    1954   A dephlogisticated species concept.
            Madroño 12.8:246-251. Berkeley.

Davis, P. H. and V. H. Heywood
    1963   Principles of angiosperm taxonomy. xx,
            556 pp. Edinburgh: Oliver and Boyd;
            Princeton: Van Nostrand.

Day, Gordon M.
    1963   The tree nomenclature of the Saint Francis
            Indians. National Museum of Canada Bulle-
            tin, No. 190:37-48. Ottawa.

De Candolle   (See Candolle.)

Delevoryas, Theodore
    1969   Paleobotany, phylogeny, and a natural sys-
            tem of classification. Taxon 18.2:204-212.
            Utrecht.

Dembeck, Adeline
    1969   Guidebook to man-made textile fibers and
            textured yarns of the world: film-to-yarn
            non-wovens. 3d edition. 345 pp. New York:
            United Piece Dye Works.

Dennler, Jorge G.
    1939   Los nombres indígenas en guaraní de los
            mamíferos de la Argentina y países limítro-
            fes y su importancia para la sistemática.
            Physis 16.48:225-244. Buenos Aires.

278

Densmore, Frances
1928   Uses of plants by the Chippewa Indians.
        Pp. 275-397 in 44th Annual Report of the
        Bureau of American Ethnology, 1926-1927.
        Washington.

Dieterlen, Germaine
1950   Les Correspondances cosmo-biologiques chez
        les Soudanais. Journal de Psychologie
        Normale et Pathologique 43.3:350-366. Paris.

1952   Classification des végétaux chez les Dogon.
        Journal de la Société des Africanistes
        22.1-2:115-158. Paris.

Dixon, Roland B.
1900   Basketry designs of the Maidu Indians of
        California. American Anthropologist 2.2:
        266-276. New York.

1921   Words for tobacco in American Indian lan-
        guages. American Anthropologist 23.1:19-49.
        Menasha.

Dodge, Bertha
1959   Plants that changed the world. 183 pp.
        Boston: Little, Brown.

Dournes, Jacques
1968   Bois-bambou (Kŏyau-ale): aspect végétal de
        l'univers jŏrai. Journal d'Agriculture
        Tropicale et de Botanique Appliquée 15.
        4-5-6:89-156; 15.9-10-11:369-498. Paris.

Dressler, Robert L.
1953   The Pre-Columbian cultivated plants of
        Mexico. Botanical Museum Leaflets, Harvard
        University 16.6:115-172. Cambridge.

Driver, Harold E.
1953   The acorn in North American Indian diet.
        Proceedings of the Indiana Academy of
        Science 62(1952):56-62. Indianapolis.

Du Rietz, G. Einar
1930   The fundamental units of biological taxono-
        my. Svensk Botanisk Tidskrift 24.3:333-428.
        Uppsala.

Elmore, Francis Hapgood
1944   Ethnobotany of the Navaho. (Monographs of
        the School of American Research, No. 8.)

136 pp.   Santa Fe: University of New Mexico Press.

Emmart, Emily Walcott
1940   The Badianus manuscript, (Codex Barberini, Latin 241), Vatican Library, an Aztec herbal of 1552; introduction, translation and annotations by Emily Walcott Emmart, with a foreword by Henry E. Sigerist. xxiv, 341 pp. Baltimore: Johns Hopkins Press.

Engler, Adolf
1898   Syllabus der Pflanzenfamilien.   Eine Uebersicht über das gesammte Pflanzensystem mit Berücksichtigung der Medicinal- und Nutzpflanzen zum Gebrauch bei Vorlesungen und Studien über specielle und medicinish-pharmeceutische Botanik. xii, 214 pp.   Berlin: Gebrüder Borntraeger.

[Engler, Adolf]; Ludwig Diels, editor
1936   A. Engler's Syllabus der Pflanzenfamilien; eine übersicht über des gesamte Pflanzensystem, mit besonderer Berücksichtigung der medizinal- und Nutzpflanzen, nebst einer Uebersicht über die Florenreiche und Florengebiete der Erde, zum Gebrauch bei Vorlesungen und Studien über spezielle und medizinisch-pharmazeutische Botanik.   xlii, 419 pp.   Berlin: Gebrüder Borntraeger.

[Engler, Adolf]; Hans Melchior and Erich Werdermann, editors
1954,   A. Engler's Syllabus der Pflanzenfamilien,
1964   mit besonderer Berücksichtigung der Nutzpflanzen nebst einer Übersicht über die Florenreiche und Florengebiete der Erde. 12., völlig neugestaltete Aufl. von Hans Melchior und Erich Werdermann.   1 Band, Allgemeiner Teil, Bakterien bis Gymnospermen, 367 pp. (1954); 2 Band, Angiospermen, Übersicht über die Florengebiete der Erde, herausgegeben von Hans Melchior, 666 pp. (1964).   Berlin-Nikolassee: Gebrüder Borntraeger.

Engler, Adolf and Karl Prantl
1887-   Die natürlichen Pflanzenfamilien nebst ihren
1909   Gattungen und wichtigeren Arten, insbesondere den Nutzpflanzen, unter Mitwirkung zahlreicher hervorragender Fachgelehrten. 32 vols.   Leipzig: Wilhelm Englemann.

Estabrook, George F.
1966   A mathematical model in graph theory for
        biological classification. Journal of
        Theoretical Biology 12.3:297-310. London
        and New York.

Estabrook, George F. and David J. Rogers
1966   A general method of taxonomic description
        for a computed similarity measure. Bio-
        science 16.11:789-793. Washington.

Fanshawe, D. B.
1953   Akawaio Indian plant names. Caribbean
        Forester 14.3-4:120-127. Rio Piedras,
        Puerto Rico.

Farris, James S.
1967   The meaning of relationship and taxonomic
        procedure. Systematic Zoology 16.1:44-51.
        Lawrence, Kans.

Faulks, Philip James
1958   An introduction to ethnobotany. 152 pp.
        London: Moredale.

Fenton, William N.
1940   An herbarium from the Allegheny Senecas.
        Pp. 787-796 in The historic annals of
        southwestern New York, edited by Doty,
        Congdon, and Thornton. New York: Lewis
        Historical Publishing Co.

1949   Medicinal plant lore of the Iroquois:
        Chauncey Johnny John and James Crow instruct
        He-lost-a-bet in the use of native plants.
        University of the State of New York, Bulle-
        tin to the Schools 35.7:233-237. Albany.

1955   The maple and the passenger pigeon in Iro-
        quois Indian life. University of the State
        of New York, Bulletin to the Schools,
        March 1955, 7 pp. Albany.

Fernald, Merritt Lyndon
1950   Gray's manual of botany: 8th (centennial)
        edition. xliv, 1632 pp. New York:
        American Book.

Fewkes, J. Walter
1896   A contribution to ethnobotany. American
        Anthropologist 9.1:14-21. Washington.

[4:22]

Fitch, Walter M. and Emanual Margoliash
   1967   Construction of phylogenetic trees.   Science
           155.3760:279-284. Washington.

Fleming, H. S. and D. J. Rogers
   1970   A classification of Manihot esculenta Crantz
           using the information carrying content of a
           character as a measure of its classificatory
           rank. Pp. 66-71 in Vol. 1 of Proceedings of
           the Second International Symposium on Tropi-
           cal Root and Tuber Crops. Honolulu: College
           of Tropical Agriculture, University of
           Hawaii.

Fosberg, F. Raymond
   1960a   Introgression in Artocarpus (Moraceae) in
           Micronesia. Brittonia 12.2:101-113. New
           York.

   1960b   Plant collecting as an anthropological field
           method. El Palacio 67.4:125-139. Santa Fe.

Fourmont, R.
   1944   Introduction à un système de nomenclature
           des variétés de pois cultivés en France.
           Comptes rendus de l'Academie de l'Agriculture
           de France 40:499-502. Paris.

Fowler, Catherine Sweeney
   1966   Environmental setting and natural resources.
           Pp. 13-31 in Southern Paiute ethnohistory,
           (Anthropological Papers No. 70; Glen Canyon
           Series No. 28), by Robert C. Euler. Salt
           Lake City: Department of Anthropology,
           University of Utah.

Fowler, Catherine Sweeney and Joy Leland
   1967   Some northern Paiute native categories.
           Ethnology 6.4:381-404. Pittsburgh.

Fox, James J.
   1971   Sister's child as plant: metaphors in an
           idiom of consanguinity. Pp. 219-256 in
           Rethinking kinship and marriage, (Associa-
           tion of Social Anthropologists Monographs,
           11), edited by R. Needham. London:
           Tavistock.

Fox, Robert B.
   1953   The Pinatubo Negritos: their useful plants
           and material culture. Philippine Journal
           of Science 81.3-4:173-414. Manila.

Frake, Charles O.
1962a   Cultural ecology and ethnography. American
         Anthropologist 64.1:53-59. Menasha.

1962b   The ethnographic study of cognitive systems
         [with "comment" by H. C. Conklin]. Pp. 72-
         93 in Anthropology and human behavior,
         edited by T. Gladwin and W. C. Sturtevant.
         Washington: Anthropological Society of
         Washington.

1964   Notes on queries in ethnography. Pp. 79-98
         in Transcultural studies in cognition,
         (American Anthropologist 66.3[Part 2],
         Special Publication), edited by A. K. Romney
         and R. G. D'Andrade. Menasha.

Frederici, Georg
1947   Amerikanistisches Wörterbuch. 722 pp.
         Hamburg: Gram, de Gruyter.

French, David H.
1957   An exploration of Wasco ethnoscience.
         Pp. 224-227 in American Philosophical
         Society, Year Book 1956. Philadelphia.

1960   Review of Indian uses of native plants, by
         Edith van Allen Murphey. Economic Botany
         14.2:164-165. Baltimore.

1965   Ethnobotany of the Pacific Northwest Indians.
         Economic Botany 19.4:378-382. Baltimore.

French, David H. and Jane W. Larson
1967   A bibliography of California Indian ethno-
         botany. 17 pp. Portland: Reed College.

Friedberg, Claudine
1959a   Contribution à l'étude ethnobotanique des
         tombes précolombiennes de Lauri (Pérou).
         Journal d'Agriculture Tropicale et de
         Botanique Appliquée 6.8-9:405-434. Paris.

1959b   Rapport sommaire sur une mission au Pérou
         (effectuée de novembre 1958 à juillet 1959).
         Journal d'Agriculture Tropicale et de
         Botanique Appliquée 6.8-9:439-450. Paris.

1968   Les Méthodes d'enquête en ethnobotanique:
         comment mettre en évidence les taxonomies
         indigènes? Journal d'Agriculture Tropicale
         et de Botanique Appliquée 15.7-8:297-324.
         Paris.

[4:24]

Friedberg, Claudine (cont.)
1970   Analyse de quelques groupements de végétaux
          comme introduction à l'étude de la classifi-
          cation botanique bunaq. Pp. 1092-1031 in
          Échanges et communications, edited by J.
          Pouillon and P. Maranda. The Hague and
          Paris: Mouton.

1971   Aperçu sur la classification botanique bunaq
          (Timor Central). Bulletin de la Société
          Botanique de France 118.3-4:255-262. Paris.

Friedberg, Claudine and Louis Berthe
1963   Note ethnobotanique sur l'utilisation
          rituelle de quelques riz balinais. Journal
          d'Agriculture Tropicale et de Botanique
          Appliquée 10.12:612-620. Paris.

Friedrich, Paul
1970   Proto-Indo-European trees. xvi, 188 pp.
          London and Chicago: University of Chicago
          Press.

Fries, Elias Magnus
1821-   Systema mycologicvm, sistens fvngorvm
1832   ordines, genera et species, hvc vsqve cogni-
          tas, gvas ad normam methodi natvralis
          determinavit, disposvit atqve descripsit
          Elias Fries... 3 vols. Gryphiswaldiae:
          svmtibvs Ernesti Mavritii. (1952 reprint,
          New York: Johnson Reprint Corp.)

Gade, Daniel W.
1970   Ethnobotany of cañihua (Chenopodium pallidi-
          caule), rustic seed crop of the Altiplano.
          Economic Botany 24.1:55-61. Lawrence, Kans.

Gates, William E.
1957   A bibliography for Yucatan medicinal plant
          studies, edited by John L. Sorensen.
          Tlalocan 3.4:334-343. Mexico City.

Gerard, W. R.
1896   Plant names of Indian origin. Garden and
          Forest 9.435-440:252-253, 262-263, 282-283,
          292-293, 302-303.

Gerth van Wijk, H. L.
1911,   A dictionary of plant names. 2 vols.
1916   Vol. 1, Alphabetized by genus, v, 1444 pp.;
          Vol. 2, Alphabetized by common name, xxxiii,
          1696 pp. The Hague: Martinus Nijhoff.

Ghirlanda, Elio
1956   La terminologica viticola mei dialetti della
Svizzera italiana. (Romanica Helvetica, Vol.
61.) 211 pp. Berne: A. Francke.

Gilmore, Melvin Randolph
1919   Uses of plants by the Indians of the Missouri
River region. Pp. 43-154 in 33rd Annual
Report of the Bureau of American Ethnology,
1911-1912. Washington.

1929   The plant tribes. Pp. 165-208 in Prairie
smoke, by M. R. Gilmore. New York: Columbia
University Press.

1932a   The ethnobotanical laboratory at the University of Michigan. (Occasional Contributions
from the Museum of Anthropology of the
University of Michigan, No. 1.) 36 pp.
Ann Arbor.

1932b   Importance of ethnobotanical investigation.
American Anthropologist 34.2:320-327.
Menasha.

Gilmour, J. S. L.
1937   A taxonomic problem. Nature 139.3529:1040-
1042. London.

1940   Taxonomy and philosophy. Pp. 461-474 in
The new systematics, edited by J. Huxley.
London: Oxford University Press.

1951   The development of taxonomic theory since
1851. Nature 168.4271:400-402. London.

1958   The species: yesterday and tomorrow.
Nature 181.4606:379-380. London.

1961a   Taxonomy. Pp. 27-45 in Contemporary
botanical thought, edited by A. Macgillivray
and L. S. Cobley. Edinburgh: Oliver and
Boyd; Chicago: Quadrangle Books.

1961b   The mathematical assessment of taxonomic
similarity, including the use of computers.
Taxon 10.4:97-101. Utrecht.

Gilmour, J. S. L. and S. M. Walters
1964   Philosophy and classification. Pp. 1-22 in
Recent researches in plant taxonomy, (Vistas
in botany, Vol. 4), edited by W. B. Turrill.
New York: Macmillan.

[4:26]

Girault, Louis
   1966   Classification vernaculaire des plantes
   [1967] médicinales chez les Callawaya, médecins
           empiriques (Bolivie). Journal de la Société
           des Américanistes 55.1:155-200. Paris.

Glick, Leonard B.
   1964   Categories and relations in Gimi natural
           science. American Anthropologist 66.4(Part
           2):273-280. Menasha.

Goodspeed, Thomas Harper
   1954   The genus Nicotiana: origins, relationships
           and evolution of its species in the light of
           their distribution, morphology and cytogenet-
           ics. 536 pp. Waltham: Chronica Botanica.

Gould, Sydney W.
   1954   Permanent numbers to supplement the binomial
           system of nomenclature. American Scientist
           42.2:269-274. New Haven.

   1962   Family names of the plant kingdom: inter-
           national plant index. Vol. 1. 111 pp.
           New Haven and New York: IPIx Office.

Grant, Verne
   1957   The plant species in theory and practice. Pp.
           39-80 in The species problem (AAAS Publica-
           tion No. 50), edited by E. Mayr. Washington.

Gray, Asa (See Fernald.)

Gray, Asa and J. Hammond Trumbull
   1883   Review of DeCandolle's Origin of cultivated
           plants; with annotations upon certain Ameri-
           can species. American Journal of Science,
           3d Series, 25.148:241-255; 25.149:370-379;
           26.152:128-138. New Haven.

[Gray Herbarium]
   1873-   Gray Herbarium card index. Cambridge, Mass.

Greene, Edward Lee
   1909   Landmarks of botanical history. (Smithsonian
           Miscellaneous Collections, Vol. 54.) 329 pp.
           Washington.

Greenman, J. M.
   1940   The concept of genus: III. Genera from the
           standpoint of morphology. Bulletin of the
           Torrey Botanical Club 67.5:371-374. New
           York. (See also Bartlett et al. 1940.)

Griaule, Marcel
1952   Le Savoir des Dogon. Journal de Société
         des Africanistes 22.1-2:27-42. Paris.

Guerra, F.
1966   La política imperial sobre las drogas de
         las Indias. Revista Indias 26.103-4:31-58.

Gunckel, Hugo
1960   Nombres indigenas relacionados con la flora
         chilena. Boletín de Filologia 11(1959):191-
         327. Santiago.

Gundersen, Alfred
1920   Plant families: a plea for an international
         sequence. New Phytologist 19.9-10:264-271.
         London.

Gunther, Erna
1945   Ethnobotany of western Washington.
         University of Washington Publications in
         Anthropology 10.1:1-61. Seattle.

Guyot, A. Lucien and Pierre Gibassier
1960a   Les Noms des plantes. (Que sais-je?, No.
         856.) 127 pp. Paris: Presses Universi-
         taires de France.

1960b   Les Noms des arbres. (Que sais-je?, No. 861.)
         127 pp. Paris: Presses Universitaires de
         France.

1960c   Les Noms des fleurs. (Que sais-je?, No.
         866.) 126 pp. Paris: Presses Universi-
         taires de France.

Guzman, H. G.
1960   Nueva localidad de importanica etnomicológi-
         ca de los hongos neurotrópicos mexicanos.
         Ciencia 20.3-4:85-88. Mexico City.

Haber, Tom Burns
1963   Canine terms in popular names of plants.
         American Speech 38.1:28-41. New York.

Hall, A. V.
1969   Giving ranks and names to subsidiary groups.
         Taxon 18.4:375-377. Utrecht.

Hall, Harvey Monroe and Fredric E. Clements
1923   The phylogenetic method in taxonomy: the
         North American species of _Artemesia_,

[4:28]

Chrysothamnus, and Atriplex. (Carnegie Institution of Washington, Publication No. 326.) iv, 355 pp. Washington.

Harlan, Jack R.
1971   Agricultural origins: centers and noncenters. Science 174:468-474. Washington.

Harrington, H. D.
1951   Identification keys in botany. Turtox News 29:166-168. Chicago.

Harrington, John P.
1932   Tobacco among the Karuk Indians of California. (Bulletins of the Bureau of American Ethnology, No. 94.) 284 pp. Washington.

Harrison, S. G.
1963   Nomenclature for cultivated plants. Taxon 12.7:259-260. Utrecht.

Harshberger, John W.
1895   Some new ideas. Philadelphia Evening Telegram, December 5, 1895.

1896a   Ethno-botanic gardens. Science 3.58:203-205. Washington.

1896b   The purposes of ethno-botany. American Antiquarian and Oriental Journal 17.2:73-81. Chicago. (Also 1896, Botanical Gazette 21.3:146-154. Chicago.)

1906   Phytogeographic influences in the arts and industries of the American aborigines. Bulletin of the Geographical Society of Philadelphia 4.3:137-153. Philadelphia.

Hart, Charles P.
1887   Piute herbalists. Proceedings of the American Association for the Advancement of Science, 35th Meeting, Buffalo, 1886, 35: 330-331. Salem, Mass.

Haudricourt, André G.
1960   Une mission linguistique et ethnobotanique en Nouvelle-Calédonie. Journal de la Société des Océanistes 16.16:100-101. Paris.

1962   Domestication des animaux, culture des plantes et traitement d'autrui. L'Homme 2.1:40-50. Paris.

1964   Nature et culture dans le civilization de
        l'igname, l'origine des clones et des clans.
        L'Homme 4.1:93-104. Paris.

Havard, V.
1884   The mesquit. American Naturalist 18.5:451-
        459. Philadelphia.

1895   Food plants of the North American Indians.
        Bulletin of the Torrey Botanical Club 22.3:
        98-123. New York.

1896   Drink plants of the North American Indians.
        Bulletin of the Torrey Botanical Club 23.2:
        33-46. New York.

Hawkes, J. G.
1947   On the origin and meaning of South American
        Indian potato names. Journal of the Linnean
        Society of London 53.350:205-250. London.

Hedrick, U. P. editor
1919   Sturtevant's notes on edible plants. (27th
        Annual Report of the New York Agricultural
        Experimental Station, Vol. 2, Part 2.)
        vii, 686 pp. Albany: J. B. Lyon.

Heider, Karl G.
1969   Sweet potato notes and lexical queries, or,
        the problem of all those names for sweet
        potatoes in the New Guinea Highlands.
        Kroeber Anthropological Society Papers 41:
        78-86. Berkeley.

Heiser, Charles B., Jr.
1969a   Taxonomy. Pp. 110-114 in A short history
        of botany in the United States, edited by
        J. Ewan. New York: Hafner.

1969b   Systematics and the origin of cultivated
        plants. Taxon 18.1:36-45. Utrecht.

Heiser, Charles B., Jr. and Barbara Pickersgill
1969   Names for the cultivated Capsicum species
        (Solanaceae). Taxon 18.3:277-283. Utrecht.

Heizer, Robert F.
1941   The use of plants for fish-poisoning by the
        California Indians. Leaflets of Western
        Botany 3.2:43-44. San Francisco.

1945   Honey-dew "sugar" in western North America.
        Masterkey 19.5:140-145. Los Angeles.

[4:30]

Henshaw, H. W.
1890   Indian origin of maple sugar. American
        Anthropologist 3.4:341-351. Washington.

Hernandez, Francisco
1942-   Historia de las plantas de Nueva España.
1946   3 vols. xx, 1104 pp. Mexico City: Imprenta
        Universitaria.

Herrera y Garmendia, Fortunato L.
1933   Botánica etnológica. La Duplicación de las
        voces en la nomenclatura indígena. Nomencla-
        tura binaria indígena. Revista del Museo
        Nacional 2.1:3-8. Lima.

1934   Botánica etnológica. Filología quechua.
        Revista del Museo Nacional 3.1-2:37-62.
        Lima.

1939   Catálogo alfabético de los nombres vulgares
        y científicos de plantas que existen en el
        Perú. vii, 363 pp. Lima: La Universidad
        Mayor de San Marcos.

Heslop-Harrison, J.
1956   New concepts in flowering-plant taxonomy.
        viii, 135 pp. Cambridge: Harvard Univer-
        sity Press.

Heyerdahl, Thor
1963   Prehistoric voyages as agencies for Melanesi-
        an and South American plant and animal dis-
        persal to Polynesia. Pp. 23-35 in Plants
        and the migrations of Pacific peoples,
        edited by J. Barrau. Honolulu: Bishop
        Museum Press.

Heyne, K.
1927   De nuttige planten van Nederlandsch-Indië.
        2d edition. 3 vols. Batavia: Gedrukt bij
        Ruygrok.

Heywood, Vernon Hilton
1967   Plant taxonomy. 60 pp. London: Arnold.

1970   Infraspecific categories: summary of
        discussion. Biological Journal of the
        Linnean Society 2.3:257-258. London.
        (See also Valentine et al. 1970.)

Heywood, Vernon Hilton, editor
1968   Modern methods in plant taxonomy. (Botanical

Society of the British Isles, Conference
Report No. 10.) xv, 312 pp. New York and
London: Academic Press.

Heywood, Vernon Hilton and Áskell Löve, editors
1963   Symposium on biosystematics; organized by
         the International Organization of Biosystem-
         atics, Montreal, October 1962. (Regnum
         Vegetabile, Vol. 27.) 72 pp. Utrecht.

Heywood, Vernon Hilton and J. McNeill, editors
[c.1964] Phenetic and phylogenetic classification;
         a symposium edited for the Association.
         (Systematics Association Publication No. 6.)
         xi, 164 pp. London.

Hiatt, Betty
1967,   The food quest and the economy of the
1968   Tasmanian aborigines, I and II. Oceania
         38.2:99-133; 38.3:190-219. Sydney.

Hilger, Inez
1937   Chippewa interpretations of natural phenom-
         ena. Scientific Monthly 45.2:178-179.
         Washington.

Hill, Albert Frederick
1945   Ethnobotany in Latin America. Pp. 176-181
         in Plants and plant science in Latin America,
         edited by F. Verdoorn. New York: Ronald
         Press.

1952   Economic botany: a textbook of useful
(1937)   plants and plant products. 2d edition.
         xii, 560 pp. New York: McGraw-Hill.

Hocking, George Macdonald
1949   Ethnobotanical notes. Rocky Mountain
         Druggist, November, p. 12. Denver.

1955   A dictionary of terms in pharmacognosy and
         other divisions of economic botany: a
         compilation of words and expressions relat-
         ing principally to natural medicinal and
         pharmaceutical materials and the plants and
         animals from which they are derived, their
         chemical composition, applications and uses,
         together with some materials derived from
         the plant, animal, and mineral kingdoms of
         current economic interest. xxv, 284 pp.
         Springfield, Ill.: C. Thomas.

[4:32]

Hodge, Walter and Douglas M. Taylor
1957   The ethnobotany of the Island Caribs of
        Dominica. Webbia 12.2:513-644. Florence.

Hollyman, K. J.
1961   The sources and developments of flora vocabu-
        lary in New Caledonian French. Te Reo 4:
        44-64. Auckland.

1966   Observations sur les noms composés en
        français calédonien. Bulletin de la Société
        de Linguistique de Paris 61.1:96-109. Paris.

1970   Nomenclature scientifique et lexique popu-
        laire. Pp. 84-91 in Melanges Marcel Cohen,
        edited by David Cohen. Paris: Mouton.

Honigman, John J.
1956   Coping with the universe. Davidson Journal
        of Anthropology 2.2:85-98. Seattle.

Hough, Walter
1897   The Hopi in relation to their plant environ-
        ment. American Anthropologist 10.2:33-44.
        Washington.

Hudson, H. J.
1970   Infraspecific categories in fungi. Biologi-
        cal Journal of the Linnean Society 2.3:211-
        219. London. (See also Valentine et al.
        1970.)

Hurd, Paul D., E. Gorton Linsley and Thomas W. Whitaker
1971   Squash and gourd bees (Peponais, Xenoglossa)
        and the origin of the cultivated Cucurbita.
        Evolution 25.1:218-234. Lawrence, Kans.

Hutchinson, John
1959   The families of flowering plants. Arranged
        according to a new system based on their
        probable phylogeny. 2d edition. 2 vols.
        Vol. 1, pp. i-xvi, 1-510; vol. 2, pp. i-x,
        511-792. Oxford: Clarendon.

Hutchinson, John and Ronald Melville
1948   The story of plants and their uses to man.
        xv, 334 pp. London: P. R. Gawthorn.

Hutchinston, Joseph, editor
1965   Essays on crop plant evolution. vii, 204
        pp. Cambridge: Cambridge University Press.

Huxley, Julian, editor
   1940   The new systematics. 583 pp. London:
           Oxford University Press. (Reprinted 1952.)

Index filicum (See Christensen.)

[Index Kewensis]
   1893   Index Kewensis: an enumeration of the
   [1895] genera and species of flowering plants from
           the time of Linnaeus to the year 1885 inclu-
           sive, together with their author's names,
           the works in which they were first published,
           their native countries and their synonyms.
           Compiled at the expense of the late Charles
           Robert Darwin under the direction of Joseph
           D. Hooker by B. Daydon Jackson. 2 vols. in
           4. Oxford: Clarendon.

   1901-   Index Kewensis plantarum phanerogamarum.
           Supplementum Primum,...by Theophilus Durand
           and B. Daydon Jackson. Brussels: Alfredum
           Castaigne. (Supplements to 1970.)

Inger, Robert F.
   1958   Comments on the definition of genera.
           Evolution 12.3:370-384. Lancaster, Pa.

Inglett, G. E. and Joann F. May
   1968   Tropical plants with unusual taste proper-
           ties. Economic Botany 24.4:326-331.
           Baltimore.

Inglis, William Grant
   1966   The observational basis of homology.
           Systematic Zoology 15.3:219-228. Lawrence,
           Kans.

International Commission for the Nomenclature of
           Cultivated Plants.
   1969   International code of nomenclature of culti-
           vated plants--1969. Edited by J. S. L.
           Gilmour et al. (Regnum Vegetabile, Vol.
           64.) 32 pp. Utrecht: International Bureau
           for Plant Taxonomy and Nomenclature of the
           International Association for Plant Taxonomy.

Irvine, F. R.
   1959   Bibliography of wild food plants of United
           States Indians. (Smithsonian Institution
           Leaflet.) 26 pp. Washington.

   1963   Bibliography of wild food plants of

293

[4:34]

Canadian Indians. (Smithsonian Institution
Leaflet.) 13 pp. Washington.

Jain, Sudhanshu Kumar
1968   Medicinal plants. xi, 176 pp. New Delhi:
National Book Trust.

James, George Wharton
1902   Indian basketry. 2d edition, revised and
enlarged. 274 pp., 360 illustrations,
bibliography of Indian basketry. New York:
H. Malkan.

Jaques, Harry Edwin
1948   Plant families: how to know them; pictured-
(1941)   keys for determining the families of nearly
all of the members of the entire plant
kingdom. 2d edition. 177 pp. Dubuque, Iowa:
Wm. C. Brown.

Jardine, Nicholas
1969   What is biological homology? Classification
Society Bulletin 2.1:2-4. Leicester,
England.

Jeffrey, Charles
1968a   Evolution, phylogeny and systematics.
Taxon 17.1:65-70. Utrecht.

1968b   Systematic categories for cultivated plants.
Taxon 17.2:109-114. Utrecht.

1968c   An introduction to plant taxonomy. 128 pp.
London: J. and A. Churchill.

Jeffreys, M. D. W.
1965   Vernacular maize names and some African
tribal migrations. Annals of the New York
Academy of Sciences 118(Art. 12):555-574.
New York.

1967   Who introduced maize into southern Africa?
South African Journal of Science 63.1(Supplement):23-40. Johannesburg.

Jepson, Willis Linn
1924   A flora of the economic plants of California,
for agricultural students, including the
important crop plants, agricultural weeds,
poisonous plants, honey plants, medicinal
plants, chaparral shrubs, native timber
trees, and the most common native plants of

[4:35]

the spring flowering. 223 pp. Berkeley:
University of California, Associated Students
Store.

c.1925   A manual of the flowering plants of California. 1238 pp. Berkeley: University of
California, Associated Student's Store.

Jirásek, Václav
1961   Evolution of the proposals of taxonomical
categories for the classification of cultivated plants. Taxon 10.2:34-45. Utrecht.

Johnson, L. A. S.
1967   Rainbow's end: the quest for an optimal
taxonomy. Proceedings of the Linnaean
Society of New South Wales 93.1:8-45.
Sydney. (Reprinted 1970, Systematic Zoology
19.3:203-239. Lawrence, Kans.)

Jones, Volney H.
1936   Some Chippewa and Ottawa uses of sweet
grass. Papers of the Michigan Academy of
Science, Arts and Letters 21(1935):21-31.
Ann Arbor.

1937   Notes on the preparation and the uses of
basswood fiber by the Indians of the Great
Lakes Regions. Papers of the Michigan
Academy of Science, Arts and Letters 22
(1936):1-14. Ann Arbor.

1941   The nature and status of ethnobotany.
Chronica Botanica 6.10:219-221. Waltham,
Mass.

1945   The use of honey-dew as food by Indians.
Masterkey 19.5:145-149. Los Angeles.

Jones, Volney H., Gordon R. Willey, and Frank H. H.
Roberts, Jr.
1946   Combined review of Plant geography and
culture history in the American Southwest,
by George F. Carter. American Antiquity
11.4:262-269. Menasha.

Jonker, F. P.
1962   Heyerdahl's Kon-Tiki theory and its relation
to ethnobotany. Pp. 535-550 in Annual Report
of the Smithsonian Institution, 1961.
Washington.

Jordan, Alexis
1873   Remarques sur le fait de l'existençe en
        sociéte, à l'état sauvage, des espèces
        végétales affines, et sur d'autres faits
        relatifs à la question de l'espèce.
        (Reprinted 1923, Revue de Botanique Appli-
        quée et d'Agriculture Coloniale 3:459-477,
        Paris.)

Jussieu, Antoine Laurent de
1789   Genera plantarum, secundum ordines naturales
        disposita, juxta methodum in Horto regio
        parisiensi exaratum, anno M.DCC.LXXIV. 24,
        lxxii, 498 pp. Paris: Herissant et Barrois.
        (Reprinted, 1964, with an introduction by
        Frans A. Stafleu. Weinheim: Cramer.)

Kaden, N. N. and M. E. Kirpicznikov
1967   Once more on fruit terminology. Taxon 16.3:
        181-183. Utrecht.

Kano, Tadao and Kokichi Segawa
1956   An illustrated ethnography of Formosan
(1945) aborigines... Vol. 1. The Yami. Revised
        edition. Tokyo: Maruzen.

Kaplan, Lawrence
1960   Historical and ethnobotanical aspects of
        domestication in Tagetes. Economic Botany
        14.3:200-202. Baltimore.

1963   Archeoethnobotany of Cordova Cave, New
        Mexico. Economic Botany 17.4:350-359.
        Baltimore.

Kell, Katharine T.
1966   Folk names for tobacco. Journal of American
        Folklore 79.3-4:590-599. Austin, Texas.

Kelsey, Harlan P. and William A. Dayton, editors
1942   Standardized plant names. 2d edition: A
        revised and enlarged listing of approved
        scientific and common names of plants and
        plant products in American commerce or use.
        xvi, 675 pp. Harrisburg, Pa.: J. Horace
        McFarland.

Kluyver, Albert Jan and C. B. van Niel
1936   Prospects for a natural system of classifi-
        cation of bacteria. Zentralblatt für Bak-
        teriologie, Parasitenkunden, Infektionskrank-
        heiten und Hygiene (Abt. II) 94:369. Jena
        and Stuttgart.

Kroeber, A. L.
1920   Review of Uses of plants by the Indians of
        the Missouri River region, by M. R. Gilmore.
        American Anthropologist 22.4:384-385.
        Menasha.

La Barre, Weston
1938a   Native American beers. American Anthropolo-
        gist 40.2:224-234. Menasha.

1938b   The peyote cult. (Yale University Publica-
        tions in Anthropology, No. 19.) 188 pp.
        New Haven.

1947a   Potato taxonomy among the Aymara Indians
        of Bolivia. Acta Americana 4.1-2:83-103.
        Mexico City.

1947b   Kiowa folk sciences. Journal of American
        Folklore 60.236:105-114. Philadelphia.

1948   The Aymara Indians of the Lake Titicaca
        Plateau, Bolivia. (American Anthropologist
        50.1[Part 2]; Memoir No. 68.) 250 pp.
        Menasha.

Lam, H. J.
1936   Phylogenetic symbols, past and present.
        Acta Biotheoretica (Series A) 2.3:153-194.
        Leiden.

1948   Classification and the new morphology.
        Acta Biotheoretica (Series A) 8.4:107-154.
        Leiden.

Lamb, F. Bruce
1968   Mahogany name controversy. Economic Botany
        22.1:84-86. Baltimore.

Lanjouw, Joseph
1959   Synopsis of proposals concerning the
        International Code of Botanical Nomenclature
        submitted to the Ninth International Botani-
        cal Congress, Montreal, 1959. (Regnum
        Vegetabile, Vol. 14.) 84 pp. Utrecht.

Lanjouw, Joseph, editor
1950   Botanical nomenclature and taxonomy. With
        a Supplement to the International Rules of
        Botanical Nomenclature, embodying the alter-
        ations made at the 6th International Botani-
        cal Congress, Amsterdam, 1935, compiled by

[4:38]

        T. A. Sprague.   Chronica Botanica 12.1-2:
        1-87. Waltham, Mass.

Lanjouw, Joseph et al., editors
    1966   International Code of Botanical Nomenclature,
            adopted by the Tenth International Botanical
            Congress, Edinburgh, August 1964 (in English,
            French, and German). 402 pp. Utrecht:
            International Bureau for Plant Taxonomy and
            Nomenclature of the International Association
            for Plant Taxonomy.

Laszlo, Henry de and Paul S. Henshaw
    1954   Plant materials used by primitive peoples
            to affect fertility.   Science 119.3097:626-
            631. Washington.

Laufer, Berthold
    1919   Sino-Iranica; Chinese contributions to the
            history of civilization in ancient Iran,
            with special reference to the history of
            cultivated plants and products.   (Field
            Museum of Natural History, Anthropological
            Series 15.3.) iv, 185-630 pp. Chicago.

Lawrence, George H. M.
    1951   Taxonomy of vascular plants. 823 pp. New
            York: Macmillan.

    1955   An introduction to plant taxonomy. 179 pp.
            New York: Macmillan.

Lawrence, George H. M. et al.
    1953   Plant genera, their nature and definition;
            a symposium. Chronica Botanica 14.3:91-160.
            Waltham, Mass.

Laydevant, François
    1942   Les Plantes et l'ethnographie au Basutoland.
            Annali Lateranensi 6:237-283. Rome.

Lea, David Alexander Maclure
    1964   Abelam land and subsistence: swidden horti-
            culture in an area of high population
            density, Maprik, New Guinea. Ph.D. disser-
            tation in geography, Australian National
            Museum, Canberra.

    1966   Yam growing in the Maprik area. Papua and
            New Guinea Agricultural Journal 18.1:5-15.
            Konedobu.

Learned, Henry Dexter
1941   The definition of <u>mahogany</u>. Language 17.3:
        256-257. Baltimore.

Legendre, P. and P. Vaillancourt
1969   A mathematical model for the entities
        species and genus. Taxon 18.3:245-252.
        Utrecht.

León, Jorge
1964   Plantas alimenticias andinas. (Bol. Tech.
        6, Instituto Interamericano de Ciencas.)
        Lima: Peru.

Leroy, Jean F.
1958   Taxon, taxonomie...querelle de mots?
        querelle de fond! Journal d'Agriculture
        Tropicale et de Botanique Appliquée 5.1-2-3:
        173-176. Paris.

Leroy, Jean-François
1970   Origine des plantes cultivées--problèmes et
        méthodes. Article A (79 pp.) in Cours de
        ethno-botanique et ethno-zoologie (1969-
        1970), Vol. 2, edited by J.-F. Leroy. Paris:
        Museum National d'Histoire Naturelle; Labora-
        toire d'Ethno-Botanique et d'Ethno-Zoologie.

Lévi-Strauss, Claude
1962   La Pensée sauvage. ii, 395 pp. Paris:
        Plon. (Translated 1966 as The savage mind,
        xii, 290 pp. London: Weidenfeld and Nicol-
        son; Chicago: University of Chicago Press.)

1970   Les Champignons dans la culture: a propos
        d'un livre de M. R. G. Wasson. L'Homme
        10.1:5-16. Paris.

Linnaeus, Carolus
1735   Systema naturae. First edition. Leiden:
(1964) Haak. (1964 facsimile of the first edition,
        with an introduction and a first English
        translation of the "Observationes" by M. S.
        J. Engel-Ledeboer and H. Engel. [Dutch
        Classics on the History of Science 8.]
        30, facsim, [9 l], Nieuwkoop: B. de Graaf.)

1754   Genera plantarum. 5th edition. (1960 fac-
(1960) simile with an introduction by William T.
        Stearn. [xxiv], xxxii, 500 pp. + index.
        Weinheim/Bergstr.: J. Cramer. [1st edition
        1737, Uppsala.].)

Linton, Ralph
    1924   Use of tobacco among North American Indians.
            (Field Museum of Natural History, Anthro-
            pology Leaflet No. 15.) 27 pp. Chicago.

Lloyd, Robert M.
    1964   Ethnobotanical uses of California pterido-
            phytes by western American Indians. Ameri-
            can Fern Journal 54.2:76-82. Baltimore.

Long, Charles A.
    1966   Dependence in taxonomy. Taxon 15.2:49-63.
            Utrecht.

Luomala, Katherine
    1953   Ethnobotany of the Gilbert Islands. (Bernice
            P. Bishop Museum Bulletin No. 213.) v, 129
            pp. Honolulu.

Mabuchi, Toichi
    1964   Tales concerning the origin of grains in the
            insular area of eastern and southeastern
            Asia. Asian Folklore Studies 13.1:1-92.
            Tokyo.

Maccacaro, G. A.
    1958   La misura delle informazione contenuta nei
            criteri di classificazione. Annali di
            Microbiologia ed Enzimologia 8:231-239.
            Milan.

McClure, Floyd A.
    1956   Bamboo in the economy of oriental peoples.
            Economic Botany 10.4:335-361. Lancaster, Pa.

    1966a   A glossary of the bamboos. Taxon 15.6:220-
            235. Utrecht.

    1966b   The bamboos: a fresh perspective. xv, 347
            pp. Cambridge: Harvard University Press.

McFarland, J. W.
    1951   Poisonous plants used for fishing. Yosemite
            Nature Notes 30:14-21. Stockton, Calif.

McKaughan, Howard P. and Batua A. Macaraya
    1965   Maranao plant names. 47 pp. Honolulu:
            University of Hawaii.

Maclet, Jean-Noël and Jacques Barrau
    1959   Catalogue des plantes utiles aujourd'hui
            présentes en Polynésie française. Journal

d'Agriculture Tropicale et de Botanique
Appliquée 6.4-5:161-184. Paris.

Maekawa, Fumio
1962   Ethnobotanical notes on Cynanchum caudatum
in Ainu. Journal of Japanese Botany 37.9:
288. Tokyo.

Mahr, August C.
1954   Aboriginal culture traits as reflected in
18th century Delaware Indian tree names.
Ohio Journal of Science 54.6:380-387.
Columbus.

1955a   Semantic analysis of eighteenth-century
Delaware Indian names for medicinal plants.
Ethnohistory 2.1:11-28. Bloomington, Ind.

1955b   Eighteenth century terminology of Delaware
Indian cultivation and use of maize: a
semantic analysis. Ethnohistory 2.3:209-
240. Bloomington, Ind.

1962   Delaware terms for plants and animals in the
eastern Ohio country: a study in semantics.
Anthropological Linguistics 4.5:1-48.
Bloomington, Ind.

Maldonado-Koerdell, Manuel
1942   Estudios etnobiológicos: notas a una bibliografía mexicana de botánica. Boletín
Bibliográfico de Anthropología Americana
6.1-3:61-74. Mexico City.

Malinowski, Bronislaw
1935   Coral gardens and their magic. 2 vols.
Vol. 1, The description of gardening, xxxv,
500 pp.; Vol. 2, The language of magic and
gardening, xxxii, 350 pp. London: Allen
and Unwin; New York: American Book Co.
(Reprinted 1965 as: Vol. 1, Soil-tilling
and agricultural rites in the Trobriand
Islands, xlv, 500 pp.; Vol. 2, The language
of magic and gardening, xliv, 350 pp.
Bloomington: Indiana University Press.)

Malone, Kemp
1940   On defining mahogany. Language 16.4:308-
318. Baltimore.

Mangelsdorf, Paul C.
1953   Review of Agricultural origins and disper-

[4:42]

        sals, by Carl O. Sauer. American Antiquity
        19.1:87-90. Salt Lake City.

Marafioti, Richard Lynn
    1970   The meaning of generic names of important
        economic plants. Economic Botany 24.2:189-
        207. Lawrence, Kans.

Marcelin, Milo
    1956   Le Maïs, son vocabulaire. Optique, Whole
        No. 24:59-70. Port-au-Prince, Haiti.

Martin, Richard T.
    1970   The role of coca in the history, religion,
        and medicine of South American Indians.
        Economic Botany 24.4:422-438. Lawrence,
        Kans.

Martín del Campo, Rafael
    1955   Productos biológicos del Valle de México.
        Revista Mexicana de Estudios Antropológicos
        14(Part 1):53-77. Mexico City.

Martínez, Maximino
    1933   Las plantas medicinales de México. 644 pp.
        Mexico City: Ediciones Botas. (Later
        edition 1969, Mexico City: La Impresora
        Azteca.)

Masefield, G. B., M. Wallis, S. G. Harrison, and J. B.
    E. Nicholson
    1969   The Oxford book of food plants. 206 pp.
        Fairlawn, N. J.: Oxford University Press.

Mason, H. L.
    1950   Taxonomy, systematic botany and biosystemat-
        ics. Madroño 10:193-208. Berkeley.

Massal, E. and Jacques Barrau
    1956   Food plants of the South Sea Islands. (South
        Pacific Commission, Technical Paper No. 94.)
        iv, 52 pp. Noumea.

Matthews, Washington
    1886   Navajo names for plants. American Natural-
        ist 20.9:767-777. Philadelphia.

Maxwell, H.
    1918   Indian medicine made from trees. American
        Forestry 24.292:205-211.

Mayr, Ernst
    1949   The species concept: semantics versus

semantics. Evolution 3.4:371-372. Lancaster, Pa.

Mead, George R.
1970 On the improper usage of common names when giving botanical data. American Antiquity 35.1:108-109. Salt Lake City.

Medsger, Oliver Perry
1939 Edible wild plants. 323 pp. New York: Macmillan.

Mellinger, Marie B.
1965 Medicine plants of the Cherokees. Tile and Till 51.4:51-53.

Mercier, André-Louis
1951- Enquête sur les végétaux dans le folklore et
1954 l'ethnographie. L'Ethnographie (n.s.) 46: 125-139; 47:86-113; 48:48-61; 49:82-92. Paris.

1964- Suite de l'enquête sur les végétaux dans le
1965 folklore et l'ethnographie. Les agrumes. L'Ethnographie (n.s.) 58-59:136-142. Paris.

Merrill, Elmer Drew
1938 On the significance of certain oriental plant names in relation to introduced species. Proceedings of the American Philosophical Society (1937) 78.1:111-146. Philadelphia. (Reprinted 1946, pp. 295-315 in Merrilleana [Chronica Botanica 10.3-4], Waltham, Mass.)

1945 Plant life of the Pacific world. xv, 295 pp. New York: Macmillan.

1946 Merrilleana: a selection from the general writings of Elmer Drew Merrill. Chronica Botanica 10.3-4:127-394. Waltham, Mass.

1950 Observations on cultivated plants with reference to certain American problems. Ceiba 1.1:3-36. Tegucigalpa, Honduras.

1954 The botany of Cook's voyages. Chronica Botanica 14.5-6:1-iv, 161-304, plates 80-93. Waltham, Mass.

Merrill, Ruth E.
1923 Plants used in basketry by the California

303

[4:44]

Indians. University of California Publications in American Archaeology and Ethnology 20.13:215-242. Berkeley.

Metcalf, Z. P.
1954   The construction of keys. Systematic Zoology 3.1:38-45. Baltimore.

Millot, Jacques
1965   Inde et bétel. Objets et Mondes 5.2:73-122. Paris.

1966a   Inde et bétel, notes complémentaires. Objets et Mondes 6.1:19-30. Paris.

1966b   Le Bétel au Nepal. Objets et Mondes 6.2: 153-168. Paris.

Möller, F.
1962   Quantitative methods in the systematics of Actinomycetales IV. The theory and application of a probabilistic identification key. Giornale de Microbiologia 10:29-47. Milan.

Mooney, James
1889   Cherokee plant lore. American Anthropologist 2.3:223-224. Washington.

Morton, C. V.
1957   The misuse of the term taxon. Taxon 6.5: 155. Utrecht. (Also 1957, Rhodora 59.698: 43-44. Boston.)

Morton, Julia F.
1968   A survey of medicinal plants of Curaçao. Economic Botany 22.1:87-102. Baltimore.

Munk, Anders
1962   An approach to an analysis of taxonomic method with main reference to higher fungi. Taxon 11.6:185-190. Utrecht.

Müntzing, Arne
1959   Darwin's views on variation under domestication in the light of present-day knowledge. Proceedings of the American Philosophical Society 103.2:190-220. Philadelphia.

Neher, Robert Trostle
1968   The ethnobotany of Tagetes. Economic Botany 22.4:317-325. Baltimore.

Newberry, John Strong
1888   Food and fiber plants of the North American
        Indians. Popular Science Monthly 32:31-46.
        New York. (Pamphlet 1887, 16 pp., New York:
        D. Appleton.)

Nickerson, G. S.
1966   Some data on Plains and Great Basin Indian
        uses of certain plants. Tebiwa 9.1:45-51.
        Pocatello: Idaho State College Museum.

Nissen, Claus
1966   Die botanische Buchillustration, ihre
        Geschichte und Bibliographie. 2d edition.
        Stuttgart: Anton Hiersemann.

Oblitas Poblete, Enrique
1969   Plantas medicinales de Bolivia. Cochabamba:
        Amigos de Libro.

Ochse, J. J. et al.
1961   Tropical and subtropical agriculture. 2
        vols. Vol. 1, pp. i-liv, 1-760; Vol. 2,
        pp. i-xxii, 761-1446. New York: Macmillan.

Ochse, J. J. and R. C. Bakhuizen van den Brink
1931a   Vruchten en vruchtenteelt in Nederlandsch-
        Oost-Indië. 181 pp. Batavia: G. Kolff.
        (Translated 1931 by C. A. Backer as Fruits
        and fruitculture in the Dutch East Indies.
        xv, 180 pp. Batavia-C.: G. Kolff.)

1931b   Vegetables of the Dutch East Indies (edible
        tubers, bulbs, rhizomes and spices included);
        survey of the indigenous and foreign plants
        serving as pot-herbs and side-dishes.
        (English edition of revised and much enlarged
        2d edition [1925] of Indische groenten;
        translation by C. A. Backer.) xxxvi, 1005
        pp. Buitenzorg, Java: Archipel Drukkerij.

Oliver, Daniel
1897   First book of Indian botany. 397 pp.
(1869) London: Macmillan.

Osgood, Cornelius
1959   Ingalik mental culture. (Yale University
        Publications in Anthropology, No. 56.)
        195 pp. New Haven.

Ossewaarde, Johannes Gijsbert and S. J. Wellensiek
1946   Capita selecta uit de algemeene plantenteelt.

Pp. 83-200 in Vol. 1 of De Landbouw in den Indischen Archipel, edited by C. J. J. van Hall and C. van Koppel. 's-Gravenhage: W. van Hoeve.

Ostwalt, Wendell Henry
1957   A western Eskimo ethnobotany. Anthropological Papers of the University of Alaska 6.1: 16-36. College.

Palmer, Edward
1871   Food products of the North American Indians. Pp. 404-428 in U.S. Department of Agriculture, Report of the Commissioner of Agriculture, 1870. Washington.

1889   Opuntia fruit as an article of food. West American Scientist 6(whole no. 45):67-69. San Diego.

Parham, H. B. Richenda
1943   Fiji native plants, with their medicinal and other uses. (Polynesian Society, Memoir No. 16; Supplement to the Journal of the Polynesian Society.) xii, 160 pp. Wellington.

Paso y Troncoso, Francisco del
1886   La botanica entre los Nahuas. Anales del Museo Nacional de México 3:140-235. Mexico City.

Patiño, Victor Manuel
1963,   Plantas cultivadas y animales domésticos en
1964   América equinoccial. 1st edition. Vol. 1, Frutales, 647 pp.; Vol. 2, Plantas alimenticias, 364 pp. Cali, Colombia: Imprenta Departmental.

Perrot, Émile
1943-   Matières premières usuelles du règne végétal.
1944   Thérapeutique--hygiène--industrie. 2 vols. Paris: Masson.

Peterson, Roger Tory and Margaret McKenny
1968   A field guide to wildflowers of northeastern and north-central North America. A visual approach arranged by color, form, and detail. (Peterson Field Guide 17.) xxviii, 420 pp. Boston: Houghton Mifflin.

Petrides, George A.
1958   A field guide to trees and shrubs: field

marks of all trees, shrubs, and woody vines
that grow wild in the northeastern and north-
central United States and in southeastern
and south-central Canada. (Peterson Field
Guide 11.) xxix, 431 pp. Boston: Houghton
Mifflin.

Phillips, John Frederick Vicars
1960   Agriculture and ecology in Africa: a study
of actual and potential development south
of the Sahara. 423 pp. New York: Praeger.

Pickering, Charles
1879   Chronological history of plants: man's
record of his own existence illustrated
through their names, uses, and companionship.
xvi, 1222 pp. Boston: Little, Brown.

Popenoe, Wilson
1920   Manual of tropical and subtropical fruits,
excluding the banana, coconut, pineapple,
citrus fruits, olive, and fig. xv, 474 pp.
New York: Macmillan.

Porter, Cedric Lambert
1967   Taxonomy of flowering plants. 2d edition.
(1959) 472 pp. San Francisco: W. H. Freeman.

Portères, Roland
1956   Taxonomie agro-botanique des riz cultivés
(Oryza sativa L. et O. glaberrima St.).
Journal d'Agriculture Tropicale et de
Botanique Appliquée 3:341-384, 541-580,
622-700, 821-856. Paris.

1961   L'Ethnobotanique: place-object-méthode-
philosophie. Journal d'Agriculture Tropicale et de Botanique Appliquée 8.4-5:102-
109. Paris.

1966   Les Noms des riz en Guinée. Journal d'Agriculture Tropicale et de Botanique Appliquée.
13.1-2-3:1-32. Paris.

[1970] Cours d'ethno-botanique générale (1969-1970).
(Vol. 1 of Cours de ethno-botanique et ethno-
zoologie.) 151 pp. Paris: Laboratoire
d'Ethno-Botanique et d'Ethno-Zoologie,
Muséum National d'Histoire Naturelle.

Porterfield, W. M., Jr.
1951   The principal Chinese vegetable foods and

food plants of Chinatown markets. Economic
Botany 5.1:3-37. Lancaster, Pa.

Pouillon, Jean and Pierre Maranda, editors
1970   Échanges et communications; mélanges offerts
        à Claude Lévi-Strauss à l'occasion de son
        60ème anniversaire. 2 vols. 1452 pp. The
        Hague and Paris: Mouton.

Prado, Bento
1970   Philosophie, musique et botanique. De Rous-
        seau à Lévi-Strauss. Pp. 571-580 in Échanges
        et communications, edited by J. Pouillon and
        P. Maranda. The Hague and Paris: Mouton.

Price, P. David
1967   Two types of taxonomy: a Huichol ethnobotan-
        ical example. Anthropological Linguistics
        9.7:1-28. Bloomington, Ind.

Pritzel, George August and C. Jessen
1884   Die deutschen Volksnamen der Pflanzen. viii,
        701 pp. Leipzig: Otto Lenz. (Reprinted
        1966.)

Proskauer, Johannes
1968a   On nomenclatural dialectics, or two blatantly
        different names are not the same. Taxon
        17.5:502-503. Utrecht.

1968b   The type method vs. relicts from the past.
        Taxon 17.5:583-584. Utrecht.

Pursh, Frederick
1814   Flora Americae Septentrionalis; or, a system-
        atic arrangement and description of the
        plants of North America. 2d edition. 2 vols.
        London: White, Cochrane.

Quinn, Vernon
1938   Roots: their place in life and legend.
        230 pp. New York: Frederick A. Stokes.

Raponda-Walker, André and Roger Sillans
1961   Les Plantes utiles du Gabon. Essai d'inven-
        taire et de concordance des noms vernacu-
        laires et scientifiques des plantes spontanées
        et introduites. Description des espèces,
        propriétés, utilisations économiques, ethno-
        graphiques et artistiques. (Encyclopédie
        Biologique 66.) x, 614 pp. Paris: Paul
        Lechevalier.

Raven, Peter H., Brent Berlin, and Dennis E. Breedlove
1971   The origins of taxonomy. A review of its
        historical development shows why taxonomy is
        unable to do what we expect of it. Science
        171.4015:1210-1213. Washington.

Raven, Peter H. and Richard W. Holm
1967   Systematics and the levels-of-organization
        approach. Systematic Zoology 16.1:1-5.
        Lawrence, Kans.

Ravin, Arnold W.
1963   Experimental approaches to the study of
        bacterial phylogeny. American Naturalist
        97.896:307-318. Tempe, Ariz.

Reichard, Gladys A.
1948   Navajo classification of natural objects.
        Plateau 21.1:7-12. Flagstaff.

Reichel-Dolmatoff, Gerardo
1968   Desana: simbolismo de los indios Tukano del
        Vaupés. xiii, 270 pp. Bogotá: Universidad
        de los Andes. (Translated 1971 by the author
        as Amazonian Cosmos, the sexual and religious
        symbolism of the Tukano Indians. xxiii,
        290 pp. Chicago: University of Chicago
        Press.)

Rickett, Harold William
1958   So what is a Taxon? Taxon 7.2:37-38.
        Utrecht.

Ring, M.
1930   Flora for an Indian garden. Masterkey
        4.3:68-77. Los Angeles.

Robbins, Wilfred William, John P. Harrington, and
        Barbara Freire-Marreco
1916   Ethnobotany of the Tewa Indians. Bulletins
        of the Bureau of American Ethnology, No. 55.)
        xii, 118 pp. Washington.

Rogers, David J.
1963   Taximetrics--new name, old concept.
        Brittonia 15.4:285-290. New York.

Rogers, David J. and S. G. Appan
1969   Taximetric methods for delimiting biological
        species. Taxon 18.5:609-624. Utrecht.

Rogers, David J. and Henry Fleming
1964   A computer program for classifying plants.

[4:50]

II. A numerical handling of non-numerical
data. Bioscience 14.9:15-28. Washington.

Rogers, David J. and Taffee T. Tanimoto
1960   A computer program for classifying plants.
        Science 132.3434:1115-1118. Washington.

Roia, Frank C., Jr.
1966   The use of plants in hair and scalp prepara-
        tions. Economic Botany 20.1:17-30. Balti-
        more.

Rolland, Eugène
1896-   Flore populaire, ou, Histoire naturelle des
1914   plantes dans leurs rapports avec la linguis-
        tique et le folklore. 11 vols. (Vols. 8-11
        edited by Henri Gaidoz.) Paris: various
        publishers. (1967 reprint, Paris: G. P.
        Maisonneuve and Larose.)

Rollins, Reed C.
1965   On the bases on biological classification.
        Taxon 14.1:1-6. Utrecht.

Romero, John B.
1954   The botanical lore of the California Indians,
        with side lights on historical incidents in
        California. vii, 82 pp. New York: Vantage
        Press.

Roon, A. C. de
1958   International directory of specialists in
        plant taxonomy, with a census of their
        current interests. (Regnum Vegetabile,
        Vol. 13.) 266 pp. Utrecht: International
        Bureau of Plant Taxonomy and Nomenclature.

Ross, R.
1958   What is a "New Taxon"? Taxon 7.3:65-68.
        Utrecht.

Roth, Walter Edmund
1924   An introductory study of the arts, crafts,
        and customs of the Guiana Indians. Pp. 25-
        745 in 38th Annual Report of the Bureau of
        American Ethnology, 1916-1917. Washington.

Rousseau, Jacques
1955   Les Noms populaires des plantes au Canada
        français. Pp. 135-173 in Études du parler
        Français au Canada. Québec.

1961   Le Champ de l'ethnobotanique. Journal
        d'Agriculture Tropicale et de Botanique
        Appliquée 8.4-5:93-101. Paris.

Roys, Ralph L.
1931   The ethno-botany of the Maya. (Tulane
        University, Middle American Research Series,
        No. 2.) 359 pp. New Orleans.

Rubin, Jerrold
1966   An approach to organizing data into homoge-
        nous groups. Systematic Zoology 15.3:169-
        182. Lawrence, Kans.

Rusby, H. H.
1906-   Wild foods of the United States in May [and
1907   other months]. Country Life in America
        10.1:66-69; 10.4:436-438; 10.5:533-535;
        11.1:82,84,86,88,90,92,94; 11.5:546.
        New York.

Rydberg, P. A.
1924   Plants used by ancient American Indians.
        Journal of the American Botanical Garden
        25.295:204-205.

Safford, William Edwin
1905   The useful plants of the island of Guam.
        (Contributions from the U.S. National
        Herbarium, Vol. 9.) 416 pp. Washington.

1916   Narcotic plants and stimulants of the
        ancient Americans. Pp. 387-424 in Annual
        Report of the Smithsonian Institution, 1916.
        Washington.

1921   Cultivated plants of Polynesia and their
        vernacular names, an index to the origin
        and migration of the Polynesians. Proceed-
        ings of the First Pan-Pacific Scientific
        Congress...1920; Bernice P. Bishop Museum,
        Special Publications, No. 7(Part 1):183-187.
        Honolulu.

Sahagún, Fray Bernardino de
1963   Florentine Codex: general history of the
        things of New Spain, Book XI, Earthly things.
        Translated from the Aztec into English, with
        notes and illustrations by Charles E. Dibble
        and Arthur J. O. Anderson. (Monographs of
        the School of American Research and the
        Museum of New Mexico, No. 14, Part 12.)

297 pp. [Salt Lake City]: University of Utah Press.

Salisbury, E. J.
1940   Ecological aspects of plant taxonomy. Pp. 329-340 in The new systematics, edited by Julian Huxley. London: Oxford University Press. (Reprinted 1952.)

Sauer, Carl O.
1936   American agricultural origins: a consideration of nature and culture. Pp. 279-297 in Essays in anthropology presented to A. L. Kroeber, edited by R. H. Lowie. Berkeley: University of California Press. (Reprinted 1969, New York: Kraus Reprint.)

1947   Early relations of man to plants. Geographical Review 37.1:1-25. New York.

1950a   Grassland climax, fire, and man. Journal of Range Management 3.1:16-21. Baltimore.

1950b   Cultivated plants of South and Central America. Pp. 487-543 in Vol. 6 of Handbook of South American Indians, (Bulletins of the Bureau of American Ethnology, No. 143), edited by J. H. Steward. Washington.

1969   Agricultural origins and dispersals: the
(1952)   domestication of animals and foodstuffs. 2d edition. xi, 175 pp. Cambridge: MIT Press. (First published in 1952, [Bowman Memorial Lectures, Ser. 2], v, 110 pp., New York: American Geographical Society.)

Saunders, Charles Francis
1911   The yucca and the Indian. American Botanist 17:1-3. Binghamton, N. Y.

Schenck, Sara M. and E. W. Gifford
1952   Karok ethnobotany. University of California Anthropological Records 13.6:377-392. Berkeley and Los Angeles.

Schery, Robert
1952   Plants for man. vii, 564 pp. New York: Prentice-Hall.

Schiemann, Elisabeth
1932   Entstehung der Kulturpfanzen. (Handbuch der Vererbungswissenschaft, Vol. 3, edited by E. Baur and M. Hartmann.) ix, 377 pp.

Berlin: Gebrüder Borntraeger.

Schneider, Albert
1906   The medicinal plants of the California
        Indians. Merck's Report 15:63-128. Rahway,
        N. J.

Schultes, Richard Evans
1937a   Peyote and plants used in the peyote ceremony.
        Botanical Museum Leaflets, Harvard University,
        4.8:129-152. Cambridge.

1937b   Peyote (Lophophora williamsii) and plants
        confused with it. Botanical Museum Leaflets,
        Harvard University, 5.5:61-88. Cambridge.

1941   La etnobotánica: su alcance y sus objectos.
        Caldasia [1].3:7-12. Bogotá.

1942   Plantae colombianae II: Yoco, a stimulant
        of southern Colombia. Botanical Museum
        Leaflets, Harvard University, 10.10:301-324.
        Cambridge.

1960   Tapping our heritage of ethnobotanical lore.
        Economic Botany 14.1:257-262. Baltimore.

1962   The role of the ethnobotanist in the search
        for new medicinal plants. Lloydia 25.4:
        257-266. Cincinnati.

1969-   The plant kingdom and hallucinogens. Bulle-
1970   tin on Narcotics 21.3:3-16; 21.4:15-27;
        22.1(1970). New York.

Schwidetzky, Ilse
1955   Etnobiología. Bases para el estudio biológi-
        co de los pueblos y el desarrollo de las
        sociedades. 444 pp. Mexico City: Fondo de
        Cultura Económica.

Seguy, Jean
1953   Les Noms populaires des plantes dan les
        Pyrénées centrales. (Monografías del
        Instituto de Estudios Pirenaicos, Filologia
        18, no. general 100.) xxv, 444 pp.
        Barcelona.

Setchell, William Albert
1921   Aboriginal tobaccos. American Anthropologist
        23.4:397-414. Menasha.

[4:54]

Setchell, William Albert (cont.)
1924   Ethnobotany of the Samoans. Pp. 191-224 in
American Samoa (Part 2), (Carnegie Institution of Washington, Publication No. 341) by
W. A. Setchell. Washington.

Sherff, Earl E.
1940   The concept of genus: IV. The delimitations
of genera from the conservative point of
view. Bulletin of the Torrey Botanical Club
67.5:375-380. New York. (See also Bartlett
et al. 1940.)

Simoons, Frederick J.
1961   East not of this flesh: food avoidances in
the Old World. 246 pp. Madison: University
of Wisconsin Press.

Smith, Albert C.
1969   Systematics and appreciation of reality.
Taxon 18.1:5-13. Utrecht.

Smith, Alexander H.
1967   The mushroom hunter's field guide revised
and enlarged. 264 pp. Ann Arbor: University
of Michigan Press.

Smith, C. Earle, Jr., Eric O. Callen, Hugh C. Cutler,
Walton C. Galinat, Lawrence Kaplan, Thomas
W. Whitaker, and Richard A. Yarnell
1966   Bibliography of American archaeological
plant remains. Economic Botany 20.4:446-460.
Baltimore.

Smith, Hobart M.
1967a   Biological similarities and homologies.
Systematic Zoology 16.1:101-102. Lawrence,
Kans.

1967b   The hierarchy of monophyly and polyphyly.
Systematic Zoology 16.1:102-103. Lawrence,
Kans.

Smith, Huron H.
1923   Ethnobotany of Menomini Indians. Bulletins
of the Public Museum of the City of Milwaukee
4.1:1-174. Milwaukee.

1928   Ethnobotany of the Meskwaki Indians. Bulletins of the Public Museum of the City of
Milwaukee 4.2:175-326. Milwaukee.

[4:55]

1932   Ethnobotany of the Ojibwa Indians. Bulletins
       of the Public Museum of the City of Milwaukee
       4.3:327-525. Milwaukee.

1933   Ethnobotany of the Forest Potawatomi Indians.
       Bulletins of the Public Museum of the City of
       Milwaukee 7.1:1-230. Milwaukee.

Smith, John
1882   A dictionary of popular names of plants
       which furnish the natural and acquired wants
       of man, in all matters of domestic and gen-
       eral economy; their history, products, and
       uses. ix, 457 pp. London: Macmillan.

Sneath, Peter H. A.
1957   Some thoughts on bacterial classification.
       Journal of General Microbiology 17.1:184-
       200. Cambridge, England.

1962   Microbial classification. Pp. 283-332 in
       Microbial classification, (12th Symposium
       of the Society for General Microbiology,
       1962), edited by G. C. Ainsworth and P. H.
       A. Sneath. Cambridge: Cambridge University
       Press.

Sokal, Robert R.
1962   Typology and empiricism in taxonomy.
       Journal of Theoretical Biology 3.2:230-267.
       London and New York.

1965   Statistical methods in systematics. Biologi-
       cal Reviews 40.3:337-391. Cambridge.

1966   Numerical taxonomy. Scientific American
       215.6:106-116. New York.

Sokal, Robert R. and Peter H. A. Sneath
1963   Principles of numerical taxonomy. xii,
       359 pp. San Francisco and London: W. H.
       Freeman.

1966   Efficiency in taxonomy. Taxon 15.1:1-21.
       Utrecht.

Speck, Frank G.
1941a Gourds of the southeastern Indians: a
       prolegomenon on the Lagenaria gourd in the
       culture of the southeastern Indians.
       (Ethnographical Series No. 1.) 113 pp.
       Boston: New England Gourd Society.

315

Speck, Frank G. (cont.)
1941b   A list of plant curatives obtained from the
         Houms Indians of Louisiana. Primitive Man
         14.4:49-73. Washington.

1944   Catawba herbals and curative practices.
         Journal of American Folklore 57.223:37-50.
         Philadelphia.

Speck, Frank G. and Ernest S. Dodge
1945   On the fable of Joe Pye, Indian herbalist,
         and Joe Pye Weed. Scientific Monthly 61.1:
         63-66. Washington.

Sporne, K. R.
1956   The phylogenetic classification of the
         angiosperms. Biology Revue 31:1-29.

Sprague, T. A.
1940   Taxonomic botany, with special reference to
         the angiosperms. Pp. 435-454 in The new
         systematics, edited by J. Huxley. London:
         Oxford University Press. (Reprinted 1952.)

Stafleu, Frans A.
1971   Linnaeus and the Linnaeans: the spreading
         of their ideas in systematic botany, 1735-
         1789. xvi, 386 pp. Utrecht: A. Oosthoek's
         Uitgeversmaatschappij N.V. for the Interna-
         tional Association for Plant Taxonomy.

Stafleu, Frans A. and Edward G. Voss
1969   Synopsis of proposals on botanical nomencla-
         ture, Seattle, 1969. (Regnum Vegetabile,
         Vol. 60.) 124 pp. Utrecht: International
         Bureau for Plant Taxonomy and Nomenclature
         of the International Association for Plant
         Taxonomy.

Stahel, Gerold
1944   Notes on the Arawak Indian names of plants
         in Surinam. Journal of the New York Botani-
         cal Garden 45.540:268-279. New York.

Stainer, R. Y. and C. B. Van Niel
1941   The main outlines of bacterial classifica-
         tion. Journal of Bacteriology 42.4:437-466.
         Baltimore.

Stearn, William T.
1952   Historical introduction. Pp. 157-159 in
         Proposed international code of nomenclature

for cultivated plants, by W. H. Camp, J. S. L. Gilmour, and W. T. Stearn. Journal of the Royal Horticultural Society 77.5:157-173. London.

1956   Keys, botanical and how to use them. Pp. 251-253 in Supplement to the dictionary of gardening, a practical and scientific encyclopaedia of horticulture, edited by P. M. Synge. Oxford: Clarendon.

1960   Notes on Linnaeus's 'Genera plantarum.' Pp. v-xxiv in 1960 facsimile of Genera plantarum, (Fifth edition 1774), by Carl Linnaeus, Weinheim/Bergstr., Germany: H. R. Engelmann (J. Cramer); and Codicote/Herts., England: Wheldon and Wesley.

1966   Botanical Latin: history, grammar, syntax, terminology, and vocabulary. xix, 566 pp. New York: Hafner; London: Nelson.

Stebbins, George Ledyard
1950   Variation and evolution in plants. (Columbia Biological Series, No. 16.) xix, 643 pp. New York: Columbia University Press.

1969   Comments on the search for a 'perfect system.' Taxon 18.4:357-359. Utrecht.

Steedman, Elsie Viault, editor
1930   The ethnobotany of the Thompson Indians of British Columbia: based on field notes by James A. Teit. Pp. 441-522 in 45th Annual Report of the Bureau of American Ethnology, 1927-1928. Washington.

Steenis-Kruseman, M. J. van
1953   Select Indonesian medicinal plants. (Organisation for Scientific Research in Indonesia, Bulletin 18.) 90 pp. Djakarta.

Steggerda, Morris
1940   One Maya Indian's knowledge of nature. Proceedings of the 8th American Scientific Congress, Washington, 1940, 2:91-92. Washington: Department of State.

1943   Some ethnological data concerning one hundred Yucatecan plants. Bulletins of the Bureau of American Ethnology, No. 136:189-226; Anthropological Paper No. 29. Washington.

[4:58]

Steiner, Mona Lisa
1961   A dictionary of vernacular names of Pacific
        food plants. 362 pp., bibliog. Pasay City:
        National Research Council of the Philippines.

Steinmetz, E. F.
1954   Materia medica vegetabilis. 3 Parts.
        Amsterdam: Stencildruck ITB.

1957   Codex vegetabilis. 2d edition. 136, 7 pp.
        Amsterdam: E. F. Steinmetz.

Stevenson, Matilda Coxe
1915   Ethnobotany of the Zuñi Indians. Pp. 31-
        102 in 30th Annual Report of the Bureau of
        American Ethnology, 1908-1909. Washington.

Stewart, K. H.
1966   Mojave Indian agriculture. Masterkey 40.1:
        4-15. Los Angeles.

Straatmans, W.
1967   Ethnobotany of New Guinea in its ecological
        perspective. Journal d'Agriculture Tropi-
        cale et de Botanique Appliquée 14.1-2-3:
        1-20. Paris.

Strathern, Marilyn
1969   Why is the Pueraria a sweet potato?
        Ethnology 8.2:189-198. Pittsburgh.

Sturtevant, E. Lewis   (See Hedrick.)

Sturtevant, William C.
1954   The Mikasuki Seminole: medical beliefs and
        practices. 538 pp. Ph.D. dissertation in
        anthropology, Yale University, New Haven.
        (Published by University Microfilms, Ann
        Arbor, Mich., 1967.)

1958   Review of The ethnobotany of the Island
        Caribs of Dominica, by W. A. Hodge and
        Douglas Taylor. American Anthropologist
        60.4:767. Menasha.

1965   Preliminary annotated bibliography on east-
        ern North American Indian agriculture.
        Pp. 1-24 in Southeastern Archaeological Con-
        ference, Bulletin 3, (Proceedings of the Twen-
        ty-First Southeastern Archaeological Confer-
        ence.) Cambridge, Mass.

1969   History and ethnography of some West Indian
        starches. Pp. 177-199 in The domestication
        and exploitation of plants and animals,
        edited by P. J. Ucko and G. W. Dimbleby.
        London: Gerald Duckworth.

Sullivan, Michael
1971   Review of Soma: divine mushroom of immor-
        tality, by R. Gordon Wasson. Journal of
        the American Oriental Society 91.2:346-349.
        New Haven.

Sumner, F. B.
1932   Genetic, distributional, and evolutionary
        studies of subspecies of deer mice (Peromys-
        cus). Bibliographia Genetica 9:1-106.
        's-Gravenhage.

Swain, T., editor
1963   Chemical plant taxonomy. ix, 543 pp.
        London and New York: Academic Press.

Talbot, P. B.
1971   Principles of fungal taxonomy. 272 pp.
        New York: St. Martin's Press.

Tantaquidgeon, Gladys
1932   Notes on the origin and uses of plants of
        the Lake St. John Montagnais. Journal of
        American Folklore 45.176:265-267. New York.

Taylor, Lyda Averill
1940   Plants used as curatives by certain south-
        eastern tribes. xi, 88 pp. Cambridge:
        Botanical Museum of Harvard University.

Te Rangi Hiroa (See Peter H. Buck.)

Theophrastus
1916   Theophrastus: Enguiry into plants and
        minor works on odours and weather signs.
        Translated and edited by Arthur Hort.
        2 vols. Vol. 1, xxviii, 475 pp.; Vol. 2,
        ix, 499 pp. London: William Heinemann;
        New York: G. P. Putnam's Sons.

Thierry, Solange
1966-   Quelques aspects du rôle culturel des fleurs
1967   en asie méridionale. L'Ethnographie 60-61:
        123-150. Paris.

Thoday, J. M.
1952   Units of evolution and units of classifica-

tion. Proceedings of the Leeds Philosophical and Literary Society 6(Part 1):61-63.
Leeds.

Thomas, Jacqueline M. C.
1959   Notes d'ethnobotanique africaine: plantes
        utilisées dans la région de la Lobaye
        (Afrique centrale). Journal d'Agriculture
        Tropicale et de Botanique Appliquée 6.8-9:
        353-390. Paris.

Thompson, H. C. and W. C. Kelly
1959   Vegetable crops. viii, 611 pp. New York:
        McGraw-Hill.

Timmermans, J. et al.
1963   La Classification dans les sciences. 236
        pp. Gembloux: J. Duculot.

Timson, J.
1966   Fruit terminology. Taxon 15.2:82. Utrecht.

Tippo, Oswald
1942   A modern classification of the plant king-
        dom. Chronica Botanica 7.5:203-206.
        Waltham, Mass.

Tournefort, Joseph Pitton de
1694   Elements de botanique. 3 vols. Paris:
        Impr. royale. (Later editions, in Latin,
        1700; 1719, see below.)

1719   Institutiones rei herbariae. Editio tertia,
        Appendicibus aucta ab Antonio de Jussieu
        Lugdunaeo. (Corollarium Institutionum rei
        herbariae, in quo plantae 1356. munificentia
        Ludovici Magni in orientalibus regionibus
        observatae recensentur, et ad genera sua
        revocantur.) 3 vols. xxxii, [16], 695 pp.,
        4 l , 58 pp. and 2 vols. of 489 plates.
        Paris: Typographia Regia.

Towle, Margaret
1961   The ethnobotany of pre-Columbian Peru.
        (Viking Fund Publications in Anthropology,
        No. 30.) xii, 180 pp. New York: Wenner-
        Gren Foundation for Anthropological Research.

Trager, George
1939   "Cottonwood-tree," a south-western linguistic
        trait. International Journal of American
        Linguistics 9.2-4:117-118. New York.

Treide, Barbara
    1967   Wildflanzen in der Ernährung der Grundbe-
            völkerung Melanesiens. (Veröffentlichungen
            des Museums für Völkerkunde zu Leipzig,
            Heft 16.) 267 pp. Berlin: Akademie-Verlag.

Trimble, Henry
    1888-   Some Indian food plants. American Journal
    1891   of Pharmacy 60(4th series vol. 18).12:593-
            595; 61(4th series vol. 19).4-6:556-558;
            62(4th series vol. 20).6:281-282, 62(4th
            series vol. 20).12:598-600; 63(4th series
            vol. 21).11:525-527. Philadelphia.

Troels-Smith, Jørgen Andreas
    1955   Pollenanalythische Untersuchungen zu einigen
            schweizerischen Pfahlbauproblemen. Med
            dansk resumé. 64 pp. Copenhagen: Eget
            Forlag.

Turrill, William Bertram, editor
    1964   Recent researches in plant taxonomy.
            (Vistas in botany, Vol. IV.) xiii, 314 pp.
            New York: Macmillan.

Turrill, William Bertram et al.
    1942   Discussion: differences in the systematics
            of plants and animals and their dependence
            on differences in structure, function, and
            behaviour in the two groups. Proceedings
            of the Linnean Society of London 153(Part
            3):272-287. London.

Ucko, Peter J. and G. W. Dimbleby, editors
    1969   The domestication and exploitation of
            plants and animals. xxxvi, 581 pp. London:
            Gerald Duckworth.

Ugent, Donald
    1968   The potato in Mexico: geography and primi-
            tive culture. Economic Botany 22.2:109-
            123. Baltimore.

Uphof, J. C. Th.
    1968   Dictionary of economic plants. 2d edition,
    (1959) revised and enlarged. 591 pp. Lehre:
            J. Cramer; New York: Stechert-Hafner.

Urban, M.
    1966   Zur Herkunft der polynesischen Kultur:
            Bemerkungen aus der Sicht der Ethnobotanik
            und Ethnozoologie des pazifischen Raumes.

[4:62]

Mitteilungen zur Kulturkunde 1:169-178.
Wiesbaden.

Uscátegui Mendoza, Néstor
1963   Notas etnobotánicas sobre el ají indígena.
Revista Colombiana de Antropología 12:89-
96. Bogotá.

Valentine, D. H. et al.
1970   Infraspecific categories. Biological Journal of the Linnean Society 2.3:209-258.
London. (See also Burtt; Crundwell; Heywood
1970; Hudson.)

Van Beek, Gus W.
1958   Frankincense and myrrh in ancient south
Arabia. Journal of the American Oriental
Society 78.3:141-151. New Haven.

Vargas C., César
1962   Phytomorphic representations of the ancient
Peruvians. Economic Botany 16.2:106-115.
Baltimore.

Vavilov, Nikolai I.
1951   The origin, variation, immunity and breeding
of cultivated plants: selected writings.
Translated from the Russian by K. Starr
Chester. (Chronica Botanica 13.1-6.)
xviii, 364 pp. Waltham, Mass.: Chronica
Botanica.

Vestal, Paul Anthony
1952   Ethnobotany of the Ramah Navaho. (Reports
of the Ramah Project Report No. 4; Papers
of the Peabody Museum of American Archaeology and Ethnology, Harvard University,
40.4.) ix, 94 pp. Cambridge.

Vestal, Paul Anthony and Richard Evans Schultes
1939   The economic botany of the Kiowa Indians as
it relates to the history of the tribe.
With a foreword by Clyde Kluckhohn. xiii,
110 pp. Cambridge: Harvard University
Botanical Museum.

Vidal, Jules
1962   Noms vernaculaires de plantes (Lao, Méo,
(1959) Kha) en usage au Laos. 2d édition, revue
et corrigée. 197 pp. Paris: École
Française d'Extrême Orient. (1959, Bulletin
de l'École Française d'Extrême-Orient 49.2:
435-608, Hanoi.)

1963-
1964
(1959-
1961)   Les Plantes utiles du Laos.   8 pts. in 1
vol.   Paris: Muséum National d'Histoire
Naturelle.   (Reprinted from Journal d'Agriculture Tropicale et de Botanique Appliquée,
vols. 6-10 [1959-1961], Paris.

1963   Systématique, nomenclature et phytonymie
botanique populaire au Laos.   Journal
d'Agriculture Tropicale et de Botanique
Appliquée 10.10-11:438-448.   Paris.

Voss, Edward G.
1952   The history of keys and phylogenetic trees
in systematic biology.   Journal of the Scientific Laboratories, Denison University
43:1-25(Art. 1).   Granville, Ohio.

Walker, André Raponda and Roger Sillans
1961   Les Plantes utiles du Gabon: essai d'inven-
taire et de concordance des noms vernaculaires et scientifiques des plantes spon-
tanées et introduites; descriptions des
espèces, propriétés, utilisations économiques, ethnographiques et artistiques.
(Encyclopédie Biologique, 56.)   xii, 614 pp.
Paris: Paul Lechevalier.

Walter, S. M.
1961   The shaping of angiosperm taxonomy.   New
Phytologist 60.1:74-84.   Oxford.

Warfield, J. O.
1911   Materia medica of the Algonquian Indians of
Virginia.   American Anthropologist 13.1:
119.   Menasha.

Warner, J. N.
1962   Sugar cane: an indigenous Papuan cultigen.
Ethnology 1.4:405-411.   Pittsburgh.

Wassén, S. Henry
1965   The use of some specific kinds of South
American Indian snuff and related parapher-
nalia.   (Etnologiska Studier 28.)   132 pp.
Gothenburg.

Wasson, R. Gordon
1968   Soma: divine mushroom of immortality.
XIII, 381 pp.   New York: Harcourt, Brace
and World.

Watson, James B.
1968   Pueraria: names and traditions of a lesser

crop of the Central Highlands, New Guinea.
Ethnology 7.3:268-279. Pittsburgh.

Watson, James Gilbert, compiler
1928   Malayan plant names. Malayan Forest Records
        No. 5:17-277. Singapore.

Watt, George
1889-   A dictionary of the economic products of
1896   India. 7 vols. in 10. Calcutta: The
        Superintendent of Government Printing,
        India; London: W. H. Allen.

1908   The commercial products of India, being an
        abridgment of "The dictionary of the econom-
        ic products of India". viii, 1189 pp.
        London: John Murray.

Weatherwax, Paul
1954   Indian corn in old America. ix, 253 pp.
        New York: Macmillan.

Wells, J. R.
1966   Toward a more colorful taxonomy. Taxon
        15.6:214-215. Utrecht.

West, George A.
1934   Tobacco, pipes and smoking customs of the
        American Indians. 2 vols. Bulletins of
        the Public Museum of the City of Milwaukee
        17(Part 1), text, pp. 1-477; 17(Part 2),
        plates, pp. 482-994. Milwaukee.

Whitaker, Thomas Wallace and Glen N. Davis
1962   Cucurbits: botany, cultivation and utiliza-
        tion. 250 pp. London: L. Hill; New York:
        Interscience.

White, Leslie A.
1944   Notes on the ethnobotany of the Keres.
        Papers of the Michigan Academy of Science,
        Arts and Letters 30(Part 4):557-570.
        Ann Arbor.

Whitford, Harry Nichols
1911   The forests of the Philippines. 2 parts.
        (Department of the Interior, Bureau of
        Forestry, Bulletin No. 10). Part 1, Forest
        types and products, viii, 94 pp.; Part 2,
        The principal forest trees, 113 pp. Manila:
        Bureau of Printing.

Whiting, Alfred F.
1939   Ethnobotany of the Hopi. (Museum of North-
        ern Arizona Bulletin No. 15.) viii, 120 pp.
        Flagstaff.

1966   The present status of ethnobotany in the
        Southwest. Economic Botany 20.3:316-325.
        Baltimore.

Williams, W. T.
1969   The problem of attribute-weighting in numeri-
        cal classification. Taxon 18.4:369-374.
        Utrecht.

Williamson, Kay
1970   Some food plant names in the Niger Delta.
        International Journal of American Linguis-
        tics 36.2:156-167. Baltimore.

Willis, John Christopher
1922   Age and area; a study in geographical
        distribution and origin of species. x,
        259 pp. Cambridge: Cambridge University
        Press.

1940   The course of evolution by differentiation
        or divergent mutation rather than by selec-
        tion. viii, 207 pp. Cambridge: Cambridge
        University Press.

1966   A dictionary of the flowering plants and
(1897) ferns. 7th edition, revised by H. K. Airy
        Shaw. xxii, 1214, liii pp. Cambridge:
        Cambridge University Press. (First edition
        1897, A manual and dictionary of the flow-
        ering plants and ferns.)

Wirth, Michael, George F. Estabrook, and David J.
        Rogers
1966   A graph theory model for systematic biology,
        with an example for the Oncidiinae (Orchi-
        daceae). Systematic Zoology 15.1:59-69.
        Lawrence, Kans.

Wit, H. C. D. de
1952   In memory of G. E. Rumphius (1702-1952).
        Taxon 1.7:101-110. Utrecht.

Witthoft, John
1947   An early Cherokee ethnobotanical note.
        Journal of the Washington Academy of Sciences
        37.3:73-75. Baltimore.

[4:66]

Wittrock, Marion A. and G. L.
1942   Food plants of the Indians: vegetables,
        grains, fruits, seasonings gleaned from
        the wild by the North American natives.
        Journal of the New York Botanical Garden
        43.507:57-71. New York.

Woodger, Joseph Henry
1937   The axiomatic method in biology. With
        appendices by Alfred Tarski and W. F. Floyd.
        x, 174 pp. Cambridge: Cambridge University
        Press.

1952   Biology and language, an introduction to
        the methodology of the biological sciences,
        including medicine. xiii, 364 pp. Cambridge.
        Cambridge University Press.

1960-   Taxonomy and evolution. La Nuova Critica
1961   3.12:67-77. Rome.

1967   Biological principles: a critical study.
(1929) Reissued (with a new introduction). xix,
        496 pp. London: Routledge and Kegan Paul;
        New York: Humanities Press. (1929, New
        York: Harcourt, Brace.)

Worsley, Peter M.
1961   The utilization of food resources by an
        Australian aboriginal tribe. Acta Ethno-
        graphica Academiae Scientiarum Hungaricae.
        10.1-2:153-190. Budapest.

Wulff, E. V.
1943   An introduction to historical plant geogra-
        phy. Authorized translation by Elizabeth
        Brissenden. Foreword by Elmer D. Merrill.
        xv, 223 pp. Waltham, Mass.: Chronica
        Botanica.

Wyatt-Smith, J.
1951   Vernacular tree name changes. Malayan
        Forester 14.2:82-88. Kuala Lumpur.

Wyman, Leland C. and Stuart K. Harris
1941   Navajo Indian medical ethnobotany. (Univer-
        sity of New Mexico Bulletin No. 366, Anthro-
        pological Series 3.5.) 76 pp. Albuquerque.

1951   The ethnobotany of the Kayenta Navaho: an
        analysis of the John and Louisa Wetherill
        ethnobotanical collection. (University of

New Mexico Publications in Biology, No. 5.)
66 pp. Albuquerque.

Yanovsky, Elios
1936   Food plants of the North American Indians.
        (United States Department of Agriculture,
        Miscellaneous Publication No. 237.)
        Washington.

Yarnell, Richard A.
1959   Prehistoric Pueblo use of datura. El
        Palacio 66.5:176-178. Santa Fe.

Yen, Douglas E.
1963   The study of variation in taros and kumaras
        and its possible ethnobotanical signifi-
        cance. Proceedings of the Ninth Pacific
        Science Congress of the Pacific Science
        Association, 1957, 3:46-47. Bangkok.

1971   Construction of the hypothesis for distribu-
        tion of the sweet potato. Pp. 328-342 in
        Man across the sea: problems of pre-Colum-
        bian contacts, edited by C. L. Riley et al.
        Austin and London: University of Texas
        Press.

Yepes Agredo, Silvio
1953   Introducción a la etnobotánica columbiana,
        Publ. de la Soc. Colomb. de Etnología,
        No. 1:5-48.

Youngken, Heber W.
1924-   The drugs of the North American Indian.
1925   American Journal of Pharmacy 96.7:485-502;
        97.3:158-185; 97.4:257-271. Philadelphia.

Zigmond, Maurice Louis
[1941] Ethnobotanical studies among California and
        Great Basin Shoshoneans. 297 pp. Ph.D.
        dissertation in anthropology, Yale Univer-
        sity, New Haven. (Published by University
        Microfilms, Ann Arbor, Mich., 1967.)

Zingg, R. M.
1934   American plants in Philippine ethnobotany.
        Philippine Journal of Science 54.2:221-274.
        Manila.

5. Ethnozoology (and systematic zoology)

[Including references to representative types
of ethnozoological reports and pertinent background works on zoological classification, as
well as analyses of specific folk systems of
animal categorization; cf. O. and 4.]

Abbott, Richard Tucker
  1968   Seashells of North America: a guide to
          field identification. Illustrated by George
          F. Sandström, under the editorship of
          Herbert S. Zim. 280 pp. New York: Golden
          Press.

Acheson, Nicholas H.
  1966   Etnozoología zinacanteca. Pp. 433-454 in
          Los zinacantecos, edited by E. Z. Vogt.
          Mexico City: Instituto Nacional Indigen-
          ista.

Alkire, William H.
  1968   Porpoises and taro. Ethnology 7.3:280-289.
          Pittsburgh.

Amadon, Dean
  1966a   Another suggestion for stabilizing nomencla-
          ture. Systematic Zoology 15.1:54-58.
          Lawrence, Kans.

  1966b   The superspecies concept. Systematic Zoology
          15.3:245-259. Lawrence, Kans.

Anderson, Eugene N., Jr.
  1967   The ethnoichthyology of the Hong Kong boat
          people. 103 pp. Ph.D. dissertation in
          anthropology, University of California,
          Berkeley.

  1969   Sacred fish. Man (n.s.)4.3:443-449. London.

Anderson, Myrdene
  1971   L'Ethnobiologie. La Recherche, No. 18:1029-
          1038. Paris.

André, Jacques
  1963   Noms de plantes et noms d'animaux en latin.
          Latomus 22.4:649-663. Brussels.

André, Marc
  1958   Les Crustacés dans les légendes anciennes et
          actuelles. L'Ethnographie (n.s.)52:107-131.
          Paris.

[5:2]

Andrew, R. J.
1956-   Intention movements of flight in certain
1957   passerines, and their uses in systematics.
         Behaviour 10:179-204. Leiden.

1963   The origin and evolution of the calls and
         facial expression of the primates. Behav-
         iour 20.1-2:1-109. Leiden.

Anonymous
1970   Atļas de biologie (Atlas zur Biologie).
         Preface by Jean Bernard. Translated by
         Anne Sebisch et al. ii, 569 pp., Paris:
         Librarie Stock and Librairie Générale
         Française.

Askew, R. R.
1970   Infraspecific categories in insects. Bio-
         logical Journal of the Linnean Society
         2.3:225-231. London. (See also Valentine
         et al. 1970.)

Austerlitz, Robert
1968   Native seal nomenclatures in South-Sahalin.
         Pp. 133-141 in Papers of the CIC Far Eastern
         Language Institute, edited by J. K. Yamagiwa.
         Ann Arbor: Panel on Far Eastern Language
         Institutes of The Committee on Institutional
         Cooperation.

Baker, John
1928   Notes on New Hebridean customs, with special
         reference to the intersex pig. Man 28:113-
         118(Art. 81). London.

Baldus, Herbert
1947   Vocabulário zoológico kaingang. (Arquivos
         Museu Paranaense 6.) 12 pp. Curitiba,
         Brazil.

Bather, Francis Arthur
1927   Biological classification, past and future.
         Quarterly Journal of the Geological Society
         of London 83(Part 2):lxii-civ. London.

Bec, Pierre
1960   Formations secondaires et motivations dans
         quelques noms d'animaux en gascon. Revue
         de Linguistique Romane 24.95-96:296-351.
         Paris.

Beckner, Morton
1959   The biological way of thought. vii, 200 pp.

330

New York: Columbia University Press.

Beidleman, Richard G.
1956   Ethnozoology of the Pueblo Indians in histor-
        ic times. Southwestern Lore 22.1:5-13;
        22.2:17-28. Boulder.

Bentley, A. and M. C. Downes
1968   Deer in New Guinea. Papua and New Guinea
        Agricultural Journal 20.1-2:1-4; 20.3-4:
        95-99. Konedobu.

Bernstein, Irwin S.
1966   Naturally occurring primate hybrid.
        Science 154.3756:1559-1560. Washington.

Blackwelder, R. E.
1955   Review of The language of taxonomy, by John
        R. Gregg. Systematic Zoology 4.1:41-42.
        Baltimore.

1967   A critique of numerical taxonomy. Systemat-
        ic Zoology 16.1:64-72. Lawrence, Kans.

Blair, W. Frank
1943   Criteria for species and their subdivision
        from the point of view of genetics. Annals
        of the New York Academy of Sciences 44(Art.
        2):179-188. New York. (See also Bogert
        et al. 1943.)

Blair, W. Frank, editor
1961   Vertebrate speciation. xvi, 642 pp. Austin:
        University of Texas Press.

Bodenheimer, Friedrich Simon
1951   Insects as human food; a chapter of the
        ecology of man. 352 pp. The Hague:
        W. Junk.

1960   Animal and man in Bible lands. Translation
        by the author of Vol. 1 of the 1950 Hebrew
        edition. (Collection de Travaux de l'Acadé-
        mie Internationale d'Histoire des Sciences
        10.) viii, 232 pp. Leiden: Brill.

Boettger, Caesar Rudolph
1958   Die Haustiere Afrikas: ihre Herkunft,
        Bedeutung und Aussichten bei der weiteren
        wirtschaftlichen Erschliessung des Kontin-
        ents. 314 pp. Jena: Fischer.

Bogert, Charles M.
1943   Introduction [to Criteria for vertebrate
        subspecies, species and genera]. Annals of
        the New York Academy of Sciences 44(Art. 2):
        107-108. New York. (See also Bogert et al.
        1943.)

Bogert, Charles M. et al.
1943   Criteria for vertebrate subspecies, species
        and genera. Annals of the New York Academy
        of Sciences 44(Art. 2):105-188. New York.
        (See also Blair; Bogert; Dunn; Hall; Hubbs;
        Mayr 1943; Simpson 1943.)

Borror, Donald J. and Richard E. White
1970   A field guide to the insects (America north
        of Mexico). (Peterson Field Guide 19.)
        xi, 404 pp. Boston: Houghton Mifflin.

Braidwood, J.
1965,   Local bird names in Ulster--a glossary.
1966   Ulster Folklife 11:98-135; 12:104-107.
        Belfast.

Brink. F. H. van den
1968   A field guide to the mammals of Britain and
        Europe. (Peterson Field Guide 18.) 221 pp.
        Boston: Houghton Mifflin.

Buchanan, Robert Earle et al., editors
1958   International code of nomenclature of
        bacteria and viruses. Revised edition.
        180 pp. Ames: Iowa State University Press.

1966   Index Bergeyana: an annotated alphabetic
        listing of names of the taxa of the bacteria.
        xiv, 1472 pp. Baltimore: Williams and
        Wilkens.

Buck, Roger C. and David L. Hull
1966   The logical structure of the Linnean hier-
        archy. Systematic Zoology 15.2:97-111.
        Lawrence, Kans.

1969   Critique of "Nomenifers: are they christened
        or classified?" Systematic Zoology 18.3:
        343-357. Lawrence, Kans.

Bulmer, Ralph N. H.
1957   A primitive ornithology. Australian Museum
        Magazine 12.7:224-229. Sydney.

1965   Review of Navaho Indian ethnoentomology,
        by Leland C. Wyman and Flora L. Bailey.
        American Anthropologist 67.6:1564-1566.
        Menasha.

1967   Why is the cassowary not a bird? A problem
        of zoological taxonomy among the Karam of
        the New Guinea Highlands. Man (n.s.)2.1:
        5-25. London.

1968a   The strategies of hunting in New Guinea.
        Oceania 38.4:302-318. Sydney.

1968b   Worms that croak and other mysteries of
        Karam natural history. Mankind 6.12:621-
        639. Sydney.

1969   Field methods in ethno-zoology with special
        reference to the New Guinea Highlands.
        28 pp. Boroko: Department of Anthropology
        and Sociology, University of Papua and New
        Guinea.

1970a   Why is the cassowary not a bird? Australian
        External Territories 10.1:7-9. Canberra.

1970b   Which came first, the chicken or the egg-
        head? Pp. 1069-1091 in Échanges et communi-
        cations, edited by J. Pouillon and P. Maranda.
        The Hague and Paris: Mouton.

Bulmer, Ralph N. H. and Michael J. Tyler
1968   Karam classification of frogs. Journal of
        the Polynesian Society 77.4:333-385.
        Wellington. (Also available as Polynesian
        Society Reprint No. 16.)

Burma, Benjamin H.
1949a   The species concept: a semantic review.
        Evolution 3.4:369-370. Lancaster, Pa.

1949b   Postscriptum [see Burma 1949a, Mayr 1949].
        Evolution 3.4:372-373. Lancaster, Pa.

1954   Reality, existence, and classification: a
        discussion of the species problem. Madroño
        12.7:193-209. Berkeley.

Burns, John M.
1968   A simple model illustrating problems of
        phylogeny and classification. Systematic
        Zoology 17.2:170-173. Lawrence, Kans.

[5:6]

Burt, William H. and Richard P. Grossenheider
1952   A field guide to mammals. (Peterson Field
        Guide 5.) xxiii, 234 pp. Boston: Houghton
        Mifflin.

Bütschli, O.
1880-   Protozoa. Dr. H. G. Bronn's Klassen und
1887   Ordnungen des Thier-Reichs, wissenschaft-
        lichdargestellt in Wort und Bilt. Band 1,
        Protozoa, Abtheilung 1, Sarkodina und
        Sporazoa, pp. I-XVIII, 1-616; Abtheilung 2,
        Mastigophora, pp. 617-1097. Leipzig and
        Heidelberg: C. F. Winter'sche Verlagshand-
        lung.

Cain, Arthur James
1954   Animal species and their evolution. ix,
        190 pp. London: Hutchinson's University
        Library, Biological Sciences. (Reprinted
        1960, New York: Harper.)

1956   The genus in evolutionary taxonomy. System-
        atic Zoology 5:97-109. Baltimore.

1958   Logic and memory in Linnaeus's system of
        taxonomy. Proceedings of the Linnean
        Society of London 169(Parts 1-2):144-163.
        London.

1959a   Deductive and inductive methods in post-
        Linnean taxonomy. Proceedings of the Linnean
        Society of London 170(Part 2):185-217.
        London.

1959b   The post-Linnaen development of taxonomy.
        Proceedings of the Linnean Society of London
        170(Part 3):234-244. London.

1959c   Taxonomic concepts. Ibis 101.3-4:302-318.
        London.

1962   The evolution of taxonomic principles. Pp.
        1-13 in Microbial classification, (12th
        Symposium of the Society for General Micro-
        biology), edited by G. C. Ainsworth and
        P. H. A. Sneath. Cambridge: Cambridge
        University Press.

Cain, A. J. and G. A. Harrison
1958   An analysis of the taxonomist's judgement of
        affinity. Proceedings of the Zoological
        Society of London 131(Part 1):85-98. London.

1960   Phyletic weighting. Proceedings of the
          Zoological Society of London 135(Part 1):
          1-31. London.

Camin, Joseph H. and Robert R. Sokal
1965   A method for deducing branching sequences
          in phylogeny. Evolution 19.3:311-326.
          Lawrence, Kans.

Camp, W. H.
1951   Biosystematy. Brittonia 7.3:113-127. New
          York.

Campbell, Bernard G.
1965   The nomenclature of the Hominidae including
          a definitive list of Hominid taxa. (Royal
          Anthropological Institute of Great Britain
          and Ireland, Occasional Paper No. 22.)
          v, 33 pp. London.

Carter, George F.
1971   Pre-Columbian chickens in America. Pp. 178-
          218 in Man across the sea: problems of pre-
          Columbian contacts, edited by Carroll L.
          Riley et al. Austin and London: University
          of Texas Press.

Castetter, Edward F. and Ruth M. Underhill
1935   The ethnobiology of the Papago Indians.
          (Ethnobiological Studies in the American
          Southwest, II; University of New Mexico
          Bulletin, No. 275, Biological Series 4.3.)
          84 pp. Albuquerque.

Chamisso, Adelbertus de
1824   Cetaceorum maris Kamschatici imagines, ab
          Aleutis e ligno fictas, adumbravit recensuit-
          que. Verhandlungen der Kaiserlichen Leo-
          poldinisch-Carolinischen Akademie der
          Naturforscher 12.1:249-263. Bonn.

Chevalier, Auguste
1923   L'Oeuvre d'Alexis Jordan et la notion
          actuelle d'espèce en systématique. Revue
          de Botanique Appliquée et d'Agriculture
          Coloniale 3:441-459. Paris.

Colless, Donald H.
1967   An examination of certain concepts in
          phenetic taxonomy. Systematic Zoology
          16.1:6-27. Lawrence, Kans.

Colless, Donald H. (cont.)
1970   Type-specimens: their status and use.
        Systematic Zoology 19.2:251-253. Lawrence,
        Kans.

Collias, Nicholas E.
1960   An ecological and functional classification
        of animal sounds. Pp. 368-391 in Animal
        sounds and communication, (AIBS Publication
        No. 7), edited by W. E. Lanyon and W. N.
        Tavolga. Washington: American Institute
        of Biological Sciences.

Collinson, J. D. H.
1970   Eroticism in Swahili bird names. Man (n.s.)
        5.4:699-700. London.

Conant, Roger
1958   A field guide to reptiles and amphibians
        (eastern North America). (Peterson Field
        Guide 12.) xv, 366 pp. Boston: Houghton
        Mifflin.

Croizat, Leon
1945   History and nomenclature of higher units of
        classification. Bulletin of the Torrey
        Botanical Club 72.1:52-75. New York.

Crowson, Roy A.
1970   Classification and biology. ix, 350 pp.
        New York: Atherton Press.

Cuvier, Georges
1817   La Règne animal distribué d'après son organi-
        sation, pour servir de base à l'histoire
        naturelle des animaux et d'introduction à
        l'anatomie comparée. 4 vols. Paris:
        Deterville.

Darlington, P. J., Jr.
1970   A practical criticism of Hennig-Brundin
        "phylogenetic systematics" and antarctic
        biogeography. Systematic Zoology 19.1:
        1-18. Lawrence, Kans.

Decary, Raymond
1950   La Faune malgache, son rôle dans les
        croyances et les usages indigènes. 236 pp.
        Paris: Payot.

Dennler, Jorge G.
1939   Los nombres indígenas en guaraní de los

mamíferos de la Argentina y países limítrofes
y su importancia para la sistemática. Physis
16.48:225-244. Buenos Aires.

Diamond, J. M.
1966   Zoological classification system of a primitive people [Fore, New Guinea]. Science
151.3714:1102-1104. Washington.

Dieterlen, Germaine
1950   Les Correspondances cosmo-biologiques chez
les Soudanais. Journal de Psychologie
Normale et Pathologique 43.3:350-366. Paris.

Dobzhansky, Theodosius
1933   Geographical variation in lady-beetles.
American Naturalist 67.709:97-126. New York.

Douglas, Mary
1957   Animals in Lele religious symbolism. Africa
27.1:46-57. London.

Downs, James F.
1960   Domestication: an examination of the changing social relationship between man and
animals. Kroeber Anthropological Society
Papers 22:18-67. Berkeley.

Dunn, Emmett Reid
1943   Lower categories in herpetology. Annals of
the New York Academy of Sciences 44(Art.2):
123-131. New York. (See also Bogert et al.
1943.)

Du Rietz, G. Einar
1930   The fundamental units of biological taxonomy.
Svensk Botanisk Tidskrift 24.3:333-428.
Uppsala.

Eichler, Wolfdietrich
1966   Two new evolutionary terms for speciation in
parasitic animals. Systematic Zoology 15.3:
216-218. Lawrence, Kans.

Estabrook, George F.
1966   A mathematical model in graph theory for
biological classification. Journal of
Theoretical Biology 12.3:297-310. London
and New York.

Evans, D.
1961   Formations secondaires parmi les noms

d'oiseaux dans le domaine gascon. Pp. 167-
173 in Actes et mémoires du IIe Congrès
International de Langue et Littérature du
Midi de la France. Aix: Centre d'Études
Provencales de la Faculté des Lettres.

Evans, Ivor H. N.
1950   Some Dusun measures and the classification
        of domestic animals. Sarawak Museum Journal
        5.17(old series),2(n.s.):193-195. Kuching,
        Sarawak.

Evans-Pritchard, E. E.
1937,   Economic life among the Nuer: cattle.
1938   Sudan Notes and Records 20.3:209-245; 21.1:
        31-77. Khartoum.

1963   Notes on some animals in Zandeland. Man
        63:139-142(Art. 173). London.

Farris, James S.
1967a   The meaning of relationship and taxonomic
        procedure. Systematic Zoology 16.1:44-51.
        Lawrence, Kans.

1967b   Definitions of taxa. Systematic Zoology
        16.2:174-175. Lawrence, Kans.

Farris, James S., Arnold G. Kluge, and Michael J.
        Eckardt
1970   A numerical approach to phylogenetic system-
        atics. Systematic Zoology 19.2:172-189.
        Lawrence, Kans.

Findeisen, Hans
1929   Die Fischerei im Leben der altsibirischen
        Völkerstämme... 73 pp. Berlin.

1956a   Mensch und Tier als Liebespartner in der
        volksliterarischen Überlieferung Nordeurasiens
        und in der amerikanischen Arktis, unter
        Berücksichtigung der Erzählung und ihrer
        Genese. (Veröffenlichungen Institut für
        Menschen und Menschenheitskunde, 29.) 28 pp.
        Augsburg.

1956b   Das Tier als Gott, Dämon und Ahne. Eine
        Untersuchung über das Erleben des Tieres
        in der Altmenschheit. 80 pp. Stuttgart.

Fischer, E.
1955   Insektenkost beim Menschen: ein Beitrag

zur Urgeschichte der menslichen Ernahrung
unter dem Bambutiden. Zeitschrift für
Ethnologie 80.1:1-37. Braunschweig.

Forman, Shepard
1967   Cognition and the catch: the location of
fishing spots in a Brazilian coastal village.
Ethnology 6.4:417-426. Pittsburgh.

Frank, Barbara
1965   Die Rolle des Hundes in afrikanischen
Kulturen. (Studien zur Kulturkunde, Vol.
17.) 256 pp. Wiesbaden: Franz Steiner
Verlag GMBH.

Freeman, J. D.
1961   Iban augury. Bijdragen tot de Taal-, Land-
en Volkenkunde. 117.1:141-167.
's-Gravenhage.

French, David H.
1957   An exploration of Wasco ethnoscience. Pp.
224-227 in American Philosophical Society,
Year Book 1956. Philadelphia.

Galtier, C.
1961   Les Noms d'oiseaux en Provence. Pp. 153-
159 in Actes et mémoires du IIe Congrès
International de Langue et Littérature du
Midi de la France. Aix: Centre d'Études
Provençales de la Faculté des Lettres.

Gay, F. J. et al.
1955   Common names of insects and allied forms
occurring in Australia. (CSIRO Bulletin
275.) 32 pp. Melbourne: Commonwealth
Scientific and Industrial Research Organization.

Gillet, Hubert
1970   Le Comportement alimentaire des animaux
sauvages. Article C (18 pp.) in Cours de
ethno-botanique et ethno-zoologie (1969-
1970), Vol. 2, edited by J.-F. Leroy.
Paris: Muséum National d'Histoire Naturelle; Laboratoire d'Ethno-Botanique et
d'Ethno-Zoologie.

Gilmore, Raymond M.
1950   Fauna and ethnozoology of South America.
Pp. 345-463 in Vol. 6 of Handbook of South
American Indians, (Bulletins of the Bureau
of American Ethnology, No. 143), edited by

[5:12]

J. Steward. Washington.

Glick, Leonard B.
1964   Categories and relations in Gimi natural
        science. American Anthropologist 66.4(Part
        2):273-280. Menasha.

Gould, Sydney W.
1954   Permanent numbers to supplement the binomial
        system of nomenclature. American Scientist
        42.2:269-274. New Haven.

Gregg, John R.
1950   Taxonomy, language and reality. American
        Naturalist 84.819:419-435. Lancaster, Pa.

1954   The language of taxonomy, an application of
        symbolic logic to the study of classificatory
        systems. xii, 70 pp. New York: Columbia
        University Press.

1967   Finite Linnaean structures. Bulletin of
        Mathematical Biophysics 29.2:191-206.
        London.

Griaule, Marcel
1941   Les Mammifères dans la région des Dogons
        (Soudan français). Mammalia 5.3-4:104-109.
        Paris.

1952   Le Savoir des Dogon. Journal Société des
        Africanistes 22.1-2:27-42. Paris.

Grunnett, Neils T.
1962   An ethnographic-ecological survey of the
        relationship between the Dinka and their
        cattle. Folk 4:5-20. Copenhagen.

Gurney, Ashley B.
1967   Descriptions of new species and the use of
        holotypes still valid. Systematic Zoology
        16.3:264-265. Lawrence, Kans.

Guyot, A. Lucien and Pierre Gibassier
1967   Les Noms des animaux terrestres. (Que sais-
        je?, No. 1250.) 126 pp. Paris: Presses
        Universitaires de France.

Hahn, Eduard
1896   Die Haustiere und ihre Beziehungen zur
        Wirtschaft des Menschen. x, 581 pp.
        Leipzig: Duncker and Humbolt.

Hale, W. G.
  1970   Infraspecific categories in birds. Biologi-
          cal Journal of the Linnean Society 2.3:239-
          255. London. (See also Valentine et al.
          1970.)

Hall, E. Raymond
  1943   Criteria for vertebrate subspecies, species
          and genera: mammals. Annals of the New
          York Academy of Sciences 44(Art. 2):141-144.
          New York. (See also Bogert et al. 1943.)

Hall, Edith Thompson
  1954   Cattle nomenclature and genealogy. Names
          2.2:113-120. Berkeley.

Harrington, John P.
  1945   Mollusca among the American Indians. Acta
          Americana 3.4:293-297. Mexico City and
          Los Angeles.

Harrisson, Tom
  1965   Punan Busang bird names. Sarawak Museum
          Journal 12.25-26(n.s.):201-206. Kuching,
          Sarawak.

Haudricourt, André G.
  1962   Domestication des animaux, culture des
          plantes et traitement d'autrui. L'Homme
          2.1:40-50. Paris.

Heincke, Friedrich
  1882   Fünfte Klasse des Thierreichs. Fische,
          Pisces. Pp. 279-552 in Vol. 2 of Illus-
          trirte Naturgeschichte der Thiere, by
          P. L. Martin et al. Leipzig: F. A. Brock-
          haus.

Heizer, Robert F.
  1941   The use of plants for fish-poisoning by the
          California Indians. Leaflets of Western
          Botany 33.2:43-44. San Francisco.

  1953   Aboriginal fish poisons. Pp. 225-283 in
          Bulletins of the Bureau of American Ethnolo-
          gy, No. 151; Anthropological Papers No. 38.
          Washington.

Henderson, Junius and John P. Harrington
  1914   Ethnozoology of the Tewa Indians. (Bulletins
          of the Bureau of American Ethnology, No. 56.)
          x, 76 pp. Washington.

[5:14]

Herald, Earl Stannard
1967   Living fishes of the world. 303 pp.
(1961)   Garden City, N. Y.: Doubleday.

Herre, Wolf
1955   Das Ren als Haustier: eine zoologische
         Monographie. 324 pp. Leipzig: Akademische
         Verlagsgesellschaft.

Heyerdahl, Thor
1963   Prehistoric voyages as agencies for Melanesi-
         an and South American plant and animal dis-
         persal to Polynesia. Pp. 23-35 in Plants
         and the migrations of Pacific peoples, edited
         by J. Barrau. Honolulu: Bishop Museum
         Press.

Heywood, Vernon Hilton
1970   Infraspecific categories: summary of discus-
         sion. Biological Journal of the Linnean
         Society 2.3:257-258. London. (See also
         Valentine et al. 1970.)

Heywood, Vernon Hilton and J. McNeill, editors
[c.1964] Phenetic and phylogenetic classification; a
         symposium edited for the Association.
         (Systematics Association Publication No. 6.)
         xi, 164 pp. London.

Hiatt, Betty
1967,   The food quest and the economy of the
1968   Tasmanian aborigines, I and II. Oceania
         38.2:99-133; 38.3:190-219. Sydney.

Hide, R. L.
1969   Worms and sickness: a note on noise-produc-
         ing worms and mystical belief among the
         Nimai of the New Guinea Highlands. Mankind
         7.2:149-151. Sydney.

Hilger, Inez
1937   Chippewa interpretations of natural phenomena.
         Scientific Monthly 45.2:178-179. Washington.

Höhn, E. O.
1962   The names of economically important or
         conspicuous mammals and birds in the Indian
         languages of the District of Mackenzie,
         N.W.T. and in Sarcee. Arctic 15.4:299-300.
         Montreal and New York.

Honigman, John J.
1956   Coping with the universe. Davidson Journal

of Anthropology 2.2:85-98. Seattle.

Hubbs, Carl L.
1943   Criteria for subspecies, species and genera,
        as determined by researches on fishes.
        Annals of the New York Academy of Sciences
        44(Art. 2):109-121. New York. (See also
        Bogert et al. 1943.)

Hull, David L.
1968   The syntax of numericlature. Systematic
        Zoology 17.4:472-474. Lawrence, Kans.

Hull, David L. and Roger Buck
1967   Definitions of taxa. Systematic Zoology
        16.4:349. Lawrence, Kans.

Hummel, Siegbert
1958   Der Hund in der religiösen Vorstellungswelt
        des Tibeters. Paideuma 6.8:500-509.
        Wiesbaden.

Huntingford, George Wynn Brereton
1950   Nandi work and culture. (Colonial Research
        Studies No. 4.) iv, 126 pp. London:
        H. M. Stationery Office for the Colonial
        Office.

Huxley, Julian, editor
1940   The new systematics. 583 pp. London:
        Oxford University Press. (Reprinted 1952.)

Huxley, Thomas Henry
1869   An introduction to the classification of
        animals. 147 pp. London: J. Churchill.

Im Thurn, E. F.
1882   Tame animals among the Red Men of (South)
        America. Timehri 1:25-43. Demerara,
        British Guiana.

Inger, Robert F.
1958   Comments on the definition of genera.
        Evolution 12.3:370-384. Lancaster, Pa.

Inglis, William Grant
1966   The observational basis of homology.
        Systematic Zoology 15.3:219-228. Lawrence,
        Kans.

1970   The purpose and judgments of biological
        classifications. Systematic Zoology 19.3:
        240-253. Lawrence, Kans.

[5:16]

International Commission of Zoological Nomenclature
1964   International code of zoological nomenclature adopted by the XV International Congress
of Zoology. xix, 175 pp. London.

Irving, Lawrence
1958   On the naming of birds in Eskimo. Anthropological Papers of the University of Alaska
6.2:61-77. College.

1962   Stability in Eskimo naming of birds on
Cumberland Sound, Baffin Island. Anthropological Papers of the University of Alaska
10.1:1-12. College.

Jahn, Theodore L.
1961   Man versus machine: a future problem in
protozoan taxonomy. Systematic Zoology
10.4:179-192. Baltimore.

Jardine, Nicholas
1969   What is biological homology? Classification
Society Bulletin 2.1:2-4. Leicester, England.

Jensen, Bent
1961   Folkways of Greenland dog-keeping. Folk
3:43-66. Copenhagen.

Johnson, L. A. S.
1968   Rainbow's end: the quest for an optimal
taxonomy. Proceedings of the Linnean
Society of New South Wales 93(Part 1).416:
8-45. Sydney. (Reprinted 1970, Systematic
Zoology 19.3:203-239, Lawrence, Kans.)

Kennedy, Kenneth A. R.
1960   The phylogenetic tree: an analysis of its
development in studies of human evolution.
Kroeber Anthropological Society Papers 23:
7-53. Berkeley.

Kinsey, Alfred C.
1929   The gall wasp genus Cynips: a study in the
origin of species. (Indiana University
Studies Vol. 16, Studies Nos. 84, 85, 86;
Contribution from the Department of Zoology,
Indiana University, No. 220, Entomological
Series No. 7.) 577 pp. Bloomington, Ind.

Kiriakoff, Sergius G.
1966   Cladism and phylogeny. Systematic Zoology
15.1:91-93. Lawrence, Kans.

1967   On the nomenclature of the super-species.
        Systematic Zoology 16.3:281-282. Lawrence,
        Kans.

Klauber, Laurence Monroe
    1956   Rattlesnakes: their habits, life histories,
            and influence on mankind. 2 vols. xxix,
            1476 pp. Berkeley and Los Angeles: Univer-
            sity of California Press.

Klots, Alexander B.
    1951   A field guide to the butterflies (eastern
            North America). (Peterson Field Guide 4.)
            xvi, 349 pp. Boston: Houghton Mifflin.

Krueger, John R.
    1961   Miscellanea Selica III: flathead animal
            names and anatomical terms. Anthropological
            Linguistics 3.9:43-52. Bloomington, Ind.

Kummer, Hans
    1968   Social organization of Hamadryas baboons:
            a field study. (Bibliotheca Primatologica,
            No. 6.) vi, 189 pp. Basel and New York:
            S. Karger; Chicago: University of Chicago
            Press.

La Barre, Weston
    1947   Kiowa folk sciences. Journal of American
            Folklore 60.236:105-114. Philadelphia.

Lai, L. Y. C. and R. J. Walsh
    1966   Observations on ear lobe types. Acta Geneti-
            ca et Statistica Medica 16:250-257. Basel
            and New York.

Lamarck, Jean Baptiste Pierre Antoine de Monet de
    1809   Philosophie zoologique; ou, Exposition des
            considérations relatives à l'histoire natur-
            elle des animaux... 2 vols. Paris.
            (Translated by Hugh Elliot, 1963, as Zoologi-
            cal philosophy; an exposition with regard to
            the natural history of animals... xcii,
            410 pp. New York: Hafner.)

Lang, Werner
    1955   Der Hund als Haustier der Polynesier. Pp.
            227-236 in Vom fremden Völkern und Kulturen,
            Beiträge zur Völkerkunde; Hans Plischke zum
            65 Geburtstage, edited by W. Lang et al.
            Düsseldorf: Drost-Verlag.

Lanyon, W. E. and W. N. Tavolga, editors
1960   Animal sounds and communication. (AIBS
         Publication No. 7.) xiii, 443 pp. + phono-
         disc. Washington: American Institute of
         Biological Sciences.

Laufer, Berthold
1914   History of the rhinoceros. Field Museum of
         Natural History Publication 177, Anthropo-
         logical Series 13.2:73-173. Chicago.

Layard, John Willoughby
1942   Pigs. Pp. 240-269 (Chapter 10) in Stone
         men of Malekula: Vao, by J. Layard.
         London: Chatto and Windus.

Leach, Edmund R.
1964   Anthropological aspects of language: animal
         categories and verbal abuse. Pp. 23-63 in
         New directions in the study of language,
         edited by E. H. Lenneberg. Cambridge:
         MIT Press.

Leach, Maria
1961   God had a dog: folklore of the dog.
         Illustrations by Mamie Harmon. xiv, 544 pp.
         New Brunswick, N. J.: Rutgers University
         Press.

Leder, Irmgard
1968   Russische Fischnamen. xix, 181 pp.
         Wiesbaden: Harrassowitz.

Leeds, Anthony and Andrew P. Vayda, editors
1965   Man, culture, and animals: the role of
         animals in human ecological adjustments.
         (AAAS Publication No. 78.) vii, 304 pp.
         Washington: American Association for the
         Advancement of Science. (Reprinted 1967.)

Leriche, A.
1952   Vocabulaire du chameau en Mauritanie.
         Bulletin de l'Institut Français d'Afrique
         Noire 14:984-995. Dakar.

Leroi-Gourhan, André
1935   Le Mammouth dans la zoologie des Eskimos.
         La Terre et la Vie 5(Deuxième semestre).1:
         3-12. Paris.

Leroy, Jean F.
1958   Taxon, taxonomie...querelle de mots?
         querelle de fond! Journal d'Agriculture

Tropicale et de Botanique Appliquée 5.1-2-3: 173-176. Paris.

Lévi-Strauss, Claude
1962   La Pensée sauvage. ii, 395 pp. Paris: Plon. (Translated 1966 as The savage mind. xii, 290 pp. London: Weidenfeld and Nicolson.)

Leye, Thierno
1963   Insectes et croyances au Sénégal. Notes Africaines, No. 98:61-63. Dakar.

Linneaus, Carolus
1735   Systema naturae. First edition. Leiden: Haak. (1964 facsimile of the first edition, with an introduction and a first English translation of the "Observationes" by M. S. J. Engel-Ledeboer and H. Engel. [Dutch Classics on the History of Science 8.] 30, facsim, [9 ℓ]. Nieuwkoop: B. de Graaf.)

Mahr, August C.
1962   Delaware terms for plants and animals in the eastern Ohio country: a study in semantics. Anthropological Linguistics 4.5:1-48. Bloomington, Ind.

Malkin, Borys
1956a   Seri ethnozoology: a preliminary report. Davidson Journal of Anthropology 2.1:73-83. Seattle.

1956b   Sumu ethnozoology: herpetological knowledge. Davidson Journal of Anthropology 2.2:165-180. Seattle.

1958   Cora ethnozoology, herpetological knowledge; a bio-ecological and cross cultural approach. Anthropological Quarterly 31.3:73-90. Washington.

1962   Seri ethnozoology. (Idaho State College Museum, Occasional Papers No. 7.) 59 pp. Pocatello.

Martín el Campo, Rafael
1961   Contribución a la etnozoología maya de Chiapas. Pp. 29-39 in Los Mayas del sur y sus relaciones con los Nahuas meridionales, (VIII Mesa Redonda, Sociedad Mexicana de Antropología). Mexico City.

Maxwell, Allen R.
1969   Kedayan ethno-ornithology--a preliminary
        report. Brunei Museum Journal 1.1:197-217.
        Brunei.

Mayr, Ernst
1942   Systematics and the origin of species from
        the viewpoint of a zoologist. (Columbia
        Biological Series, No. 13.) xiv, 334 pp.
        New York: Columbia University Press.
        (Reprinted 1949.)

1943   Criteria for subspecies, species and genera
        in ornithology. Annals of the New York
        Academy of Sciences 44(Art. 2):133-319.
        New York. (See also Bogert et al. 1943.)

1946   The naturalist in Leidy's time and today.
        Proceedings of Academy of Natural Science
        Philadelphia 98:271-276. Philadelphia.

1949   The species concept: semantics versus
        semantics. Evolution 3.4:371-372. Lancas-
        ter, Pa.

1954   Notes on nomenclature and classification.
        Systematic Zoology 3.2:86-89. Baltimore.

1955   The species as a systematic and as a biologi-
        cal problem. Pp. 3-12 in Biological system-
        atics, 16th Annual Biological Colloquium,
        edited by E. Mayr. Corvallis: Oregon State
        College.

1957a   Species concepts and definitions. Pp. 1-22
        in The species problem, (AAAS Publication
        No. 50), edited by E. Mayr. Washington:
        American Association for the Advancement
        of Science.

1957b   Difficulties and importance of the biologi-
        cal species concept. Pp. 371-388 in The
        species problem, (AAAS Publication No. 50),
        edited by E. Mayr. Washington: American
        Association for the Advancement of Science.

1963   Animal species and evolution. xiv, 797 pp.
        Cambridge, Mass.: Belknap Press.

1969a   The biological meaning of species. Biologi-
        cal Journal of the Linnean Society 1.3:311-
        320. London.

1969b   Principles of systematic zoology. xi, 428
         pp. New York: McGraw-Hill.

Mayr, Ernst, editor
1955   Biological systematics, 16th Annual Biologi-
         cal Colloquium. iv, 51 pp. Corvallis:
         Oregon State College.

1957   The species problem: a symposium presented
         at the Atlanta meeting of the American Associ-
         ation for the Advancement of Science, 1955.
         (AAAS Publication No. 50.) ix, 395 pp.
         Washington: American Association for the
         Advancement of Science.

Mayr, Ernst, E. Gorton Linsley, and Robert L. Usinger
1953   Methods and principles of systematic zoology.
         x, 328 pp. New York: McGraw-Hill.

Mearns, Edger A.
1896   Ornithological vocabulary of the Moki Indians.
         American Anthropologist 9.12:391-403.
         Washington.

Metcalf, Z. P.
1954   The construction of keys. Systematic
         Zoology 3.1:38-45. Baltimore.

Middelkoop, P.
1956   About the translation of the word nachash
         into Timorese. The Bible Translator 7:
         130-133. London.

Miller, David
1952   The Insect People of the Maori. Journal of
         the Polynesian Society 61.1-2:1-61. Well-
         ington.

Millot, Jacques
1964   De quelques erreurs zoologiques. Objets et
         Mondes 4.3:199-208. Paris.

Modell, Walter
1969   Horns and antlers. Scientific American
         220.4:114-122. New York.

Molet, Louis
1953   Les Boeuf dans l'Ankaizinana: son importance
         sociale et économique. (Mémoires de l'Insti-
         tut Scientifique de Madagascar, Série C,
         Sciences humaines, Vol. 2.) 218 pp. Paris:
         P. André.

Montalban, H. R., G. J. Blanco, and I. A. Ronquillo
[1955]   Philippine fishes. (Popular Bulletin No.
49.) Manila: Department of Agriculture
and National Resources.

Moore, Ian
1966   The endings of specific names. Systematic
Zoology 15.4:350-351. Lawrence, Kans.

Moore, John A.
1957   An embryologist's view of the species concept. Pp. 325-338 in The species problem,
(AAAS Publication No. 50), edited by E.
Mayr. Washington: American Association
for the Advancement of Science.

Morrill, Warren T.
1967   Ethnoicthyology of the Cha-Cha. Ethnology
6.4:405-416. Pittsburgh.

Morris, Percy A.
1947   A field guide to the shells (Atlantic and
Gulf Coasts). (Peterson Field Guide 3.)
xix, 236 pp. Boston: Houghton Mifflin.

1952   A field guide to shells of the Pacific
Coast and Hawaii (and including the Gulf
of California). (Peterson Field Guide 6.)
xxxiii, 297 pp. Boston: Houghton Mifflin.

Moss, Wayne W.
1967   Some new analytic and graphic approaches to
numerical taxonomy, with an example from
the Dermanyssidae (Acari). Systematic
Zoology 16.3:177-207. Lawrence, Kans.

Mounin, Georges
1965   Un champ sémantique: la dénomination des
animaux domestiques. La Linguistique 1.1:
31-54. Paris.

Munro, Ian S. R.
1967   The fishes of New Guinea. xxxvii, 651, 78
pp. Port Moresby: Department of Agriculture,
Stock and Fisheries.

Müntzing, Arne
1959   Darwin's views on variation under domestication in the light of present-day knowledge.
Proceedings of the American Philosophical
Society 103.2:190-220. Philadelphia.

Murie, Olaus J.
1954   A field guide to animal tracks. (Peterson
        Field Guide 9.) xxii, 374 pp. Boston:
        Houghton Mifflin.

Neave, Sheffield Airey, editor
1939-   Nomenclator Zoologicus: a list of the names
1940   of genera and subgenera in zoology from the
        tenth edition of Linnaeus 1758 to the end of
        1935. 4 vols. London: Zoological Society
        of London.

Nissen, Claus
1953   Die illustrierte Vogelbücher ihre Geschichte
        und Bibliographie. 222 pp. Stuttgart:
        Anton Hiersemann.

1966   Die zoologische Buchillustration, ihre
        Bibliographie und Geschichte. Stuttgart:
        Anton Hiersemann.

Oldroyd, Harold
1966   The future of taxonomic entomology. System-
        atic Zoology 15.4:253-260. Lawrence, Kans.

1967   On comments concerning the future of taxonom-
        ic entomology. Systematic Zoology 16.3:274-
        275. Lawrence, Kans.

Parker-Rhodes, A. F.
1957   Review of The language of taxonomy, by
        John R. Gregg. Philosophical Review 66.1:
        124-125. Ithaca.

Parkes, Kenneth C.
1967   A qualified defense of traditional nomencla-
        ture. Systematic Zoology 16.3:268-273.
        Lawrence, Kans.

Peter, Revo, Sivari Udia, et al.
1967   Motu-Koitabu beliefs and practices about
        snakes and snakebite. Journal of the Papua
        and New Guinea Society 1.2:36-46. Port
        Moresby.

Peters, James Lee
1931   Check list of birds of the world. 2 vols.
        Cambridge: Harvard University Press.

Peterson, Roger Tory
1947   A field guide to birds. (Peterson Field
(1934) Guide 1.) xxiv, 230 pp. Boston: Houghton
        Mifflin.

1960   A field guide to the birds of Texas and adjacent states. (Peterson Field Guide 13.) xxx, 304 pp. Boston: Houghton Mifflin.

1969   A field guide to western birds. (Peterson (1941)   Field Guide 2.) xxvi, 366 pp. Boston: Houghton Mifflin.

Peterson, Roger Tory, Guy Mountfort and P. A. D. Hollom
1954   A field guide to the birds of Britain and Europe. (Peterson Field Guide 8.) xxxv, 344 pp. Boston: Houghton Mifflin.

Pickens, A. L.
1943   A comparison of Cherokee and Pioneer bird nomenclature. Southern Folklore Quarterly 7.4:213-221. Gainesville.

Plischke, Hans
1954   Das Kuhblasen: eine völkerkundliche Miszelle zu Herodot. Zeitschrift für Ethnologie 79:1-7. Braunschweig.

Poppe, N.
1962   Pferdenamen in der Geschichte und Sage der Nomaden Zentralasiens. Oriens Extremus 9:97-104. Wiesbaden.

Pouillon, Jean and Pierre Maranda, editors
1970   Échanges et communications; mélanges offerts à Claude Lévi-Strauss à l'occasion de son 60ème anniversaire. 2 vols. 1452 pp. The Hague and Paris: Mouton.

Pujol, Raymond
1970   Initiation a l'ethno-zoologie--methodes. Article D (38 pp.) in Cours de ethno-botanique et ethno-zoologie (1969-1970), Vol. 2, edited by J.-F. Leroy. Paris: Muséum National d'Histoire Naturelle; Laboratoire d'Ethno-Botanique et d'Ethno-Zoologie.

Ramírez Granados, Rodolfo
1957   El medio biológico de los seris. Acción Indigenista, No. 50:1, 4. Mexico City.

Rand, Austin Loomer and E. Thomas Gilliard
1967   Handbook of New Guinea birds. x, 612 pp. London: Weidenfeld and Nicolson.

Raven, Peter H., Brent Berlin, and Dennis E. Breedlove
1971   The origins of taxonomy, a review of its

historical development shows why taxonomy is unable to do what we expect of it. Science 174.4015:1210-1213. Washington.

Raven, Peter H. and Richard W. Holm
1967   Systematics and the levels-of-organization approach. Systematic Zoology 16.1:1-5. Lawrence, Kans.

Reichard, Gladys A.
1948   Navajo classification of natural objects. Plateau 21.1:7-12. Flagstaff.

Reichel-Dolmatoff, Gerardo
1968   Desana: simbolismo de los indios Tukano del Vaupés. xiii, 270 pp. Bogotá: Universidad de los Andes. (Translated by the author 1971 as Amazonian Cosmos, the sexual and religious symbolism of the Tukano Indians. xxiii, 290 pp. Chicago: University of Chicago Press.)

Reim, Helmut
1962   Die Insektennahrung der australischen Ureinwohner: eine Studie zur Frühgeschichte menschlicher Wirtschaft und Ernährung. (Veröffentlichungen des Museums für Völkerkunde zu Leipzig, No. 13.) 158 pp. Berlin: Akademie-Verlag.

Ringenson, Karin
1957   Les Noms de la chèvre en français. Studia Neophilologica 29:13-38. Uppsala.

Rohlf, F. James and Robert R. Sokal
1962   The description of taxonomic relationships by factor analysis. Systematic Zoology 11.1:1-16. Baltimore.

Rolland, Eugène
1877-   Faune popularie de la France. 13 vols.
1915   (Continued by H. Gaidoz from vol. 9 on.) Vol. 1, Les mammifères sauvages, (noms vulgaires, dictons, proverbes, contes et superstitions), xiii, 179 pp., 1877; Vol. 2, Les oiseaux sauvages, xv, 421 pp., 1879; Vol. 3, Les reptiles, les poissons, les mollusques, les crustacés, et les insectes, xv, 365 pp., 1881; Vol. 4, Les mammifères domestiques, Première partie, 276 pp., 1881; Vol. 5, Les mammifères domestiques, Deuxième partie, vi, 266 pp., 1882; Vol. 5, Les

oiseaux domestiques et al fauconnerie, xi,
243 pp., 1883, vols. 1-6 published Paris:
Maisonneuve; Vol. 7, Les mammifères sauvages, complément, 272 pp., Paris: Chez
l'Auteur, 1906; Vol. 8, Les mammifères
sauvages (suite et fin), le loup, le renard,
et les cétacés, 175 pp., Paris: Chez l'Auteur, 1908; Vol. 9, Oiseaux sauvages, Première partie, vii, 252 pp., Paris: En Vente
chez les Libraires-Commissionnaires, 1911;
Vol. 10, Oiseaux sauvages, Seconde partie,
viii, 245 pp., Paris: En Vente chez les
Libraires-Comissionnaires, 1915; Vol. 11,
Reptiles et poissons, Première partie, vii,
255 pp., Paris: En Vente chez les Libraires-
Commissionnaires, 1910; Vol. 12, Les mollusques, les crustacés, les arachnides et
les annélides, 205 pp., Paris: Chez l'Auteur,
(n.d.); Vol. 13, Les insectes, Première
partie, 217 pp., Paris: En Vente chez les
Libraires-Commissionnaires, 1911.

Rostlund, Erhard
  1952   Freshwater fish and fishing in native North
          America. (University of California Publica-
          tions in Geography, Vol. 9.) x, 313 pp.
          Berkeley.

Rousseau, Michel
  1963   L'Animal civilisateur de l'homme. 176 pp.
          Paris: Masson.

Roux, Jean-Paul
  1959   Le Chameau en Asie centrale; son nom--son
          élévage--sa place dans la mythologie.
          Central Asiatic Journal 5.1:35-76. The
          Hague and Wiesbaden.

  1966   Faune et flore sacrées dans les sociétés
          attaïques. x, 478 pp. Paris: Maison-
          neuve.

Rubin, Jerrold
  1966   An approach to organizing data into homoge-
          nous groups. Systematic Zoology 15.3:169-
          182. Lawrence, Kans.

Saint-Dennis, Eugène de
  1947   Le Vocabulaire des animaux marins en Latin
          classique. (Études et commentaires 2.)
          xxxii, 120 pp. Paris: Klincksieck.

Schenk, Edward Theodore and John H. McMasters
1956   Procedure in taxonomy, including a reprint in
        translation of the Regles internationales de
        la nomenclature zoölogique (International Code
        of Zoölogical Nomenclature) with titles and
        notes on the opinions rendered to the present
        date (1907-1956). 3d edition, enlarged and in
        part rewritten by A. Myra Keen and Siemon
        William Muller. xii, 119 pp. Stanford:
        Stanford University Press.

Schlee, Dieter
1969   Hennig's principle of phylogenetic systemat-
        ics, an "intuitive, statistico-phenetic
        taxonomy?" Systematic Zoology 18.1:127-134.
        Lawrence, Kans.

Schmeltz, Johannes Dietrich Eduard
1894   Schnecken und Muscheln im Leben der Völker
        Indonesiens und Oceaniens. 43 pp. Leiden.

Schwidetzky, Ilse
1955   Etnobiología. Bases para el estudio biológi-
        co de los pueblos y el desarrollo de las
        sociedades. 444 pp. Mexico City: Fondo de
        Cultural Económica.

Sebeok, Thomas A.
1968   Zoosemiotics: a guide to its literature.
        Language Sciences 3:7-14. Bloomington, Ind.

Sherborn, Charles Davies
1902-   Index animalium; sive, Index nominum quae ab
1933   A. D. MDCCLVIII generibus et speciebus
        animalium imposita sunt, societatibus eru-
        ditorium adiuvantibus, a Carolo Davies
        Sherborn confectus... London: Cambridge
        University Press.

Sibree, James
1883   The oratory, songs, legends, and folk-tales
        of the Malagasy. Folk-lore Journal 1:1-15,
        33-40, 65-77, 97-106, 169-174, 201-211,
        233-243, 273-279, 305-316, 337-343. London.

1891   The folk-lore of Malagasy birds. Folk-lore
        2.3:336-366. London.

Simoons, Frederick J.
1961   Eat not of this flesh: food avoidances in
        the Old World. xiii, 241 pp. Madison:
        University of Wisconsin Press.

[5:28]

Simpson, George Gaylord
1943   Criteria for genera, species and subspecies
          in zoology and palaeozoology. Annals of the
          New York Academy of Sciences 44(Art. 2):145-
          178. New York. (See also Bogert et al.
          1943.)

1945   The principles of classification and a classi-
          fication of mammals. (Bulletin of the Ameri-
          can Museum of Natural History, Vol. 85.)
          xvi, 350 pp. New York.

1952   How many species? Evolution 6.3:342.
          Lancaster, Pa.

1959   Anatomy and morphology: classification and
          evolution: 1859 and 1959. Proceedings of
          the American Philosophical Society 103.2:286-
          306. Philadelphia.

1961   Principles of animal taxonomy. (Columbia
          Biological Series, No. 20.) xii, 247 pp.
          New York: Columbia University Press.
          (Reprinted 1967.)

1963   The meaning of taxonomic statements. Pp. 1-
          31 in Classification and human evolution,
          (Viking Fund Publications in Anthropology,
          No. 37), edited by S. Washburn. New York:
          Wenner-Gren Foundation for Anthropological
          Research.

Simpson, George Gaylord, Anne Roe, and Richard C.
          Lewontin
1960   Quantitative zoology. Revised edition.
(1939)   440 pp. New York: Harcourt, Brace.
          (1st edition, 1939, Quantitative zoology:
          numerical concepts and methods in the study
          of recent and fossil animals, by George
          Gaylord Simpson and Ann Roe. xvii, 414 pp.
          New York and London: McGraw-Hill.)

Sklar, Abe
1964   On category overlapping in taxonomy. Pp.
          395-401 in Form and strategy in science,
          edited by J. R. Gregg and F. T. C. Harris.
          Dordrecht: Reidel.

Smith, Hobart M.
1967a   Biological similarities and homologies.
          Systematic Zoology 16.1:101-102. Lawrence,
          Kans.

1967b   The hierarchy of monophyly and polyphyly.
         Systematic Zoology 16.1:102-103. Lawrence,
         Kans.

1967c   Classification of non-nomenclatural ranges
         of biological variation. Systematic Zoology
         16.2:171. Lawrence, Kans.

1969   Parapatry: sympatry or allopatry? System-
         atic Zoology 18.2:254-259. Lawrence, Kans.

Sokal, Robert R.
1966   Numerical taxonomy. Scientific American
         215.6:106-116. New York.

Sokal, Robert R. and Joseph H. Camin
1965   The two taxonomies: areas of agreement and
         conflict. Systematic Zoology 14.3:176-195.
         Lawrence, Kans.

Sokal, Robert R. and Peter H. A. Sneath
1963   Principles of numerical taxonomy. xvi, 359
         pp. San Francisco and London: W. H.
         Freeman.

1966   Efficiency in taxonomy. Taxon 15.1:1-21.
         Utrecht.

Speck, Frank G.
1921   Bird-lore of the northern Indians. Pp. 349-
         380 in Vol. 7 of University of Pennsylvania,
         University Lectures, delivered by members of
         the faculty in the free public lecture
         course, 1919-1920. Philadelphia.

1923   Reptile lore of the northern Indians.
         Journal of American Folklore 36.141:273-280.
         Lancaster, Pa.

1925   Dogs of the Labrador Indians. Natural
         History 25.1:58-64. New York.

1946a   Ethnology: bird nomenclature and song
         interpretation of the Canadian Delawares:
         an essay in ethno-ornithology. Journal of
         the Washington Academy of Sciences 36.8:
         249-258. Menasha.

1946b   Ethnology: ethnoherpetology of the Catawba
         and Cherokee Indians. Journal of the
         Washington Academy of Sciences 36.10:355-
         360. Menasha.

[5:30]

Speck, Frank G. and Ralph W. Dexter
1946   Molluscan food items of the Houma Indians.
        Nautilus 60.1:34. Philadelphia.

1948   Ethnology: utilization of marine life by
        the Wampanoag Indians of Massachusetts.
        Journal of Washington Academy of Sciences
        38.8:257-265. Menasha.

Speck, Frank G. and Ernest S. Dodge
1945   Amphibian and reptile lore of the Six Nations
        Cayuga. Journal of American Folklore 58.230:
        306-309. Philadelphia.

Stearns, Robert E. C.
1889   Ethno-conchology: a study of primitive
        money. Pp. 297-334 in Part 2 of Annual
        Report of the U.S. National Museum, 1887.
        Washington.

Stebbins, Robert C.
1966   A field guide to western reptiles and
        amphibians. (Peterson Field Guide 16.)
        xiv, 279 pp. Boston: Houghton Mifflin.

Steggerda, Morris
1940   One Maya Indian's knowledge of nature.
        Proceedings of the 8th American Scientific
        Congress, Washington 1940, 2:91-92.
        Washington: Department of State.

Stevenson, Elmo
1942   Key to the nests of Pacific Coast birds.
        (Oregon State Monographs, Studies in
        Zoology 4.) 71 pp. Corvallis.

Steyskal, George C.
1967   Another view of the future of taxonomy.
        Systematic Zoology 16.3:265-268. Lawrence,
        Kans.

1970   The language of zoological names. Systematic
        Zoology 19.1:94-97. Lawrence, Kans.

Sturtevant, William C. and Richard H. Manville
1966   Early specimens of the eastern wolf, Canis
        lupus lycaon. Chesapeake Science 7.4:218-
        220. Solomons, Md.

Swann, Harry Kirke
1913   A dictionary of English and folk-names of
        British birds; with their history, meaning,

and first usage; and the folk-lore, weatherlore, legends, etc., relating to the more
familiar species. xii, 266 pp. London:
Witherby. (Reprinted 1968, Detroit: Gale
Research Co.)

Tambiah, S. J.
1969   Animals are good to think and good to prohi-
bit. Ethnology 8.4:423-459. Pittsburgh.

Theuwis, Alfons
1966   Notes d'ethnographie et de folklore [des
oiseaux de Tunisie]. IBLA (Revue de
l'Institut des belles lettres arabes) 29.
116:409-411. Tunis.

Thoday, J. M.
1952   Units of evolution and units of classification. Proceedings of the Leeds Philosophical
and Literary Society 6(Part 1):61-63. Leeds.

Thomas, Dorothy
1966   Chrau zoology: an ethnolinguistic study.
Pp. 1-14 in Papers in four Vietnamese languages, edited by D. D. Thomas. Auckland:
Linguistic Society of New Zealand. (Also
1964, Te Reo, 7:1-14, Auckland.)

Timmermans, J. et al.
1963   La Classification dans les sciences. 236 pp.
Gembloux: J. Duculot.

Tomlinson, Jack T.
1968   Improper use of the word bisexual. Systematic Zoology 17.2:212. Lawrence, Kans.

Turner, John R. G.
1967   Goddess changes sex, or the gender game.
Systematic Zoology 16.4:349-350. Lawrence,
Kans.

Turrill, William Bertram et al.
1942   Differences in the systematics of plants and
animals and their dependence on differences
in structure, function, and behaviour in the
two groups. Proceedings of the Linnean
Society of London 153(Part 3):272-287.
London.

Tyler, Michael J.
1961   A preliminary note on herpetological data
obtained from natives in the Central Highlands of New Guinea. British Journal of

[5:32]

Herpetology 2.12:219-220.   London.

Ucko, Peter J. and G. W. Dimbleby, editors
  1969   The domestication and exploitation of plants
          and animals.   xxxvi, 581 pp.   London: Gerald
          Duckworth.

Urban, M.
  1966   Zur Herkunft der polynesischen Kultur:
          Bemerkungen aus der sicht der Ethnobotanik
          und Ethnozoologie des pazifischen Raumes.
          Mitteilungen zur Kulturkunde 1:169-178.
          Wiesbaden.

Valentine, D. H. et al.
  1970   Infraspecific categories.   Biological Journal
          of the Linnean Society 2.3:209-258.   London.
          (See also Askew; Hale; Heywood.)

Vanzolini, P. E.
  1956-   Notas sôbre a zoologia dos Índios Canela.
  1958   Revista do Museu Paulista (n.s.)10:155-171.
          São Paulo.

Verheijen, J. A. J.
  1963   Bird-names in Manggarai, Flores, Indonesia.
          Anthropos 58.5-6:677-718.   Fribourg.

Voss, Edward G.
  1952   The history of keys and phylogenetic trees
          in systematic biology.   Journal of the
          Scientific Laboratories, Denison University,
          43:1-25(Art. 1).   Granville, Ohio.

Walker, Ernest Pillsbury et al.
  1968   Mammals of the world.   2d edition, revision
  (1964) by John L. Paradiso.   2 vols.   Baltimore:
          Johns Hopkins Press.   (1964, 3 vols.)

Warburton, Frederick E.
  1967   The purposes of classifications.   Systematic
          Zoology 16.3:241-245.   Lawrence, Kans.

Washburn, Sherwood L., editor
  1963   Classification and human evolution.   (Viking
          Fund Publications in Anthropology, No. 37.)
          vii, 371 pp.   New York: Wenner-Gren Founda-
          tion for Anthropological Research.

Weisel, George F.
  1952   Ethnology: animal names, anatomical terms,
          and some ethnozoology of the Flathead

Indians. Journal of the Washington Academy of Sciences 42.11:345-355. Baltimore.

Widstrand, Carl Gösta
    1964   Lapp reindeer terminology, I. A collection of horn terms from Karasjok, Norway. Pp. 331-357 in Lapponica, (Studia Ethnographica Upsaliensia 21), edited by Arne Furumark et al. Lund.

Willis, John Christopher
    1922   Age and area: a study in geographical distribution and origin of species. x, 259 pp. Cambridge: Cambridge University Press.

    1940   The course of evolution by differentiation or divergent mutation rather than by selection. viii, 207 pp. Cambridge: Cambridge University Press.

Witthoft, John
    1946a   Ethnology: some eastern Cherokee bird stories. Journal of the Washington Academy of Sciences 36.6:177-180. Menasha.

    1946b   Ethnology: birdlore of the eastern Cherokee. Journal of the Washington Academy of Sciences 36.11:372-384. Menasha.

Woodger, Joseph Henry
    1937   The axiomatic method in biology. With appendices by A. Tarski and W. F. Floyd. x, 174 pp. Cambridge: Cambridge University Press.

    1952   Biology and language, an introduction to the methodology of the biological sciences, including medicine. xiii, 364 pp. Cambridge: Cambridge University Press.

    1960-   Taxonomy and evolution. La Nuova Critica
    1961   3.12:67-77. Rome.

    1967   Biological principles: a critical study.
    (1929)   Reissued, with a new introduction. xix, 496 pp. London: Routledge and Kegan Paul; New York: Humanities Press. (1929, New York: Harcourt, Brace.)

Worsley, Peter M.
    1961   The utilization of food resources by an Australian aboriginal tribe. Acta

[5:34]

        Ethnographica Academiae Scientiarium
        Hungaricae 10.1-2:153-190. Budapest.

Wyman, Leland C. and Flora L. Bailey
    1964   Navaho Indian ethnoentomology. (University
        of New Mexico Publications in Anthropology,
        No. 12.) 158 pp. Albuquerque.

Yochelson, Ellis L.
    1966   Nomenclature in the machine age. Systematic
        Zoology 15.1:88-91. Lawrence, Kans.

Zeuner, Friedrich Eberhard
    1963   A history of domesticated animals. 560 pp.
        London: Hutchinson; New York: Harper and
        Row.

6. Ethnomedicine (and medical classification)

[Including references to ethnomedical and
related medical works on disease categorization and treatment, anatomical classification, and similar topics; cf. 4.]

Aberle, David F.
    1966   The peyote religion among the Navaho. (Vik-
            ing Fund Publications in Anthropology, No.
            42.) xxvi, 454 pp. New York: Wenner-Gren
            Foundation for Anthropological Research.

Aberle, David F. and Omer C. Stewart
    1957   Navaho and Ute peyotism: a chronological
            and distributional study. (University of
            Colorado Studies, Series in Anthropology
            No. 6.) 129 pp. Boulder.

Abrahams, Harold J.
    1970   The Compendium Pharmaceuticum of Jean François
            Coste. Economic Botany 24.4:374-398. Law-
            rence, Kans.

Ackerknecht, Erwin H.
    1942a   Problems of primitive medicine. Bulletin of
            the History of Medicine 11.5:503-521.
            Baltimore.

    1942b   Primitive medicine and culture pattern.
            Bulletin of the History of Medicine 12.4:
            545-574. Baltimore.

    1943a   Primitive autopsies and the history of
            anatomy. Bulletin of the History of Medi-
            cine 13.3:334-339. Baltimore.

    1943b   Psychopathology, primitive medicine and
            primitive culture. Bulletin of the History
            of Medicine 14.1:30-67. Baltimore.

    1945   On the collecting of data concerning primi-
            tive medicine. American Anthropologist
            47.3:427-431. Menasha.

    1946a   Natural diseases and rational treatment of
            primitive medicine. Bulletin of the History
            of Medicine 19.5:467-497. Baltimore.

    1946b   Contradictions of primitive surgery. Bulle-
            tin of the History of Medicine 20:184-187.
            Baltimore.

Ackerknecht, Erwin H. (cont.)
 1946c Primitive medicine. Transactions of the New
 York Academy of Sciences, Series II, 8.1:
 26-37. New York.

 1946d Primitive medicine: a contrast with modern
 practice. Merck Report, July, pp. 4-8.
 Rahway, N. J.

 1947 Primitive surgery. American Anthropologist
 49.1:25-45. Menasha.

 1955 A short history of medicine. xviii, 258 pp.
 New York: Ronald Press.

 1958 Primitive medicine's social function. Pp. 3-
 7 in Vol. 1, Miscellanea Paul Rivet, Octo-
 genario Dicata. Mexico City: Universidad
 Nacional Autónoma de Mexico.

Adam, Tassilo
 1946a Amok and mata gelapocher Malay diseases.
 Knickerbocker Weekly 5.4:18-21. New York.

 1946b Latah, a peculiar Malay disease. Knickerbocker Weekly 6.4:21-23. New York.

Adams, Richard Newbold
 1951 Un analisis de las enfermedades y sus cura-
 ciones en una población indígena de Guatemala (con sugerencias relacionadas con la
 práctica de medicina en el area maya).
 Guatemala City: Instituto de Nutrición de
 Centro América y Panamá.

 1952 Un análisis de las creencias y prácticas
 médicas en un pueblo indígena de Guatemala
 (con sugerencias relacionadas con la práctica
 de medicina en la área Maya). (Publicaciones
 especiales del Instituto Indigenista Nacional,
 No. 17.) Guatemala City: Editorial del
 Ministerio de Educación Pública.

Adams, William R.
 1951 Aboriginal American medicine and surgery.
 Proceedings of the Indiana Academy of
 Sciences 61:49-53. Indianapolis.

Ajose, Oladele A.
 1957 Preventive medicine and superstition in
 Nigeria. Africa 27.3:268-274. London.

Altschul, Siri von Reis
 1970 Ethnogynecological notes in the Harvard

University Herbaria. Botanical Museum
Leaflets, Harvard University 22.10:333-343.
Cambridge.

Anderson, E. N., Jr. and Marja L. Anderson
1969   Folk medicine in rural Hong Kong. Ethnoiatria
        2.1:(7). Varese, Italy.

Andros, F.
1883   The medicine and surgery of the Winnebago
        and Dakota Indians. Journal of American
        Medical Association 1.4:116-118; 1.13:402.
        Chicago.

Anonymous
1966   Survey of medicines and medicinal plants of
        the South Pacific. South Pacific Bulletin
        16.3:54. Noumea.

Anson, B. J.
1947   Saints, animals, stars and demons in mediae-
        val medicine. Quarterly Bulletin of North-
        western University Medical School 21:1-17.
        Chicago.

Argumosa, J. A. de
1963   La anestesia en la medicina aborigen.
        Boletín Indigenista Venezolana 8:129-153.
        Caracas.

Aufenanger, Heinrich
1959   How children's faeces are preserved in the
        Central Highlands of New Guinea. Anthropos
        54.1-2:236-237. Fribourg.

Baker, Frank
1969   Review of general systems concepts and their
        relevance for medical care. Systematics
        7.3:209-229. London.

Bartlett, Harley Harris
1929   The labors of the Datoe: Part I, an anno-
        tated list of religious, magical and medical
        practices of the Batak of Asahan. (Papers
        of the Michigan Academy of Science, Arts and
        Letters, Vol. 12.) 74 pp. Ann Arbor.

1930   The labors of the Datoe: Part II, directions
        for the ceremonies. (Papers of the Michigan
        Academy of Science, Arts and Letters, Vol.
        14.) 34 pp. Ann Arbor.

Bartlett, Harley Harris   (cont.)
    1940   The geographic distribution, migration, and
            dialectical mutation of certain plant names
            in the Philippines and Netherlands India,
            with special reference to the materia medica
            of a Mangyan mediquillo. Proceedings of the
            Sixth Pacific Science Congress of the Pacific
            Science Association 6:85-110. Berkeley and
            Los Angeles.

Bouteiller, Marcelle
    1959   Cosmologie et médecine magique selon notre
            folklor rurale: esquisse d'analyse struc-
            turale. L'Ethnographie (n.s.) 53:91-95.
            Paris.

Bradley, Will T.
    1936   Medical practices of the New England aborig-
            ines. Journal of the American Pharmaceutical
            Association 25.2:138-147. Easton, Pa.

Brendle, Thomas R. and Claude W. Unger
    1935   Folk medicine of the Pennsylvania Germans.
            (Proceedings of the Pennsylvania German
            Society, 45.) 303 pp. Norristown, Pa.

Brothwell, Don R. and A. T. Sandison, editors
    1967   Diseases in antiquity: a survey of the
            diseases, injuries and surgery of early
            populations. xix, 766 pp. Springfield,
            Ill.: C. C. Thomas.

Brown, Robert
    1868   On the vegetable products used by the north-
            west American Indians, as food and medicine,
            in the arts, and in superstitious rites.
            Botanical Society of Edinburgh Transactions
            (1866-1868), 9(May):378-396. Edinburgh.

Browne, Ray B.
    1958   Popular beliefs and practices from Alabama.
            (University of California Publications,
            Folklore Studies 9.) 271 pp. Berkeley and
            Los Angeles: University of California Press.

Buchanan, Scott Milrosse
    1938   The doctrine of signatures: a defence of
            theory in medicine. xiv, 205 pp. London:
            Kegan Paul, Trench, Trubner; New York:
            Harcourt, Brace.

Burkill, I. H. and M. Haniff
    1930   Malayan village medicine. Gardens' Bulletin

6:165-321. Singapore.

Burton-Bradley, B. G. and Charles Julius
1965   Folk psychiatry of certain villages in the
        Central District of Papua. Pp. 9-26 in
        South Pacific Commission Technical Report
        No. 146. Noumea.

Campbell, T. N.
1951   Medicinal plants used by Choctaw, Chickasaw,
        and Creek Indians in the early nineteenth
        century. Journal of the Washington Academy
        of Sciences 41.9:285-290. Baltimore.

Cárdenas, Martín
1969   Manual de plantas económicas de Bolivia.
        421 pp. Cochabamba: Imprenta Icthus.

Carter, George F.
1938   Aboriginal use of medicinal plants in south-
        ern California. California Garden 29.9:4,
        8; 29.11:4-5.

Chamberlain, Alexander F.
1894   Primitive anthropometry and its folklore.
        Proceedings of the American Association for
        the Advancement of Science 43:348-349.
        Salem.

Chattopadhyay, P. K.
1968   Mode de croisement des mains et des bras,
        droiterie, gaucherie et camptodactylie chez
        les Bengalis. L'Anthropologie 72.3-4:317-
        324. Paris.

Clements, Forrest E.
1932   Primitive concepts of disease. University
        of California Publications in American
        Archaeology and Ethnology 32.2:185-252.
        Berkeley.

Comas, Juan
1954   Influencia indígena en la medicina hipocrática
        en la Nueva España del siglo XVI. América
        Indígena 14.4:327-361. Mexico City.

Culley, John
1936   The California Indians: their medical
        practices and their drugs. Journal American
        Pharmaceutical Association 25.4:332-339.
        Easton, Pa.

[6:6]

Currier, R. L.
1966 The hot-cold syndrome and symbolic balance in Mexican and Spanish-American folk medicine. Ethnology 5.3:251-263. Pittsburgh.

Curtin, Leonora Scott Muse
1948 Healing herbs of the upper Río Grande. 281 pp. Santa Fé: Laboratory of Anthropology. (Reprinted 1965, Los Angeles: Southwest Museum.)

Dailey, Robert Clifton
1957 Medical practices among the Plains Indians: a study in culture. 350 pp. Ph.D. dissertation in the University of Toronto. Toronto, Ontario.

Dastur, Jehangir Fardunji
1962 Medicinal plants of India and Pakistan; a concise work describing plants used for drugs and remedies according to Ayurvedic, Unani and Tibbi systems and mentioned in British and American pharmacopoeias. 2d edition. vi, 212 pp. India: D. B. Taraporevala Sons.

Dávalos Hurtado, E. and J. M. Ortiz de Zárate
1953 La plástica indígena y la patología. Revista Mexicana de Estudios Antropológicos 13.2-3: 95-104. Mexico City.

Devereaux, George
1948a Mohave pregnancy. Acta Americana 6.1-2:84-116. Mexico City.

1948b Mohave Indian obstetrics. American Imago 5.2:99-139. Boston.

1955 A study of abortion in primitive societies: a typological, distributional, and dynamic analysis of the prevention of birth in 400 preindustrial societies. x, 394 pp. New York: Julian Press.

1961 Mohave ethnopsychiatry and suicide: the psychiatric knowledge and the psychic disturbances of an Indian tribe. (Bulletin of the Bureau of American Ethnology, No. 175.) vi, 586 pp. Washington.

Dieterlen, H.
1930 La Médecine et les médecins au Lessouto.

(Les Cahiers missionnaires, No. 17.) 72 pp.
Paris: Société des Missions Évangéliques.

Dobkin, Marlene
1969   Fortune's magic: divination, psychotherapy,
and folk medicine in Peru. Journal of American Folklore 82.2:132-141. Austin.

Dobrec, Erich
1952   Heilkunde bei den Eingeborenen Australiens.
Weiner Beiträge zur Kulturgeschichte und
Linguistik 9:280-307. Vienna.

Dubos, René
1961   Mirage of health, utopias, progress, and
biological change. 235 pp. New York:
Doubleday Anchor Books.

Eaton, Joseph W. and Robert J. Weil
1955   Culture and mental disorders. 254 pp.
Glencoe, Ill.: Free Press.

Ellis, Edgar S.
1946   Ancient anodynes. Primitive anaesthesia and
allied conditions. 187 pp. London: W.
Heinemann.

Elmendorf, William W.
1952   Soul loss in western North America. Pp. 104-
114 in Indian tribes of aboriginal America,
(Selected Papers of the 29th International
Congress of Americanists), edited by S. Tax.
Chicago: University of Chicago Press.

Erasmus, Charles J.
1952   Changing folk beliefs and the relativity of
empirical knowledge. Southwestern Journal
of Anthropology 8.4:411-428. Albuquerque.

Eron, Leonard D., editor
1966   The classification of behavior disorders.
xii, 180 pp. Chicago: Aldine.

Evans-Pritchard, E. E.
1937   Witchcraft, oracles and magic among the
Azande. xxv, 558 pp. Oxford: Clarendon.

Fabrega, Horacia, Jr.
1970   On the specificity of folk illnesses.
Southwestern Journal of Anthropology 26.3:
305-314. Albuquerque.

Feinstein, Alvan R.
1963   Boolean algebra and clinical taxonomy, 1. Analytic synthesis of the general spectrum of a human disease. New England Journal of Medicine 269.18:929-938. Boston.

1964a Symptomatic patterns, biologic behavior, and prognosis in cancer of the lung: practical application of Boolean algebra and clinical taxonomy. Annals of Internal Medicine 61.1:27-43. Philadelphia.

1964b Scientific methodology in clinical medicine. 1. Introduction, principles, and concepts. Annals of Internal Medicine 61.3:564-579. 2. Classification of human disease by clinical behavior. Annals of Internal Medicine 61:757-781. Philadelphia.

1967   Clinical judgment. 414 pp. Baltimore: Williams and Wilkins.

1969   Taxonomy and logic in clinical data. Annals of the New York Academy of Sciences 161(Art. 2):450-459. New York.

1970a The pre-therapeutic classification of co-morbidity in chronic disease. Journal of Chronic Diseases 23:455-468. Oxford.

1970b Taxonorics. 1. Formulation of criteria. Archives of Internal Medicine 126:679-693. 2. Formats and coding systems for data processing. Archives of Internal Medicine 126:1053-1067. Chicago.

Fenton, William N.
1941   Masked medicine societies of the Iroquois. Pp. 397-430 in Smithsonian Institution Annual Report for 1940. Washington.

1942   Contacts between Iroquois herbalism and colonial medicine. Pp. 503-526 in Smithsonian Institution Annual Report for 1941. Washington.

1949   Medicinal plant lore of the Iroquois: Chauncey Johnny John and James Crow instruct He-lost-a-bet in the use of native plants. University of the State of New York, Bulletin to the Schools 35.7:233-237. Albany.

Field, Margaret Joyce
1960   Search for security: an ethnopsychiatric
         study of rural Ghana. (Northwestern Uni-
         versity African Studies, No. 5.) 478 pp.
         Evanston, Ill.: Northwestern University
         Press.

Forbes, Thomas R.
1953   The social history of the caul. Yale Journal
         of Biology and Medicine 25:495-508. New
         Haven.

Fortune, R. F.
1960   Folk medicine in the Dobuan Islands. Jour-
         nal of the Polynesian Society 69.1:31-33.
         Wellington.

Foster, George
1944   Nagualism in Mexico and Guatemala. Acta
         Americana 2.1-2:85-103. Mexico City.

Fox, Robert B.
1952   The Pinatubo Negritos: their useful plants
         and material culture. Philippine Journal
         of Science 81.3-4:173-414. Manila.

Frake, Charles O.
1961   The diagnosis of disease among the Subanun.
         American Anthropologist 63.1:11-32. Menasha.

Frake, Charles O. and Carolyn M. Frake
1957   Post-natal care among the eastern Subanun.
         Silliman Journal 4.3:207-214. Dumaguete
         City, Philippines.

Franklin, Karl J.
1963   Kewa ethnolinguistic concepts of body parts.
         Southwestern Journal of Anthropology 19.1:
         54-63. Albuquerque.

Freeland, L. S.
1923   Pomo doctors and poisoners. University of
         California Publications in American
         Archaeology and Ethnology 20.4:57-73.
         Berkeley.

Friedrich, Paul
1969   Metaphor-like relations between referential
         subsets. Lingua 24.1:1-10. Amsterdam.

Gajdusek, D. Carleton
1961   Cybernetics of human development: apologia

of an ethno-pediatrician. Pp. 76-77 in Program and abstracts of the Society of Pediatric Research, 31st Annual Meeting. Atlantic City.

Galdston, Iago, editor
1959 Anthropology and medicine. 165 pp. New York: International Universities Press.

1961 Man's image in medicine and anthropology. (Transactions of Arden House Conference on Medicine and Anthropology, 1961.) xvii, 525 pp. New York: International Universities Press.

Gates, William Edmond
1957 A bibliography for Yucatan medicinal plant studies, edited by John L. Sorensen. Tlalocan 3.4:334-343. Mexico City.

Gates, William Edmond, translator and editor
1939 De la Cruz-Badiano Aztec herbal of 1552. 48 pp. Baltimore: Maya Society.

Gayton, A. H.
1930 Yokuts-Mono chiefs and shamans. University of California Publications in American Archaeology and Ethnology 24.8:361-420. Berkeley.

Gelfand, Michael
1947 African medical handbook; an outline of medicine and hospital practice for African nurses, orderlies, and medical assistants. 202 pp. Cape Town: African Bookman.

1956 Medicine and magic of the Mashona. 206 pp. Cape Town: Juta.

1964 Witch doctor; traditional medicine man of Rhodesia. 191 pp. London: Harvill Press.

Gerste, A.
1910 Notes sur la médecine et la botanique des anciens Mexicains... 2d edition. 191 pp. Rome: Impr. Polyglotte Vaticane.

Gerstner, Andreas
1955 Die glaubensmässige Einstellung der Wewäk-Boikin-Leute zu den Krankheiten und deren Heilung (Nordost-Neuguinea). Anthropos 50.1-3:319-336. Fribourg.

Gilges, W.
    1955   Some African poison plants and medicines of
            Northern Rhodesia. (Rhodes-Livingstone
            Museum, Occasional Papers No. 11.) 33 pp.
            Livingstone, Northern Rhodesia.

Gillin, John
    1956   The making of a witch doctor. Psychiatry
            19.2:131-136. Baltimore.

Gimlette, John Desmond
    1929   Malay poisons and charm cures. 3d edition.
    (1915) xiv, 301 pp. London: Churchill. (Previous
            editions in 1915, 1923.)

    1939   A dictionary of Malayan medicine. Edited
            and completed by H. W. Thomson; foreword by
            Malcolm Walton. xvi, 259 pp. New York:
            Oxford University Press.

Gimlette, J. D. and I. H. Burkhill
    1930   The medical book of Malayan medicine.
            Gardens' Bulletin 6:323-474. Singapore.

Girault, Louis
    1966   Classification vernaculaire des plantes
    [1967] médicinales chez les Callawaya, médecins
            empiriques (Bolivie). Journal de la Société
            des Americanistes 55.1:155-200. Paris.

Githens, Thomas Stotesburg
    1948   Drug plants of Africa. (African Handbooks
            8.) vii, 125 pp. Philadelphia: University
            of Pennsylvania Press.

Glick, Leonard B.
    1967   Medicine as an ethnographic category: the
            Gimi of the New Guinea Highlands. Ethnology
            6.1:31-56. Pittsburgh.

Good, Irving John
    1965   Categorization of classification. Pp. 115-
            128 in Mathematics and computer science in
            biology and medicine, (Proceedings of
            conference held by Medical Research Council).
            London: Her Majesty's Stationery Office.

Gordon, Benjamin Lee
    1949   Medicine throughout antiquity. xvii, 818 pp.
            Philadelphia: F. A. Davis.

Gould, Harold A.
    1957   The implications of technological change for

373

folk and scientific medicine. American
Anthropologist 59.3:507-518. Menasha.

Greenlee, Robert F.
1944   Medicine and curing practices of the modern
        Florida Seminole. American Anthropologist
        46.3:317-328. Menasha.

Grinnell, George Bird
1905   Some Cheyenne plant medicines. American
        Anthropologist 7.1:37-43. Menasha.

Guerra, Francisco
1950   Bibliografía de la materia médica mexicana.
        423 pp. Mexico City: La Prensa Médica
        Mexicana.

Guerrero, Leon M.
1921   Medicinal uses of Philippine plants. Minor
        Products of Philippine Forests 3:149-246.
        Manila.

Guiang, Rodolfo V.
1959   The end of quackery? Philippines Free Press
        52.30:42. Manila.

Hagar, Stansbury
1896   Micmac magic and medicine. Journal of
        American Folklore 9.34:170-177. Boston and
        New York.

Hallowell, A. Irving
1961   Ojibwa world view and disease. In Man's
        image in medicine and anthropology, edited
        by I. Galdston. New York: International
        University Press.

Hanson, F. Allan
1970   The Rapan theory of conception. American
        Anthropologist 72.6:1444-1447. Menasha.

Harley, George W.
1941   Native African medicine. xvi, 294 pp.
        Cambridge: Harvard University Press.

Hart, Charles P.
1886   Piute herbalists. Proceedings of the Ameri-
        can Association for the Advancement of Sci-
        ence 35:330-331. Salem, Mass.

Hart, Donn V.
1969   Bisayan Fililpino and Malayan humoral

pathologies: folk medicine and ethnohistory in Southeast Asia. (Data Paper No. 76.) x, 96 pp. Ithaca: Cornell University Southeast Asia Program.

Harwood, Alan
1971   The hot-cold theory of disease, implications for treatment of Puerto Rican patients. Journal of the American Medical Association 216.7:1153-1158. Chicago.

Haskin, Leslie L.
1929   Frontier foods, ipo or yampa sustained the pioneers. Nature Magazine 14.9:171-172. London.

Henry, Jules
1949   Anthropology and psychosomatics. Psychosomatic Medicine 11.4:216-222. Richmond, Va.

Hernández, Francisco
1942-   Historia de las plantas de Nueva España.
1946   3 vols. Mexico City: Imprenta Universitaria.

Heuse, G. A.
1955   L'Ethno-psychologie médicale. Revue de Psychologie des Peuples 10.2:192-200. Le Havre.

Hide, R. L.
1969   Worms and sickness; a note on noise-producing worms and mystical belief among the Nimai of the New Guinea Highlands. Mankind 7.2:149-151. Sydney.

Higbee, E. C. and Atherton Lee
1945   Drug and medicinal crops. Pp. 129-160 in New crops for the New World, edited by C. M. Wilson. New York: Macmillan.

Himes, Ron
1971   Kinship, disease, property, and time in the Tagalog area, Philippines: a study in ethnoscience. Doctoral dissertation in anthropology, University of Hawaii, Honolulu.

Hocking, George M.
1956   Some plant materials used medicinally and otherwise by the Navaho Indians in the Chaco Canyon, New Mexico. El Palacio 63.5-6: 146-165. Santa Fe.

[6:14]

Holland, William R. and Roland G. Tharp
   1964   Highland Maya psychotherapy. American
           Anthropologist 66.1:41-52. Menasha.

Honko, Lauri
   1959   Krankheitsprojektile. Untersuchung über
           eine urtümliche Krankheitserklärung.
           (FF Communications 178.) 258 pp. Helsinki.

Hosack, David
   1821   A system of practical nosology to which is
           prefixed a synopsis of the systems of Sauv-
           ages, Linnaeus, Vogel, Sagar, MacBride,
           Cullen, Darwin, Chrichton, Pinel, Parr,
           Swediaur, Young, and Good. 2d edition.
           366 pp. New York: C. S. Van Winkle.

Hrdlička, Ales
   1932   Disease, medicine and surgery among the
           American aborigines. Journal of the American
           Medical Association 99.20:1661-1666. Chicago.

Huard, Pierre
   1957   La Médecine japonaise traditionelle. Concours
           Medical 79:687-692. Paris.

Huard, P. and M. Wong
   1957   Structure de la médecine chinoise. Bulletin
           de la Société des Études Indochinoises (n.s.)
           32.4:299-376. Saigon.

   1959a   La Médecine chinoise au cours des siècles.
           192 pp. Paris: Dacosta.

   1959b   Histoire de l'acupuncture chinoise. Bulletin
           de la Société des Études Indochinoises (n.s.)
           34.4:403-423. Saigon.

Inlow, William DePrez
   1946   Medicine: its nature and definition. Bulle-
           tin of the History of Medicine 19.3:249-273.
           Baltimore.

Jain, Sudhanshu Kumar
   1968   Medicinal plants. xi, 176 pp. New Delhi:
           National Book Trust.

Jamuh, G.
   1959   Melanau healing. Sarawak Museum Journal
           9:186-194. Kuching.

Jenkins, C. David and Stephen J. Zyzanski
   1968   Dimensions of belief and feeling concerning

three diseases, poliomyelitis, cancer, and
mental illness: a factor analytic study.
Behavioral Science 13.5:372-381. Ann Arbor.

Kanner, Leo
    1942   Contemporary folk treatment of sternutation.
            Bulletin of the History of Medicine 11.3:
            273-291. Baltimore.

Kaplan, Lucille N. and Lawrence Kaplan
    1960   Medicinal plant and food use as related to
            health and disease in coastal Oaxaca. Pp.
            452-458 in Men and Cultures, Selected Papers
            of the Fifth International Congress of
            Anthropological and Ethnological Sciences,
            1956, edited by A. F. C. Wallace. Philadel-
            phia: University of Pennsylvania Press.

Katz, Martin M., Jonathan O. Cole, and Walter E. Barton,
            editors
    1968   Conference on the role and methodology of
            classification in psychiatry and psychopath-
            ology. (U.S. Public Health Service Publica-
            tion 1584.) ix, 590 pp. Washington:
            Government Printing Office.

Kilpatrick, Jack Frederick and Anna Gritts Kilpatrick
    1964   Cherokee burn conjurations. Journal of the
            Graduate Research Center, Southern Methodist
            University 33.1:17-21. Dallas.

Kloos, Peter
    1970   Search for health among the Maroni River
            Caribs: etiology and medical care in a
            20th century Amerindian group in Surinam.
            Bijdragen tot de Land-, Taal- en Volkenkunde
            126.2:115-141. 's-Gravenhage.

Koty, John
    1933   Die Behandlung der Alten und Kranken bei der
            Naturvolkern. (Forschungen zur Völkenpsy-
            chologie und Soziologie, Vol. 13.) xxxix,
            373 pp. Stuttgart: Kohl Hammer.

Krojman, Wilton M.
    1939   Medical practices and diseases of the aborig-
            inal American Indians. Ciba Symposia 1.1:
            11-18. Basel.

La Barre, Weston
    1942   Folk medicine and folk science. Journal of
            American Folklore 55.218:197-203. Phila-
            delphia.

La Barre, Weston (cont.)
1947   Primitive psychotherapy in native American cultures: peyotism and confession. Journal of Abnormal and Social Psychology 43.3:301-307. Albany.

1951   Aymara biologicals and other medicines. Journal of American Folklore 64.252:171-178. Philadelphia.

1959   Materia medica of the Aymara, Lake Titicaca Plateau, Bolivia. Webbia 15.1:47-94. Florence.

1960   Twenty years of peyote studies. Current Anthropology 1.1:45-60. Chicago.

Landar, Herbert and Joseph B. Casagrande
1962   Navaho anatomical reference. Ethnology 1.3: 370-373. Pittsburgh.

Landes, Ruth
1963   Potawatomi medicine. Transactions of the Kansas Academy of Sciences 66.4:553-599. Topeka.

Lantis, Margaret
1959   Folk medicine and hygiene: Lower Kuskokwin and Nunivale-Nelson Island areas. Anthropological Papers of the University of Alaska 8.1:1-75. College.

Laszlo, Henry de and Paul S. Henshaw
1954   Plant materials used by primitive peoples to affect fertility. Science 119.3097:626-631. Washington.

Leighton, Alexander H. and Dorothea C. Leighton
1941   Elements of psychotherapy in Navaho religion. Psychiatry 4.4:515-523. Baltimore.

Lenormand, Maurice H.
1950   Connaissance du corps et prise de conscience de la personne chez le Mélanésien de Lifou (Iles Loyalty). Journal de la Société des Océanistes 6:33-65. Paris.

Lessa, William A.
1952   Somatomancy: precursor of the science of human constitution. Scientific Monthly 75.6:355-365. Lancaster, Pa.

Lestrade, A.
1955   La Médecine indigène au Ruanda et lexique
        des termes médicaux français-urunyarwanda.
        (Mémoires de l'Académie royale des Sciences
        coloniales, Classe des Sciences morales et
        politiques, [n.s.] 8.1.) 277 pp. Brussels.

Lévi-Strauss, Claude
1962   La Pensée sauvage. 395 pp. Paris: Plon.
        (Translated 1966 as The savage mind. xii,
        290 pp. London: Wiedenfeld and Nicolson;
        Chicago: University of Chicago Press.)

Lieban, Richard W.
1960   Sorcery, illness, and social control in a
        Philippine municipality. Southwestern
        Journal of Anthropology 16.2:127-143.
        Albuquerque.

1967   Cebuano sorcery: malign magic in the Philip-
        pines. x, 163 pp. Berkeley and Los Angeles:
        University of California Press.

Lloyd, John Uri
1922   Origin and history of all the pharmacopeial
        vegetable drugs, chemicals, and preparations.
        449 pp. Washington: American Drug Manufac-
        turer's Association.

Loeb, Edwin M.
1929   Shaman and seer. American Anthropologist
        31.1:60-84. Menasha.

Lowie, Robert H.
1948   Primitive religion. Revised edition. xxiii,
(1924) 382 pp. New York: Liveright.

Luzbetak, Louis J.
1958   Treatment of disease in the New Guinea high-
        lands. Anthropological Quarterly 31.2:42-55.
        Washington.

McDermott, Walsh, Kurt Deuschle, John Adair, Hugh
        Fulmer, and Bernice Loughlin
1960   Introducing modern medicine in a Navajo
        community: physicians and anthropologists
        are cooperating in this study of changing
        patterns of culture and disease. Parts I
        and II. Science 131.3395:197-205; 131.3396:
        279-288. Washington.

[6:18]

Magnus, Hugo
1905   Die Volksmedizin, ihre geschichtliche
        Entwickelung und ihre Bezeihungen zur
        Kultur. 112 pp. Breslau: J. V. Kern
        (M. Müller).

Mahr, August C.
1951   Materia medica and therapy among the North
        American forest Indians. Ohio State Archae-
        ological and Historical Quarterly 60.4:331-
        354. Columbus, Ohio.

1955   Semantic analysis of eighteenth century
        Delaware Indian names for medicinal plants.
        Ethnohistory 2.1:11-28. Poughkeepsie.

1960   Anatomical terminology of the eighteenth
        century Delaware Indians: a study in
        semantics. Anthropological Linguistics
        2.5:1-65. Bloomington, Ind.

Major, Robert C.
1938   Aboriginal American medicine north of Mexico.
        Annals of Medical History 10.6:534-549. New
        York.

Mak, Cornelia
1959   Mixtec medical beliefs and practices.
        América Indígena 19.2:125-161. Mexico City.

Marsh, Gordon H. and William S. Laughlin
1956   Human anatomical knowledge among the Aleutian
        Islanders. Southwestern Journal of Anthropol-
        ogy 12.1:38-78. Albuquerque.

Martin, Richard T.
1970   The role of coca in the history, religion,
        and medicine of South American Indians.
        Economic Botany 24.4:422-438. Lawrence, Kans.

Martín del Campo, Rafael
1956   La anatomía entre los mexicanos. Revista
        de la Sociedad Mexicana de Historia Natural
        17:145-167. Mexico City.

Martinez, Maximino
1969   Plantas medicinales de Mexico. Mexico City:
        La Impresora Azteca.

Martinez Cortés, Fernando
1965   Las ideas en la medicina náhuatl. 110 pp.
        Mexico City: La Prensa Médica Mexicana.

Metzger, Duane and Gerald Williams
    1963   Tenejapa medicine: the curer. Southwestern
            Journal of Anthropology 19.2:216-234.
            Albuquerque.

Monachino, Joseph
    1956   Chinese herbal medicine--recent studies.
            Economic Botany 10.1:42-48. Lancaster, Pa.

Moody, D. P.
    1965   Chemotherapeutic consequence of culture
            collisions. Proceedings of the Royal Anthro-
            pological Institute, 1965, pp. 33-45. London.

Mooney, James
    1890   Cherokee theory and practice of medicine.
            Journal of American Folklore 3.8:44-50.
            Boston and New York.

    1891   The sacred formulas of the Cherokee. Pp. 301-
            397 in 7th Annual Report of the Bureau of
            American Ethnology. Washington.

Mooney, James and Frans M. Olbrechts
    1932   The Swimmer manuscript: Cherokee sacred
            formulas and medicinal prescriptions.
            (Bulletin of the Bureau of American Ethnology,
            No. 99.) xv, 319 pp. Washington.

Morton, Julia F.
    1968   A survey of medicinal plants in Curaçao.
            Economic Botany 22.1:87-102. Baltimore.

Moss, Leonard W. and Stephen C. Cappannari
    1960   Folklore and medicine in an Italian village.
            Journal of American Folklore 73.288:95-102.
            Montpelier.

Murand, M. M. du
    1948   Médications campagnardes. Mémoires de la
            Société des Sciences Naturelles et Arché-
            ologiques de la Creuse 30:353-357. Creuse,
            France.

Nadkarni, Krishnarao Mangeshrao
    1955   The Indian materia medica. 3d edition.
    (1927) 1142 pp. Bombay: Popular Book Depot.
            (1st edition 1927, Bombay: K. M. Nadkarni.)

Nelson, Alexander
    1951   Medical botany. xii, 544 pp. Edinburgh:
            E. and S. Livingston.

[6:20]

Nguyen-tran-Huan
    1957   Esquisse d'une histoire de la biologie
            chinoise des origines jusqu'au IVe siècle.
            Revue de l'Histoire des Sciences et de
            leurs Applications 10:1-37. Paris.

Nickell, Louis G.
    1956   The root that relieves blood pressure.
            Natural History 65.1:16-19. New York.

Nurge, Ethel
    1958   Etiology of illness in Guinhangdan. American
            Anthropologist 60.6:1158-1172. Menasha.

Oblitas Poblete, Enrique
    1969   Plantas medicinales de Bolivia. Cochabamba:
            Amigos de Libro.

Olbrechts, Frans
    1929   Some notes on Cherokee treatment of disease.
            Janus 33:18-22. Leiden.

Opler, Morris E.
    1936   Some points of comparison and contrast
            between the treatment of functional disorders
            of Apache shamans and modern psychiatric
            practice. American Journal of Psychiatry
            92.6:1371-1387. Baltimore.

    1963   The cultural definition of illness in village
            India. Human Organization 22.1:32-35. New
            York.

Palunin, Evon
    1953   The medical natural history of Malaya.
            Medical Journal of Malaya 8.1-2. Singapore.

Panoff, Françoise
    1970   Maenge remedies and conception of disease.
            Ethnology 9.1:68-84. Pittsburgh.

Parenti, F. and F. Fiorenzola
    1965   Ipnosi e suggestione nella medicina primitiva
            e popolare. Revista de Etnografia 19:97-104.
            Naples.

Paul, Benjamin D., editor
    1955   Health, culture and community: case studies
            of public reactions to health programs.
            viii, 493 pp. New York: Russell Sage Foun-
            dation.

382

Penfound, William T.
1953   The relation of plants to public health.
          Economic Botany 7.2:182-194. Lancaster, Pa.

Perrot, Émile
1943-   Matières premières usuelles du règne végétal.
1944   Thérapeutique-hygiène-industrie. 2 vols.
          Paris: Masson.

Perrot, Émile and H. Froin
1906   Matières premières usuelles d'origine végétale
          indigènes et exotiques. 44 pp. Paris:
          Vigot Frères.

Perry, Lily M.
1961   Problems in the compilation of a native
          medicinal flora of southeastern Asia.
          Economic Botany 5.3:241-244. Baltimore.

Pharmacopeia of the United States
1951   Epitome of the pharmacopeia of the United
          States and the national formulary, with
          comments. 9th edition. 255 pp. Philadel-
          phia: Lippincott.

Philips, Jane
1958   Lebanese folk cures. 2 vols. Ph.D. disser-
          tation in Columbia University, New York.

Polgar, Steven
1962   Health and human behavior: areas of inter-
          est common to the social and medical sciences.
          Current Anthropology 3.2:159-205. Chicago.

Price-Williams
1962   A case study of ideas concerning disease
          among the Tiv. Africa 32:123-131. London.

Quisumbing, Eduardo
1951   Medicinal plants of the Philippines. (Depart-
          ment of Agriculture and Natural Resources,
          Technical Bulletin 16.) 1234 pp. Manila.

1954   Botanical research of Philippine medicinal
          plants. Proceedings of the Eighth Pacific
          Science Congress of the Pacific Science
          Association 4:107-112. Quezon City.

Ramírez Aguirre, Adrián
1959   Medicina precortesiana en México. Revista
          de la Sociedad Médica 1.1:47-55. Mexico
          City.

Redfield, Robert
1928   Remedial plants of Tepotzlan: a Mexican
        folk herbal. Journal of the Washington
        Academy of Sciences 18.8:216-226. Baltimore.

Resner, Gerald and Joseph Hartog
1970   Concepts and terminology of mental disorder
        among Malays. Journal of Cross-Cultural
        Psychology 1.4:369-381. Bellingham, Wash.

Ritzenthaler, Robert E.
1953   Chippewa preoccupation with health: change
        in a traditional attitude resulting from
        modern health problems. Bulletins of the
        Public Museum of the City of Milwaukee
        19.4:175-258. Milwaukee.

Rivers, W. H. R.
1924   Medicine, magic and religion. viii, 146 pp.
        New York: Harcourt, Brace.

Robb-Smith, A. H. T.
1970   The international classification of diseases.
        Classification Society Bulletin 2.2:3-22.
        Leicester, England.

Rogers, Spencer L.
1942   Primitive theories of disease. Ciba Symposia
        4.1:1190-1201. Summit, N. J.

1944   Disease concepts in North America. American
        Anthropologist 46.4:559-564. Menasha.

Rogers, Spencer L. and A. J. O. Anderson
1966   La Terminología anatómica de los mexicas
        precolombinos. Proceedings of the 36th
        International Congress of Americanists 2:
        69-76. Seville.

Roia, Frank C., Jr.
1966   The use of plants in hair and scalp prepara-
        tions. Economic Botany 20.1:17-30. Balti-
        more.

Romano-V., Octavio Ignacio
1965   Charismatic medicine, folk-healing, and folk-
        sainthood. American Anthropologist 67.5(Part
        1):1151-1173. Menasha.

Rubel, Arthur J.
1960   Concepts of disease in Mexican-American
        culture. American Anthropologist 62.5:
        795-814. Menasha.

Santa Maria, Fernando de
  1915   Manual de medicinas caseras para consuelo
          de los pobres. 2d edition. 188 pp. Manila:
          Imprenta y Libreria de J. Martinez.

Schiefenhoevel, W.
  1964-   Die Anwendung von Heilpflanzen und die
  1969   traditionelle Geburtenkontrolle bei Einge-
          borenen Neuguineas. Sitzungsberichte der
          Physikalisch-medizinischen Sozietät zu
          Erlangen 83-84:114-133, 179-182. Munich.

  1969   Medizinmann, Magier und Arzt. Zeitschrift
          für Medizin-Studenten und Assistenten
          1.2:20-24. Erlangen.

  1971   Vorläufiger Symptomenkatalog für die ethno-
          medizinische Feldforschung. Ethnomedizin
          1.1:123-127.

Schneider, Albert
  1906   The medicinal plants of the California
          Indians. Merck's Report 15:63-128. Rahway,
          N. J.

Schofield, F. D. and A. D. Parkinson
  1963   Social medicine in New Guinea: beliefs and
          practices affecting health among the Abelam
          and Wam peoples of the Sepik District, I and
          II. Medical Journal of Australia 1.1:1-8;
          1.2:29-33. Sydney.

Sigerist, Henry Ernest
  1951-   A history of medicine. 2 vols. New York:
  1961   Oxford University Press.

Silver, Daniel B.
  1966   Enfermedad y curación en Zinacantan: esquema
          provisional. Pp. 455-473 in Los zinacantecos,
          edited by E. Z. Vogt. Mexico City: Insti-
          tuto Nacional Indigenista.

Simmons, Leo W.
  1945   A prospectus for field-research in the
          position and treatment of the aged in primi-
          tive and other societies. American Anthro-
          pologist 47.3:433-438. Menasha.

Simmons, Ozzie G.
  1955   Popular and modern medicine in Mestizo
          communities of coastal Peru and Chile.
          Journal of American Folklore 68.267:57-71.
          Philadelphia.

Skingle, D. C.
1970   Some medicinal herbs used by the natives of
        New Guinea. Mankind 7.3:223-225. Sydney.

1950   Disease concepts and plant medicines in
        native South America. Ph.D. dissertation
        in anthropology, University of California,
        Berkeley.

Smith, Harlan I.
1929   Materia medica of the Bella Coola and neigh-
        boring tribes of British Columbia. Pp. 47-
        68 in National Museum of Canada, Annual
        Report for 1927. Ottawa.

Sodi Morales, Demetrio
1960   Las investigaciones con plantas alucinantes
        mexicanas. Boletín del Centro de Investi-
        gaciones Antropológicas de México 7:14-18.
        Mexico City.

Sorgdrager, P.
1947   Enkele Indische geneeskruiden. Utrecht.

Soulié de Morant, Georges
1939-   L'Acupuncture chinoise. 2 vols. Vol. 1,
1941   L'Énergie (points, méridiens, circulation),
        300 pp.; Vol. 2, Le Maniement de l'énergie,
        274 pp. Paris: Mercure de France.

Speck, Frank G.
1917   Medicine practices of the northeastern
        Algonquians. Pp. 303-321 in Proceedings of
        the 19th International Congress of American-
        ists, edited by F. W. Hodge. Washington.

1937   Catawba medicines and curative practices.
        Pp. 179-197 in Twenty-fifth anniversary
        studies, (Publications of the Philadelphia
        Anthropological Society, No. 1), edited by
        D. S. Davidson. Philadelphia.

Speck, Frank G. et al.
1942   Rappahanock herbals, folklore, and science
        of cures. (Proceedings of the Delaware
        County Institute of Science 10.1.) Media,
        Pa.

Spence, Donald P.
1968   The processing of meaning in psychotherapy:
        some links with psycholinguistics and infor-
        mation theory. Behavioral Science 13.5:
        349-361. Ann Arbor.

Spencer, Dorothy Mary
    1941   Disease, religion and society in the Fiji
            Islands. (Monograph of the American Ethno-
            logical Society, No. 2.) ix, 82 pp. New
            York: J. J. Augustin.

Spicer, C. C.
    1970   The objectives of medical taxonomy. Classi-
            fication Society Bulletin 2.2:29-32.
            Leicester, England.

Stark, Louis R.
    1969   The lexical structure of Quechua body parts.
            Anthropological Linguistics 11.1:1-15.
            Bloomington, Ind.

Steenis-Kruseman, M. J. van
    1953   Select Indonesian medicinal plants. (Organ-
            isation for Scientific Research in Indonesia,
            Bulletin 18.) 90 pp. Djakarta.

Sterly, Joachim
    1970   Heilpflanzen der Einwohner Melanesiens;
            Beiträge zur Ethnobotanik des südwestlichen
            Pazifik. 341 pp. Hamburg: Arbeitsgemein-
            schaft Ethnomedizin.

Stewart, Kilton Riggs
    1948   Magico-religious beliefs and practices in
            primitive society--a sociological interpre-
            tation of their therapeutic aspects. Ph.D.
            dissertation in the University of London.
            London.

Stone, Eric
    1932   Medicine among the American Indians. 139 pp.
            New York: Hafner.

    1934   Medicine among the Iroquois. Annals of
            Medical History 6.6:529-539. New York.

Stopp, Klaus
    1963   Medicinal plants of the Mt. Hagen people
            (Mbowamb) in New Guinea. Economic Botany
            17.1:16-22. Baltimore.

Stuhr, Ernst T.
    1933   Manual of Pacific Coast drug plants. 189 pp.
            Lancaster: Science Press.

Sturtevant, William C.
    1954a   The medicine bundles and busks of the Florida

Seminole. Florida Anthropologist 7.2:31-70. Gainesville.

Sturtevant, William C. (cont.)
1954b   The Mikasuki Seminole: medical beliefs and practices. 538 pp. Ph.D. dissertation in Anthropology, Yale University, New Haven. (Published by University Microfilms, Ann Arbor, Mich., 1967.)

1960   A Seminole medicine maker. Pp. 505-532 in In the company of man, edited by J. B. Casagrande. New York: Harper and Row.

1962   Bibliography on American Indian medicine and health. (Smithsonian Information Leaflet 99.) 39 pp. Washington.

Sulit, Mamerto
1950   Possibilities of some Philippine plants for medicinal uses. Journal of the Philippine Pharmaceutical Association 37.11-12:434-448. Manila.

Swanton, John R.
1928   Religious beliefs and medical practices of the Creek Indians. Annual Report of the Bureau of American Ethnology 42:473-672. Washington.

Tantaquidgeon, Gladys
1942   A study of Delaware Indian medicine practice and folk beliefs. xi, 91 pp. Harrisburg: Pennsylvania Historical Commission.

Taylor, Lyda Averill
1940   Plants used as curatives by certain southeastern tribes. 88 pp. Cambridge: Harvard University Botanical Museum.

Thomas, Caroline Bendell
1966   An atlas of figure drawings: studies on the psychological characteristics of medical students--III. 922 pp. Baltimore: Johns Hopkins Press.

Tiglao, Teodora V.
1964   Health practices in a rural community. 232 pp. Quezon City: Community Development Research Council, University of the Philippines.

Train, Percy, James R. Henrichs, and W. Andrew Archer
1957   Medicinal uses of plants by Indian tribes of
(1941) Nevada. Revised edition, with summary of
        pharmacological research by W. A. Archer.
        (Contributions toward a flora of Nevada, No.
        45.) 139 pp. Beltsville, Md.: Crops
        Research Service, U.S. Department of Agri-
        culture Plant Industry Station. (Original
        edition 1941, Contributions toward a flora
        of Nevada, No. 33, 199 pp., Washington.)

Underhill, Ruth
1955   A classification of religious practices among
        North American Indians. Actes du IVe Congres
        International des Sciences Anthropologiques
        et Ethnologiques, 1952, 2:320-324. Vienna.

Valcárcel, Luis E.
1958   Símbolos mágico-religiosos en la cultura
        andina. Miscellanea Paul Rivet Octogenario
        Dicata 2:563-581. Mexico City: Universidad
        Nacional Autónoma de México.

Vallee, Frank G.
1966   Eskimo theories of mental illness in the
        Hudson Bay region. Anthropologica (n.s.)
        8.1:53-83. Ottawa.

Vargas Castelazo, Manuel
1955   La patología y la medicina entre los mexicas.
        Revista Mexicana de Estudios Antropológicos
        14:119-143. Mexico City.

Veith, Ilza
1945   Health and disease among the Mangyans.
        Bulletin of the History of Medicine 17.4:
        377-384. Baltimore.

1955   Psychiatric thought in Chinese medicine.
        Journal of the History of Medicine and Allied
        Sciences 10.3:261-268. New Haven.

1966   Huang Ti Nei Ching Su Wen (The Yellow Emperor's
        classic of internal medicine). 2d edition.
        [Chapters 1-38, translated from Chinese with
        an introductory study by Ilza Veith.] xxi,
        260 pp. Berkeley: University of California
        Press. (Earlier edition 1949, Baltimore:
        Williams and Wilkens.)

Vogel, Virgil J.
1970   American Indian medicine (The Civilization

of the American Indian Series, 95.) xx,
593 pp. Norman: University of Oklahoma
Press.

Wada, K.
1965   Names of diseases in the Ainu language--
manuscripts left by the late Mr. Wada
Bunjiro (2). Japanese Journal of Ethnology
30.1:47-67. Tokyo.

Wallace, Anthony F. C.
1959   The institutionalization of cathartic and
control strategies in Iroquois religious
psychotherapy. Pp. 63-96 in Culture and
mental health: cross-cultural studies,
edited by M. K. Opler. New York: Macmillan.

Wallis, Ruth Sawtell and Wilson D. Wallis
1953   The sins of the fathers: concept of disease
among the Canadian Dakota. Southwestern
Journal of Anthropology 9.4:431-435.
Albuquerque.

Wallis, Wilson D.
1922   Medicines used by the Micmac Indians.
American Anthropologist 24:24-30. Menasha.

Wassén, S. Henry
1964   Some general viewpoints in the study of
native drugs especially from the West Indies
and South America. Ethnos 29.1-2:97-120.
Stockholm.

Watson, James B. and Harold E. Nelson
1967   Body-environment transactions: a standard
model for cross-cultural analysis. Southwestern Journal of Anthropology 23.3:292-
309. Albuquerque.

Watt, John Mitchell and Marie G. Brandwijk
1927- Suto (Basuto) medicines. Bantu Studies
1929   3.1:73-100; 3.2:155-178; 3.3:297-319.
Johannesburg.

Watt, John Mitchell and Maria Gerdina Breyer-Brandwijk
1962   The medicinal and poisonous plants of southern and eastern Africa. 2d edition. xii,
1457 pp. Edinburgh: E. and S. Livingstone.

Webb, L. J.
1969   The use of plant medicines and poisons by
Australian aborigines. Mankind 7.2:137-146.
Sydney.

Wedgwood, Camilla H.
1934,   Sickness and its treatment in Manam Island,
1935   New Guinea. Oceania 5.1:64-79; 5.3:280-
        307. Sydney.

Weigl, Egon
1970   Neuropsychological studies of structure and
        dynamics of semantic fields with the deblock-
        ing method. Pp. 287-290 in Sign·language·
        culture, (Janua Linguarum, Series Maior 1),
        edited by A. J. Greimas et al. The Hague
        and Paris: Mouton.

Werner, Oswald
1965   Semantics of Navaho medical terms: I.
        International Journal of American Linguis-
        tics 31.1:1-17. Baltimore.

Werner, Oswald and Kenneth Y. Begishe
1966   The anatomical atlas of the Navaho. 3d
        revised preliminary version. 179 pp.
        Evanston, Ill.

1970   A lexemic typology of Navajo anatomical
        terms, I: the foot. International Journal
        of American Linguistics 36.4:247-265.
        Baltimore.

Wildschut, William
1960   Crow Indian medicine bundles, edited by
        John C. Ewers. (Contributions from the
        Museum of the American Indian, Vol. 17.)
        ix, 178 pp. New York: Heye Foundation.

Witthoft, John
1964   The Cherokee green corn medicine and the
        green corn festival. Journal of the Washing-
        ton Academy of Sciences 36.7:213-219.
        Menasha.

Wood, Philip H. N.
1970   Peculiarities of medical characters for
        taxonomic purposes. Classification Society
        Bulletin 2.2:23-28. Leicester, England.

World Health Organization, Expert Committee on the
        International Pharmacopoea
1951-   Pharmacopoea Internationalis. (Bulletin of
1959   the World Health Organization, Supplement
        2.) 2 vols., plus Supplement. Geneva.

Wyman, Leland C. and Flora K. Bailey
1944   Two examples of Navajo physiotherapy.

[6:30]

        American Anthropologist 46.3:329-337.
        Menasha.

Wyman, Leland C. and Stuart K. Harris
    1941   Navajo Indian medical ethnobotany. (University of New Mexico Bulletin 366; Anthropological Series 3.5.) 76 pp. Albuquerque.

Youngken, H. W.
    1924,   Drugs of North American Indians. American
    1925   Journal of Pharmacy 96:485-502; 97:158-185; 98:257-271. Philadelphia.

Zubin, Joseph
    1967   Classification of the behavioral disorders. Annual Review of Psychology 18:373-406. Palo Alto.

7. Orientation

[Including references to folk systems of time
reckoning, spatial location and measurement,
navigation, astronomy, meteorology, nonbiotic
environmental factors, and similar ecological
phenomena; cf. O.]

Adam, Paul
  1957   Archéologie navale et récents voyages au
           long cours en radeaux primitifs. La Revue
           Maritime 132 (3d series):413-434. Paris.

Adams, Robert P.
  1970   Contour mapping and differential systematics
           of geographical variation. Systematic
           Zoology 19.4:385-390. Lawrence, Kans.

Adler, Bruno
  1911   Maps of primitive peoples. Translation
           from Russian, and résume, by H. de Hutoro-
           wicz. Bulletin of the American Geographi-
           cal Society 43.9:669-679. New York. (First
           published 1910, Bulletin of the Imperial
           Society of Students of Natural History,
           Anthropology and Ethnography 119. viii,
           350 pp. St. Petersburg.)

Alford, Violet
  1934   Cantabrian calendar customs and music.
           Musical Quarterly 20.10:435-451. New York.

  1937   Pyrenean festivals: calendar customs, music
           and magic, drama and dance. 286 pp. Lon-
           don: Chatto and Windus.

Alkire, William H.
  1970   Systems of measurement on Woleai Atoll,
           Caroline Islands. Anthropos 65.1-2:1-73.
           Fribourg.

Altmann, G., Z. Dömötör, and A. Riška
  1967   The partition of space in Nimboran.
           Beiträge zur Linguistik und Informationsver-
           arbeitung 12:56-71. Munich.

Alwis, C.
  1856   On the principles of Sinhalese chronology.
           Journal of the Royal Asiatic Society, Ceylon
           Branch 3:163-176. Colombo.

American Commission on Stratigraphic Nomenclature
    1961   Code of stratigraphic nomenclature. Bulletin
            of the American Association of Petroleum
            Geologists 45.5:645-665. Tulsa.

American Geological Institute
    1960   Glossary of geology and related sciences.
    (1957) 2d edition with supplement. xii, 325, 72 pp.
            Washington: American Geological Institute.

Amiran, D. H. K. and A. P. Schick, compilers and editors
    1961   Geographical conversion tables (all sections
            in English, French, German, Russian, and
            Spanish). XXVI, 315 pp. Zürich: Inter-
            national Geographical Union.

Anderson, Johannes
    1942   Maori place-names; also personal names and
            names of colours, weapons, and natural
            objects. (Polynesian Society, Memoir 20.)
            494 pp. Wellington.

Andree, Richard
    1893   Die Pleiaden im Mythus und in ihrer
            Beziehung zum Jahresbeginn und Landbau.
            Globus 64.22:362-366. Braunschweig.

Angyal, Andreas
    1930   Ueber die Raumlage vorgestellter Oerter.
            Archiv für die Gesamte Psychologie 78.1-2:
            47-94. Leipzig.

Anonymous
    1928   The Samoan division of time. Journal of
            the Polynesian Society 37:228-240. Well-
            ington.

    1933   The countryman's calendar. (Letters to the
            editor, August 14-23.) The Times 46.522:11;
            46.524:11; 46.525:11; 46.526:11; 46.527:9;
            46.528:11; 46.530:11. London.

    n.d.   The story of our calendar. (Achievements
            of Civilization, No. 4.) Washington:
            American Council on Education.

    n.d.   Telling time throughout the centuries.
            (Achievements of Civilization, No. 5.)
            Washington: American Council on Education.

Apenes, Ola
    1936   Possible derivation of the 260 day period

of the Maya calendar. Ethnos 1.1:5-8.
Stockholm.

1937a   Abbreviated method for calculating Maya
calendar round dates. Ethnos 2.1:16-20.
Stockholm.

1937b   Table for determination of Maya calendar
round positions. Ethnos 2.4:97-101. Stockholm.

Appleyard, Donald, Kevin Lynch, and John R. Myer
1964   The view from the road. 64 pp. Cambridge:
MIT Press.

Ardener, Edwin
1957   Numbers in Africa. Man 57:176(Art. 226).
London.

Arnold, Dean E.
1971   Ethnomineralogy of Ticul, Yucatan potters:
etics and emics. American Antiquity 36.1:
20-40. Washington.

Astin, Allen V.
1968   Standards of measurement. Scientific
American 218.6:50-62. New York.

Aufenanger, Heinrich
1938   Etwas über Zahl and Zählen bei den Gende
im Bismarckgebirge Neuguineas. Anthropos
33.1-2:273-277. Vienna.

1960   The Ayom pygmies' myth of origin and their
method of counting. Anthropos 55.1-2:247-
249. Fribourg.

Austen, Leo
1939   The seasonal gardening calendar of Kiriwina,
Trobriand Islands. Oceania 9.3:237-253.
Sydney.

Bach, Adolf
1953   Deutsche Namenkunde. 3 vols. xx, 2149 pp.
Heidelberg: Winter.

Bal, Willy
1952   Le Temps et ses divisions. Les Dialectes
Belgo-Romans 9.1:5-31. Brussels.

Balint, Andras
1968   Cultural conflicts in the time concepts of

[7:4]

New Guinea speakers: a linguistic view.
Kivung 1.1:29-37. Boroko, T.P.N.G.

Ballard, Arthur C.
1950   Calendric terms of the southern Puget Salish.
        Southwestern Journal of Anthropology 6:79-99.
        Albuquerque.

Barrett, Samuel Alfred
1908   The ethno-geography of the Pomo and neighbor-
        ing Indians. (University of California
        Publications in American Archaeology and
        Ethnology 6.) 245 pp. Berkeley.

Barthel, Thomas S.
1962   Zur Sternkunde der Osterinsulaner. Zeit-
        schrift für Ethnologie 87.1:1-3. Braunschweig

Beda Venerabilis (673-735)
1505   De ratione temporum. Edited by Petrus
        Marenus Aleander. [100] pp. Rome.

Beeler, Madison S.
1957   On etymologizing Indian place-names. Names
        5.4:236-240. Berkeley.

Beidelman, T. O.
1963   Kaguru time reckoning: an aspect of the
        cosmology of an East African people.
        Southwestern Journal of Anthropology 19.1:
        9-20. Albuquerque.

Bekombo, Manga
1966-   Note sur le temps. Conceptions et attitudes
1967   chez les Dwala. L'Ethnographie 60-61:60-64.
        Paris.

Bennett, David C.
1968   English prepositions: a stratificational
        approach. Journal of Linguistics 4.1:153-
        172. London.

Benton, Richard A.
1968   Numeral and attributive classifiers in
        Trukese. Oceanic Linguistics 7.2:104-146.
        Honolulu.

Berg, Gösta
1966   Die Merkbücher auf Gotland. Folk-Liv
        30:48-62. Stockholm.

Berkhofer, Robert F., Jr.
1969   Conceptions of time: their variety and uses.

Pp. 211-242 in A behavioral approach to
historical analysis, by R. F. Berkhofer, Jr.
New York: Free Press.

Berlin, Brent
1968   Tzeltal numeral classifiers: a study in
          ethnographic semantics. 243 pp. The Hague:
          Mouton.

Berlin, Heinrich and David H. Kelley
1961   The 819-day count and color-direction
          symbolism among the Classic Maya. Pp. 9-20
          in Tulane University Middle American Research
          Institute, No. 26. New Orleans.

Berry, Brian Joe Lobley
1958   A note concerning methods of classification.
          Annals of the Association of American Geogra-
          phers 48.3:300-303. Albany.

Best, Elsdon
1910,   Maori star names. Journal of the Polynesian
1911   Society 19.74:97-99; 20.1:10-11. New
          Plymouth.

1918   The Maori system of measurement. New
          Zealand Journal of Science and Technology
          1:26-32. Wellington.

1922a   The astronomical knowledge of the Maori.
          (Dominion Museum Monograph No. 3.) Welling-
          ton. (New edition 1955, 80 pp. Wellington:
          R. E. Owen.)

1922b   The Maori division of time. (Dominion
          Museum Monograph No. 4.) 45 pp. Wellington.
          (New edition 1959.)

1923   Polynesian voyagers: the Maori as a deep-
          sea navigator, explorer and colonizer.
          (Dominion Museum Monograph No. 5.) 54 pp.
          Wellington. (New edition 1954, 67 pp.,
          Wellington: R. E. Owen.)

1924   The Maori. 2 vols. xv, 528; ix, 637 pp.
          Wellington: H. H. Tombs.

Beyer, Hermann
1931   Mayan hieroglyphs: the variable element of
          the introducing glyphs as month indicator.
          Anthropos 26.1-2:99-108. Vienna.

[7:6]

Binet, M. Alfred
1894   Reverse illusions of orientation.   Psychologi-
        cal Review 1.4:337-350.   New York.

Blaut, James M.
1970   Geographic models of imperialism.   Antipode:
        A Radical Journal of Geography 2.1:65-85.
        Worcester, Mass.

Blaut, James M., George F. McCleary, Jr., and America
        S. Blaut
1970   Environmental mapping in young children.
        Environment and Behavior 2.3:335-350.
        Beverly Hills, Calif.

Blok, H. P.
1956   Localism and deixis in Bantu linguistics.
        Lingua 5.4:382-419.   Amsterdam.

Board, Christopher, Richard J. Chorley, Peter Haggett,
        and David R. Stoddart, editors
1969   Progress in geography: international reviews
        of current research, Vol. 1.   222 pp.   London:
        Edward Arnold.

Boas, Franz
1934   Geographical names of the Kwakiutl Indians.
        (Columbia University Contribution to Anthro-
        pology, No. 20.)   83 pp.   New York.

Bock, Philip K.
1966   Social time and institutional conflict.
        Human Organization 25.2:96-102.   Lexington,
        Ky.

Bogoras, Waldemar
1904-   The Chukchee.   (Memoirs of the American
1909   Museum of Natural History 11 [Parts 1, 2,
        and 3]; The Jesup North Pacific Expedition,
        Publication No. 7.)   xvii, 733 pp.   Leiden:
        Brill; New York: Stechert.

1925   Ideas of space and time in the conceptions
        of primitive religion.   American Anthropolo-
        gist 27.2:205-266.   Menasha.

Bohannan, Paul
1953   Concepts of time among the Tiv of Nigeria.
        Southwestern Journal of Anthropology 9.3:
        251-262.   Albuquerque.

Borchardt, Ludwig
1920   Altägyptische Zeitmessung.   Berlin.

Bourdieu, Pierre
    1963   The attitude of the Algerian peasant towards
            time. Pp. 55-72 in Mediterranean countrymen:
            essays in the social anthropology of the
            Mediterranean, edited by J. A. Pitt-Rivers.
            Paris: Mouton.

Bowditch, Charles P.
    1910   The numeration, calendar systems, and
            astronomical knowledge of the Mayas. xvi,
            346 pp. Cambridge: Cambridge University
            Press.

Bowditch, Charles P., editor
    1904   Mexican and Central American antiquities,
            calendar systems, and history: twenty-four
            papers by Eduard Seler, E. Förstemann, Paul
            Schellhas, Carl Sapper, and E. P. Diesel-
            dorff. (Bulletins of the Bureau of American
            Ethnology, No. 28.) 682 pp. Washington.

Boxwell, Maurice
    1967   Weri pronoun system. Linguistics 29:34-43.
            The Hague.

Brainerd, B.
    1966   Grammars for number names. Foundations of
            Language 2.2:109-133. Dordrecht.

Bramsen, William
    1910   Japanese chronology and calendars. Trans-
            actions of the Asiatic Society of Japan
            37(Supplement):1-47. Yokohama.

Brandt, John H.
    1963   By dunung and bouj: water movements, stick
            charts, and magic help natives stay on
            course. Natural History 72.2:26-29. New
            York.

Brearley, Harry Chase
    1919   Time telling through the ages. 294 pp.
            New York: Doubleday, Page.

Breasted, James Henry
    1935   The beginnings of time measurement and the
            origins of our calendar. Scientific
            Monthly 41.10:289-304. New York.

Bright, William
    1958   Karok names. Names 6.3:173-179. Berkeley.

Brincken, Anna-Dorothee van den
    1957   Weltären. Archiv für Kulturgeschichte
            39.2:133-149. Cologne.

Brinton, Daniel G.
    1876   The myths of the New World. 2d revised
            edition. 331 pp. New York: Henry Holt.

Brookfield, Harold C.
    1969   On the environment as perceived. Pp. 51-80
            in Vol. 1 of Progress in geography: inter-
            national reviews of current research, edited
            by Christopher Board et al. London: Edward
            Arnold.

Brown, Roger W. and Albert Gilman
    1960   The pronouns of power and solidarity. Pp.
            253-276 in Aspects of style in language,
            edited by T. A. Sebeok. Cambridge: MIT
            Press; New York: John Wiley.

Brown, Warner
    1932   Spatial integrations in a human maze.
            University of California Publications in
            Psychology 5.5:123-134. Berkeley.

Brunswik, Egon
    1956   Perception and the representative design of
            psychological experiments. xii, 154 pp.
            Berkeley and Los Angeles: University of
            California Press.

Buchler, Ira R. and R. Freeze
    1966   The distinctive features of pronominal
            systems. Anthropological Linguistics 8.8:
            78-105. Bloomington, Ind.

Buchler, Ira R. and Henry A. Selby
    1970   Animal, vegetable, or mineral? Pp. 213-234
            in Échanges et communications, edited by
            J. Pouillon and P. Maranda. The Hague and
            Paris: Mouton.

Buck, Fritz
    1937   El calendario Maya en la cultura de
            Tiahuanacu. xi, 210 pp. La Paz, Bolivia:
            Unidas.

Bull, William E.
    1960   Time, tense, and the verb: a study in
            theoretical and applied linguistics, with
            particular attention to Spanish. (Univer-

sity of California Publications in Linguistics, Vol. 19.) xiii, 120 pp. Berkeley and Los Angeles: University of California Press.

Bunge, William Wheeler
1962   Theoretical geography. (Lund Studies in Geography, Series C, General and Mathematical, No. 1.) xii, 210 pp. Lund: Royal University of Lund, Department of Geography.

Burkitt, Robert
1930,   The calendar of Solóma and of other Indian
1931   towns. Parts I, II. Man 30.6:103-107(Art. 80). Part III. Man 31.8:146-150(Art. 160). London.

Burling, Robbins
1965   How to choose a Burmese numeral classifier. Pp. 243-264 in Context and meaning in cultural anthropology, edited by M. E. Spiro. New York: Free Press; London: Collier-Macmillan.

Burrill, Meredith F.
1956   Toponymic generics, I and II. Names 4.3: 129-137; 4.4:226-240. Potsdam, N. Y.

1968   The language of geography. Annals of the Association of American Geographers 58.1: 1-11. Lawrence, Kans.

Callomon, J. H. and D. T. Donovan
1966   Stratigraphic classification and terminology. Geological Magazine 103.1:97-99. Hertford, England.

Calvet, Louis-Jean
1970   Arbitraire du signe et langues en contact: les systèmes de numération en bambara, dioula et malinké. La Linguistique 6.2: 119-123. Paris.

Carpenter, Edmund
1955   Space concepts of the Aivilik Eskimos. Explorations 5:130-145. Toronto.

1959   Eskimo. (Explorations 9.) [67] pp. Toronto: University of Toronto Press.

Casamajor, Jean
1927   Le Mystérieux sens de l'espace. Revue Scientifique 65.18:554-565. Paris.

Caso, Alfonso
   1953   Calendarios de los totonacos y huastecos.
           Revista Mexicana de Estudios Anthropológicos
           13.2-3:337-350. Mexico City.

   1956   El Calendario mixteco. Historia Mexicana
           5.20:481-497. Mexico City.

   1958   El calendario mexicano. Memorias de la
           Academia Mexicana de la Historia 17.1:41-96.
           Mexico City.

   1965a   Zapotec writing and calendar. Pp. 931-947
           in Vol. 3, Part 2 of Handbook of Middle
           American Indians, edited by G. R. Willey.
           Austin: University of Texas Press.

   1965b   Mixtec writing and calendar. Pp. 948-961
           in Vol. 3, Part 2 of Handbook of Middle
           American Indians, edited by G. R. Willey.
           Austin: University of Texas Press.

Cassidy, Frederic G.
   1947   The place-names of Dane County, Wisconsin.
           (American Dialect Society, Publication No.
           7.) Greensboro, N. C.

Chattopadhyay, P. K.
   1968   Mode de croisement des mains et des bras,
           droiterie, gaucherie et camptodactylie
           chez les Bengalis. L'Anthropologie 72.3-4:
           317-324. Paris.

Chavero, Alfredo
   1905   Palemke calendar. Pp. 41-65 in Proceedings
           of the International Congress of American-
           ists, 13th session, edited by M. H. Saville,
           F. W. Putnam and Franz Boas. Easton, Pa.:
           Eschenbach.

Chilkovsky, Nadia
   1961   Techniques for the choreologist. Ethno-
           musicology 5.2:121-217. Middletown, Conn.

Chisholm, Michael
   1964   Problems in the classification and use of
           the farming type region. Transactions of
           the Institute of British Geographers
           35:91-103. London.

Clapariede, Edouard
   1943   L'Orientation lointaine. Nouveau Traité
           de Psychologie 8.3. Paris.

Clement, Ernest W.
1902   Japanese calendars. Transactions of the
        Asiatic Society of Japan 30:1-88. Tokyo.

Coe, Michael D.
1965   A model of ancient community structure in
        the Maya lowlands. Southwestern Journal
        of Anthropology 21.2:97-129. Albuquerque.

Cohen, John
1964   Psychological time. Scientific American
        211.5:116-122. New York.

Cole, Michael, John Gay, Joseph A. Glick, Donald W.
        Sharp, et al.
1971   The cultural context of learning and think-
        ing, an exploration in experimental anthro-
        pology. 304 pp. New York: Basic Books.

Collis, D. R. F.
1969-   On the establishment of visual parameters
1970   for the formalization of Eskimo semantics.
        Folk, Nos. 11-12:309-328. Copenhagen.

Collocott, E. E. V.
1922   Tongan astronomy and calendar. (Occasional
        Papers of the Bernice P. Bishop Museum, 8.4.)
        19 pp. Honolulu.

Colson, E.
1957   Numbers in northern Rhodesia. Man 57.7:
        112(Art.141). London.

Colucci, Cesare
1902   Sui disturbi dell'orientamento topografico.
        Annali di Neurologia 20:555-596. Naples.

Condominas, Georges
1957   Nous avons mangé la forêt de la Pierre-
        Génie Gôo. 495 pp. Paris: Mecure de France.

Conklin, Harold C.
1957   Hanunóo agriculture: a report on an inte-
        gral system of shifting cultivation in the
        Philippines. (FAO Forestry Development
        Paper No. 12.) xii, 209 pp. Rome: Food
        and Agriculture Organization of the United
        Nations.

1960   The cultural significance of land resources
        among the Hanunóo. Bulletin of the Phila-
        delphia Anthropological Society 13.2:38-42.
        Philadelphia.

Conklin, Harold C. (cont.)
  1962   Lexicographical treatment of folk taxonomies.
          Pp. 119-141 in Problems in lexicography:
          report of the Conference on Lexicography
          held at Indiana University, November 11-12,
          1960, (International Journal of American
          Linguistics 28.2[Part 4]; Publication 21,
          Indiana University Research Center in
          Anthropology, Folklore, and Linguistics),
          edited by F. W. Householder and S. Saporta.
          Bloomington. (Volume reprinted with addi-
          tions and corrections 1967.)

  1963   El estudio del cultivo de roza--The study
          of shifting cultivation. (Estudios y
          Monografías, XI--Studies and Monographs,
          VI.) iii, 185[215] pp., bibliog., indices.
          Washington: Pan American Union.

  1967   Some aspects of ethnographic research in
          Ifugao. Transactions of the New York
          Academy of Sciences, Series 2, 30.1:99-121.
          New York.

Cook, Edwin Aubrey
  1967   A preliminary statement of Narak spatial
          deixis. Anthropological Linguistics 9.6:
          1-29. Bloomington, Ind.

Cope, Leona
  1919   Calendars of the Indians north of Mexico.
          University of California Publications in
          American Archaeology and Ethnology 16:
          119-176. Berkeley.

Coppet, Daniel de
  1970   1, 4, 8; 9, 7. La Monnaie: présence des
          morts et mesure du temps. L'Homme 10.1:17-
          39. Paris.

Cornetz, V.
  1913   Le Cas élémentaire du sens de la direction
          chez l'homme. Bulletin de la Société de
          Géographie d'Alger 18:742-756. Algiers.

Court, Christopher
  1967   Pointing and asking: a note on deixis in
          Mentu land Dayak. Bijdragen tot de Taal-,
          Land- en Volkenkunde 123.4:520-521.
          's-Gravenhage.

Cowan, Harrison J.
  1958   Time and its measurement from the Stone

Age to the nuclear age. 159 pp. Cleveland: World.

Cunningham, Clark E.
1964 Order in the Atoni house. Bijdragen tot de Taal-, Land- en Volkenkunde 120.1:34-68. 's-Gravenhage.

Cunnison, Ian George
1951 History of the Luapula; an essay on the historical notions of a central African tribe. (Rhodes-Livingstone Papers, No. 21.) viii, 42 pp. Manchester, England.

1957 History and genealogies in a conquest state. American Anthropologist 59.1:20-31. Menasha.

Dangel, Richard
1928 Die Zeitrechnung der kalifornischen Indianer. Anthropos 23.1-2:110-134. Vienna.

Davenport, William
1960 Marshall Islands navigational charts. Imago Mundi 15:19-26. 's-Gravenhage.

1964a Notes on Santa Cruz voyaging. Journal of the Polynesian Society 73.2:134-142. Wellington.

1964b Marshall Islands cartography. Expedition 6.4:10-13. Philadelphia.

Day, Gordon M.
1964 Review of Indian place names of New England, compiled by John C. Huden. American Anthropologist 65.5:1198-1199. Menasha.

d'Azavedo, Warren L.
1962 Uses of the past in Gola discourse. Journal of African History 3.1:11-34. London.

DeCamp, David
1967 African day-names in Jamaica. Language 43.1:139-149. Baltimore.

Delaby, Laurence
1968 Un calendrier yakoute. Objets et Mondes 8.4:311-320. Paris.

Delafosse, Maurice
1921 L'Année agricole et le calendrier des Soudanais. L'Anthropologie 31:105-113. Paris.

[7:14]

Dening, G. M.
    1962   The geographical knowledge of the Polynesians
        and the nature of inter-island contact.
        Journal of the Polynesian Society 71.4(Supple-
        ment):102-131. Wellington.

Diamond, Stanley
    1960   Anaguta cosmography: the linguistics and
        behavioral implications. Anthropological
        Linguistics 2.2:31-38. Bloomington, Ind.

Dicks, D. R.
    1966   Solstices, equinoxes, and the Presocratics.
        Journal of Hellenistic Studies 86:26-40.
        London.

Dieterlen, Germaine
    1970   La Serrure et sa clef (Dogon, Mali). Pp. 7-
        28 in Échanges et communications, edited by
        J. Pouillon and P. Maranda. The Hague and
        Paris: Mouton.

Dixon, Roland B.
    1899   The color-symbolism of the cardinal points.
        Journal of American Folk-lore 12.44:10-16.
        Boston.

Doke, C. M.
    1956   The points of the compass in Bantu languages.
        The Bible Translator 7:104-113. London.

Donaldson, Bess Allen
    1938   The wild rue: a study of Muhammadan magic
        and folklore in Iran. 216 pp. London:
        Luzac.

Donovan, Desmond Thomas
    1966   Classification. Pp. 141-164 (Chapter 7) in
        Stratigraphy, an introduction to principles,
        by D. T. Donovan. London: Murby.

Douglas, George W.
    1940   The American book of days: a compendium of
        information about holidays, festivals,
        notable anniversaries, and Christian and
        Jewish holy days, with notes on other Ameri-
        can anniversaries worthy of remembrance.
        xxiii, 666 pp. New York: W. Wilson.

Dow, James W.
    1967   Astronomical orientations at Teotihuacán,
        a case study in astro-archaeology. American
        Antiquity 32.2:326-334. Salt Lake City.

Dröber, Wolfgang
    1903   Kartographie bei den Naturvölkern. 80 pp.
            Erlangen: Buchdruckerei von Junge und Sohn.
            (Reprinted 1964, Amsterdam: Meridian.)

Dubs, Homer H.
    1958   The beginnings of Chinese astronomy. Journal
            of the American Oriental Society 78.4:295-
            300. New Haven.

Dunbar, Carl Owen and John Rodgers
    1957   The stratigraphic system. Pp. 289-307
            (Chapter 17) in Principles of stratigraphy,
            by C. O. Dunbar and J. Rodgers. New York:
            John Wiley.

Dundas, Charles
    1926   Chagga time reckoning. Man 26.8:140-143
            (Art. 88). London.

Dundes, Alan
    1969   Thinking ahead: a folkloristic reflection
            of the future orientation in American
            world view. Anthropological Quarterly
            42.2:53-72. Washington.

Dunn, J. S.
    1960   Fante star lore. Nigerian Field 25.2:52-64,
            6 star charts. Bath, England.

Du Toit, Brian M.
    1965   Pictorial depth perception and linguistic
            relativity. Psychologia Africana 11.2:
            51-63. Johannesburg.

Ehrenfels, U. R.
    1959   North-up, south-down. Tamil Culture 8:163-
            171. Madras.

Eisenstadt, S. N.
    1949   The perception of time and space in a situa-
            tion of culture-contact. Journal of the
            Royal Anthropological Institute 79.1-2:63-
            68. London.

Ekvall, Robert B.
    1959   Significance of thirteen as a symbolic
            number in Tibetan and Mongolian cultures.
            Journal of the American Oriental Society
            79.3:188-192. New Haven.

Eliade, Mircea
    1949   Le Mythe de l'éternel retour. 254 pp.

Paris: Gallimard. (Translated 1954 by
Willard R. Trask as The myth of the eternal
return, [Bollingen Series 46], 195 pp.
New York: Pantheon Books.)

Elliott, Henry Wood
1886   Our arctic province. xv, 473 pp. New York:
Scribner.

Erdland, August
1910   Die Sternkunde bei den Seefahren der Marshall
Inseln. Anthropos 5:16-26. Vienna.

1914   Die Marshall-Insulaner: Leben und Sitte,
Sinn und Religion eines Südsee-Volkes.
(Anthropos, Ethnologische Bibliothek 2.1.)
viii, 376 pp. Münster: Aschendorff.

Evans-Pritchard, E. E.
1939   Nuer time reckoning. Africa 12:189-216.
London.

1946   Topographical terms in common use among the
Bedouin of Cyrenaica. Journal of the Royal
Anthropological Institute 76.2:177-188.
London.

Eyde, David B.
1969   On Tikopia social space. Bijdragen tot de
Taal-, Land- en Volkenkunde 125.1:40-70.
's-Gravenhage.

Eyzaguirre S., C. Delfín
1956   Astronomia aymara. Khana 3.19-20:82-98.
La Paz.

Faublée, Marcelle and Jacques Faublée
1950   Pirogues et navigation chez les Vezo du
sud-ouest de Madagascar. L'Anthropologie
54.5-6:432-454. Paris.

Fillenbaum, Samuel and Amnon Rapoport
1971   Structures in the subjective lexicon. 278
pp. New York and London: Academic Press.

Fillmore, Charles J.
1966a   Deictic categories in the semantics of 'come.'
Foundations of Language 2.3:219-227.
Dordrecht.

1966b   A proposal concerning English prepositions.
Georgetown University Monograph Series on

Languages and Linguistics, No. 19:19-33. Washington.

1968   Lexical entries for verbs. Foundations of Language 4.4:373-393. Dordrecht.

Finsch, Otto
1888-   Ethnologische Erfahrungen und Belegstücke
1893   aus der Südsee. Annalen des K. K. Natur-
         historischen Hofmuseum 3:83-160, 293-364;
         6:13-36, 37-130; 8:1-106, 119-275, 295-437.
         Vienna.

Firth, Raymond
1936   We, the Tikopia. xxv, 605 pp. London:
         Allen and Unwin.

1969   Tikopia social space--a commentary. Bij-
         dragen tot de Taal-, Land- en Volkenkunde
         125.1:64-70. 's-Gravenhage.

1970   Postures and gestures of respect. Pp. 188-
         209 in Échanges et communications, edited
         by J. Pouillon and P. Maranda. The Hague
         and Paris: Mouton.

Fischer, John L.
1964   Words for self and others in some Japanese
         families. American Anthropologist 66.6(Part
         2):115-126. Menasha.

Fischer, M. H.
1931   Die Orientierung im Raume bei Wirbeltieren
         und beim Menschen. Pp. 909-1022 in Handbuch
         der Normalen und Pathologischen Physiologie
         (XV.2), edited by A. Bethe et al. Berlin:
         Springer.

Flanagan, Thomas
1957   Amid the wild lights and shadows. Columbia
         University Forum 1.1:7-10. New York.

Fletcher, Alice C.
1902   Star cult among the Pawnee, a preliminary
         report. American Anthropologist 4.4:730-
         736. Menasha.

1903   Pawnee star lore. Journal of American
         Folklore 16.60:10-15. Boston.

Förstemann, E.
1891   Zur Maya-Chronologie. Zeitschrift für
         Ethnologie 23:141-155. Berlin.

[7:18]

Fortes, Meyer and Germaine Dieterlen, editors
1965   African systems of thought. viii, 392 pp.
          London and New York: Oxford University
          Press.

Foster, George
1960   Culture and conquest: America's Spanish
          heritage. (Viking Fund Publications in
          Anthropology, No. 27.) ix, 272 pp. New
          York: Wenner-Gren Foundation for Anthro-
          pological Research.

Foster, George M. and Gabriel Ospina
1948   Empire's children: the people of Tzin-
          tzuntzan. (Smithsonian Institution, Insti-
          tute of Social Anthropology, No. 6.) v, 297
          pp. Mexico City: Impr. Nuevo Mundo.

Frankel, J. P.
1962   Polynesian navigation. Journal of the
          Institute of Navigation 9:40-43. London.

1963   Polynesian migration voyages: accidental
          or purposeful. American Anthropologist
          65.1:125-127. Menasha.

Frantz, Donald G.
1966   Person indexing in Blackfoot. International
          Journal of American Linguistics 32.1:50-58.
          Baltimore.

Freed, Ruth S. and Stanley A. Freed
1964   Calendars, ceremonies, and festivals in a
          north Indian village: necessary calendric
          information for fieldwork. Southwestern
          Journal of Anthropology 20.1:67-90.
          Albuquerque.

Friederici, Georg
1925-   Der Charakter der Entdeckung und Eroberung
1936   Amerikas durch die Europäer. 3 vols. xliv,
          1670 pp., (native maps, 1:157-161). Stutt-
          gart: F. A. Perthes.

Friedrich, Paul
1969   On the meaning of the Tarascan suffixes of
          space. (Supplement to International Journal
          of American Linguistics 35.4[Part 2]; Memoir
          23.) 48 pp. Baltimore.

1970   Shape in grammar. Language 46.2(Part 1):
          379-407. Baltimore.

1971   The Tarascan suffixes of locative space: meaning and morphotactics. (Indiana University Publications, Language Science Monographs, Vol. 9.) 324 pp. Bloomington, Ind.: Indiana University; The Hague: Mouton.

Frikel, Protasio
1956   Sinais e marcos de orientacão e advêrtencia indígenas. Revista de Antropologia 4.2: 103-110. São Paulo.

Gale, Richard M., editor
1967   The philosophy of time: a collection of essays. xii, 507 pp. Garden City, N. Y.: Doubleday.

Gandz, Solomon
1949   The origin of the two new moon days. Jewish Quarterly Review 40.2:157-172. Philadelphia.

Gatty, Harold
1958   Nature is your guide. 287 pp. New York: E. P. Dutton.

Gatty, Margaret Scott
1900   The book of sun-dials. 4th edition. 529 pp. London: Bell.

Gautier, Emile Félix and R. Chudeau
1908   Missions au Sahara. 2 vols. Paris: A. Colin.

Gay, John
1716   Trivia, or, the art of walking the streets of London. 80 pp. London: B. Lintott. (Reprinted 1922, 91 pp. London: D. O'Connor.)

Gay, John and Michael Cole
1967   The new mathematics and an old culture: a study of learning among the Kpelle of Liberia. x, 100 pp. New York: Holt, Rinehart and Winston.

Gayton, A. H.
1946   Culture-environment integration: external references in Yokuts life. Southwestern Journal of Anthropology 2.3:252-268. Albuquerque.

Gemelli, Agostino
1933   L'Orientazione lontana ne volo in aeroplano.

Revista di Psicologia 29.4:297.

Gemelli, Agostino, Giulio Tessier, and Arcangelo Galli
    1920   La Percezione della posizione del nostro
            corpo e dei suoi spostamenti. Archivio
            Italiano de Psicologia 1.1-2:107-182.
            Torino.

Gennep, Arnold van
    1911   Du sens d'orientation chez l'homme.
            (Religions, Moeurs, et Légendes, 3e Series.)
            47 pp. Paris: Société du Mercure de France.

Geoghegan, Richard Henry
    1944   The Aleut language. 169 pp. Washington:
            Department of the Interior.

Ghosh, Samir
    1968   Idiom and Bengali numbers. Anthropological
            Linguistics 10.4:11-14. Bloomington, Ind.

Gilman, Albert and Roger Brown
    1958   Who says "tu" to whom. Etc. 15.3:169-174.
            Bloomington, Ill.

Ginzel, Friedrich Karl
    1914   Handbuch der mathematischen und technischen
            Chronologie. 3 vols. Leipzig: J. C.
            Hinrichs.

Girard, Françoise
    1968-   Les Notions de nombre et de temps chez les
    1969   Buang de Nouvelle Guinée (District du
            Morobe). L'Ethnographie 62-63:160-178.
            Paris.

Girard, Rafael
    1948   El calendario Maya-Mexica, origen, función,
            desarrollo y lugar de procedencia. 195 pp.
            (Colección Cultura Precolombina.) Mexico
            City: Stylo.

    1966   Los mayas. 507 pp. Mexico City: Libro Mex.

Gladwin, Thomas
    1964   Culture and logical process. Pp. 167-177
            in Explorations in cultural anthropology,
            essays in honor of George Peter Murdock,
            edited by W. H. Goodenough. New York:
            McGraw-Hill.

    1970   East is a big bird: navigation and logic

on Puluwat Atoll. 241 pp. Cambridge: Harvard University Press.

Golson, Jack, editor
1963   Polynesian navigation: a symposium on Andrew Sharp's theory of accidental voyages. (Polynesian Society, Memoir 34.) viii, 153 pp. Wellington.

Goodenough, Ward H.
1951   Native astronomy in Micronesia: a rudimentary science. Scientific Monthly 73.2:105-110. New York.

1953   Native astronomy in the central Carolines. (University of Pennsylvania Museum Monograph.) 45 pp. Philadelphia.

1965   Personal names and modes of address in two oceanic societies. Pp. 265-276 in Context and meaning in cultural anthropology, edited by M. E. Spiro. New York: Free Press; London: Collier-Macmillan.

1966   Notes on Truk's place names. Micronesia 2:95-129, separate fold-out map. Tokyo.

Gossen, Gary Hamilton
1970   Time and space in Chamula oral tradition. Ph.D. dissertation in Harvard University, Cambridge.

Graebner, F.
1920   Alt- und neuweltliche Kalender. Zeitschrift für Ethnologie 52:6-37. Berlin.

Granpré-Molière, M. J.
1955   Landscape of the N. E. Polder. Forum 10: 1-2. Hilversum.

Griaule, Marcel and Germaine Dieterlen
1950   Un système soudanais de Sirius. Journal de la Société des Africanistes 20.2:273-294. Paris.

Griffin, Donald R.
1953   Sensory physiology and the orientation of animals. American Scientist 41.2:209-244. New Haven.

Griffin, Margie
1970   Buin directionals. Pacific Linguistics,

Series A, Occasional Papers, No. 26:13-22.
Canberra.

Griffith, Craven
    1952   Indian moons. Journal of Calendar Reform
            22.1:24-25. New York.

Grigg, David
    1965   The logic of regional systems. Annals of
            the Association of American Geographers
            55.3:465-491. Albany.

    1967   Regions, models and classes. Pp. 461-509
            in Models in geography, edited by R. J.
            Chorley and P. Haggett. London: Methuen.

Grimble, Arthur
    1924   Canoes in the Gilbert Islands. Journal of
            the Royal Anthropological Institute 54:101-
            139. London.

    1931   Gilbertese astronomy and astronomical
            observations. Journal of the Polynesian
            Society 40:197-235. Wellington.

Groenke, Ulrich
    1967   Spurious attribution of meaning in place-
            name translations. Names 15.2:119-125.
            Potsdam, N. Y.

Groom, Arthur William
    1961   How we weigh and measure. viii, 160 pp.
            London: Routledge and Kegan Paul.

Grünbaum, Adolph
    1955   Time and entropy. American Scientist 43.4:
            550-572. New Haven.

Gudde, Erwin G.
    1955   Naming storms. Names 3.1:34-37. Berkeley.

Gulick, John
    1963   Images of an Arab city. Journal of the
            American Institute of Planners 29.3:179-
            198. Baltimore.

Guthe, Carl E.
    1921   A possible solution of the number series on
            pages 51 to 58 of the Dresden codex.
            (Papers of the Peabody Museum of American
            Archaeology and Ethnology, Harvard University
            6.4.) 31 pp. Cambridge.

Gutmans, Théodore
    1970   Une terminologie occidentale unifée dès le
            Moyen Age: les quatre points cardinaux.
            La Linguistique 6.1:147-151. Paris.

Haas, Mary R.
    1942   The use of numeral classifiers in Thai.
            Language 18.3:201-206. Baltimore.

    1951   The use of numeral classifiers in Burmese.
            University of California Publications in
            Semitic Philology 11:191-200. Berkeley.

    1969   'Exclusive' and 'Inclusive': a look at
            early usage. International Journal of
            American Linguistics 35.1:1-6. Baltimore.

Haddon, A. C. and James Hornell
    1936-   Canoes of Oceania. 3 vols. (Bernice P.
    1938   Bishop Museum Special Publications, Nos.
            27-29.) Vol. 1, The canoes of Polynesia,
            Fiji and Micronesia, by James Hornell, 454
            pp.; Vol. 2, The canoes of Melanesia,
            Queensland, and New Guinea, by A. C. Haddon,
            342 pp.; Vol. 3, Definition of terms,
            general survey and conclusions, by A. C.
            Haddon and James Hornell, 88 pp. Honolulu.

Haddon, A. C. and W. H. R. Rivers
    1912   Science and astronomy [including Directions
            of space], with a calendar by S. H. Ray.
            Reports of the Cambridge Anthropological
            Expedition to the Torres Straits 4:218-237.
            Cambridge, England.

Hager, Stansbury
    1900   The Celestial Bear. Journal of American
            Folklore 13.49:92-103. Boston.

    1906   Cherokee star lore. Pp. 354-366 in Anthro-
            pological papers, written in honor of
            Franz Boas. New York: Stechert.

Haile, Berard
    1947   Starlore among the Navaho. 44 pp. Santa
            Fe: Museum of Navajo Ceremonial Art.

Hall, Edward T., Jr.
    1959   The silent language. 240 pp. New York:
            Doubleday.

    1960   A microcultural analysis of time. Pp. 118-

415

122 in Men and cultures, (Selected Papers of
the Fifth International Congress of Anthropological and Ethnological Sciences, Philadelphia, 1956), edited by A. F. C. Wallace.
Philadelphia: University of Pennsylvania
Press.

Hall, Edward T., Jr. (cont.)
1963   A system for the notation of proxemic
behavior. American Anthropologist 65.5:
1003-1026. Menasha.

1966   The hidden dimension. 201 pp. Garden City,
N. Y.: Doubleday.

1968   Proxemics. Current Anthropology 9.2-3:83-
108. Utrecht.

Hall, Richard N.
1966   Recent progress in international standardiza-
tion of geographical names. Pp. 224-229 in
Proceedings of the Eighth International
Congress of Onomastic Sciences, (Janua
Linguarum, Series Maior 17), edited by
D. P. Blok. The Hague: Mouton.

Hallowell, A. Irving
1955   Culture and experience. xvi, 434 pp.
Philadelphia: University of Pennsylvania
Press.

1958   Ojibwa metaphysics of being and the perception of person. Pp. 63-85 in Person
perception and interpersonal behavior,
edited by R. Togiui and L. Petrullo.
Stanford: Stanford University Press.

Ham, William Eugene, editor
1962   Classification of carbonate rocks. (American Association of Petroleum Geologists,
Memoir 1.) 279 pp. Tulsa.

Hamp, Eric P.
1967   On the notions of 'stone' and 'mountain'
in Indo-European. Journal of Linguistics
3.1:83-90. London.

Harrington, John P.
1916   The ethnogeography of the Tewa Indians.
Annual Reports of the Bureau of American
Ethnology 29:29-618. Washington.

1957   Valladolid Maya enumeration. Bulletins of
        the Bureau of American Ethnology, No. 164:
        245-278. Washington.

Harrisson, Tom
1965   Three 'secret' communications systems among
        Borneo nomads (and their dogs). Journal of
        the Royal Asiatic Society, Malaysian Branch,
        38.2:67-86. Singapore.

Hartson, L. D.
1939   Contrasting approaches to the analysis of
        skilled movements. Journal of General
        Psychology 20.2:263-293. Worcester, Mass.

Haugen, Einar
1957   The semantics of Icelandic orientation.
        Word 13.3:447-459. New York.

Hawkins, Gerald S.
1965a   Sun, moon, men, and stones. American
        Scientist 53.4:391-408. New Haven.

1965b   Stonehenge decoded. 202 pp. New York:
        Dell.

Hedberg, Hollis D., editor
1961   Stratigraphic classification and terminology.
        (Report of the XXI International Geological
        Congress, Norden, 1960, Part 25.) 38 pp.
        Copenhagen.

Heizer, Robert F.
1958   Aboriginal California and Great Basin
        cartography. Papers on California Archaeol-
        ogy No. 63; Reports of the University of
        California Archaeological Survey 41:1-9.
        Berkeley.

Henry, David and Kay Henry
1969   Koyukon locationals. Anthropological
        Linguistics 11.4:135-142. Bloomington, Ind.

Henry, Jules
1965   White people's time, colored people's time.
        Trans-action 2.3:31-35. St. Louis, Mo.:
        Washington University.

Hewes, Gordon W.
1955   World distribution of certain postural habits.
        American Anthropologist 57.2:231-244. Menasha.

Hewes, Gordon W. (cont.)
    1957   The anthropology of posture. Scientific
            American 196.2:122-132. New York.

    1966   The domain posture. Anthropological Linguis-
            tics 8.8:106-112. Bloomington, Ind.

Heyen, G. H.
    1962   Primitive navigation in the Pacific. Journal
            of the Polynesian Society 71.3(Supplement):
            64-79. Wellington.

Hilder, Brett
    1959   Polynesian navigation stones. Journal of
            the Institute of Navigation 12.1:90-97.
            London.

    1962   Primitive navigation in the Pacific. Jour-
            nal of the Polynesian Society 71.4(Supple-
            ment):81-97. Wellington.

    1963   Primitive navigation in the Pacific. Naviga-
            tion 2:77-89. Sydney.

Himes, Ron
    1971   Kinship, disease, property, and time in the
            Tagalog area, Philippines: a study in
            ethnoscience. Ph.D. dissertation in
            anthropology, University of Hawaii.
            Honolulu.

Hinze, Oscar Marcel
    1966   Studien zum Verständnis der archaischen
            Astronomie. Symbolon 5:162-219. Basel.

Hirschberg, Walter
    1929   Die viertägige Marktwoche in Africa.
            Anthropos 24.3-4:613-619. Vienna.

    1931a   Der "Mondkalender" in der Mutterrechtskultur.
            Anthropos 26.3-4:461-467. Vienna.

    1931b   Die Zeitrechnung der Wadschagga. Inter-
            nationales Archiv für Ethnographie 31.3-4:
            51-78. Leiden.

    1934   Die Zeitrechnung der Masai und verwandter
            Völker. Zeitschrift für Ethnologie 65.4-6:
            241-264. Berlin.

Hiskett, M.
    1967   The Arab star-calendar and planetary system

in Hausa verse. Bulletin of the School of Oriental and African Studies, University of London, 30.1:158-176. London.

Hoagland, Hudson
1951   Consciousness and the chemistry of time. Pp. 164-200 in Problems of consciousness, (Transactions of the First Conference), edited by H. A. Abramson. New York: Josiah Macy Foundation.

Hoerschelmann, Werner von
1922   Flächendarstellungen in altmexicanischen Bilderschriften. Pp. 187-204 in Festschrift Eduard Seler, edited by Walter Lehmann. Stuttgart: Strecker und Schröder.

Hogbin, H. Ian
1935   Trading expeditions in northern New Guinea. Oceania 5.4:375-407. Sydney.

Höltker, P. Georg
1928   Zeit und Zahl in Nordwestafrika. Pp. 282-302 in Publication d'hommage offerte au P. W. Schmidt, edited by W. Koppers. Vienna: Mechitharisten-Congratulations-Buchdruckerei.

Hooke, Samuel Henry
1928   New Year's Day. ix, 78 pp. New York: Morrow.

Hops, A.
1956   Ueber die Einmaligkeit der Marshall-Stabkarten im Stillen Ozean. Zeitschrift für Ethnologie 81.1:104-110. Braunschweig.

Hornell, James
1943   Outrigger devices: distribution and origin. Journal of the Polynesian Society 52.3:91-100. Wellington.

1946   Water transport; origins and early evolution. 308 pp. London: Cambridge University Press.

Hose, Charles
1905   Various methods of computing the time for planting among the races of Borneo. Journal of the Royal Asiatic Society, Straits Branch, 42:1-5, 209-210. Singapore.

Hough, Walter
    1893   Time keeping by light and fire. American
            Anthropologist 6.2:207-210. Washington.

Huddleston, Rodney
    1969   Some observations on tense and deixis in
            English. Language 45.4:777-806. Baltimore.

Jaccard, Pierre
    1926   Une enquête sur la désorientation en mon-
            tagne. Bulletin de la Société Vaudoise des
            Sciences Naturelles 56.217:151-159. Lau-
            sanne.

    1932   Le Sens de la direction et l'orientation
            lointaine chez l'homme. 354 pp. Paris:
            Payot.

Jackendoff, Ray S.
    1968   Quantifiers in English. Foundations of
            Language 4.4:422-442. Dordrecht.

Jackson, John Brinckerhoff
    1956-   Other-directed houses. Landscape 6.2:
    1957   29-35. Santa Fe.

Jaspan, M. A.
    1967   Symbols at work--aspects of kinetic and
            mnemonic representation in Redjang ritual.
            Bijdragen tot de Taal-, Land- en Volkenkunde
            123.4:476-516. 's-Gravenhage.

Jones, Steve
    1966   Tracking Indian time. Masterkey 40.2:75-77.
            Los Angeles.

Jonghe, Ed. de
    1906   Der altmexikanische Kalender. Zeitschrift
            für Ethnologie 38.4-5:485-512. Berlin.

Kahane, Henry and Renée Kahane
    1957   Toponyms as anemonyms. Names 5.4:241-245.
            Berkeley.

Kahlo, Gerhard
    1962   Astronomie im alten Indonesien und Polynesi-
            en. Osiris 14:193-197. Bruges.

Kaneko, E.
    1956   The numeral systems of the Formosan lan-
            guages as compared with those of other
            Austronesian languages. Wiener Völkerkund-
            liche Mitteilungen 4.1.56:37-77. Vienna.

Kasmar, Joyce V.
    1970   The development of a usable lexicon of
            environmental descriptors. Environment and
            Behavior 2.2:153-169. Beverly Hills, Calif.

Kayan, Carl F., editor
    1959   Systems of units, national and international
            aspects. (AAAS Publication No. 57.) x,
            297 pp. Washington: American Association
            for the Advancement of Science.

Kaye, George Rusby
    1924   Hindu astronomy. (Memoirs of the Archaeo-
            logical Survey of India.) ii, 134 pp.
            Calcutta: Government of India, Central
            Publication Branch.

Kelley, David H.
    1960   Calendar animals and deities. Southwestern
            Journal of Anthropology 16.3:317-337.
            Albuquerque.

    1962a   A history of the decipherment of Maya script.
            Anthropological Linguistics 4.8:1-48.
            Bloomington, Ind.

    1962b   Review of Arithmetic in Maya, by G. I.
            Sánchez. American Anthropologist 64.5:
            1104-1105. Menasha.

Kemeny, John G., Hazleton Mirkil, J. Lauris Snell and
            Gerald L. Thompson
    1959   Introduction to finite mathematics. 372 pp.
            Englewood Cliffs, N. J.: Prentice-Hall.

Kenny, Hamill
    1964   Place-names on the moon: a report. Names
            12.2:73-81. Youngstown, Ohio.

Kepes, Gyorgy
    1956   The new landscape in art and science.
            383 pp. Chicago: P. Theobald.

Key, Mary Ritchie
    1970   Preliminary remarks on paralanguage and
            kinesics in human communication. La
            Linguistique 6.2:17-36. Paris.

Kilpatrick, Franklin P.
    1954   Recent experiments in perception. Trans-
            actions of the New York Academy of Sciences
            16.8:420-425. New York.

Kirschbaum, F. J.
1938   Ueber Zahlensysteme im Zentralgebirge von
        Neuguinea. Anthropos 33.1-2:278-279.
        Vienna.

Kisch, Bruno
1965   Scales and weights: a historical outline.
        297 pp. New Haven: Yale University Press.

Kluge, Theodor
1939   Die Zahlenbegriffe der Völker Amerikas,
        Nordeurasiens, der Munda und der Paläoafri-
        caner. Berlin.

Kniffen, Fred B.
1939   Pomo geography. University of California
        Publications in American Archaeology and
        Ethnology 36.6:353-400. Berkeley.

Knight, C. Gregory
1971   Ethnography and change. Journal of Geogra-
        phy 70.1:47-51. Chicago.

Knorozov, Juri V.
1952   Drevnjaja pis'mennost' Central'noj Ameriki.
        Sovetskaja etnografija 1952, 3:100-118.
        Moscow.

1963   Pis'mennost' indejcev Majja. 663 pp.
        Moscow: USSR Academy of Sciences.

Knox, Alexander
1968   Glossary of geographical and topographical
(1904) terms, and of words of frequent occurrence
        in the composition of such terms and of
        place-names. xl, 432 pp. Detroit: Gale
        Research Co. (Original edition 1904,
        London: E. Stanford.)

Kobayashi, T.
1957   Mongol jin no saigetsu-mei ni tsuite (The
        Mongol nomenclature of the years and the
        months). Minzokugaku Kenkyu 21.1-2:55-65.
        Tokyo.

Kopytoff, Igor
1966   Review of La Division du temps et le calen-
        drier rituel des peuples lagunaires de Côte
        d'Ivoire, by Georges Niangoran-Bouah.
        American Anthropologist 68.1:249-250.
        Menasha.

Krahe, Hans
    1949   Ortsnamen als Geschichtsquelle. 30 pp.
            Heidelberg: Winter.

Kranz, Peter
    1970   What do people do all day? Behavioral
            Science 15.3:286-291. Ann Arbor.

Krapf-Askari, Eva
    1966   Time and classifications: an ethnographic
            and historical case study of the Yoruba.
            Odu (n.s.)2.2:3-18. Ibadan, Nigeria.

Kreichgauer, Dam.
    1927   Anschluss der Maya-Chronologie an die
            julianische. Anthropos 22.1-2:1-15.
            Vienna.

Krusch, Bruno
    1880   Studien zur christlich-mittelalterlichen
            Chronologie; der 84 jährige Ostercyclus und
            seine Quellen. viii, 349 pp. Leipzig:
            Veit.

Kubitschek, Wilhelm
    1928   Grundriss der antiken Zeitrechnung. viii,
            241 pp. Munchen: Beck.

Kubler, George
    1962   The shape of time: remarks on the history
            of things. 136 pp. New Haven and London:
            Yale University Press.

Kugler, Franz Xaver
    1900   Die babylonische Mondrechnung. xv, 214 pp.
            Fribourg: Herder.

Kutscher, Gerdt
    1962   Die Flurkarte des Chiquatzin Tecuihtli.
            Baessler-Archiv (n.f.)10.1:129-244. Berlin.

LaFarge, Oliver and Douglas Byers
    1931   The Year Bearer's people. (Tulane University,
            Middle American Research Series, No. 3.)
            xii, 379 pp. New Orleans.

Lagercrantz, Sture
    1968-   African tally-strings. Anthropos 63-64.1-2:
    1969   115-128. Fribourg.

Lahee, Frederic H.
    1961   Field geology. 6th edition. 926 pp. New
            York: McGraw-Hill.

Lakoff, Robin
1970   Tense and its relation to participants.
        Language 46.4:838-849. Baltimore.

Langdon, Stephen Herbert
1935   Babylonian monologies and the semitic
        calendars. vi, 169 pp. London: Milford.

Langer, Suzanne K.
1953   Feeling and form: a theory of art. xvi,
        431 pp. New York: Scribner.

Larsen, Helga
1936   The 260 day period as related to the agri-
        cultural life of the ancient Indian. Ethnos
        1.1:9-12. Stockholm.

Laubenfels, M. W. de
1950   Oceanic currents in the Marshall Islands.
        Geographical Review 40.2:254-259. New York.

Leach, Edmund R.
1950   Primitive calendars. Oceania 20.4:245-262.
        Sydney.

1953   Cronus and chronos. Explorations 1:15-23.
        Toronto. (Reprinted 1961, pp. 124-132 in
        Rethinking anthropology, [London School of
        Economics Monographs on Social Anthropology,
        No. 22], by E. R. Leach. London: Athlone.)

1954   Primitive time-reckoning. Pp. 110-127
        (Chapter 5) in A history of technology,
        edited by Charles Singer et al. London
        and New York: Oxford University Press.

1955   Time and false noses. Explorations 5:30-35.
        Toronto. (Reprinted 1961, pp. 132-136 in
        Rethinking anthropology, (London School of
        Economics Monographs on Social Anthropology,
        No. 22), by E. R. Leach. London: Athlone.)

1957   A possible method of intercalation for the
        calendar of the Book of Jubilees. Vetus
        Testamentum 7.4:392-397. Leiden.

Lee, Terence
1968   Urban neighbourhood as a socio-spatial
        schema. Human Relations 21.3:241-267.
        Wembley, England.

Lehmann, Walter
1908   Der sogennante Kalender Ixtlilxochitls.

Anthropos 3:988-1004. Vienna.

1911 Der Kalender der Quiché-Indianer Guatemalas.
      Ein Kapitel aus dem unveröffentlichten
      Manuskriptwerk des Padre Ximenez über die
      Geschichte von Chiapas und Guatemala.
      Anthropos 6:403-410. Vienna.

Lenoir, Raymond
1924 Les Expéditions maritimes, institution
      sociale en Mélanésie occidentale. L'Anthro-
      pologie 34:387-410. Paris.

Leriche, A.
1951 Mesures maures. Bulletin de l'Institut
      Français d'Afrique Noire 14:1229-1256.
      Dakar, Senegal.

Lessa, William A.
1950 Ulithi and the outer native world. American
      Anthropologist 52.1:27-52. Menasha.

1959 Divining by knots in the Carolines. Journal
      of the Polynesian Society 68:188-210.
      Wellington.

Lévi-Strauss, Claude
1967 The story of Asdiwal. Pp. 1-47 in The
      structural study of myth and totemism,
      (Association of Social Anthropologists
      Monographs, 5), edited by E. R. Leach.
      London: Tavistock.

Lewis, David
1964 Polynesian navigational methods. Journal
      of the Polynesian Society 73.4:364-374.
      Wellington.

1966 Stars of the sea road. Journal of the
      Polynesian Society 75:84-94. Wellington.

Lincoln, J. Steward
1942 The Maya calendar of the Ixil of Guatemala.
      Carnegie Institution of Washington, Contri-
      butions to American Archaeology and History
      7.38:97-128. Washington.

Lind, Gerald
1971 A preliminary study of the pronouns of
      address in Swedish. Stanford Occasional
      Papers in Linguistics 1:101-130. Stanford.

Littlefield, George Emery
1914   Notes on the calendar and the almanac.
        Proceedings of the American Antiquarian
        Society 24:11-64. Worcester, Mass.

Lloyd, G. E. R.
1964   The hot and the cold, the dry and the wet
        in Greek philosophy. Journal of Hellenic
        Studies 84:92-106. London.

Long, Richard C. E.
1920   The setting in order of Pop in the Maya
        calendar. Man 20:37-40(Art. 22). London.

1923a   Maya high numbers. Man 23.5:66-69(Art. 39).
        London.

1923b   Maya and Christian chronology. Journal of
        the Royal Anthropological Institute 53:
        36-41. London.

1924a   Some Maya time periods. Proceedings of the
        International Congress of Americanists 21:
        574-581. The Hague.

1924b   A link between the earlier and later Mayan
        chronologies. Man 24.6:89-91(Art. 66).
        London.

1924c   The age of the Maya calendar. Journal of
        the Royal Anthropological Institute 54:
        353-362. London.

1925   The Bowditch and Morley correlations of
        Maya chronology. Man 25.1:7-11(Art. 2).
        London.

1934   The dates in the annals of the Cakchiquels,
        and a note on the 260-day period of the Maya.
        Journal of the Royal Anthropological Insti-
        tute 64.1:57-68. London.

Lotz, John
1955   On language and culture. International
        Journal of American Linguistics 21.2:187-
        189. Baltimore.

Loud, Llewellyn L.
1918   Ethnogeography and archaeology of the Wiyot
        territory. University of California Publi-
        cations in American Archaeology and Ethnolo-
        gy 14.3:221-436. Berkeley.

Lounsbury, Floyd G.
1946   Stray number systems among certain Indian
        tribes. American Anthropologist 48.4:
        672-675. Menasha.

1960   Iroquois place-names in the Champlain valley.
        Pp. 21-66 in Report of the New York-Vermont
        Interstate Commission on the Lake Champlain
        Basin. New York State Legislative Document,
        1960, No. 9. Albany. (Reprinted 1965 by
        the University of the State of New York,
        State Education Department, Albany.)

Lounsbury, Floyd G. and Michael D. Coe
1968   Linguistic and ethnographic data pertinent
        to the "cage" glyph of Dresden 36c. Pp.
        269-284 in Vol. 7 of Estudios de Cultura
        Maya. Mexico City.

Lowery, Woodbury
1901   Indian Charts. Pp. 436-437 (Appendix E) in
        Spanish settlements within the present limits
        of the United States, 1513-1561, by W.
        Lowery. New York and London: G. P. Putnam.

Ludendorff, Hans
1930   Ueber die Entstehung der Tzolkin-Periode im
        Kalender der Maya. Sitzungsberichten der
        Preussischen Akademie der Wissenschaften.
        Berlin.

Lynch, Kevin
1954   The form of cities. Scientific American
        190.4:54-63. New York.

1960   The image of the city. vii, 194 pp., bibliog.,
        index, illus. Cambridge: Harvard University
        Press.

1965   The city as environment. Pp. 192-201 in
        Cities (articles originally published in
        September 1965 issue of Scientific American.)
        New York: Knopf.

Lyons, Henry
1928   The sailing charts of the Marshall Islanders.
        Royal Geographical Journal 72.4:325-388.
        London.

Maass, Alfred
1910   Wahrsagekalender (kutikå) im Leben der
        Malaien Zentral-Sumatras. Zeitschrift für
        Ethnologie 42.5:750-775. Berlin.

Maass, Alfred (cont.)
1924,   Sternkunde und Stern deuterei im malaiischen
1926   Archipel. Tijdschrift voor Indische Taal-,
          Land- en Volkenkunde 64:1-172; 64:347-461;
          66:618-670. Batavia.

1933   Die Sterne im Glauben der Indonesier.
          Zeitschrift für Ethnologie 65.4-6:264-303.
          Berlin.

Mabuchi, Toichi
1936   Rituals and picture-calendar of the Bunun
          (Central Formosa). Japanese Journal of
          Ethnology 2.3:58-80. Tokyo.

1941   Sanchi Takasago-zoku no chiriteki chishiki
          to shakaiseiji soshiki (Geographical
          knowledge and socio-political organization
          of the mountain peoples of Formosa: their
          correlation). Minzokugaku Nempo 3:267-311.
          Tokyo.

1966   Sphere of geographical knowledge and socio-
          political organization among the mountain
          peoples of Formosa. Pp. 101-146 in Folk
          cultures of Japan and East Asia, (Monumenta
          Nipponica Monographs, No. 25.) Tokyo:
          Sophia University Press.

McClelland, E. M.
1966   Two studies of Ifa divination. II, The
          significance of number in the Odu of Ifa.
          Africa 36.4:421-431. London.

Mackay, L. D. and P. L. Gardner
1969   Conceptual and vocabulary difficulties in
          physical science amongst Papua and New
          Guinea High School students. Papua and
          New Guinea Journal of Education 6.2:3-11.
          Sydney.

MacNaughton, Duncan
1932   A scheme of Egyptian chronology. xii, 405
          pp. London: Luzac.

Maegraith, Brian G.
1932   The astronomy of the Aranda and Luritja
          tribes. Transactions of the Royal Society
          of South Australia 56:19-26. Adelaide.

Makemson, Maud Worcester
1938,   Hawaiian astronomical concepts. American
1939   Anthropologist 40.3:370-383; 41.4:589-596.

Menasha.

1941   The morning star rises. xii, 301 pp. New
        Haven: Yale University Press.

1942   The Maya calendar. Popular Astronomy 50.1:
        6-15. Northfield, Minn.

1943   The astronomical tables of the Maya.
        Carnegie Institution of Washington, Contri-
        butions to American Anthropology and History
        8:183-221. Washington.

Malinowski, Bronislaw
    1920   Kula; the circulating exchange of valuables
            in the archipelagoes of eastern New Guinea.
            Man 20.7:97-105(Art. 51). London.

    1921   Primitive economics of the Trobriand Islands.
            Economic Journal 31.1:1-16. Cambridge,
            England. (Available in Bobbs-Merrill Re-
            print Series.)

    1922   Argonauts of the Western Pacific. xxxi,
            527 pp. London: Routledge.

    1927   Lunar and seasonal calendar in the Trobri-
            ands. Journal of the Royal Anthropological
            Institute 57.1:203-215. London.

    1935   The language of magic and gardening. (Coral
            gardens and their magic, Vol. 2.) xxxii,
            350 pp. London: Allen and Unwin; New York:
            American Book. (Republished 1965, Blooming-
            ton: Indiana University Press.)

Mallery, Garrick
    1877   A calendar of the Dakota nation. (U. S.
            Geological and Geographical Survey, Bulletin
            3, No. 1.) 25 pp. Washington.

    1882-   Pictographs of the North American Indians.
    1883   Annual Reports of the Bureau of American
            Ethnology 4:100-146. Washington.

Malo, David
    1951   Hawaiian antiquities. (Bernice P. Bishop
            Museum Special Publications, No. 2.) xxii,
            278 pp. Honolulu.

Maranda, Pierre and Elli Köngäs Maranda
    1970   Le Crâne et l'utérus. Deux théorèmes nord-
            malaitains. Pp. 829-861 in Échanges et

communications, edited by J. Pouillon and P. Maranda. The Hague and Paris: Mouton.

Marie, Pierre and P. Behague
1919   Syndrome de désorientation dans l'espace. Revue Neurologique 26.1:1-14. Paris.

Marsh, Gordon H. and William S. Laughlin
1936   Human anatomical knowledge among the Aleutian Islanders. Southwestern Journal of Anthropology 12.1:38-78. Albuquerque.

Marti, Palau
1964   Calendriers dahoméens du Musée de L'Homme. Objets et Mondes 4.1:29-38. Paris.

Martí, Samuel
1960   Simbolismo de los colores, deidades, números y rumbos. Estudios de Cultura Náhuatl 2:93-127. Mexico City.

Martin, Anfos
1916   Les Mythes stellaires des ourses. Bulletin de la Société Préhistorique Française 13: 541. Paris.

Marvin, Charles F.
1932   Simplifying our calendar. Scientific Monthly 34.4:366-368. New York.

Mason, Herbert L. and Jean H. Langenheim
1957   Language analysis and the concept environment. Ecology 38.2:325-340. Durham.

Mathiot, Madeleine
1968   An approach to the cognitive study of language. (International Journal of American Linguistics 34.1[Part 2]; Publication 45, Indiana University Research Center in Anthropology, Folklore, and Linguistics.) 224 pp. Bloomington, Ind.

Mauss, Marcel
1935   Les Techniques du corps. Journal de Psychologie 32.3-4:271-293. Paris.

1966   Une catégorie de l'esprit humain: la notion de personne, celle de "moi." Pp. 333-365 in Sociologie et anthropologie, by M. Mauss. Paris: Presses Universitaires de France.

Meer, Petrus Emmanuel Van Der
1947   The ancient chronology of western Asia and

Egypt. (Documenta et monumenta orientis antiqui, 2.) 71 pp. Leiden: Brill.

Meggitt, Mervyn J.
1958   Mae Enga time-reckoning and calendar, New Guinea. Man 58.5:74-77(Art. 87). London.

Meier, Joseph
1912   Die Feier der Sonnenwende auf der Insel Vuatam, Bismarckarchipel, Südsee. Anthropos 7:706-721. Vienna.

Menninger, Karl
1969   Number words and number symbols: a cultural history of numbers. Translated by Paul Broneer from Zahlwort und Ziffer, the 1938 revised German edition. xiii, 480 pp. Cambridge, Mass. and London: MIT Press.

Menzel, Donald H.
1964   A field guide to the stars and planets. (Peterson Field Guide 15.) xiv, 397 pp. Boston: Houghton Mifflin.

Merriam, D. F. and R. H. Lippert
1966   Geologic model studies using trend-surface analysis. Journal of Geology 74.3:344-357. Chicago.

Merriam, D. F. and P. H. A. Sneath
1966   Quantitative comparison of contour maps. Journal of Geophysical Research 71.4:1105-1115. Richmond, Va.

Miller, Cecil
1967   Number origin and linguistics. Linguistics 34:26-34. The Hague.

Mintz, Sidney W.
1961   Standards of value and units of measure in the Fond-des-Nègres market place, Haiti. Journal of the Royal Anthropological Institute 91.1:23-38. London.

Monod, T.
1963   Le Ciel austral et l'orientation. Bulletin of the Institute of Africa Noire, Series B, 25.3-4:415-426. Dakar.

Monteil, Vincent
1949   Notes sur la toponymie, l'astronomie et l'orientation chez les Maures. Hesperis 36.1-2:189-219. Paris.

Mooney, James
     1898   Calendar history of the Kiowa Indians.
              Annual Reports of the Bureau of American
              Ethnology 17:141-444. Washington.

Morley, Sylvanus Griswold
     1915   An introduction to the study of the Maya
              hieroglyphs. (Bulletins of the Bureau of
              American Ethnology, No. 57.) xvi, 284 pp.
              Washington.

     1924   The earliest Mayan dates. Proceedings of
              the International Congress of Americanists
              21:655-667. The Hague.

Moulton, J. C.
     1921   Points of the compass in Brunei Malay.
              Journal of the Royal Asiatic Society,
              Straits Branch, 83:75. Singapore.

Murdoch, John
     1890a   Notes on counting and measuring among the
              Eskimo of Point Barrow. American Anthro-
              pologist 3.1:37-43. Washington.

     1890b   Notes on the names of heavenly bodies and
              the points of the compass among the Point
              Barrow Eskimo. American Anthropologist
              3.2:136. Washington.

Needham, Joseph
     1965   Time and eastern man. (Royal Anthropologi-
              cal Institute of Great Britain and Ireland,
              Occasional Paper No. 21.) ix, 52 pp.
              London.

Needham, Rodney
     1967   Right and left in Nyoro symbolic classifica-
              tion. Africa 37.4:425-452. London.

Neugebauer, Otto
     1969   The exact sciences in antiquity. 2d edi-
     (1957)   tion. xviii, 240 pp. New York: Dover.

Neugebauer, Otto, editor
     1955   Astronomical cuneiform texts. 3 vols.
              London: Lund Humphries.

Neyret, J. M.
     1950   Notes sur la navigation indigène aux Iles
              Fidji. Journal de la Société des Oceanistes
              6:5-31. Paris.

Niangoran-Bouah, Georges
1964   La Division du temps et le calendrier rituel
        des peuples lagunaires de Côte d'Ivoire.
        (Université de Paris, Travaux et Mémoires
        de l'Institut d'Ethnologie, No. 68.) 164
        pp. Paris.

Nicolaisen, W. F. H.
1957   The semantic structure of Scottish hydronomy.
        Scottish Studies 1:211-240. Edinburgh.

Nicolas, Guy
1966   Essai sur les structures fondamentales de
        l'espace dans la cosmologie Hausa. Journal
        de la Société des Africanistes 36.1:65-107.
        Paris.

Nilsson, Martin P.
1920   Primitive time-reckoning: a study of the
        origins and first development of the art of
        counting time among the primitive and early
        culture peoples. 384 pp. London: Oxford
        University Press.

1926   La Computation du temps chez les peuples
        primitifs et l'origine du calendrier.
        Scientia 39.6:393-400. Bologna.

1934   Calendar. Encyclopaedia of the Social
        Sciences 3:140-144. New York.

Norona, Delf
1950   Maps drawn by Indians in the Virginias.
        West Virginia Archaeologist (1950):12-19.

1951   Maps drawn by North American Indians.
        Bulletin of the Eastern States Archaeologi-
        cal Federation 10:6. Harrisburg, Pa.

Nuttall, Zelia
1901   The fundamental principles of Old and New
        World civilizations. (Papers of the Pea-
        body Museum of American Archaeology and
        Ethnology, Harvard University, Vol. 2.)
        602 pp. Cambridge.

Öhman, Suzanne
1951   Wortinhalt und Weltbild; vergleichende und
        methodologische Studien zu Bedeutungslehre
        und Wortfeldtheorie. 194 pp. Stockholm:
        Norstedt.

Ollier, C. D., D. P. Drover, and M. Godelier
1971   Soil knowledge amongst the Baruya of
        Wonenara, New Guinea. Oceania 42.1:33-41.
        Sydney.

Olson, Cynthia R.
1959   Master skipper, signs and the weather.
        Micronesian Reporter 7.2:10-12. Saipan,
        Mariana Islands.

Orloci, L.
1966   Geometric models in ecology. 1. The theory
        and application of some ordination methods.
        Journal of Ecology 54.1:193-215. Oxford.

Ortiz, Alfonso
1969   The Tewa world: space, time, being and
        becoming in a Pueblo society. xviii, 197
        pp. Chicago: University of Chicago Press.

Osborn, Henry
1969   The Warao self. The Bible Translator 20:
        74-83. London.

Panoff, Michel
1969   The notion of time among the Maenge people
        of New Britain. Ethnology 8.2:153-166.
        Pittsburgh.

1970   Father arithmetic: numeration and counting
        in New Britain. Ethnology 9.4:358-365.
        Pittsburgh.

Parker, Richard A.
1950   The calendars of ancient Egypt. xiii, 83
        pp. Chicago: University of Chicago Press.

Parsons, Terence
1970   An analysis of mass terms and amount terms.
        Foundations of Language 6.3:362-388.
        Dordrecht.

Partee, Barbara Hall
1970   Negation, conjunction, and quantifiers:
        syntax vs. semantics. Foundations of
        Language 6.2:153-165. Dordrecht.

Paterson, Andrew and O. L. Zangwill
1945   A case of topographic disorientation.
        Brain 68.3:188-212. London.

Peñafiel, Antonio
1885   Nombres geográficos de México; catálogo

alfabético de los nombres de lugar
pertenecientes al idioma Náhuatl; estudio
jeroglífico de la matrícula de los tributos
del Códice Mendocino. 260 pp.; atlas.
Mexico City: Oficina tip. de la Secretaría
de fomento.

Peng, Fred C. C. and Barron Brainerd
    1970   A grammar of Ainu number names. Lingua
            25.4:381-397. Amsterdam.

Perchonock, Norma and Oswald Werner
    1969   Navaho systems of classification: some
            implications for ethnoscience. Ethnology
            8.3:229-242. Pittsburgh.

Peterson, Joseph
    1916   Illusions of direction orientation. Journal
            of Philosophy, Psychology and Scientific
            Methods 8.9:225-236. New York.

Philip, Alexander
    1924   The calendar: its history, structure and
            improvement. xi, 104 pp. London: Cambridge
            University Press.

Phillips, D.
    1970   Where is Heaven, to the Wahgi? Notes on
            Translation, No. 36:30, 31-36. Hidalgo,
            Mexico.

Pike, Kenneth L. and Ivan Lowe
    1969   Pronominal reference in English conversation
            and discourse--a group theoretical treatment.
            Folia Linguistica 3:68-106. The Hague.

Pocock, David F.
    1964   The anthropology of time-reckoning. Contri-
            butions to Indian Sociology 7:18-29. Paris.

Poppe, Roger
    1970   "The time has come" (the Walrus said).
            Western Canadian Journal of Anthropology
            1.2:12-34. Edmonton, Alberta.

Porteus, Stanley David
    1931   The psychology of a primitive people. xv,
            438 pp. New York: Longmans, Green.

Pough, Frederick H.
    1953   A field guide to rocks and minerals. (Peter-
            son Field Guide 7.) xv, 349 pp. Boston:
            Houghton Mifflin.

Pouillon, Jean and Pierre Maranda, editors
   1970   Échanges et communications; mélanges offerts
          à Claude Lévi-Strauss à l'occasion de son
          60ème anniversaire. 2 vols. 1452 pp. The
          Hague and Paris: Mouton.

Pratolini, Vasco
   1947   Il Quartiere. New edition. 221 pp.
          Florence: Valleschi.

Preuss, Konrad Theodor
   1956   El concepto de la estrella matutina, según
          textos recogidos entre los mexicanos del
          Estado de Durango. El México Antiguo
          8:375-395. Mexico City.

   1960   La diosa de la tierra y de la luna de los
          antiguos mexicanos en el mito actual.
          Boletín del Centro de Investigaciones
          Antropológicas de Mexico 10:6-10. Mexico
          City.

Price, Derek J. de Solla and Leopold Pospisil
   1966   A survival of Babylonian arithmetic in New
          Guinea? Indian Journal of History of Science
          1.1:30-33. Calcutta.

Prince, J. R.
   1967   Science concepts among New Guinea school
          children: a pilot survey. Journal of the
          Papua and New Guinea Society 1.2:119-127.
          Port Moresby.

   1968a   Cultural conflicts in the time concepts of
          New Guinea speakers: an educational view.
          Kivung 1.1:18-28. Boroko, T.P.N.G.

   1968b   Science concepts among school children.
          South Pacific Bulletin 18.4:21-28. Sydney.

   1970   Views of physical causality in New Guinea
          students. Journal of the Papua and New
          Guinea Society 4.1:99-107. Port Moresby.

Pritchett, William Kendrick and Otto Neugebauer
   1947   The calendars of Athens. 115 pp. Cambridge:
          Harvard University Press.

Pukui, Mary Kawena and Samuel H. Elbert
   1968   Place names of Hawaii. x, 53 pp. Honolulu:
          University of Hawaii Press.

Rabaud, Etienne
    1927   L'Orientation lointaine et la reconnaissance
            des lieux. 112 pp. Paris: Alcan.

Rasmussen, Knud Johan Victor
    1931   The Netsilik Eskimos; social life and
            spiritual culture. (Report of the Fifth
            Thule Expedition 1921-1923, 8.1-2.)
            Copenhagen: Gyldendal.

Rattray, Robert Sutherland
    1927   Religion and art in Ashanti. xviii, 414 pp.
            Oxford: Clarendon.

Ray, S. H.
    1912   Calendar of Western Islands of Torres Straits.
            Reports of the Cambridge Anthropological
            Expedition to the Torres Straits 4:228.
            Cambridge, England

Rayner, J. H.
    1966   Classification of soil by numerical methods.
            Journal of Soil Science 17.1:79-92. Oxford.

Reche, E.
    1927   Die Dreisternnavigation der Polynesier.
            Marine-Rundschau 32:214-219, 261-271.
            Frankfurt.

Reichard, Gladys A.
    1948   Navajo classification of natural objects.
            Plateau 21.1:7-12. Flagstaff.

    1950   Navaho religion, a study of symbolism. 2
            vols. xxxvi, 800 pp. New York: Pantheon.

Reisenberg, S. H.
    1965   Table of voyages affecting Micronesian
            islands. Oceania 36.2:155-170. Sydney.

Rentenaar, Robert
    1967   Metrologische Bemerkungen zu niederländischen
            Flurnamen. Beiträge zur Namenforschung II,
            2.1:46-64. Heidelberg.

Richards, Cara B. and Henry F. Dobyns
    1957   Topography and culture: the case of the
            changing cage. Human Organization 16.1:
            16-20. Ithaca.

Ricketson, Oliver
    1928   Astronomical observatories in the Maya area.

Geographical Review 18.2:215-225. New York.

Riley, E. B. and S. H. Ray
    1924   Kiwai seasons. Man 24.5:73-75(Art. 56).
            London.

Ritchie-Calder, Lord
    1970   Conversion to the metric system. Scientific
            American 223.1:17-25. New York.

Robels, Cecilio
    1911   Origen del calendario Nahuatl. Anales del
            Museo Nacional de Arguelogia, Historia y
            Etnologia 3:339-350. Mexico City.

Roberts, John M., Wayne E. Thompson, and Brian Sutton-
            Smith
    1966   Expressive self-testing in driving. Human
            Organization 25.1:54-63. New York.

Röck, Fritz
    1928   Kalenderkreise und Kalenderschichten im
            alten Mexiko und Mittelamerika. Pp. 610-
            628 in Publication d'hommage offerte au
            P. W. Schmidt, edited by W. Koppers.
            Vienna: Mechitharisten-Congratulations-
            Buchdruckerei.

    1929   Zahlen-, Welt- und Kalenderbilder. Mannus
            21.3-4:201-219. Leipzig.

    1930   Das Jahr von 360 Tagen und seine Gliederung.
            (Weiner Beiträge zur Kulturgeschichte und
            Linguistik, I.) Vienna.

Rogers, M.
    1966   The navigation of Lough Erne. Ulster
            Folklife 12:97-103. Belfast.

Rousseau, Jacques
    1949   Mistassini calendar. The Beaver, 1949, 280:
            33-37. Winnipeg.

Rubel, Arthur J.
    1965   Prognosticative calendar systems. American
            Anthropologist 67.1:107-109. Menasha.

Ruesch, Jurgen and Weldon Kees
    1961   Nonverbial communication: notes on the
            visual perception of human relations. 205
            pp. Berkeley and Los Angeles: University
            of California Press.

Ryan, T. A. and M. S. Ryan
    1940   Geographical orientation. American Journal
            of Psychology 53.2:204-215. Austin.

Salzman, Zdenek
    1950   A method for analyzing numerical systems.
            Word 6.1:78-83. New York.

Sánchez, George I.
    1961   Arithmetic in Maya. viii, 74 pp. Austin:
            George I. Sanchez.

Sandström, Carl Ivar
    1951   Orientation in the present space. 193 pp.
            Stockholm: Almqvist and Wiksell.

Sapir, Edward
    1912   Language and environment. American Anthro-
            pologist 14.2:226-242. Menasha.

Saraf, Samarendra
    1970   The trichotomous theme: a ritual category
            in Hindu culture. Anthropos 65.5-6:948-972.
            Fribourg.

Sarfert, E.
    1911   Zur Kenntnis der Schiffahrtskunde der
            Karoliner. (Korrespondenzblatt der
            deutschen Gesellschaft für Anthropologie,
            Ethnologie, und Urgeschichte 42.)

Sastri, Madugula I.
    1968   Prepositions in Chemical Abstracts: a
            sememic study. Linguistics 38:42-51. The
            Hague.

Sather, Clifford A.
    1965   Bajau numbers and adjectives of quantity.
            Sabah Society Journal 2.4:194-197. Jessel-
            ton, Sabah, Malaysia.

Satterthwaite, Linton
    1965   Calendrics of the Maya lowlands. Pp. 603-
            631 in Vol. 3, Part 2 of Handbook of Middle
            American Indians, edited by G. R. Willey.
            Austin: University of Texas Press.

Sauer, Martin
    1802   An account of a geographical and astronomi-
            cal expedition to the northern parts of
            Russia. xxvi, 332, 58 pp. London: T.
            Cadell.

Saussure, Léopold de
    1920   Le Système astronomique des Chinois.
            Archives des Sciences Physiques et Natur-
            elles, 5m période, 2:325-350. Geneva.

    1930   Les Origines de l'astronomie chinoise.   x,
            594 pp. Paris: Librairie Orientale et
            Américaine Maisonneuve Frères.

Scherer, Anton
    1957   Die Erfassung des Raumes in der Sprache.
            Studium Generale 10.9:574-582. Berlin.

Schidlowski, Manfred
    1966   Ein lokaler Meteoritenkult aus der Calabar-
            Region von Ost-Nigeria. Zeitschrift für
            Ethnologie 91.1:141-143. Braunschweig.

Schilder, Paul
    1950   The image and appearance of the human body.
            353 pp. New York: International Universi-
            ties Press.

Schulz, R. P. C.
    1936   Beiträge zur Chronologie und Astronomie des
            alten Zentralamerika. Anthropos 31.5-6:
            758-788. Vienna.

Scott, William Henry
    1958   Some calendars of northern Luzon. American
            Anthropologist 60.3:563-570. Menasha.

Scully, Vincent
    1962   The earth, the temple, and the gods. 257
            pp., illus. New Haven: Yale University
            Press.

Sebeok, Thomas A.
    1968   Zoosemiotics: a guide to its literature.
            Language Sciences 3:7-14. Bloomington, Ind.

Sechefo, Justinus
    1910   The twelve lunar months among the Basuto.
            Anthropos 5.1:71-81. Vienna.

Seely, F. A.
    1888   The development of time-keeping in Greece
            and Rome. American Anthropologist 1:25-49.
            Washington.

Segall, Marshall H., Donald T. Campbell, and Melville
            Herskovits
    1963   Cultural differences in the perception of

geometric illusions. Science 139.3556:769-711. Washington.

1966   The influence of culture on visual perception: an advanced study in psychology and anthropology. 268 pp. New York: Bobbs-Merrill.

Seler, Eduard
1891   Zur mexicanischen Chronologie mit besonderer Berücksichtigung des zapoteksischen Kalenders. Zeitschrift für Ethnologie 23:89-133. Berlin.

1903   Die Korrekturen der Jahreslänge und der Länge der Venusperiode in den mexicanischen Bilderschriften. Zeitschrift für Ethnologie 35.1:27-49. Berlin.

1904   The Mexican chronology. Bulletins of the Bureau of American Ethnology, No. 28:11-55. Washington.

Serruys, Henry
1958   A note on arrows and oaths among the Mongols. Journal of the American Oriental Society 78.4:279-294. New Haven.

Sewell, Robert and Sankara B. Dīkshit
1896   The Indian calendar. With Appendix: Eclipses of the sun in India, by Robert Schram. 169 pp. London: Swan, Sonnen-schein.

Sharp, Andrew
1956   Ancient voyagers in the Pacific. (Polynesian Society, Memoir 32.) 191 pp. Wellington.

1961   Polynesian navigation to distant islands. Journal of the Polynesian Society 70.2: 219-226. Wellington.

1963   Polynesian navigation: some comments. Journal of the Polynesian Society 72.4:384-396. Wellington.

1966   Early Micronesian voyaging. Oceania 37.1: 64-65. Sydney.

Shirokogoroff, Sergei M.
1926   The Northern Tungus terms of orientation. Rocznik Orjentalistyczny 4:167-187. Lwów.

Shirokogoroff, Sergei M. (cont.)
1935   Psychomental complex of the Tungus. xvi,
        469 pp. London: Kegan Paul, Trench,
        Trubner.

Silva, Harry R. de
1931   A case of a boy possessing an automatic
        directional orientation. Science 73.1893:
        393-394. New York.

Sköld, Trygve
1964   The Scandinavian nordr and the Lappish
        system of orientation. Pp. 267-283 in
        Lapponica, (Studia Ethnographica Upsali-
        ensia 21), edited by Arne Furumark et al.
        Lund.

Smart, J. J. C., editor
1964   Problems of space and time. 436 pp. New
        York: Macmillan.

Smith, Albert Hugh
1956   English place-name elements. 2 vols. 305,
        417 pp. Cambridge: Cambridge University
        Press.

Smith, Elsdon C.
1956   West north versus east south. Names 4.3:
        166-167. Berkeley.

Smith, M. Elisabeth
1966   Mixtec place signs: a study of the Lienzos
        of Zacatepec and Jicayan. Ph.D. disserta-
        tion in Yale University, New Haven.

Smith, Robert J.
1961   Cultural differences in the life cycle and
        the concept of time. In Aging and leisure:
        a research perspective into the meaningful
        use of time, edited by R. W. Kleemeier.
        New York: Oxford University Press.

Smith, S. Percy
1918   Guiding stars in navigation. Journal of the
        Polynesian Society 27.108:226. New Plymouth,
        N. Z.

Sneath, P. H. A.
1969   Problems of homology in geology and related
        fields. Classification Society Bulletin
        2.1:5-11. Leicester, England.

Solenberger, Robert R.
1953   Recent changes in Chamorro direction termi-
        nology. Oceania 24.2:132-141. Sydney.

Sølver, C. V.
1957   Eskimo maps from Greenland. Archaeology
        10.4:188-190. Cincinnati.

Sommer, Robert
1969   Personal space: the behavioral basis of
        design. 177 pp. Englewood Cliffs, N. J.:
        Prentice-Hall.

Sorokin, Pitirim A.
1943   Sociocultural causality, space, time. ix,
        246 pp. Durham: Duke University Press.

Sorokin, Pitirim A. and Robert K. Merton
1937   Social time. American Journal of Sociology
        42.5:615-629. Chicago.

Soustelle, Jacques
1939   La Pensée cosmologique des anciens Mexi-
        cains. 95 pp. Paris: Hermann.

Spence, Lewis
1912   Les Systèmes des calendriers des tribus
        indiennes de l'Amérique. Revue Scientifique,
        1912(2).14:424-428. Paris.

Spencer, Baldwin and Francis James Gillin
1899   The native tribes of Central Australia.
        671 pp. London: Macmillan.

Spinden, Herbert Joseph
1924   The reduction of Mayan dates. (Papers of
        the Peabody Museum of American Archaeology
        and Ethnology, Harvard University, 6.4.)
        xiii, 286 pp. Cambridge.

1930   Maya dates and what they reveal. 111 pp.
        Brooklyn: Museum of the Brooklyn Institute
        of Arts and Sciences.

1948   Mexican calendars and the solar year. Pp.
        393-405 in Annual Report of the Smithsonian
        Institution. Washington.

Spiro, Melford E., editor
1965   Context and meaning in cultural anthropology.
        xxii, 442 pp. New York: Free Press; London:
        Collier-Macmillan.

Spoehr, Alexander
1949   Majuro: a village in the Marshall Islands.
(Fieldiana: Anthropology, Vol. 39.)   266 pp.
Chicago: Chicago Natural History Museum.

Sprenger, A.
1859   Ueber den Kalender der Araber vor Mohammed.
Zeitschrift der Deutschen Morgenländischen
Gesellschaft 13:134-175.   Leipzig.

Springer, Max
1927   Mensch, Zeit, Uhr: zur Geschichte der
Zeitmessung.   150 pp.   Berlin: Ullstein.

Stefánsson, Vihljlámur
1914   The Stefánsson-Anderson Arctic Expedition
of the American Museum; preliminary ethnological report.   Anthropological Papers of
the American Museum of Natural History 14.1:
1-395, corrections and comments, pp. 445-
457.   New York.

Stewart, George R.
1943   What is named?--towns, islands, mountains,
rivers, capes.   University of California
Publications in English 14:223-232.
Berkeley.

1954   A classification of place names.   Names 2.1:
1-13.   Youngstown, Ohio.

1962   Leah, woods, and deforestation as an influence on place-names.   Names 10.1:11-20.
Youngstown, Ohio.

Stewart, Omer C.
1943   Notes on Pomo ethnogeography.   University
of California Publications in American
Archaeology and Ethnology 40.2:29-62.
Berkeley.

1954   The forgotten side of ethnogeography.   Pp.
221-248 in Methods and perspectives in
anthropology, papers in honor of Wilson D.
Wallis, edited by R. F. Spencer.   Minneapo-
lis: University of Minnesota Press.

Stimson, J. Frank
1928   Tahitian names for the nights of the moon.
Journal of the Polynesian Society 37.3:326-
337.   New Plymouth, N. Z.

Størmor, Lief
1966   Concepts of stratigraphical classification
         and terminology. Earth-Science Reviews
         1.5:5-28. Amsterdam.

Strathern, Andrew
1970   Wiru penthonyms. Bijdragen tot de Taal-,
         Land- en Volkenkunde 12.1:59-74.
         's-Gravenhage.

Strehlow, Carl
1907-   Die Aranda und Loritja-stämme in Zentral-
1920   Australien. 5 vols. Frankfurt am Main:
         J. Baer.

Stuchlik, Milan
1970   Categorías de terrenos entre los Batakos de
         Sumatra Central, un problema taxonómico.
         Rehue 3:27-37. Concepcion, Chile.

Swainson, Charles
1873   A handbook of weather folk-lore. x, 275 pp.
         London: W. Blackwood.

Swellengrebel, J. L.
1951   Further translation questions on Bali. The
         Bible Translator 2:25-30. London.

Szaley, Loránd
1962   Untersuchungen zur semantischen Struktur
         der Zeitwörter. Zeitschrift für Experimen-
         telle und Angewandte Psychologie 9.1:140-
         163. Göttingen.

Tallqvist, Knut
1928   Himmelsgegenden und Winde; eine semasiolo-
         gische Studie. Societas Orientalis Fennica,
         Studia Orientalia 2:105-185. Helsinki.

Tantaquidgeon, Gladys
1928   Mohegan medicinal practices, weatherlore,
         and superstitions. Pp. 264-275 in Native
         tribes and dialects of Connecticut, (Annual
         Reports of the Bureau of American Ethnology
         43), edited by F. G. Speck. Washington.

Taylor, Douglas
1946   Notes on the star-lore of the Caribbees.
         American Anthropologist 48.2:215-222.
         Menasha.

Ten Raa, Eric
1969   The moon as a symbol of life and fertility

in Sandawe thought. Africa 39.1:24-53.
London.

Thái-Van-Kiem
1962   Interprétation d'une carte ancienne de
        Saigon. Bulletin de la Société des Études
        Indo-Chinoises de Saigon (n.s.)37.4:407-431.
        Saigon.

Thilenius, Georg
1905   Die Bedeutung der Meeresströmungen für die
        Besiedelung-Melanesiens. Jahrbuch der
        Hamburgischen Wissenschaftlichen Austalten
        23.5. Hamburg. (Also, 1906, Mitteilungen
        aus dem Museum für Völkerkunde 1:1-21.
        Hamburg.)

Thomas, Cyrus
1882   Notes on certain Maya and Mexican manuscripts.
        Annual Reports of the Bureau of American
        Ethnology 3:3-65. Washington.

1894   The Maya Year. (Bulletins of the Bureau of
        American Ethnology, No. 18.) 64 pp.
        Washington.

1894-   Day symbols of the Maya Year. Annual Re-
1895   ports of the Bureau of American Ethnology
        16:199-265. Washington.

1900   Numeral systems of Mexico and Central
        America. Annual Reports of the Bureau of
        American Ethnology 19(Part 2). Washington.

1900-   Mayan calendar systems. Annual Reports of
1904   the Bureau of American Ethnology 22.1:203-
        305 (1901-1902); 26:197-305 (1904).
        Washington.

Thomas, Northcote W.
1920   The Edo week. Man 20.10:152-153(Art. 73).
        London.

1924   The week in west Africa. Journal of the
        Royal Anthropological Institute 54:183-210.
        London.

Thompson, J. Eric S.
1925   The meaning of the Mayan months. Man 25.8:
        121-123(Art. 71). London.

1928   Some new dates from Pusilha. Man 28.6:95-
        97(Art. 70). London.

1934a   Sky bearers, colors, and directions in Maya and Mexican religion. Carnegie Institution of Washington, Contributions to American Archaeology 2.10:209-242. Washington.

1934b   Maya chronology: the fifteen Tun Glyph. Carnegie Institution of Washington, Contributions to American Archaeology 2.11:243-254. Washington.

1941   Maya arithmetic. Carnegie Institution of Washington, Contributions to American Anthropology and History 36:37-62. Washington.

1944   The fish as a Maya symbol for counting and further discussion of the direction glyphs. (Carnegie Institution of Washington, Division Historical Research, Theoretical Approaches to Problems, No. 2.) Cambridge, Mass.

1950   Maya hieroglyphic writing: introduction. (Carnegie Institution of Washington, Publication 589.) xvi, 347 pp. Washington.

1962   A catalog of Maya hieroglyphs. xiv, 458 pp. Norman: University of Oklahoma Press.

Timmermans, Jean et al.
1963   La Classification dans les sciences. 236 pp. Gembloux: J. Duculot.

Tozzer, Alfred M.
1908   A note on star-lore among the Navajos. Journal of American Folklore 21:28-32. Boston.

Tozzer, Alfred M., translator and annotator
1941   Landa's Relación de las cosas de Yucatan. (Papers of the Peabody Museum of American Archaeology and Ethnology, Harvard University, Vol. 18.) xiii, 394 pp. Cambridge.

Trager, George L.
1939   Days of the week in the language of Taos Pueblo, New Mexico. Language 15.1:51-55. Baltimore.

1967   A componential morphemic analysis of English personal pronouns. Language 43.1:372-378. Baltimore.

Trager, George L. and Felicia Harben Trager
1970   The cardinal directions at Taos and Picuris.
        Anthropological Linguistics 12.2:31-37.
        Bloomington, Ind.

Trowbridge, C. C.
1913   On fundamental methods of orientation and
        "imaginary maps." Science 38.990:888-897.
        Washington.

Troyer, Lester O.
1966-   Linguistics as a window into man's mind:
1967   Gaddang time segmentation. Pp. 109-118 in
        Anthropology for non-anthropologists,
        (General Education Journal, No. 12), edited
        by M. D. Zamora and R. Lawless. Quezon
        City: University of the Philippines.

U. S. Department of Agriculture, Westher Bureau
            Committee on Clouds and Cloud Forms
1938   Cloud forms, according to the international
        system of classification. 3d edition.
        8 pp., 32 figs. Washington: Government
        Printing Office.

U. S. Geographic Board
1967   Sixth report of the United States Geographic
(1933) Board, 1890 to 1932. ix, 834 pp. Detroit:
        Gale Research Co. (1933, Washington:
        Government Printing Office.)

Vaillant, George Clapp
1940   A sacred almanac of the Aztecs, Tonalamatl
        of the Codex Borbonicus. New York: American
        Museum of Natural History.

Vest, Eugene B.
1968   Names on the ocean bottom, or some observa-
        tions on the invisible landscape. Names
        16.2:79-88. Potsdam, N. Y.

Vilkuna, Kustaa
1957-   Zur ältesten Geschichte der Woche. Folk-Liv
1958   21-22:197-215. Stockholm.

Villiers, Alan John
1940   Sons of Sinbad. xv, 429 pp. New York:
        Scribner.

Wallace, Anthony F. C.
1965   Driving to work. Pp. 277-292 in Context
        and meaning in cultural anthropology, edited

by M. E. Spiro. New York: Free Press;
London: Collier-Macmillan.

Waller, G. F.
1971   Transition in Renaissance ideas of time and
place of Giordano Bruno. Neophilologus
55.1:3-15. Groningen.

Wallman, Sandra
1965   The communication of measurement in Basuto-
land. Human Organization 24.3:236-243.
Ithaca.

Wang, Teh-Ming
1959   A study on astronomy: the magnet theory of
cosmoses. Note from W. W. Watson. xiii,
76 pp. Manila: published by the author.

Waterman, T. T.
1916   The delineation of the day-signs in the
Aztec manuscripts. University of California
Publications in American Archaeology and
Ethnology 11.6:297-398. Berkeley.

1920   Yurok geography. University of California
Publications in American Archaeology and
Ethnology 16.5:177-314. Berkeley.

1922   The geographical names used by the Indians
of the Pacific coast. Geographical Review
12.2:175-194. New York.

Watson, O. Michael
1969   On proxemic research. Current Anthropology
10.2-3:222-224; including reply by Edward
T. Hall. Glasgow.

Watson, Richard A. and Patty Jo Watson
1969   Man and nature: an anthropological essay in
human ecology. xii, 172 pp. New York:
Harcourt, Brace and World.

Webster, Hutton
1916   Rest days; a sociological study. Nebraska
University Studies 11.1-2:1-158. Lincoln.

Wedel, Waldo R.
1967   The council circles of central Kansas: were
they solstice registers? American Antiquity
32.1:54-63. Salt Lake City.

Weill, Raymond
1926   Bases, méthodes et résultats de la

chronologie égyptienne. 216 pp. Paris: Geuthner.

Werner, Helmut
1952   Klassische Sternbilder am Himmel der Tschuktschen. Zeitschrift für Ethnologie 77.1:139-141. Braunschweig.

West, Robert C.
1954   The term "Bayou" in the United States: a study in the geography of place names. Annals of Association of American Geographers 44.1:63-74. Lancaster, Pa.

White, Taylor
1907   On the use of birds in navigation. Journal of the Polynesian Society 16.62:92-93. New Plymouth, N. Z.

Whitrow, Gerald James
1961   The natural philosophy of time. xi, 324 pp. New York: Harper and Row.

Whorf, Benjamin Lee
1950   An American Indian model of the universe. International Journal of American Linguistics 16.2:67-72. Baltimore.

Williams, H. W.
1928   The nights of the moon. Journal of the Polynesian Society 37.3:338-356. New Plymouth, N. Z.

Willson, Robert W.
1924   Astronomical notes on the Maya codices. (Papers of the Peabody Museum of American Archaeology and Ethnology, Harvard University, 6.3.) 46 pp. Cambridge.

Wilson, Philip Whitwell
1937   The romance of the calendar. viii, 351 pp. New York: Norton.

Winkler, Captain
1901   On sea charts formerly used in the Marshall
(1898) Islands, with notices on the navigation of these islanders in general. Translation, pp. 487-508 in Smithsonian Institution Annual Report for 1899. (Original publication 1898, Marine-Rundschau 10:1418-1439. Berlin.)

Winkler, S. Johannes
1913   Der Kalender der Toba-Bataks auf Sumatra.
        Zeitschrift für Ethnologie 45:435-447.
        Berlin.

1925   Die Toba-Batak auf Sumatra in gesunden und
        kranken Tagen. 234 pp. Stuttgart: Belfer.

Witherspoon, Gary J.
1971   Navajo categories of objects at rest.
        American Anthropologist 73.1:110-127.
        Menasha.

Witkin, H. A.
1949   Orientation in space. Research Reviews,
        Office of Naval Research, (December).
        Washington.

Wolfers, Edward P.
1971   The original counting systems of Papua and
        New Guinea. The Arithmetic Teacher (1971):
        77-83.

Wonderly, William L.
1952   Semantic components in Kechua person
        morphemes. Language 28.3:366-376.
        Baltimore.

Wurm, S. A.
1960   The question of aboriginal place names.
        Cartography 3.3:134-139. Melbourne.

Wylie, Laurence
1965   The life and death of a myth. Pp. 164-185
        in Context and meaning in cultural anthro-
        pology, edited by M. E. Spiro. New York:
        Free Press; London: Collier-Macmillan.

Yung, Emile
1918   Le Sens de la direction. Echo des Alpes
        4:110-143. Geneva.

Zimmermann, Günter
1935   Einige Erleichterungen beim Berechnen von
        Maya-Daten. Anthropos 30.5-6:707-715.
        Vienna.

1956   Die Hieroglyphen der Maya-Handschriften.
        174 pp. Hamburg: Cram.

Zinner, Ernst
1931   Die Geschichte der Sternkunde von den

[7:60]

ersten Anfängen bis zur Gegenwart.   673 pp.
Berlin: Springer.

Zinsli, Paul
1945   Grund und Grat, die Bergwelt im Spiegel der
schweitzerdeutschen Alpenmundarten.   352 pp.
Bern: A. Francke.

Zuidema, R. T.
1962   The relationship between mountains and coast
in ancient Peru. Mededelingen van het Rijks-
museum voor Volkenkunde, Leiden, 15:156-165.
Leiden.

Zupko, Ronald Edward
1968   A dictionary of English weights and measures;
from Anglo-Saxon times to the nineteenth
century. xvi, 224 pp. Madison: University
of Wisconsin Press.

Zusne, Leonard
1971   Visual perception of form. xii, 548 pp.
New York: Academic Press.

8. Color

[Including references to varying systems of
color categorization, comparative studies,
and pertinent technical research on color in
psychophysics, colorimetry, etc.]

Albers, Josef
    1963   Interaction of color. Text (vol.), 80 pp.;
            Commentary (vol.), 48 pp; Folders IV-XXV.
            New Haven and London: Yale University Press.
            (Text of the original edition with selected
            plates republished 1971. xiv, 74 pp. New
            Haven and London: Yale University Press.)

Allen, Grant
    1879   The colour-sense: its origin and develop-
            ment. xii, 282 pp. Boston: Houghton;
            London: Trübner. (Reprinted 1892 as
            "second edition," London: Kegan Paul,
            Trench, and Trübner.)

Anderson, Johannes
    1942   Maori place-names, also personal names and
            names of colours, weapons and natural objects.
            (Polynesian Society, Memoir 20.) xi, 494 pp.
            Wellington.

André, Jacques
    1949   Étude sur les termes de couleur dans la
            langue latine. 427 pp. Paris: C. Klinck-
            sieck.

Andree, H.
    1878   Ueber den Farbensinn der Naturvölker.
            Zeitschrift für Ethnologie 10:323-334.
            Berlin.

Arber, Agnes
    1940   The colouring of 16th century herbals.
            Nature 154:803-804. London.

Ardener, Edwin
    1971   Introductory essay: social anthropology and
            language. Pp. ix-ci in Social anthropology
            and language, (Association of Social Anthro-
            pologists Monographs, 10), edited by E.
            Ardener. London: Tavistock.

Aristotle (See Hett 1936, Lovejoy and Forster 1913,
            Prantl 1881, and Webster 1931.)

Arnheim, Rudolf
  1969   Art and visual perception; a psychology of
          the creative eye. xi, 485 pp. Berkeley:
          University of California Press.

Arnold, Dean Edward
  1967   Sak lu'um in Maya culture: and its possible
          relation to Maya blue. (University of
          Illinois Department of Anthropology Research
          Reports 2.) 53 pp. Urbana.

Balaraman, Shakuntala
  1962   Color vision research and the trichromatic
          theory: a historical review. Psychological
          Bulletin 59.5:434-448. Menasha.

Bartholomaeus Anglicus
  1582   De coloribus. Numbered lvs. 387-396 (First
  (c.1250) part of Book 19) in Batman vppon Bartholome,
          his book De proprietatibus rerum... London:
          Thomas East. (1398 John de Trevisa English
          translation, enlarged and amended by Stephan
          Batman.)

  1601   De rerum accidentibus, in quo de coloribus,
  (c.1250) odoribus, saporibus et liquoribus agitur.
          Pp. 1133-1161 in De rerum proprietatibus
          (Medieval Latin encyclopedia by Bartholemew
          the Englishman). Frankfurt: Wolfgang
          Richter. (Facsimile reprint, Frankfurt:
          Minerva, G.M.B.H, 1964.)

Bartleson, C. J.
  1960   Memory colors of familiar objects. Journal
          of the Optical Society of America 50.1:73-
          77. Lancaster, Pa.

Bartlett, F. C.
  1937   Psychological methods and anthropological
          problems. Africa 10.4:401-419. London.

Bartlett, Harley Harris
  1929   Color nomenclature in Batak and Malay.
          Papers of the Michigan Academy of Science,
          Arts, and Letters 10:1-52. Ann Arbor.

Battig, William F. and William E. Montague
  1969   Category norms for verbal items in 56
          categories: a replication and extension
          of the Connecticut category norms. Journal
          of Experimental Psychology Monograph 80.3
          (Part 2):1-46. Lancaster, Pa.

Beaglehole, Ernest
1939   Tongan colour-vision. Man 39:170-172.
        London.

Beaglehole, Ernest and Pearl Beaglehole
1938   Ethnology of Pukapuka. (Bulletins of the
        Bernice P. Bishop Museum, No. 150.) 419 pp.
        Honolulu.

Beare, Aleeza Cerf
1963   Color-name as a function of wave-length.
        American Journal of Psychology 76.2:248-256.
        Austin.

1968   Colour names as response criteria.
        Ergonomics 11.6:565-575. London.

Beare, Aleeza C. and Michael H. Siegal
1967   Color name as a function of wavelength and
        instruction. Perception and Psychophysics
        2.11:521-527. Goleta, Calif.

Beck, Brenda E. F.
1969   Colour and heat in South Indian ritual.
        Man (n.s.)4.4:553-572. London.

Bello, Francis
1959   Astonishing new theory of color. Fortune
        59(May):144-148. Jersey City.

Berlin, Brent
1970   A universalist-evolutionary approach in
        ethnographic semantics. Bulletins of the
        American Anthropological Association 3.3
        (Part 2):3-18. Washington.

Berlin, Brent and Paul Kay
1969   Basic color terms: their universality and
        evolution. xi, 178 pp. Berkeley and Los
        Angeles: University of California Press.

Berlin, Heinrich and David H. Kelley
1961   The 819-day count and color-direction
        symbolism among the Classic Maya. Pp. 9-20
        in Tulane University, Middle American
        Research Institute, No. 26. New Orleans.

Bernardo, Angelo G.
1967-   Matigsalug color categories. Anthropology
1968   Bulletin 3.1:11-13. Diliman, Quezon City,
        Philippines.

Best, Elsdon
1905   Notes on the colour-sense of the Maori.
        Pp. 637-642 in New Zealand Official Yearbook,
        1905. Wellington.

Billmeyer, Fred W., Jr. and Max Saltzman
1966   Principles of color technology. x, 181 pp.
        New York: John Wiley.

Birren, Faber
1937   Functional color. 124 pp. New York:
        Crimson Press.

1966   Color in your world. 121 pp. New York:
        Collier Books; London: Collier-Macmillan.

1969a   Light, color and environment. 131 pp. New
        York: Van Nostrand Reinhold.

1969b   (See Ostwald 1969.)

Bohannan, Paul
1963   Social anthropology. 421 pp. New York:
        Holt, Rinehart and Winston.

Boring, Edwin G.
1942   Sensation and perception in the history of
        experimental psychology. xv, 644 pp. New
        York: Appleton-Century-Crofts.

Bourma, Pieter Johannes
1946   Kleuren en kleurindrukken. 320 pp. Amster-
        dam: Meulenhoff. (Translated 1948 as
        Physical aspects of colour. 312 pp.
        Eindhoven: Philips Gloeilampenfabricken;
        also translated 1948 as Les Couleurs et leur
        perception visuelle. 348 pp. Eindhoven:
        Philips Gloeilampenfabricken.)

Bouman, M. A. and P. L. Walraven
1957   Some color naming experiments for red and
        green monochromatic lights. Journal of the
        Optical Society of America 47.9:834-839.
        Lancaster, Pa.

Boyle, Robert
1664   Experiments and considerations touching
        colours....as the beginning of an experimen-
        tal history of colours. [40], 423 pp.
        London: Printed for Henry Herringham.

Boynton, Robert M.
1971   Color vision. Pp. 315-368 in Woodworth and

Schlosberg's Experimental psychology, 3d
edition, edited by J. W. Kling and L. A.
Riggs. New York: Holt, Rinehart and Winston.

Boynton, Robert M. and James Gordon
1965   Bezold-Brucke hue shift measured by a color-
        naming technique. Journal of the Optical
        Society of America 55.1:78-86. Lancaster, Pa.

Boynton, Robert M., William Schafer and Mary Ellen Nuen
1964   Hue-wavelength relation measured by color
        naming method for three retinal locations.
        Science 146.3644:666-668. Washington.

Bradley, Morton C., Jr.
1938   Systems of color classification. Technical
        Studies in the Field of Fine Arts 6.4:240-
        275. Lancaster, Pa.

British Colour Council
1938-   Horticultural colour chart. 2 vols. 800
1942   color samples. London.

Broadbent, Donald Eric
1958   Perception and communication. 338 pp.
        London: Pergamon.

Bromley, Myron
1967   The linguistic relationships of Grand River
        Dani: a lexicostatistical classification.
        Oceania 37.4:286-308. Sydney.

Brown, Roger W.
1965   The semantic system; language, thought, and
        society. Pp. 306-349 (Chapter 7) in Social
        psychology, by R. W. Brown. New York: Free
        Press; London: Collier-Macmillan.

Brown, Roger W. and Eric H. Lenneberg
1954   A study in language and cognition. Journal
        of Abnormal and Social Psychology 49.3:454-
        462. Baltimore.

1966   Studies in linguistic relativity. Pp. 244-
        252 in Basic studies in social psychology,
        edited by H. Proshansky and B. Seidenberg.
        New York: Holt, Rinehart and Winston.

Bühler, Alfred
1962   The significance of colour among primitive
        peoples. Palette 9:2-8. Basel.

[8:6]

Bulmer, R. N. H.
1968   Karam colour categories.   Kivung 1.3:119-134.
        Boroko, T.P.N.G.

Burling, Robbins
1970   Man's many voices: language in its cultural
        context. xi, 222 pp. New York: Holt,
        Rinehart and Winston.

Burnham, Robert W. and Joyce R. Clark
1955   A test of hue memory. Journal of Applied
        Psychology 39.3:164-172. Lancaster, Pa.

Caprile, Jean-Pierre
1971   La Dénomination des "couleurs": méthode
        d'enquête, avec application à une langue
        du Tchad, le Mbay de Moïssala. Pp. 1-22
        in Méthodes d'enquête et de description des
        langues sans tradition écrite (colloques
        internationaux des C.N.R.S.). Nice.

[Carpenter, Edmund]
1955   Colour and communication. Explorations 5:
        97-102. Toronto.

Carpenter, Henry Barrett
1933   Colour, a manual of its theory and practice.
        86 pp. New York: Scribner.

Carroll, John B.
1964   Words, meanings, and concepts. Harvard
        Educational Review 34:178-202. Cambridge.

Chapanis, Alphonse
1965   Color names for color space. American
        Scientist 53.3:327-346. New Haven.
        (Reprinted 1967, pp. 105-132 in Science in
        progress, 16th Series, edited by W. R.
        Brode. New Haven: Yale University Press.)

1968   Vision III: Color vision and color blindness.
        International Encyclopedia of the Social
        Sciences 16:329-336. New York: Macmillan
        and Free Press.

Chiri, M.
1953   Bunrui Ainu-go jiten-daiikkan shokubutsu-
        hen (Dictionary of Ainu. Vol. 1, Plants).
        Tokyo: Nihon Jômin Bunka Kenkyûsho.

Clark, W. E. LeGros
1947   Anatomical pattern as the essential basis

for sensory discrimination. (Robert Boyle
Lecture, No. 49.) 16 pp. Oxford: Basel
Blackwell.

Clements, Forrest
1930   Racial differences in color blindness.
        American Journal of Physical Anthropology
        14.3:417-432. Philadelphia.

Colenso, W.
1882   On the fine perception of colours possessed
        by the ancient Maoris. Transactions of the
        New Zealand Institute 14:49-76. Wellington.

Collier, George Allen
1966   Categorías del color en Zinacantan. Pp. 414-
        432 in Los Zinancantecos, edited by E. Z.
        Vogt. Mexico City: Instituto Nacional
        Indigenista.

Conklin, Harold C.
1955   Hanunóo color categories. Southwestern
        Journal of Anthropology 11.4:339-344.
        Albuquerque. (Reprinted 1963 as Bobbs-
        Merrill Reprint Series in Social Sciences,
        No. A-42, Indianapolis; reprinted 1964,
        pp. 189-192 in Language in culture and
        society, edited by D. H. Hymes, New York:
        Harper and Row.)

Corso, John F.
1967   The experimental psychology of sensory
        behavior. xii, 628 pp. New York: Holt,
        Rinehart and Winston.

Cuervo Marquez, Carlos
1924   La percepción de los colores en algunas
        tribus indígenas de Colombia. Twentieth
        International Congress of Americanists
        Proceedings 1:49-51. Rio de Janiero.

Cuisenaire, Georges and Caleb Gattegno
1957   Numbers in colour, a new method of teaching
(1954) arithmetic in primary schools. 3d edition.
        xi, 63 pp. London: Wilheim Heinemann.

1960   Initiation à la méthode: les nombres en
        couleurs. Revised and augmented edition.
        98 pp. Neuchâtel, Switz.: Delachaux.

Dale, Philip S.
1969   Color naming, matching, and recognition by

preschoolers. Child Development 40.4:1135-1144. Chicago.

Davies, Peter
1971   New views of lexicon. Pp. xli-liv in The American Heritage word frequency book, by J. B. Carroll, P. Davies and B. Richman. Boston: Houghton Mifflin; New York: American Heritage.

Davson, Hugh
1962   The eye. 4 vols. New York: Academic Press.

De Reuck, Anthony V. S. and Julie Knight, editors
1965   Colour vision: physiology and experimental psychology; Ciba Foundation symposium. xiii, 382 pp. Boston: Little, Brown.

DeValois, Russell L. and Israel Abramov
1966   Color vision. Annual Review of Psychology 17:337-362. Palo Alto.

DeValois, Russell L., Israel Abramov, and Gerald H. Jacobs
1966   Analysis of response patterns of LGN cells. Journal of the Optical Society of America 56.7:966-977. Lancaster, Pa.

Dimmick, Forrest Lee
1938   Color nomenclature and specification. Psychological Bulletin 35.8:473-486. Columbus, Ohio.

1939   Spectral components of psychologically unique red. American Journal of Psychology 52.3:348-353. Ithaca.

Dimmick, Forrest Lee and Margaret R. Hubbard
1939   The spectral location of psychologically unique yellow, green, and blue. American Journal of Psychology 52.2:242-254. Ithaca.

Ditchburn, Robert William
1965   Light. 2d edition. xxvi, 833 pp. New York: Interscience.

Dixon, R. M. W.
1970   Where have all the adjectives gone? An essay in universal semantics. 53 pp. London.

Dixon, Roland B.
    1899   The color-symbolism of the cardinal points.
            Journal of American Folk-lore 12:10-16.
            Philadelphia.

Doob, Leonard W.
    1960   The effect of codability upon the afferent
            and efferent functioning of language.
            Journal of Social Psychology 52.1:3-15.
            Provincetown, Mass.

Ekman, Gösta
    1954   Dimensions of color vision. Journal of
            Psychology 38:467-474. Provincetown, Mass.

Ellis, Havelock
    1900   The psychology of red. Popular Science
            Monthly 57.4(340):365-375; 57.5(341):517-
            526. New York.

    1906   The psychology of yellow. Popular Science
            Monthly 68.5(409):456-463. New York.

Ellis, Willis Davis
    1967   A source book of Gestalt psychology. With
    (1938) an introduction by K. Koffka. 403 pp.
            London: Routledge; New York: Humanities
            Press.

Ervin, Susan M.
    1961   Semantic shift in bilingualism. American
            Journal of Psychology   74.2:233-241.
            Austin.

Evans, Ralph M.
    1948   Introduction to color. x, 340 pp. New
            York: John Wiley.

Fairlee, Susan
    1965   Dyestuffs in the eighteenth century.
            Economic History Review, Second Series
            17.3:488-510. Utrecht.

Farnsworth, Dana L.
    1949   The Farnsworth-Munsell 100 hue test for the
            examination of color discrimination:
            manual. Baltimore: Munsell Color Co.

Fillenbaum, Samuel and Amnon Rapoport
    1971   Structures in the subjective lexicon. viii,
            266 pp. New York and London: Academic
            Press.

Fisher, S. Caroline, Chester Hull, and Paul Holtz
1956   Past experience and perception: memory
        color. American Journal of Psychology
        69.4:546-560. Austin.

Forge, Anthony
1970   Learning to see in New Guinea. Pp. 269-291
        in Socialization, the approach from social
        anthropology, (Association of Social Anthro-
        pologists Monographs, 8), edited by P. Mayer.
        London: Tavistock.

Franciscan Fathers
1910   An ethnologic dictionary of the Navaho
        language. 536 pp. Saint Michaels, Ariz.

French, David H.
1963   The relationship of anthropology to studies
        in perception and cognition. Pp. 388-428
        in Vol. 6 of Psychology: a study of a
        science, edited by S. Koch. New York:
        McGraw-Hill.

Frieling, H.
1960   Psychologie der Farben. Studium Generale
        13.7:435-446. Berlin.

1962   Color experience and color occurrence in
        chronological order. Palette 10:3-8. Basel.

Fries, Charles C.
1947   Teaching and learning English as a foreign
        language. (Publications of the English
        Language Institute, University of Michigan,
        No. 1.) xii, 153 pp. Ann Arbor.

Frisch, Karl von
1950   Bees: their vision, chemical senses, and
        language. xiii, 119 pp. Ithaca: Cornell
        University Press.

Fuchs, Wilhelm
1967   The influence of form on the assimilation of
(1938) colours. Pp. 95-103 in A source book of
        Gestalt psychology, by W. D. Ellis. London:
        Routledge; New York: Humanities Press.

Gartrell, Richard B.
1971   Review of Basic color terms: their univer-
        sality and evolution, by Brent Berlin and
        Paul Kay. Journal of Communication 21.2:
        190-191. Lawrence, Kans.

Gatschet, Albert S.
  1879a   Adjectives of color in Indian languages.
          American Naturalist 13:475-485. Philadelphia.

  1879b   Farbenbenennungen in nordamerikanischen
          Sprachen. Zeitschrift für Ethnologie 11:293-
          302. Berlin.

Geddes, William R.
  1946   The colour sense of Fijian natives. British
          Journal of Psychology 37.1:30-36. London.

Geer, J. P. van de
  1960   Studies in codability I. Identification and
          recognition of colors. Paper E 001-60,
          pp. 1-8. Leiden: Psychological Institute,
          University of Leiden.

Geiger, Lazarus
  1871   Zur Entwickelungsgeschichte der Menschheit.
          2d German edition. Stuttgart. (Translated
          1880 by David Ascher as Contributions to
          the history of the development of the human
          race. xiii, 156 pp. London: Trübner.)

  1872   Ursprung und Entwickelung der menschlichen
          Sprache und Vernuft. 2 vols. Stuttgart:
          J. G. Cotta.

Gelb, Adhémar
  1967   Colour constancy. Pp. 196-209 in A source
  (1938) book of Gestalt psychology, by W. D. Ellis.
          London: Routledge; New York: Humanities
          Press.

Gibson, Eleanor Jack
  1968   Principles of perceptual learning and de-
          velopment. viii, 537 pp. New York:
          Appleton-Century-Crofts.

Gibson, James Jerome
  1950   The perception of the visual world.
          Cambridge, Mass.: Riverside Press.

  1966   The senses considered as perceptual systems.
          xiv, 335 pp. Boston: Houghton Mifflin.

Gifford, Edward S.
  1958   The evil eye: studies in the folklore of
          vision. 216 pp. New York: Macmillan.

Gipper, Helmut
  1964   Purpur. Glotta 42.1-2:39-69. Göttingen.

[8:12]

Gladstone, William Ewart
1858   Homer's perceptions and use of colour. Pp.
        457-499 in Vol. 3 of Studies on Homer and
        the Homeric age, by W. E. Gladstone. Oxford:
        Oxford University Press.

Gleason, Henry A., Jr.
1961   An introduction to descriptive linguistics.
        Revised edition. 503 pp. New York: Holt.

Glenn, James J. and James T. Killian
1940   Trichromatic analysis of the Munsell book
        of color. Journal of the Optical Society of
        America 30.12:609-616. Lancaster, Pa.

Goeje, C. H. de
1928   The Arawak language of Guiana. Verhande-
        lingen der Koninklijke Akademie van Weten-
        schappen te Amsterdam, Afdeeling Letterkunde,
        Nieuwe Reeks 28.2:1-309. Amsterdam.

Godlove, I. H., compiler
1957   Bibliography on color, from the Inter-
        Society Color Council News Letter, 1936-1954.
        Arranged by Margaret N. Godlove. vi, 357 pp.
        Cleveland, Ohio: Inter-Society Color Council.

Goethe, Johann Wolfgang von
1810   Zur Farbenlehre. 2 vols. and atlas. Vol. 1:
        5 p. l., [ix]-xlviii, 654 pp.; vol. 2:
        xxviii, 757, [I] pp.; atlas: 24 pp., xvi
        plates. Tübingen: J. G. Cotta'sche Buch-
        handlung.

Goodenough, Florence L.
1947   Psychology and anthropology: some problems
        of joint import for the two fields. South-
        western Journal of Anthropology 3.1:5-14.
        Albuquerque.

Goodman, John Stuart
1963   Malayalam color categories. Anthropological
        Linguistics 5.4:1-12. Bloomington, Ind.

Göthlin, Gustav F.
1944   Experimental determination of the short wave
        fundamental color in man's color sense.
        Journal of the Optical Society of America
        34.3:147-158. Lancaster, Pa.

Graham, Clarence Henry
1958   Sensation and perception in an objective

psychology. Psychological Review 65.2:65-76. Lancaster, Pa.

1959   Color theory. Pp. 145-287 in Vol. 1 of Psychology, a study of a science, edited by S. Koch. New York: McGraw-Hill.

Graham, Clarence Henry, editor
1965   Vision and visual perception. vii, 637 pp. New York: John Wiley.

Granit, Ragnar
1955   Receptors and sensory perception. 369 pp. New Haven: Yale University Press.

Gudschinsky, Sarah Caroline
1967   How to learn an unwritten language. 64 pp. New York: Holt, Rinehart and Winston.

Halliday, David and Robert Resnick
1966   Physics. xxvi, 1214, 110 pp. New York: John Wiley.

Hallowell, A. Irving.
1954   Cultural factors in the structuralization of perception. Pp. 164-195 in Social psychology at the crossroads, edited by J. H. Rohrer and M. Sherif. New York: Harper.

Halsey, Rita M. and Alphonse Chapanis
1951   On the number of absolutely identifiable spectral hues. Journal of the Optical Society of America 41.12:1057-1058. Lancaster, Pa.

Hamly, D. H.
1949   The Ridgway color standards with a Munsell notation key. Journal of the Optical Society of America 39.7:592-599. Lancaster, Pa.

Hamp, Eric P.
1971   Some colour words in -no-. International Journal of Slavic Linguistics and Poetics 14.1:1-4. The Hague.

Hardy, Arthur Cobb
1936   Handbook of colorimetry. 87 pp. Cambridge: MIT Press. (Reprinted 1948.)

Helm, Carl E. and Ledyard R. Tucker
1962   Individual differences in the structure of

color-perception. American Journal of Psychology 75.3:437-444. Austin.

Helmholtz, Hermann Ludwig Ferdinand von
1866   Handbuch der physiologischen Optik. xiv, 874 pp. Leipzig: L. Voss. (2d edition of 1896 retains all color vision contributions; 1911 edition does not.)

Henneman, Richard H.
1935   Photometric study of the perception of object color. 88 pp. New York: Columbia University Library.

Hering, Ewald
1878   Zur Lehre vom Lichtsinne. 141 pp. Vienna: C. Gerold's Sohn.

1964   Outline of a theory of light sense. Translated by Leo M. Hurvich and Dorothea Jameson. xxvii, 317 pp. Cambridge: Harvard University Press. (Original publication in German, 1920.)

Herne, Gunnar
1954   Die slawischen Farbenbennungen, eine semasiologischetymologische Untersuchung. (Publications de l'Institut Slave, No. 9.) 147 pp. Uppsala, Sweden.

Herskovits, Melville J.
1948   Man and his works: the science of cultural anthropology. xviii, 678 pp. New York: Alfred A. Knopf.

Hess, Eckhard H.
1965   Attitude and pupil size. Scientific American 212.4:46-54. New York.

Hett, W. S., translator
1936   On colours (de coloribus). Pp. 1-45 in Aristotle, minor works, on colors..., translated by W. S. Hett. (Loeb Classical Library.) London: William Heineman; Cambridge: Harvard University Press.

Hickerson, Nancy P.
1953   Ethnolinguistic notes from lexicons of Lokono (Arawak). International Journal of American Linguistics 19.3:181-190. Baltimore.

1971 Review of Basic color terms: their universality and evolution, by Brent Berlin and Paul Kay. International Journal of American Linguistics 37.4(Part 1):257-270. Baltimore.

Hiler, Hilaire
1942 Color harmony and pigments. 61 pp. Chicago and New York: Favor, Ruhl.

Hill Jane H. and Kenneth C. Hill
1970 A note on Uto-Aztecan color terminologies. Anthropological Linguistics 12.7:231-238. Bloomington, Ind.

Hjelmslev, Louis
1961 Prolegomena to a theory of language. Revised
(1943) English edition, translated by Francis J. Whitfield. v, 144 pp. Madison: University of Wisconsin Press. (First translation published in 1953; original Danish edition, 1943.)

Hollander, Camilla
1966 Field work on color concepts. Ethnos 31 (Supplement, The Fourth Conference of Nordic Anthropologists, Stockholm, 1965):92-98. Stockholm.

Holmer, Nils M.
1955- Amerindian color semantics. International
1956 Anthropological and Linguistic Review 2: 158-166. Miami.

1957 Los colores en la semántica de las lenguas indígenas de América. Pp. 5-18 in Arsbók utgiven av Seminarierna i slaviska sprak, jämförande sprakforskning, finskugriska sprak och ostasiatska sprak vid Lunds Universitet, 1951-1952. Lund.

Hulstaert, G.
1969 Les Couleurs chez les Mongo. Académie Royale des Sciences d'Outre-Mer, Bulletin des Sciences 2:236-237.

Hurvich, Leo M. and Dorothea Jameson
1953 The spectral sensitivity of the fovea. I. Neutral adaptation. Journal of the Optical Society of America 43.6:485-494. Lancaster, Pa.

1957 An opponent-process theory of color vision. Psychological Review 64.6:384-404. Lancaster.

Hurvich, Leo M. and Dorothea Jameson (cont.)
1966   The perception of brightness and darkness.
        ix, 141 pp. Boston: Allyn and Bacon.

Indow, Tarow and Kimiko Ohsumi
1971   Multidimensional mapping of sixty Munsell
        colors by nonmetric procedure. 10 pp.
        Driebergen, Netherlands: International
        Color Association.

Ingling, Carl R., Horst M. O. Schreibner, and Robert
        M. Boynton
1970   Color naming of small foveal fields. Vision
        Research 10:501-511. Oxford.

International Printing Ink Corporation
1935   Three monographs on color: color chemistry,
        color as light, color in use. 18 pp., 21
        pp., 40 color plates. New York: Research
        Laboratories of the International Printing
        Ink Corporation.

Istomina, Z. M.
1963   Perception and naming of color in early
        childhood. Soviet Psychology and Psychiatry
        1.2:37-45. New York.

Itten, Johannes
[1961] The art of color: the subjective experience
        and objective rationale of color. Translated
        by Ernst van Hagen. 155 pp. New York:
        Van Ostrand Reinhold.

Jakobson, Roman, C. Gunnar, M. Fant and Morris Halle
1951   Preliminaries to speech analysis: the
        distinctive features and their correlates.
        53 pp. Cambridge: MIT Press.

Jakobson, Roman and Morris Halle
1955   Fundamentals of language. 87 pp. The Hague:
        Mouton.

Jameson, Dorothea and Leo M. Hurvich
1959   Perceived color and its dependence on focal,
        surrounding, and preceding stimulus varia-
        bles. Journal of the Optical Society of
        America 49.9:890-898. Lancaster, Pa.

Joergensen, Joergen
1951   The development of logical empiricism.
        (International Encyclopedia of Unified
        Science, 2.9.) 100 pp. Chicago: Univer-
        sity of Chicago Press.

Judd, Deane Brewster
    1939   Specification of color tolerances at the
             National Bureau of Standards. American
             Journal of Psychology 52.3:418-428. Ithaca.

    1960   Appraisal of Land's work on two-primary
             color projections. Journal of the Optical
             Society of America 50.3:254-268. Lancaster,
             Pa.

Judd, Deane Brewster et al.
    1940   Colorimetric and psycho-physical data on
             colors of the Munsell book of colors.
             Journal of the Optical Society of America
             30.12:573-645. Lancaster, Pa.

Judd, Deane Brewster and Kenneth L. Kelly
    1939   Method of designating colors. Journal of
             Research of the National Bureau of Standards
             23:355-385. Washington.

Judd, Deane Brewster and Günter W. Wyszecki
    1967   Color in business, science and industry.
             2d edition. x, 500 pp. New York: John
             Wiley. (1st edition by senior author, 1952.)

Judson, J. A. V.
    1935   A handbook of colour. viii, 95 pp. Leices-
             ter, England: Dryad Press.

Julesz, Bela
    1965   Texture and visual perception. Scientific
             American 212.2:38-48. New York.

Kallay, Ubul von
    1939   Die zweierlei Farbenortungen einiger
             Indianerstämme Nordamerikas. Mitteilungen
             der Anthropologischen Gesellschaft 49:11-23.
             Vienna.

Katz, David
    1911   Die Erscheinungsweisen der Farben und ihre
             Beeinflussung durch die individuelle
             Erfahrung. 425 pp. Leipzig: J. A. Barth.

    1935   The world of colour. Translated from the
             German by R. B. MacLeod and C. W. Fox.
             xvi, 300 pp. London: Kegan Paul, Trench,
             Trubner. (Translation of Der Aufbau der
             Farbwelt, 1930; in turn a 2d edition of
             Katz 1911.)

[8:18]

Kay, Paul
1917   Some theoretical implications of ethnographic
        semantics. Bulletins of the American Anthro-
        pological Association 3.3(Part 2):19-31.
        Washington.

Kelly, Kenneth L.
1943   Color designations for lights. Journal of
        Research of the National Bureau of Standards
        31:271-278. Washington.

1965   A universal color language. Color Engineer-
        ing 3.2:16-21. New York. (Abbreviated
        version 1965, Museum News 43.10:47-54.
        Washington.)

Kelly, Kenneth L., Kasson S. Gibson and Dorothy Nickerson
1943   Tristimulus specification of the Munsell
        book of color from spectrophotometric meas-
        urements. Journal of the Optical Society
        of America 33.7:355-376. Lancaster, Pa.

Kelly, Kenneth L. and Deane Brewster Judd
1955   The ISCC-NBS method of designating colors
        and a dictionary of color names. (Circulars
        of the National Bureau of Standards, 553.)
        v, 158 pp. Washington: Government Printing
        Office.

Kennedy, Donald Gilbert
1930   Field notes on the culture of Vaitupu,
        Ellice Islands. Journal of the Polynesian
        Society 39.1(Memoir Supplement):101-124.
        Wellington.

Kepner, William A.
1905   Observations on color perception among the
        Visayans of Leyte Island, P. I. Science
        22.569:680-683. New York.

Kimura, T.
1950   Apparent warmth and heaviness of colours.
        Japanese Journal of Psychology 20:33-36.
        Tokyo.

Kluckhohn, Clyde
1954   Culture and behavior. Pp. 921-976 in Vol. 2
        of Handbook of social psychology, edited by
        G. Lindzey. Cambridge, Mass.: Addison-
        Wesley.

Koch, Gerd
1965   "Farbenindifferenz" bei pazifischen Völkern.

470

Pp. 235-242 in Festschrift Alfred Bühler, (Basler Beiträge zur Geographie und Ethnologie, Ethnologische Reihe, Band 2), edited by C. A. Schmitz and W. Wildhaber. Basel.

Koffka, K. and M. R. Harrower
1931 Colour and organization, I and II. Psychologische Forschung 15:145-192; 15: 193-275. Berlin.

Kohlrausch, K. W. F.
1920 Beitraege zur Farbenlehre. Physikalische Zeitschrift 21:396-403, 423-426, 473-477. Leipzig.

König, Arthur
1896 Uebersicht über de gesammte physiologisch-optische Litteratur bis zum Schlusse des Jahres 1894. Pp. 1009-1334 [7833 titles] in Handbuch der physiologischen Optik by H. L. F. von Helmholtz, 2d edition, edited by A. König. Hamburg and Leipzig: L. Voss.

Kopp, James and Harlan Lane
1968 Hue discrimination related to linguistic habits. Psychonomic Science 11.2:61-62. Goleta, Calif.

Krause, Robert M.
1968 Language as a symbolic process in communication. American Scientist 56.3:265-278. New Haven.

Krauskopf, John
1964 Color appearance of small stimuli and the spatial distribution of color receptors. Journal of the Optical Society of America 54.9:1171. Lancaster, Pa.

Krauskopf, John and Richard Srebro
1965 Spectral sensitivity of color mechanisms: derivation from fluctuations of color appearance near threshold. Science 150. 3702:1477-1479. Washington.

Kučera, Henry and W. Nelson Francis
1967 Computational analysis of present-day American English. xxv, 424 pp. Providence: Brown University Press.

Kunihiro, Tetsuya
1970 A contrastive study of vocabulary--with

471

special reference to English and Japanese. Pp. 325-347 in Studies in general and Oriental linguistics: presented to Shirô Hattori on the occasion of his sixtieth birthday, edited by R. Jakobson and S. Kawamoto. Tokyo: TEC Co.

Kuttner, R.
1960   Primitive color perception. Perceptual and Motor Skills 11:220. Missoula, Mont.

Ladd-Franklin, Christine
1901   Color-introspection on the part of the Eskimo. Psychological Review 8:396-402. Lancaster, Pa.

1929   Colour and colour theories. xv, 287 pp. New York: Harcourt, Brace.

Land, Edwin H.
1959a   Experiments in color vision. Scientific American 200.5:84-99. New York.

1959b   Color vision and the natural image, Parts 1 and 2. Proceedings of the National Academy of Sciences 45.1:115-129; 45.4:636-645. Chicago.

Landar, Herbert J.
1965   Language and culture. xiv, 274 pp. New York: Oxford University Press.

Landar, Herbert J., Susan M. Ervin, and Arnold E. Horowitz
1960   Navaho color categories. Language 36.3(Part 1):368-382. Baltimore.

Lantz, DeLee and Volney Stefflre
1964   Language and cognition revisited. Journal of Abnormal and Social Psychology 69.5:472-481. Lancaster, Pa.

Laude, Ilse
1960   The use of color designations in Turkic dialects. 168 pp. Wiesbaden: Harrassowitz.

Laude-Cirtautas, Ilse
1961   Der Gebrauch der Farbbezeichnungen in den Türkdialekten. 137 pp. Wiesbaden: Harrassowitz.

Laudermilk, Jerry
1949   The bug with a crimson past. Natural History

58.3:114-118. New York.

Le Grand, Yves
1959   About theories of color vision. Proceedings
        of the National Academy of Sciences 45.1:
        89-96. Easton, Pa.

1968   Light, colour and vision. Translated by
        R. W. G. Hunt, J. W. T. Walsh, and F. R. W.
        Hunt. 2d edition. xiii, 564 pp. London:
        Chapman and Hall.

Lenneberg, Eric H.
1953   Cognition in ethnolinguistics. Language
        29.4:463-471. Baltimore.

1957   A probabilistic approach to language
        learning. Behavioral Sciences 2.1:1-12.
        Ann Arbor and Baltimore.

1961   Color naming, color recognition, color
        discrimination: a reappraisal. Perceptual
        and Motor Skills 12:375-382. Missoula, Mont.

1967   Biological foundations of language. xvi,
        489 pp., appendices (by Noam Chomsky and
        Otto Marx). New York: John Wiley.

Lenneberg, Eric H. and John M. Roberts
1956   The language of experience, a study in
        methodology. (Supplement to International
        Journal of American Linguistics 22.2; Memoir
        13.) vi, 33 pp. Baltimore.

Lerner, L. D.
1951   Colour words in Anglo-Saxon. Modern Language
        Review 46.2:246-249. Cambridge, England.

Lévi-Strauss, Claude
1948   La Vie familiale et sociale des Indiens
        Nambikwara. Journal de la Société des
        Américanistes de Paris 37:1-131. Paris.

Liggett, W. F.
1944   Origins of color names. Dyestuffs 38:194-
        197. New York.

Linton, William
1852   Ancient and modern colours from the earliest
        periods to the present time. London: Long-
        man, Brown, Green, and Longman.

Loken, Robert D.
    1942   The Nela test of color vision. (Comparative
            Psychology Monographs 17.6, Serial No. 90.)
            37 pp. Baltimore: Williams and Wilkins.

Longacre, Robert E.
    1956   Review of Language and reality, by W. M.
            Urban; and Four articles on metalinguistics,
            by B. L. Whorf. Language 32.2:298-308.
            Baltimore.

Lounsbury, Floyd G.
    1953   Introduction [to section on linguistics and
            psychology]. Pp. 47-49 in Results of the
            Conference of Anthropologists and Linguists,
            (International Journal of American Linguis-
            tics, Memoir No. 8). Baltimore.

Lovejoy, T. and E. S. Forster
    1913   De coloribus. Pp. 791^a-799^b in Vol. 6 of
            The works of Aristotle, translated into
            English under the editorship of W. D. Ross.
            Oxford: Clarendon.

Luckey, George Washington Andrew
    1895   Comparative observations on the indirect
            color range of children, adults, and adults
            trained in color. American Journal of
            Psychology 6.4:489-504. Worcester, Mass.

Luckiesh, Matthew
    1921   Color and its applications. 2d edition.
            419 pp. New York: Van Nostrand.

    1938   Color and colors. 206 pp. New York: Van
            Nostrand.

Luria, S. M.
    1967   Color-name as a function of stimulus--
            intensity and duration. American Journal
            of Psychology 80.1:14-27. Austin.

Lüscher, Max
    1969   The Lüscher color test. Translated and
            edited by Ian A. Scott, based on the original
            German text by Max Lüscher. 185 pp., cards,
            end papers. New York: Random House.

Lyons, John
    1968   Introduction to theoretical linguistics.
            x, 519 pp. Cambridge: Cambridge University
            Press.

1970   The meaning of meaning. Times Literary
         Supplement No. 3569(23 July):795-797.
         London.

Maass, A.
1908   363 Farbenuntersuchungen bei den Malaien
         Zentral-Sumatras. Appendix (22 pp.) in
         Johannes Pieter Kleiwag de Zwaan, Bydrage
         tot de anthropologie der Menangkabau-
         Maleiers. Amsterdam.

1912   Ueber das Farbenempfindungsvermögen bei den
         Minangkabauern. Pp. 135-152 in Vol. 2 of
         Durch Zentral-Sumatra. Berlin: Süsserott.

MacAdam, David L., editor
1970   Sources of color science. x, 282 pp.
         Cambridge: MIT Press.

Mach, Edmund
1914   The analysis of sensations and the relation
         of the physical to the psychical. Trans-
         lated by C. M. Williams from the 1900 German
         original. xv, 380 pp. London: Open Court.

MacNichol, Edward F., Jr.
1964a   Retinal mechanisms in color vision. Vision
         Research 4:119-133. Oxford.

1964b   Three-pigment color vision. Scientific
         American 211.6:48-56. New York.

Maerz, Aloys and M. Rea Paul
1930   A dictionary of color. 1st edition. 207 pp.,
         58 plates with 144 blocks of different
         colors on each. New York: McGraw-Hill.

Magnus, Hugo
1877   Die geschichtliche Entwicklung des Farben-
         sinnes. 56 pp. Leipzig: Veit.

1878   Histoire de l'évolution de sens des couleurs.
         1v, 130 pp. Paris.

1880   Untersuchungen über den Farbensinn der
         Naturvölker. iii, 50 pp. Jena: Fischer.

1883   Ueber ethnologische Untersuchungen des
         Farbensinnes. 36 pp. Berlin: C. Habel.

Mann, Ida and Cecil Turner
1956   Color vision in native races in Australasia.

[8:24]

American Journal of Ophthamology 41:797-800.
Chicago.

Marriott, F. H. C.
1959   Color naming experiments and the two-quanta
         theory. Journal of the Optical Society of
         America 49.10:1022. Lancaster, Pa.

Martí, Samuel
1960   Simbolismo de los colores, deidades,
         números y rumbos. Estudios de Cultura
         Náhuatl 2:93-127. Mexico City.

Matoré, Georges
1958   A propos du vocabulaire des couleurs.
         Annales de l'Université de Paris 28:137-150.
         Paris.

Mauss, Marcel
1964   On language and primitive forms of classifi-
(1923)   cation. Pp. 124-127 in Language in culture
         and society, edited by D. H. Hymes. New
         York: Harper and Row. (Originally published
         in French in 1923 in Journal de Psychologie:
         Normale et Pathologique 20:944-947. Paris.)

Mead, William E.
1899   Color in Old English poetry. Publications
         of the Modern Language Association of
         America 14(n.s. 7).2:169-206. Baltimore.

Merrifield, W. R.
1971   Review of Basic color terms, by Brent Berlin
         and Paul Kay. Journal of Linguistics 7.2:
         259-268. London.

Meyerson, Ignace, editor
1957   Problèmes de la couleur. 372 pp. Paris:
         Centre de Psychologie Comparative.

Miller, George A. and David McNeill
1968   Psycholinguistics. Pp. 666-794 in Vol. 3 of
         The handbook of social psychology, 2d edition,
         edited by G. Lindzey and E. Aronson. Reading,
         Mass.: Addison-Wesley.

Mollison, Th. M.
1913   Eine neue Methode zur Prüfung des Farben-
         sinnes und ihre Ergebnisse an Europäern
         und Somali. Archiv für Anthropologie
         40:26-43. Brunswick.

Monberg, Torben
    1971   Tikopia color classification. Ethnology
            10.3:349-358. Pittsburgh.

Morrill, W. T.
    1971   Review of Basic color terms, by Brent
            Berlin and Paul Kay. Man 6.1:151-152.
            London.

Moskovich, V. A.
    1960   Sistema cvetooboznachenij v sovremennom
            anglijskom jazyke (The system of words
            denoting color in modern English). Voprosy
            jazykoznanija 9.1:83-87. Moscow.

Munsell, Albert Henry
    1915   Atlas of the Munsell color system. 16 pp.,
            illustrated. Boston: Wadsworth, Howland.

    1929   Munsell book of color. 42 pp., 26 color
            plates. Baltimore: Munsell Color Company.

    1942   The atlas of the Munsell color system
            (Munsell book of color). Revised library
            edition (earlier abridged edition, 1929).
            2 vols. Baltimore: Munsell Color Company.

Munsell Color Company
    1946   A color notation, an illustrated system
            defining all colors and their relations.
            10th revised edition. 74 pp. Baltimore:
            Munsell Color Company.

    1966   Munsell book of color; glossy finish
            collection. 2 parts (chiefly illustrated).
            Baltimore: Munsell Color Company.
            (Cf. Munsell, earlier dates.)

    1967   Munsell book of color; matte finish
            collection. Neighboring hues edition.
            1 vol. (chiefly illustrated). Baltimore:
            Munsell Color Company.

Murray, Humphrey Desmond, editor
    1952   Colour in theory and practice. New edition,
            enlarged and rewritten by R. Donaldson
            et al. 309 pp. London: Chapman and Hall.

Myers, Charles S.
    1908   Some observations on the development of the
            colour sense. British Journal of Psychology
            2.4:353-362. Cambridge.

National Academy of Sciences
    1959   Symposium on new developments in the study
            of color vision. (Proceedings of the
            National Academy of Sciences 45.1.) Chicago.

Newcomer, Peter and James Faris
    1971   Basic color terms. International Journal
            of American Linguistics 37.4:270-274.
            Baltimore.

Newhall, Sidney M.
    1940   Preliminary report of the Optical Society
            of America Subcommittee on the Spacing of
            the Munsell Colors. Journal of the Optical
            Society of America 30.12:617-645. Lancaster,
            Pa.

Newhall, Sidney M., Dorothy Nickerson, and Deane B. Judd
    1943   Final report of the Optical Society of
            America Subcommittee on the Spacing of
            the Munsell Colors. Journal of the Optical
            Society of America 33.7:385-418. Lancaster,
            Pa.

Newton, Isaac
    1671   A letter of Mr. Isaac Newton...containing
            his theory about light and colours. London.
            (Microprint, Landmarks of Science.)

    1672   A new theory about light and colours.
            Philosophical Transactions of the Royal
            Society of London, No. 80, Feb. 19, 1672;
            (republished in 1965, pp. 3075-3084 in
            Historiae scientarum elementa, fasc. 2.
            München: W. Fritsch).

    1704   Opticks: or, a treatise of the reflexions,
            refractions, inflexions and colours of
            light. 144 and 211 pp., 19 folding dia-
            grams. London: Printed for William and
            John Innys. (Later editions: 1718, 1721,
            1730; 1952 reprinting of 1730 edition,
            New York: Dover.)

    1728   Optical lectures read in the publick schools
            of the University of Cambridge, Anno Domini,
            1669. xi, 212 pp., 13 plates. Cambridge,
            England.

Nickerson, Dorothy and Sidney M. Newhall
    1943   A psychological color solid. Journal of
            the Optical Society of America 33.7:419-422.
            Lancaster, Pa.

Nickerson, Dorothy, Josephine J. Tomaszewski, and
        Thomas F. Boyd
    1953   Colorimetric specifications of Munsell
            repaints. Journal of the Optical Society
            of America 43.3:163-171. Lancaster, Pa.

Nida, Eugene A.
    1959   Principles of translation as exemplified by
            bible translating. Pp. 11-31 in On transla-
            tion, edited by R. A. Brower. Cambridge:
            Harvard University Press.

Noell, Werner K. and S. Howard Bartley
    1968   Vision. Encyclopaedia Britannica 23:60-76.
            Chicago.

Oblath, Oscar
    1929   Color vision tests. (International Labor
            Office, Studies and Reports, Series F,
            Industrial Hygiene, No. 12.) 47 pp.
            Geneva.

Öhman, Suzanne
    1951   Wortinhalt and Weltbild. Vergleichende und
            methodologische Studien zu Bedeutungslehre
            und Wortfeldtheorie. 194 pp. Stockholm:
            University of Stockholm.

O'Neale, Lila M. and Juan Dolores
    1943   Notes on Papago color designations. Ameri-
            can Anthropologist 45.3:387-397. Menasha.

Optical Society of America Committee on Colorimetry
    1953   The science of color. 385 pp. New York:
            Crowell.

Osgood, Charles E.
    1953   Method and theory in experimental psychology.
            808 pp. New York: Oxford University Press.

Ostwald, [Fredrich] Wilhelm
    1917   Die Farbenfibel. 8, 46 pp. Leipzig.
            (7th edition, 1928.)

    1920-   Der Farbnormenatlas. 4 pp. diagrams.
    1925   Leipzig.

    1931-   Colour science; a handbook for advanced
    1933   students in schools, colleges....
            Authorized translation with an introduction
            and notes by John Scott Taylor. 2 vols.
            London: Winsor and Newton.

Ostwald, [Fredrich] Wilhelm (cont.)
1969   The color primer: a basic treatise on the
        color system of Wilhelm Ostwald. Edited
        reprinting, in translation, by Farber Birren,
        of Die Farbenfibel. 96 pp., illus. New
        York: Van Nostrand.

Otto, A. G.
1899   Étude sur les couleurs en vieux français.
        Paris: Bouillon.

Paclt, Jurag
1958   Farbenbestimmung in der Biologie. 76 pp.
        Jena: Fischer.

Panoff-Eliet, Françoise
1971   Review of Basic color terms, by Brent Berlin
        and Paul Kay. L'Homme 11.4:100-103. Paris.

Pastore, Nicholas
1960   Color phenomena. Science 132:1396-1397.
        Washington.

Pickford, Ralph William
1951   Individual differences in colour vision.
        xviii, 386 pp. London: Routledge and
        Kegan Paul.

Pierce, Watson O'Dell
1933   Individual differences in normal color
        vision: a survey of recent experimental
        work (1910-1931). 96 pp. London: Her
        Majesty's Stationery Office.

Pirenne, M. H. L.
1967   Vision and the eye. 2d edition. xvi, 224
        pp. London: Chapman and Hall.

Plateau, J.
1878   Bibliographie analytique des principaux
        phénomènes subjectifs de la vision, depuis
        les temps anciens jusqu'à la fin du XVIIIe
        siècle, suivie d'une bibliographie simple
        pour la partie écoulée du siècle actuel.
        (Mémoires de l'académie royale des sciences,
        des lettres et des beaux-arts de Belgique,
        Vol. 42.) Brussels: F. Hayez, Imprimeur
        de L'Academie Royale.

Platnauer, Maurice
1921   Greek colour-perception. Classical Quarterly
        15.3:153-162. London.

Plochere, Gladys and Gustave Plochere
    1946   Color and color names. 64 plates with 1,536
            colors. Los Angeles: G. Plochere.

Pollack, Robert H.
    1969   Some implications of ontogenetic changes in
            perception. In Studies in cognitive devel-
            opment; essays in honor of Jean Piaget,
            edited by D. Elkind and J. H. Flavell. New
            York: Oxford University Press.

Prantl, Carl von
    1881   Aristotelis quae feruntur De coloribus,
            de audibilibus, physiognomonica recensuit
            Carolus Prantl. IV, 67 pp. Leipzig:
            B. G. Treubneri. (English translations of
            this 4th century B.C. Greek work were pub-
            lished in 1913 and 1936; see Lovejoy and
            Forster, and Hett.)

Rabl-Rückhard, H. J. J.
    1880   Zur historischen Entwicklung des Farbensinnes.
            Zeitschrift für Ethnologie 12:210-221.
            Berlin.

Ray, Verne F.
    1932   The Sanpoil and Nespelem. (University of
            Washington Publications in Anthropology,
            Vol. 5.) 237 pp. Seattle.

    1952   Techniques and problems in the study of
            human color perception. Southwestern
            Journal of Anthropology 8.3:251-259.
            Albuquerque.

    1953a   Human color perception and behavioral
            response. Transactions of the New York
            Academy of Sciences, Series 2, 16.2:98-104.
            New York.

    1953b   Comments [on lack of correlation of color
            naming systems and other aspects of cultures].
            P. 49 in Results of the Conference of
            Anthropologists and Linguists, (International
            Journal of American Linguistics, Memoir No.
            8). Baltimore.

Remoli, F.
    1933   Farbenkenntnis und Farbenverwendung bei
            Hilfsschülern. Zeitschrift für pädagogische
            Psychologie und Jungendkunde 34.10:372-377.
            Leipzig.

Richter, Manfred
1952   Internationale Bibliographie der Farben-
           lehre und ihrer Grenzgebiete, Nr. 1:
           Berichtszeit 1940-1949. Göttingen:
           Musterschmidt.

1963   Internationale Bibliographie der Farben-
           lehre und ihrer Grenzgebiete, Nr. 2:
           Berichtszeit 1950-1954. Göttingen:
           Musterschmidt.

Ridgway, Robert
1886   A nomenclature of colors for naturalists,
           and compendium of useful knowledge for
           ornithologists. 129 pp. Boston: Little,
           Brown.

1912   Color standards and color nomenclature.
           53 colored plates, 1,115 named colors.
           Washington: The author.

Riley, Carroll L.
1963   Color-direction symbolism: an example of
           Mexican-south-western contacts. America
           Indigena 23.1:49-58. Mexico City.

Ripps, H. and R. A. Weale
1969   Color vision. Annual Review of Psychology
           20:193-216. Palo Alto.

Rivers, W. H. R.
1901a   Colour vision. Pp. 48-96 (Chapter 3) in
           Part 1, Introduction and vision, of Vol. 2,
           Physiclogy and psychology, of Reports of
           the Cambridge Anthropological Expedition to
           the Torres Straits, edited by A. C. Haddon.
           Cambridge: Cambridge University Press.

1901b   Primitive color vision. Popular Science
           Monthly 59.1:44-58. New York.

1901c   The color vision of the natives of upper
           Egypt. Journal of the Royal Anthropological
           Institute (n.s.) IV:229-247. London.

1902   The colour vision of the Eskimo. Proceed-
           ings of the Cambridge Philosophical Society
           11:142. Cambridge, England.

1905   Observations on the senses of the Todas.
           British Journal of Psychology 1.4:321-396.
           Cambridge, England.

Rösch, S.
1960   Der Regenbogen in der Malerei. Studium
        Generale 13.7:418-426. Berlin.

Ross, Denman Waldo
1919   The painter's palette: a theory of tone
        relations, and instrument of expression.
        41 pp. Boston: Houghton Mifflin.

Saul, Ezra V. and Charles E. Osgood
1950   Perceptual organization of materials as a
        factor influencing ease of learning and
        degree of retention. Journal of Experimen-
        tal Psychology 40:372-379. Lancaster, Pa.

Schachtel, E. G.
1943   On color and affect. Psychiatry 6:393-409.
        Baltimore.

Schuster, Meinhard
1969   Farbe motiv funktion: zur Malerei von
        Naturvölkern. Führer durch das Museum für
        Völkerkunde und Schweizerische Museum für
        Völkskunde. 40 pp., + 82 plates. Basel:
        G. Krebs AG.

Segall, Marshall H., Donald T. Campbell, and Melville
        J. Herskovits
1966   The influence of culture on visual percep-
        tion: an advanced study in psychology and
        anthropology. 268 pp. New York: Bobbs-
        Merrill.

Séguy, E.
1936   Code universel des couleurs. 68 pp., 55
        plates, 720 colors. Paris: P. Lechevalier.

Seligman, Charles Gabriel
1901   Colour vision. Pp. 135-140 in Appendix in
        Part 1 of Vol. 2 of Reports of the Cambridge
        Anthropological Expedition to the Torres
        Straits, edited by A. C. Haddon. Cambridge:
        Cambridge University Press.

Shemjakin, F. N.
1959   K voprosu ob istoricheskom razvitii nazvanij
        tcveta (On the historical development of
        color names). Voprosy psikhologii 5.4:16-29.
        Moscow.

Shepard, Anna O.
1957   Review of the ISCC-NBS method of designating

colors and a dictionary of color names, by
K. L. Kelley and D. B. Judd. American
Antiquity 22.3:309-310. Salt Lake City.

Shepard, R. N.
   1962   The analysis of proximities: multidimen-
           sional scaling with an unknown distance
           function, II. Psychometrika 27:219-246.
           Richmond, Va.

Simon, Hilda
   1971   The splendor of iridescence: structural
           colors in the animal world. 268 pp. New
           York: Dodd, Mead.

Simon, K.
   1951   Colour vision of Buganda Africans. East
           African Medical Journal 28.1:75-79. Nairobi.

Skard, Sigmund
   1946   The use of color in literature, a survey of
           research. Proceedings of the American
           Philosophical Society 90.3:163-249, (includ-
           ing 1083-item bibliography). Philadelphia.

Smith, Damien P.
   1971   Derivation of wavelength discrimination from
           colour-naming data. Vision Research 11:739-
           742. Oxford.

Smith, H. C.
   1943   Differences in color discrimination. Journal
           of Genetic Psychology 29:191-226. Worcester,
           Mass.

Southall, James Powell Cooke
   1937   Introduction to physiological optics. v,
           426 pp. New York: Oxford University Press.

Squires, B. T.
   1942   Colour vision and colour discrimination
           amongst the Bechuana. Transactions of the
           Royal Society of South Africa 29:29-34.
           Cape Town.

Staples, Ruth
   1931   Color vision and color preference in infancy
           and childhood. Psychological Bulletin 28.4:
           297-308. Lancaster, Pa.

   1932   The responses of infants to color. Journal
           of Experimental Psychology 15.2:119-141.
           Lancaster, Pa.

Sternheim, C. S. and R. M. Boynton
1966   Uniqueness of perceived hues investigated
         with a continuous judgement technique.
         Journal of Experimental Psychology 72.5:
         770-776. Lancaster, Pa.

Stevens, Stanley S., editor
1951   Handbook of experimental psychology.
         xi, 1,436 pp. New York: John Wiley.

Stilling, J.
1910   Pseudo-isochromatische Tafeln zur Prüfung
         des Farbensinnes. 12 pp. Leipzig: Thieme.
         (English edition 1936, translated and edited
         by James Drever, Leipzig: Thieme.)

Straube, H.
1960   Gedanken zur Farbensymbolik in afrikanischen
         Eingeborenen-Kulturen. Studium Generale
         13.7:392-418. Berlin.

Swadesh, Morris
1971   Color terms: an example of the need to
         separate ancient and recent vocabulary.
         Pp. 202-205 in The origin and diversification
         of language, by M. Swadesh, edited by J.
         Shertzer. Chicago: Aldine-Atherton.

Tajfel, Henri
1968   Social and cultural factors in perception.
         Pp. 315-393 in Vol. 3 of The handbook of
         social psychology, 2d edition, edited by
         G. Lindzey and E. Aronson. Reading, Mass.:
         Addison-Wesley.

Taylor, G. A.
1934   Primitive colour vision. NADA (The Southern
         Rhodesian Native Affairs Department, Annal),
         No. 12:64-67.

Taylor, John Scott
n.d.   The Ostwald colour album: a complete
         collection of colour standards for use in
         colour specification and the study of
         colour harmony. London.

Teevan, Richard Collier and Robert C. Birney
1961   Color vision; an enduring problem in psy-
         chology. Selected readings. viii, 214 pp.
         Princeton: D. van Nostrand.

Thompson, John Eric S.
    1934   Sky bearers, colors, and directions in Maya
            and Mexican religion. Carnegie Institution
            of Washington, Contributions to American
            Archaeology 2.10:209-242. Washington.

Thomson, L. C.
    1954   Sensations aroused by monochromatic stimuli
            and their prediction. Optica Acta 1.2:93-
            102. Paris.

Thorndike, Edward L. and Irving Lorge
    1952   The teacher's word book of 30,000 words.
            274 pp. New York: Teacher's College,
            Columbia University.

Time-Life Books Editors
    1970   Color. 240 pp. (Life Library of Photogra-
            phy.) New York: Time-Life Books.

Titchener, Edward Branford
    1916   On ethnological tests of sensation and
            perception, with special reference to tests
            of color, vision, and tactile discrimination
            described in the Reports of the Cambridge
            Anthropological Expedition to the Torres
            Straits. Proceedings of the American Philo-
            sophical Society 55.3:204-236. Philadelphia.

Triandis, Harry C.
    1964   Cultural influences upon cognitive processes.
            Advances in Experimental Social Psychology
            1:2-48. New York.

Turner, Victor Witter
    1966   Colour classification in Ndembu ritual.
            Pp. 47-87 in Anthropological approaches to
            the study of religion, (Association of So-
            cial Anthropologists Monographs, 3), edited
            by M. Banton. London: Tavistock.

Uemura, Rokurō and Katsuhiro Yamazaki
    1943   Nihon shikimei taikan (Dictionary of Japan-
            ese color terms). Tokyo: Kōchō Shorin.

Uhlenbeck, Eugenius Marius
    1956   De studie der zgn. exotische talen in
            verband met de algemene taalwetenschap.
            Museum 61.2:65-80. Leiden.

United States National Bureau of Standards
    1955   (See Kelly, Kenneth L. and Deane B. Judd.)

Urry, J. W.
1969   Cherokee colour symbolism. Man (n.s.)4.3:
459. London.

Villalobos-Domínquez, D. and Julio Villalobos
1947   Atlas de los colores, colour atlas. 7,279
colors, with designations, on 38 plates with
explanatory text. Buenos Aires: Librería
El Ateneo Editorial.

Virchow, Rudolf
1878   In Berlin anwesenden Nubier. Zeitschrift
für Ethnologie 10:333-356. Berlin.

1879   Nubier. Zeitschrift für Ethnologie 11:449-
456. Berlin.

Vries, Jan de
1965   Rood-wit-zwaart. Pp. 351-359 in Kleine
Schriften, by Jan de Vries. Berlin:
Walter de Gruyter.

Wald, George
1945   Human vision and the spectrum. Science
101.2635:653-658. Washington.

1964   The receptors of human color vision. Science
145.3636:1007-1016. Washington.

1968   The molecular basis of visual excitation.
Nobel Lecture. 21 pp. Stockholm: Norstedt.

Wald, George et al.
1958   Visual problems of colour. (Forty papers
presented at the British National Physical
Laboratory's Eighth Symposium, 1957.)
2 vols. London: Her Majesty's Stationery
Office.

Walker, D. E., J. J. Jenkins and T. A. Sebeok
1954   Language, cognition and culture. Journal
of Abnormal and Social Psychology 49(Part
2).2:192-203. Baltimore.

Wallach, Hans
1963   The perception of neutral colors. Scientific
American 208.1:107-116. New York.

Warneck, Johannes Gustav
1906   Tobabataksch-Deutsches Wörterbuch. 253 pp.
Batavia: Landsdrukkerij.

Webster, E. W.
    1931   Meterologica. Pp. 338^a-390^b in Vol. 3 of
            The works of Aristotle translated into
            English under the editorship of W. D. Ross.
            Oxford: Clarendon.

Weisgerber, Leo
    1953   Vom Weltbild der deutschen Sprache.
            1. Halband: Die inhaltbezogene Grammatik.
            267 pp. Düsseldorf: Schwann.

Wells, James R.
    1966   Toward a more colorful taxonomy. Taxon
            15.6:214-215. Utrecht.

Wescott, Roger W.
    1970   Bini color terms. Anthropological Linguis-
            tics 12.9:349-360. Bloomington, Ind.

Wheeler, Lawrence
    1962   Color-naming responses to red light of
            varying luminance and purity. Journal of
            the Optical Society of America 52.9:1058-
            1066. Lancaster, Pa.

White, Leslie A.
    1943   Keresan Indian color terms. Papers of the
            Michigan Academy of Science, Arts, and
            Letters 28:559-563. Ann Arbor.

Wijk, H. A. C. W. van
    1959   A cross-cultural theory of colour and
            brightness nomenclature. Bijdragen tot de
            Taal-, Land- en Volkenkunde 15.2:113-137.
            's-Gravenhage.

Williams, J. E., J. K. Morland, and W. L. Underwood
    1970   Connotations of color names in the United
            States, Europe and Asia. Journal of Social
            Psychology 82.1:3-14. Worcester, Mass.

Willmer, Edward Nevill
    1946   Retinal structure and colour vision. xii,
            231 pp. London: Cambridge University Press.

Winick, Charles
    1963   Taboo and disapproved colors and symbols in
            various foreign countries. Journal of
            Social Psychology 59:361-368. Worcester,
            Mass.

Woodworth, Robert Sessions
1905-   Color sense in different races of mankind.
1906   Proceedings of the Society for Experimental
         Biology and Medicine 3:24-26. New York.

1910   The puzzle of color vocabularies. Psycho-
         logical Bulletin 7.10:325-334. Lancaster, Pa.

Woodworth, R. S. and H. Schlosberg
1956   The perception of color. Pp. 428-454 (Chap-
         ter 15) in Experimental psychology, by R. S.
         Woodworth and H. Schlosberg. New York:
         Holt.

Wright, Anthony A. and William W. Cumming
1970   Color-naming functions for the pigeon.
         Journal of the Experimental Analysis of
         Behavior 15.1:7-17. Bloomington, Ind.

Wright, William David
1946   Researches in normal and defective colour
         vision. xvi, 383 pp. London: Kempton.

1969   The measurement of colour. 4th edition.
(1944)   x, 340 pp. New York: Van Nostrand Reinhold.

Wyszecki, G. W. and W. S. Stiles
1967   Color science, concepts and methods, quanti-
         tative data and formulas. xvi, 628 pp.
         New York: John Wiley.

Yilmaz, Hüseyin
1967,   A theory of speech perception, I and II.
1968   Bulletin of Mathematical Biophysics 29.4:
         793-825; 30.3:455-479. London.

Zahan, Dominique
1951   Les Couleurs chez les Bambara du Soudan
         Français. Notes Africaines 50:53-56. Paris.

9. Sensation

[Including references to folk classifications
of sound, smell, taste, touch, visual form,
and related topics, but not of orientation (7.)
or color (8.); and to some nonethnographic
background sources.]

Amoore, John E., James W. Johnston, Jr., and Martin Rubin
1964   The stereochemical theory of odor. Scientific
        American 210.2:42-49. New York.

Anderson, Eugene N.
1969   Cantonese hoptology. Ethnos 1-4:107-117.
        Stockholm.

1970   Réflexions sur la cuisine. L'Homme 10.2:
        122-124. Paris.

Arnheim, Rudolf
1969   Visual thinking. xi, 345 pp. Berkeley and
        Los Angeles: University of California Press.

Aschmann, Herman
1946   Totonac categories of smell. Tlalocan 2.2:
        187-189. Azcapotzalco, D. F., Mexico.

Astrov, Margot
1950   The concept of motion as the psychological
        Leitmotif of Navajo life and literature.
        Journal of American Folklore 63.247:45-56.
        Philadelphia.

Barker, Roger G. and Herbert F. Wright
1954   Midwest and its children: the psychological
        ecology of an American town. viii, 532 pp.
        Evanston, Ill.: Row, Peterson.

Barthes, Roland
1967   Système de la mode. 327 pp. Paris:
        Éditions du Seuil.

Bartholomaeus Anglicus
1601   De rerum accidentibus, in quo de coloribus,
(c.1250) odoribus, saporibus liquoribus agitur.
        Pp. 1133-1161 in De rerum proprietatibus
        (Medieval Latin encyclopedia by Bartholemew
        the Englishman). Frankfurt: Wolfgang
        Richter. (Facsimile reprint, Frankfurt:
        Minerva, G.M.B.H., 1964.)

Bartoshuk, Linda M., Donald H. McBurney, and Carl
    Pfaffmann
    1964   Taste of sodium chloride solutions after
            adaptation to sodium chloride: implications
            for the "water taste." Science 143.3609:
            967-968. Washington.

Basso, Keith H.
    1970   To give up on words: silence in western
            Apache culture. Southwestern Journal of
            Anthropology 26.3:213-230. Albuquerque.

Bedichek, Roy
    1960   The sense of smell. 264 pp. New York:
            Doubleday.

Berlin, Brent
    1967   Categories of eating in Tzeltal and Navaho.
            International Journal of American Linguis-
            tics 33.1:1-6. Baltimore.

Birdwhistell, Ray L.
    1952   Introduction to kinesics: an annotation
            system for analysis of body motion and
            gesture. 75 pp. Louisville: University
            of Kentucky.

Bloomfield, Leonard
    1944   Secondary and tertiary responses to language.
            Language 20.2:45-55. Baltimore.

Boilés, Charles L.
    1967   Tepehua thought-song: a case of semantic
            signaling. Ethnomusicology 11.3:267-292.
            Middletown, Conn.

Bright, William
    1963   Language and music: areas for cooperation.
            Ethnomusicology 7.1:26-32. Middletown, Conn.

Browne, C. A.
    1935   The chemical industries of the American
            aborigines. Isis 23.2:406-424. Bruges.

Bukofzer, Manfred
    1942   Speculative thinking in medieval music.
            Speculum 17.2:165-180. Cambridge, Mass.

Casagrande, Joseph B.
    1964   On "round objects" a Navaho covert category.
            Actes du VIe Congres International des
            Sciences Anthropologiques et Ethnologiques,

Paris, 1960, Tome 2, Ethnologie (deuxième volume):49-54. Paris.

Chamberlain, Alexander Francis
1903   Primitive taste-words. American Journal of Psychology 14.3-4:146-153. Worcester, Mass.

1905   Primitive hearing and "hearing-words." American Journal of Psychology 16.1:119-130. Worcester, Mass.

Chenoweth, Vida
1966   Song structure of a New Guinea Highlands tribe. Ethnomusicology 10.3:285-297. Middletown, Conn.

1969   An investigation of the singing styles of the Dunas. Oceania 39.3:218-230. Sydney.

Chilkovsky, Nadia
1961   Techniques for the choreologist. Ethnomusicology 5.2:121-127. Middletown, Conn.

Collias, Nicholas E.
1960   An ecological and functional classification of animal sounds. Pp. 368-391 in Animal sounds and communication, (Publication No. 7), edited by W. E. Lanyon and W. N. Tavolga. Washington: American Institute of Biological Sciences.

Conklin, Harold C.
1958   Betel chewing among the Hanunóo. 41 pp. Quezon City: National Research Council of the Philippines.

Conklin, Harold C. and William C. Sturtevant
1953   Seneca singing tools at Coldspring Longhouse: musical instruments of the modern Iroquois. Proceedings of the American Philosophical Society 97.3:262-290. Philadelphia.

Cook, Sherburne Friend
1941   The mechanism and extent of dietary adaptation among certain groups of California and Nevada Indians. (University of California Publications in Ibero-Americana, Vol. 18.) 59 pp. Berkeley and Los Angeles.

Cunningham, Clark E.
1964   Order in the Atoni house. Bijdragen tot de Taal-, Land- en Volkenkunde 120.1:34-68.

's-Gravenhage. (Revised and reprinted 1968 in Right and left, edited by R. Needham. London.)

Dournes, Jacques
1965   La Musique chez les Jörai. Objets et Mondes 5.4:211-244. Paris.

1969   Modèle structural et réalité ethnographique, (A propos du "Triangle culinaire"). L'Homme 9.1:42-48. Paris.

Durkheim, Emile and Marcel Mauss
1903   De quelques formes primitives de classifica-tion; contribution à l'étude des représenta-tions collectives. L'Année Sociologique 6:1-72. Paris.

1963   Primitive classification. Translated and edited with an introduction by Rodney Needham. xlvii, 96 pp. Chicago: University of Chicago Press.

Ellis, Catherine J.
1969   Structure and significance in aboriginal song. Mankind 7.1:3-14. Sydney.

Emery, Irene
1966   The primary structures of fabrics, an illustrated classification. xxvi, 339 pp. Washington: Textile Museum.

Evans-Pritchard, E. E.
1961   A note on bird cries and other sounds in Zande. Man 61.7:19-20. London.

Fantz, Robert L.
1961   The origin of form perception. Scientific American 204.5:66-72. New York.

Frake, Charles O.
1962   The ethnographic study of cognitive systems. Pp. 72-93 in Anthropology and human behavior, edited by T. Gladwin and W. C. Sturtevant. Washington: Anthropological Society of Wash-ington.

1964   How to ask for a drink in Subanun. American Anthropologist 66.6(Part 2):127-132. Menasha.

Frisch, Jack A.
1968   Maricopa foods: a native taxonomic system.

International Journal of American Linguistics 34.1:16-20. Baltimore.

Gayton, Anna Hadwick
1946   Culture-environment integration: external references in Yokuts life. Southwestern Journal of Anthropology 2.3:252-268. Albuquerque.

Greenberg, Joseph H.
1967   The first (and perhaps only) non-linguistic distinctive feature analysis. Word 23.1-2-3 (Part 1):214-220. New York.

Hall, Edward T.
1966   The hidden dimension. 201 pp. Garden City, N. Y.: Doubleday.

Hall, Fernau
1967   Benesh notation and ethnochoreology. Ethnomusicology 11.2:188-198. Middletown, Conn.

Harper, R.
1966   On odour classification. Journal of Food Technology 1:167-176.

Harweg, Roland
1968   Language and music--an immanent and sign theoretical approach. Some preliminary remarks. Foundations of Language 4.3:270-281. Dordrecht.

Hause, H. E.
1948   Terms for musical instruments in the Sudanic languages: a lexicographical inquiry. (Supplement to the Journal of the American Oriental Society 7.) 71 pp. New Haven.

Hayashi, Takashi, editor
1967   Olfaction and taste II: Proceedings of the Second International Symposium, Tokyo, 1965. viii, 835 pp. London: Pergamon.

Henning, Hans
1916   Die Qualitätenreihe des Geschmacks. Zeitschrift für Psychologie und Physiologie der Sinnesorgane 74.3-4:203-219. Leipzig.

Hewes, Gordon W.
1966   The domain posture. Anthropological Linguistics 8.8:106-112. Bloomington, Ind.

Ho, Ping-yü and Joseph Needham
    1959   Theories of categories in early medieval
             Chinese alchemy. Journal of the Warburg
             and Courtauld Institutes 22:173-210.
             London.

Hoernle, A. W. T.
    1923   The expression of the social value of water
             among the Naman of south-west Africa. South
             African Journal of Science 20.2:514-526.
             Johannesburg.

Hudson, W.
    1960   Pictorial depth perception in sub-cultural
             groups in Africa. Journal of Social Psy-
             chology 52:183-208. Provincetown, Mass.

Hymes, Dell H., editor
    1964   Language in culture and society: a reader
             in linguistics and anthropology. 764 pp.
             New York: Harper and Row.

Inglett, G. E. and Joann F. May
    1968   Tropical plants with unusual taste proper-
             ties. Economic Botany 22.4:326-331.
             Baltimore.

Jones, A. M.
    1962   Venda note-names. African Music 3.1:49-53.
             Roodepoort, Transvaal, South Africa.

Kakumasu, Jim
    1968   Urubú sign language. International Journal
             of American Linguistics 34.4:275-281.
             Baltimore.

Katz, Ruth
    1970   Mannerism and cultural change: an ethnomusi-
             cological example. Current Anthropology
             11.4-5:465-475. Glasgow.

Keil, Charles and Angeliki Keil
    1966   Musical meaning: a preliminary report (the
             perception of Indian, Western and Afro-
             American musical moods by American students).
             Ethnomusicology 10.2:153-173. Middletown,
             Conn.

Key, Mary Ritchie
    1970   Preliminary remarks on paralanguage and
             kinesics in human communication. La
             Linguistique 6.2:17-36. Paris.

Knobloch, F., J. Juna, H. Junová, and Z. Koutsky
    1968   On an interpersonal hypothesis in the
            semiotic of music. Kybernetika 4.4:364-
            382. Prague.

Landar, Herbert J.
    1964   Seven Navaho verbs of eating. International
            Journal of American Linguistics 30.1:94-98.
            Baltimore.

Lehrer, Adrienne
    1969   Semantic cuisine. Journal of Linguistics
            5.1:39-55. London.

Lévi-Strauss, Claude
    1962   La Pensée sauvage. 395 pp. Paris: Plon.
            (Translated 1966 as The savage mind. xii,
            290 pp. London: Wiedenfeld and Nicolson.)

    1964   Mythologiques 1: le cru et le cuit. 402 pp.
            Paris: Plon. (Translated 1969 by John and
            Doreen Weightman as The raw and the cooked:
            introduction to a science of mythology, I.
            xiii, 387 pp. New York and Evanston:
            Harper and Row.)

    1965   Le Triangle culinaire. L'Arc, No. 26:19-29.
            Aix-en-Provence.

List, George
    1963   The boundaries of speech and song. Ethno-
            musicology 7.1:1-16. Middletown, Conn.

Lloyd, G. E. R.
    1964   The hot and the cold, the dry and the wet in
            Greek philosophy. Journal of Hellenistic
            Studies 84:92-106. London.

Lomax, Alan
    1967   The good and the beautiful in folksong.
            Journal of American Folklore 80.3:213-235.
            Austin.

    1968   Folk song style and culture. xix, 308 pp.
            Washington: American Association for the
            Advancement of Science.

McAllester, David P.
    1954   Enemy Way music: a study of social and
            aesthetic values as seen in Navaho music.
            (Papers of the Peabody Museum of Archaeology
            and Ethnology, Harvard University 41.3.)
            ix, 96 pp. Cambridge.

Merriam, Alan P.
1960   Ethnomusicology; discussion and definition
        of the field. Ethnomusicology 4.3:107-114.
        Middletown, Conn.

1964   The anthropology of music. xi, 358 pp.
        Evanston, Ill.: Northwestern University
        Press.

Montagu, Jeremy and John Burton
1971   A proposed new classification system for
        musical instruments. Ethnomusicology 15.1:
        49-70. Middletown, Conn.

Myers, Charles S.
1904   The taste-names of primitive peoples.
        British Journal of Psychology 1(Part 2):
        117-126. London.

Needham, Joseph, editor
1925   Science, religion and reality. 396 pp.
        New York: Macmillan.

Needham, Rodney
1967   Percussion and transition. Man (n.s.)2.4:
        606-614. London.

Nettl, Bruno
1964   Theory and method in ethnomusicology.
        xiii, 306 pp. New York: Free Press.

Nketia, J. H. Kwabena
1962   The problem of meaning in African music.
        Ethnomusicology 6.1:1-7. Middletown, Conn.

Ortiz, Fernando
1952-   Los instrumentos de la música afrocubana.
1955   5 vols. Havana: Dirrecion de Cultura,
        Publicaciones del Ministerio de Educación.
        Vols. 4-5 published by Cardenas y Cia.

Palmer, Edward
1878a   Notes on Indian manners and customs.
        American Naturalist 12.5:308-313. Philadel-
        phia.

1878b   Indian food customs. American Naturalist
        12.6:402-403. Philadelphia.

Pike, Kenneth L.
1943   Phonetics: a critical analysis of phonetic
        theory and a technic for the practical

description of sounds. (University of Michigan Publications, Language and Literature, Vol. 21.) 182 pp. Ann Arbor.

Pitts, Walter and Warren S. McCulloch
1947   How we know universals; the perception of auditory and visual form. Bulletin of Mathematical Biophysics 9:127-147. Chicago.

Prado, Bento
1970   Philosophie, musique et botanique. De Rousseau à Lévi-Strauss. Pp. 571-580 in Échanges et communications; mélanges offerts à Claude Lévi-Strauss à l'occasion de son 60ème anniversaire, edited by J. Pouillon and P. Maranda. The Hague and Paris: Mouton.

Preuss, Konrad Theodore
1914   Die geistige Kultur der Naturvoelker. 112 pp. Leipzig and Berlin: B. G. Teubner.

Sachs, Kurt
1953   Rhythm and tempo. 391 pp. New York: Norton.

Schapiro, M.
1970   On some problems in the semiotics of visual art: field and vehicle in image-signs. Pp. 487-502 in Sign·language·culture, (Janua Linguarum, Series Maior 1), edited by A. J. Greimas et al. The Hague and Paris: Mouton.

Sebeok, Thomas A.
1967   On chemical signs. Pp. 1775-1782 in To honor Roman Jakobson, essays on the occasion of his seventieth birthday, (Janua Linguarum, Series Maior 31). The Hague and Paris: Mouton.

Seeger, Charles
1961   Semantic, logical and political considerations bearing upon research in ethnomusicology. Ethnomusicology 5.2:77-80. Middletown, Conn.

1962   Music as a tradition of communication, discipline, and play, I. Ethnomusicology 6.3: 156-163. Middletown, Conn.

Segall, Marshall H.
1963   Cultural differences in the perception of geometric illusions. Science 139.3556: 769-771. Washington.

Segall, Marshall H., Donald T. Campbell, and Melville
    J. Herskovits
  1966   The influence of culture on visual perception:
          an advanced study in psychology and anthro-
          pology. 268 pp. New York: Bobbs-Merrill.

Sturtevant, William C.
  1968   Categories, percussion and physiology.
          Man (n.s.)3.1:133-134. London.

Thomas, L. V.
  1960   Essai d'analyse structurale appliquée à la
          cuisine diola. Bulletin de l'Institut
          Français d'Afrique Noire 22.1-2:328-345.
          Dakar.

Timmermans, J. et al.
  1963   La Classification dans les sciences. 236 pp.
          Gembloux: J. Duculot.

Valentine, Charles A.
  1963   Men of anger and men of shame: Lakalai
          ethnopsychology and its implications for
          sociopsychological theory. Ethnology
          2.4:441-477. Pittsburgh.

Verdier, Yvonne
  1966   Repas Bas-Normands. L'Homme 6.3:92-111.
          Paris.

  1969   Pour une ethnologie culinaire. L'Homme
          9.1:49-57. Paris.

Watson, J. B.
  1943   How the Hopi classify their food. Plateau
          15.4:49-52. Flagstaff.

Waugh, Frederick Wilkerson
  1916   Iroquois foods and food preparation.
          (Canada Department of Mines, Geological
          Survey, Memoir 86; No. 12, Anthropological
          Series.) v, 235 pp. Ottawa.

Wenzel, Bernice M.
  1968   Taste and smell. International Encyclopedia
          of the Social Sciences 15:514-516. New York:
          Macmillan and Free Press.

Wiser, Charlotte Viall
  1937   The foods of a Hindu village of north India.
          vi, 121 pp. Allahabad: Superintendent of
          Printing and Stationery, United Provinces.

Wyman, Leland C. and Clyde Kluckhohn
   1938   Navaho classification of their song ceremon-
           ials. (Memoirs of the American Anthropologi-
           cal Association, No. 50.) 38 pp. Menasha.

Yamaguchi, Osamu
   1968   The taxonomy of music in Palau. Ethnomusi-
           cology 12.3:345-351, large tip-in folded
           chart. Middletown, Conn.

Zinsli, Paul
   1945   Grund und Grat, die Bergwelt im Spiegel der
           schweitzerdeutschen Alpenmundarten. 352 pp.
           Bern: A. Francke.